5/18

D0783198

Footprint Handbook
Colombia

HUW & CAITLIN HENNESSY

This is
Colombia

Colombia has finally put its stereotype image into the past, and has rediscovered its identity as one of Latin America's most progressive and dynamic nations. Boasting a variety of untouched natural landscapes, from arid deserts and vast savannahs to snow-capped volcanoes and white-sand beaches, Colombia offers inexhaustible opportunities for exploration and adventure. Adrenalin junkies can brave the raging rivers of San Gil, while nature-lovers can travel south deep into Amazonia, where the Great River yields an abundance of flora and fauna, including pink dolphins, caimans and the world's smallest primate. Visitors to the Zona Cafetera, Colombia's largest coffee-producing region, can stay at working coffee fincas and do a bit of birding – the country boasts nearly 2000 species – while learning the finer points of 'black gold' production. Seekers of urban culture will find satisfaction walking the historic ramparts of Cartagena or visiting Bogotá's Gold Museum. And, when the sun goes down, Cali's famous salsa clubs and Medellín's upscale discos and downscale tango bars come into their own. Those eager to relax and recharge have their pick of either a Pacific coastline, where humpback whales cruise near the shore, or a Caribbean coast washed by crystalline waters and sprinkled with coral islands.

It was on the coast that Afro-Caribbean rhythms first took hold in Colombia, leading to a musical diversity perhaps unsurpassed by any other country on the continent. *Vallenato*, *cumbia*, *salsa*: these sounds are heard everywhere from village bars to big-city festivals. The vigorous musical pulse of the country is a testament to the mixed-heritage of the population, the result of indigenous, European and African cultures co-mingling for centuries. But the Colombian experience is in the texture and the text as much as it is in the land and the music. Witness the voluminous figures sculpted by Fernando Botero or the dreamlike prose offered up by literary lion Gabriel García Márquez.

Huw & Caitlin Hennessy

Best of
Colombia

❶ La Candelaria

Much of Bogotá is crowded, noisy, polluted and chaotic. However, it is also an endearing cosmopolitan hub, rich in culture. La Candelaria, in the historic centre, is a well-preserved colonial neighbourhood notable for its churches and old houses, and the Museo del Oro (Gold Museum) possesses a dazzling collection of pre-Columbian art. Page 42.

❷ San Gil

The town of San Gil has become the unofficial capital of the Colombian adventure sports scene. Three whitewater rivers flow through or near it, offering a range of rafting to satisfy everyone, from timid beginners to big water veterans. There are also opportunities for abseiling, caving and paragliding, including a flight over the spectacular Chicamocha Canyon. Page 90.

❸ Cartagena

Cartagena is colonial Spain's finest legacy in the Americas, impressive in every respect. Spend several days exploring the fortified old centre, teeming with historic buildings, then laze on the city's beautiful beaches. It is the best base for visits to the Caribbean coast and the islands, and there are strange mud volcanoes nearby. Page 108.

❹ Ciudad Perdida

Located in the jungle in the far north of the country is the Lost City of the Tayrona people. The multi-day trek to this hidden archaeological site ranks alongside the Inca Trail in Peru and Roraima in Venezuela, as one of the classic South American adventures and is a truly memorable experience. Page 161.

❺ Guajira Peninsula

South America's northernmost point is an otherworldly landscape of arid desert and salt flats that is nonetheless home to vast flocks of flamingos and to the best-preserved indigenous culture in Colombia. Visit Cabo de la Vela, where the turquoise Caribbean laps against a desolate shore, and the Parque Nacional Natural Macuira, which provides a welcome splash of green in the desert. Page 170.

❻ Medellín

Medellín has shrugged off its notorious past and is now a vibrant city with a spring-like climate. There is plenty of modern art to see and fascinating places to visit in the surrounding countryside. At night, take a turn in the city's tango bars or party till dawn in Parque Lleras. The best way to get an overview of the city is to ride a *teleférico* into the hillside suburbs. Page 189.

❼ Pacific coast

Whale watching off Colombia's pristine Pacific coast is a definite highlight. Humpback whales swim up from the Antarctic Ocean every year to feed and raise their young. Page 215.

❽ Zona Cafetera

Colombia's main coffee-producing region is characterized by rolling green hills, blanketed in plantations and forests. Stay on a coffee finca to learn about Colombia's 'black gold' and to appreciate the region's rich flora and fauna, particularly its prolific birdlife. Page 219.

❾ Los Nevados National Park

Easily accessible from Bogotá is a range of snow-covered volcanic peaks that rival any along the Andean chain. Three huge volcanoes form the centre of the park, but there are also hot springs, volcanic lakes and vast tracts of *páramo* to explore. Page 222.

⑩ Cali

The 'capital' of the south, Cali has had an unhappy past but has now rediscovered its sensual side with a vibrant popular music scene and an unrivalled passion for salsa. The popular excursion to San Cipriano is a couple of hours away. Page 244.

⑪ Popayán

Popayán is one of the oldest Spanish towns in Colombia. Its whitewashed colonial houses have been beautifully restored and gleam in the southern sunshine. Visit at Easter to witness the famous Semana Santa parades, or at other times to soak up the cultured atmosphere and the fresh, mountain air. The sulphurous pools of Puracé National Park are a short trip to the east. Page 254.

⑫ Tierradentro and San Agustín

Two unmissable pre-Columbian sites are located in beautiful scenery in the south of the country. The burial tombs of Tierradentro are spread across remote hillsides east of Popayán, while the mysterious statues at San Agustín are surrounded by subtropical vegetation, with the raging Río Magdalena nearby. Pages 257 and 264.

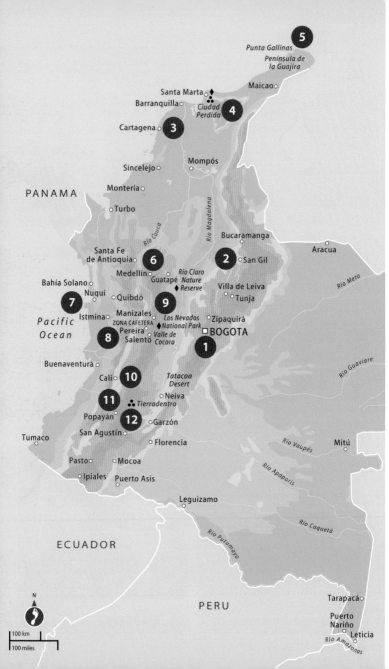

Caribbean Sea

VENEZUELA

Puerto
Carreño

Río Orinoco

Puerto
Inírida

BRAZIL

Route
planner

A country as large and varied as Colombia has a great many sights worth visiting. A comprehensive tour will require a good deal of planning. If you have limited time and want to see as much as possible, you could consider air travel; cheap fares can be found through most local carriers. If you have more time, there are good long-distance bus services and minibuses.

Seven to ten days

a whistle-stop tour

Even if you only have time for a short visit, you can still experience some of Colombia's most dazzling highlights. Start by exploring **Bogotá** and its colonial sector, La Candelaria. A visit to the Gold Museum is a must. For spectacular panoramic views over the whole city and beyond, take a cable car or funicular up to **Monserrate**. From Bogotá fly to Armenia in the **Zona Cafetera** where you can either stay at a coffee finca outside

Below: Zona Cafetera
Opposite page: Isla Rosario

the city or head to **Salento**, a great base for exploring the **Valle de Cocora** and its famous wax palms. Finally, fly to **Cartagena**, where you can spend the last days unwinding in the historic walled city and relaxing on the beaches of the coral **Islas del Rosario**.

Two to three weeks

Start in Bogotá as described above, and from there it's a short bus ride to **Villa de Leiva**, with the magnificent Zipaquirá Salt Cathedral as a convenient stopover. Soak up the colonial atmosphere in Villa de Leiva over a couple of days and explore its many surrounding attractions, such as the *páramo* and lakes near Iguaque, before heading up to **San Gil** for some rafting, kayaking and hiking. The neighbouring village of **Barichara** will provide more colonial architecture and sweeping views of the Cordillera Oriental. From San Gil, make your way

Top: Bogotá
Above: Salt Cathedral, Zipaquirá
Opposite page: Tayrona National Park

up to **Bucaramanga** and fly to **Medellín**, soaking up the cosmopolitan buzz of Colombia's second city and its surroundings. After a few days here, fly up to **Santa Marta** and plunge into the sparkling seas off **Tayrona National Park**'s beautiful beaches. Finally, hop along the coast to **Cartagena**; explore the historic city's walled ramparts and take a boat to the coral **Islas del Rosario**.

Four weeks or more

the figure of eight

A month or more will give you the opportunity to see a good chunk of the country – and taking a few internal flights will give you more time in each destination.

Start from **Bogotá**, following the two- to three-week itinerary described above as far as **Medellín**. After spending a few days here, fly up to the historic city of **Cartagena** and soak up its relaxed, Caribbean ambience. Fly back to Bogotá, and continue by bus due south, stopping off at the **Tatacoa Desert** for a night under the stars. From nearby **Neiva** it's a hard day's slog (but a worthwhile one) to **Tierradentro**. Spend a couple of days exploring the extraordinary tombs in the surrounding hills before dropping down to **San Agustín** for more pre-Columbian archaeology and then a well-earned rest in one of the town's many comfortable *hostales*. From San Agustín enjoy the spectacular drive to the dazzling white city of **Popayán**, which has several nearby attractions, including the market at **Silvia** and the **Puracé National Park**. From here, head to the salsa-mad city of **Cali** for the weekend and hit the dance floor with the locals. Next make your way to the **Zona Cafetera** for a stay on a coffee finca. A visit to **Salento** and the **Valle de Cocora** (see above), as well as the snowy peaks of **Los Nevados National Park** are highlights of this region. From here it's a long bus journey or a short flight back to Bogotá.

Best
national parks

El Cocuy
The Sierra Nevada del Cocuy is a premier climbing and hiking destination, with over 22 snow-capped peaks rising up to 5322 m and the largest expanse of glaciers in South America north of the equator. El Cocuy also offers plenty for nature lovers thanks to its biodiversity. Look out for *frailejón* shrubs and cardoon cactus, spectacled bear, wild boar, puma and several types of monkey. Page 88.

Macuira
At the northeast tip of the remote La Guajira Peninsula, Macuira is an oasis of cloudforest in the middle of a semi-desert. The park is named after the Makui people, ancestors of the indigenous Wayúu who almost exclusively inhabit the peninsula. The park boasts over 140 species of bird, as well as insects, iguanas, toads and frogs. Page 171.

Old Providence
The Caribbean island of Providencia has the third-longest barrier reef in the world and forms part of the UNESCO Seaflower Biosphere Reserve, along with neighbouring San Andrés. The archipelago is rich in marine life, including parrotfish, triggerfish, surgeonfish, the masked hamlet and several species of coral, plus on-shore mangroves and well-preserved tropical forest. Page 181.

Ensenada de Utría
This marine park on the northern Pacific coast is a migratory home to humpback whales, as well as many other aquatic species, birds and coral. Award-winning eco-lodges run boat trips from Nuquí and Bahía Solano. Page 214.

Los Nevados

The snow-capped peaks of Los Nevados rise sharply from the coffee heartland surrounded by cloudforest, glaciers, volcanic lakes and *páramo*. The highest of the three volcanoes is Nevado del Ruiz, which last erupted in 1985. Los Nevados is home to the Andean condor, golden eagle and various species of hummingbird. Page 222.

Amacayacu

Amacayacu is surrounded by waterways that feed into the Amazon and Putumayo rivers. It is home to over 500 species of bird and around 150 species of mammal, including pink dolphin, danta and manatí, plus giant Victoria regia water lilies. Large sections of the park are flooded for part of the year and can only be explored in dug-out canoes. Page 278.

Opposite page: El Cocuy
Left: Pygmy marmoset, Amacayacu
Top: Los Nevados

Long-tailed sylph

When to go

… and when not to

Climate

The climate varies little in Colombia, and, other than in the Chocó (northwest Colombia) where it rains almost daily, you will see plenty of sun year-round. There are no seasons to speak of and temperatures are dictated mainly by altitude. However, travellers should take note that March to September is the rainy season in the western departments, which can make travel difficult because of landslides and flooding. See page 313 for more detailed information on climate.

December to February are, on average, the driest months. It's worth remembering, though, that this is holiday season for many Colombians; prices rise significantly in the most popular places, and transport, including domestic flights, can be busy. During this period, a number of major annual fiestas are held, including the Días de los Blancos y Negros in January in Popayán and Pasto, and the Barranquilla Carnival in February. These events bring the locals out in force and it is a fun but crowded time to visit. Easter is also a local holiday time and almost every town has superb celebrations. In July and August, accommodation prices tend to rise because of school holidays.

Weather Colombia

January	February	March	April	May	June
24°C	24°C	24°C	24°C	24°C	24°C
17°C	17°C	18°C	18°C	18°C	18°C
81mm	86mm	110mm	178mm	193mm	163mm

July	August	September	October	November	December
24°C	24°C	24°C	24°C	24°C	23°C
17°C	17°C	17°C	17°C	17°C	17°C
133mm	137mm	159mm	217mm	195mm	111mm

Festivals

García Márquez once said, "five Colombians in a room invariably turns into a party". It could also be said that a couple of hundred Colombians in a village invariably turns into a fiesta. Colombians will use almost anything as a pretext for a celebration; there are more festivals, parties and carnivals than days in the year. Every city, town and village has at least three or four annual events in which local products and traditions are celebrated with music, dancing and raucous revelry (these are listed throughout the book). Below are some of the most significant. See also Public holidays, page 334.

January

Early January Feria de Manizales, Facebook: Feria de Manizales. Festivities in Manizales include horse parades, beauty pageants, bullfighting and general celebration of all things coffee.

Carnaval de los Blancos y Negros, www.carnavaldepasto.org. The city of Pasto celebrates one of Latin America's oldest carnivals in which everyone daubs each other with black grease and white flour to commemorate the emancipation of black slaves. Celebrations begin late December with communal water fights and floats. There is dancing, parades and lots of costumes.

Carnaval del Diablo. The town of Riosucio in Caldas has celebrated this homage to the devil every two years since 1915. The whole town effectively becomes a masked ball as locals dress up as devils and other characters in a festival in which Hispanic, black and indigenous traditions collide.

End January Hay Festival Cartagena, www.hayfestival.com/cartagena. A branch of the UK's Hay Literary Festival turns Cartagena into a focus for all things bookish for four days.

February

2 February Fiesta de Nuestra Señora de la Candelaria. Celebrated in several towns, including Cartagena and Medellín, this religious cult festival was inherited from the Canary Islands, where two goat herders witnessed the apparition of the Virgin Mary holding a green candle.

February-March Barranquilla Carnival (movable), www.carnavaldebarranquilla. org. Beginning four days before Ash Wednesday, this is one of the best carnivals in South America and involve parades and plenty of dancing. Four days of partying are compulsory by law.

March-April

Concurso Mundial de la Mujer Vaquera, The women of the Llanos prove their cowboy skills during three days.

Semana Santa (Holy Week) (movable). Celebrated all over Colombia, but the processions in Popayán, Mompós and Pamplona are particularly revered.

Late April Festival de la Leyenda Vallenata, www.festivalvallenato.com. One of the most important music festivals in Colombia, four days of hard partying in Valledupar culminate in the selection of the best *vallenato* musician.

June-July

Festival Folclórico y Reinado Nacional del Bambuco. The city of Neiva hosts *Bambuco* dancing competitions and various parades in which bikini-clad beauty queens float downriver on boats while up to 5000 (often) drunken women ride horses through Neiva's streets. It culminates in the crowning of a *Bambuco* queen.

Torneo Internacional del Joropo. The city of Villavicencio gives itself over to a celebration of *llanero* culture, with more than 3000 couples dressed in traditional outfits dancing *joropo* in the streets, a large horse parade, a beauty contest and *coleo* (a type of rodeo).

August

First fortnight Feria de las Flores. Concerts, street parties, antique car parades, a *Paso Fino* horse parade and the *Desfile de Silleteros*, in which flower-growers file through the streets carrying their elaborate displays mounted on wooden 'chairs', have made this festival in Medellín a world-renowned event.

Festival del Viento y de las Cometas (windiest weekend in August). Villa de Leiva's enormous cobbled plaza fills with hundreds of kite-fliers displaying models of all shapes and sizes. Competition is fierce.

September

Jazz al Parque, www.jazzalparque.gov.co. Bogotá's parks resonate to the sound of pianos, saxophones and trumpets during this festival that has grown exponentially since it began in 1996. Musicians from all over the world converge on Colombia's capital for a weekend.

20 September-9 October Fiestas de San Pacho. For 20 days in late September/early October, the streets of Quibdó in Chocó convert themselves into a big party venue to commemorate the death of Saint Francis of Assisi. Religious processions, parades and *sancocho* cookouts all combine in this fusion of Catholicism and African customs.

October

Encuentro Mundial del Coleo, www.mundialcoleo.com.co. More than 40,000 people descend on Villvicencio each year to watch mounted cowboys display their skills at *coleo*, a sport not dissimilar to rodeo that involves upending bulls by grabbing them by the tail and twisting until they fall over.

November

First fortnight Independencia and Concurso Nacional de la Belleza. Cartagena celebrates being the first department to win Independence from the Spanish each 11 November with parades and traditional dancing in the streets. This has been somewhat supplanted by the National Beauty Pageant in which the winner will go on to represent Colombia at Miss Universe.

Late November-early December El Pirarucú de Oro. This music festival in Leticia reflects the Colombian Amazon capital's position on the edge of two frontiers. With influences from Brazil and Peru, the festival celebrates music from the region.

December

7-9 December Festival de Luces. The skies above Villa de Leiva are lit by one of the best pyrotechnic shows in Colombia while the streets are illuminated by hundreds of candles in this most picturesque of festivals.

25-30 December Feria de Cali, www. feriadecali.com. What started as a bullfighting festival involving the best Spanish and South American matadors is now a city-wide party where Cali's self-imposed title of 'capital of salsa' is reaffirmed every year. The festival is opened by an impressive *Paso Fino* horse parade.

What to do

Colombia's disparate landscapes mean it really can offer something for everyone: tropical getaway, wildlife safari, metropolitan cultural tour, island hop, desert excursion, or all of the above. Adventurers have their pick of outdoor pursuits from hiking and climbing to rafting and parasailing, while others can eschew adrenaline for relaxation in the form of mud baths and white-sand beaches. Operators are listed in the relevant places throughout the book.

Birdwatching

With almost 1900 confirmed bird species, Colombia is a hotspot for birders and wildlife enthusiasts. Top of the list of birding locales is Parque Ecológico Río Blanco, a 4343-ha protected cloudforest near Manizales, which is home to 335 species in its own right, including 33 species of hummingbird. There are also butterflies, orchids and rare mammals, such as spectacled bears, ocelots and white-tailed deer.

Diving

Colombia's 2 extensive coastlines and numerous offshore islands offer myriad diving opportunities. Top of the list for aficionados must be the San Andrés and Providencia archipelago, which boasts the third-largest barrier reef in the world. There are several dive shops dotted around the two islands offering huge choice for exploring this underwater wonderland. Off the mainland, the Caribbean coast is known for its large brain coral. There are coral islands off Cartagena and Tolú. The fishing village of Taganga has established itself as a dive centre, and Capurganá on the Darién coast also has some excellent dive sites. On the Pacific coast, Bahía Solano offers the chance to explore a scuttled navy vessel. Further south the ex-prison island of Gorgona has countless exotic fish and turtles, while the remote island of Malpelo is a mecca for hammerhead sharks.

Hiking and walking

Colombia's varied topography offers a wealth of options for the hiking enthusiast. Everything from jungle treks and scampers over glacier fields to leisurely strolls through Arcadian landscapes can be enjoyed here. The most famous long-distance hike is the six-day return trek through the jungle to the Ciudad Perdida in the north. For high-altitude trekking the mountains of Los Nevados and El Cocuy national

ON THE ROAD

Visiting the national parks

Colombia has 42 Parques Nacionales Naturales (PNN), as well as numerous other sanctuaries and reserves (see Background, page 319), spread throughout the country, covering virtually every type of terrain, and comprising more than 20% of the national territory. Although some are very remote and difficult to access, others offer visitors the best chance to get to know the country's diverse landscapes, flora and fauna.

Colombia's national parks are administered by the Unidad Administrativa Especial del Sistema de Parques Nacionales Naturales (UAESPNN), with the exception of Parque Nacional Natural Puracé, which is now being run by the local indigenous people (see page 262, for details). If you intend to visit the parks, a good place to start is the main office at the **Ministerio del Medio Ambiente y Desarrollo Sostenible**, Calle 37, No 8-40, Bogotá, T1-353 2400 ext 3011/12, www.parquesnacionales.gov.co, Monday-Friday 0800-1700. Staff can issue permits (see below), provide information about facilities and accommodation, and hand out maps. There is a library and research unit (Centro de Documentación) for more information. The National Parks Guide is attractive and informative, providing lavishly illustrated scientific information. Permits (usually free) are required to visit the parks and are usually obtainable at offices near the parks themselves. Admission is charged at park entrances and may vary according to season, with higher prices at weekends, on public holidays, in June and July, December and January and Semana Santa (Easter week). Accommodation in many of the more popular parks is run as a concession by Aviatur, www.aviaturecoturismo.com.

Volunteers can apply to work as park rangers for a minimum of 30 days at 20 or so national parks in Colombia; details are available from the UAESPNN office in Bogotá (see above). Corales del Rosario National Park has been particularly recommended. If you have a specific or professional scientific interest and would like to study in one of the parks, bring a letter from an educational or research institution in your home country indicating your specialism.

Other useful addresses include: **Asociación Red Colombiana de Reservas Naturales de la Sociedad Civil**, Calle 39, No 16-39, Teusaquillo, Bogotá, www. resnatur.org.co, a network of privately owned nature reserves that work with local people to build a sustainable model of environmentally friendly tourism. **Instituto Colombiano de Antropología e Historia**, Calle 12, No 2-41, Bogotá, T1-444 0544 ext 118, www.icanh.gov.co, Monday-Friday 0800-1700, also has useful information.

parks rival any along the Andean chain. Other national parks such as Puracé offer countless waterfalls, lakes and trails to explore. To get up close and personal with tropical wildlife the Colombian Amazon is the place to go. Reserva Natural Palmarí (actually in Brazil but best accessed from Leticia) offers guided jungle walks ranging from one to 72 hours.

Conexion Natural, T320-206 3523, http://yeduardo.wixsite.com/conexionnatural, and **Corporación Clorofila Urbana**, T1-6168711, www.clorofilaurbana.org, are two of several walking clubs that organize walks in the countryside just outside Bogotá and further afield.

Parapenting and paragliding

Squeezed between the Andean mountain ranges of the Central and Eastern cordilleras, which create a very effective wind tunnel, the Mesa de Ruitoque near Bucaramanga is the perfect place for parapenting. There are two very professional schools, **Voladero Las Aguilas**, T300-7622662, www.voladerolasaguilas.com, and **Colombia Paragliding**, T312-432 6266, www.colombiaparagliding.com, which also has a hostel.

Rafting and kayaking

The town of San Gil has access to three whitewater rivers that offer various levels of rafting and kayaking. Several companies in the town offer professional and safety-conscious guidance and equipment, as well as new thrills such as hydrospeed, best described as whitewater boogie boarding. In southern Colombia, the village of San Agustín catches the Magdalena river at its wildest, while Cubarral on the Ariari River near Villavicencio is another popular rafting destination.

Shopping tips

Colombia takes pride in its artisanal prowess, which can be seen in the handcrafted items on sale everywhere in the country, but with distinctive differences depending on the region. Ráquira in Boyacá Department is regarded as the centre of Colombian pottery, but the popular, brightly coloured folk art ceramics most associated with the country are made in Pitalito in the south and can be bought all over. Colombian emeralds are famous worldwide, but you should go to a reputable dealer, as they vary widely in price and quality, not to mention the abundant fake stones; Bogotá has many jewellery shops, including outlets in the Emerald Trade Centre (see page 61). Other good buys include hammocks in the north (especially in San Jacinto and around the Guajira Peninsula), leather goods in the south around Pasto, sisal-based textiles (known as *fique*), Panama and *vueltiao* (woven black and white) hats, basketwork, gold (notably in Bogotá, Cartagena and Mompós) and filigree silver, made in Mompós but sold everywhere. In most cases these items are very good value. A traditional handwoven Wayuu mochila handbag, for example, which can cost hundreds of euros in Paris or Milan, can be bought for a song in Cartagena or Medellín. Bear this in mind when buying a handcrafted item in Colombia and do not haggle too much; your bargain may well be the only source of income for the vendor.

Improve your travel photography

Taking pictures is a highlight for many travellers, yet too often the results turn out to be disappointing. Steve Davey, author of Footprint's *Travel Photography*, sets out his top rules for coming home with pictures you can be proud of.

Before you go
Don't waste precious travelling time and do your research before you leave. Find out what festivals or events might be happening or which day the weekly market takes place, and search online image sites such as Flickr to see whether places are best shot at the beginning or end of the day, and what vantage points you should consider.

Get up early
The quality of the light will be better in the few hours after sunrise and again before sunset – especially in the tropics when the sun will be harsh and unforgiving in the middle of the day. Sometimes seeing the sunrise is a part of the whole travel experience: sleep in and you will miss more than just photographs.

Stop and think
Don't just click away without any thought. Pause for a few seconds before raising the camera and ask yourself what you are trying to show with your photograph. Think about what things you need to include in the frame to convey this meaning. Be prepared to move around your subject to get the best angle. Knowing the point of your picture is the first step to making sure that the person looking at the picture will know it too.

Compose your picture
Avoid simply dumping your subject in the centre of the frame every time you take a picture. If you compose with it to one side, then your picture can look more balanced. This will also allow you to show a significant background and make the picture more meaningful. A good rule of thumb is to place your subject or any significant detail a third of the way into the frame; facing into the frame not out of it.

This rule also works for landscapes. Compose with the horizon two-thirds of the way up the frame if the foreground is the most interesting part of the picture; one-third of the way up if the sky is more striking.

Don't get hung up with this so-called Rule of Thirds, though. Exaggerate it by pushing your subject out to the edge of the frame if it makes a more interesting picture; or if the sky is dull in a landscape, try cropping with the horizon near the very top of the frame.

Fill the frame
If you are going to focus on a detail or even a person's face in a close-up portrait, then be bold and make sure that you fill the frame. This is often a case of physically getting in close. You can use a telephoto setting on a zoom lens but this can lead to pictures looking quite flat; moving in close is a lot more fun!

Interact with people

If you want to shoot evocative portraits then it is vital to approach people and seek permission in some way, even if it is just by smiling at someone. Spend a little time with them and they are likely to relax and look less stiff and formal. Action portraits where people are doing something, or environmental portraits, where they are set against a significant background, are a good way to achieve relaxed portraits. Interacting is a good way to find out more about people and their lives, creating memories as well as photographs.

Focus carefully

Your camera can focus quicker than you, but it doesn't know which part of the picture you want to be in focus. If your camera is using the centre focus sensor then move the camera so it is over the subject and half press the button, then, holding it down, recompose the picture. This will lock the focus. Take the now correctly focused picture when you are ready.

Another technique for accurate focusing is to move the active sensor over your subject. Some cameras with touch-sensitive screens allow you to do this by simply clicking on the subject.

Leave light in the sky

Most good night photography is actually taken at dusk when there is some light and colour left in the sky; any lit portions of the picture will balance with the sky and any ambient lighting. There is only a very small window when this will happen, so get into position early, be prepared and keep shooting and reviewing the results. You can take pictures after this time, but avoid shots of tall towers in an inky black sky; crop in close on lit areas to fill the frame.

Bring it home safely

Digital images are inherently ephemeral: they can be deleted or corrupted in a heartbeat. The good news though is they can be copied just as easily. Wherever you travel, you should have a backup strategy. Cloud backups are popular, but make sure that you will have access to fast enough Wi-Fi. If you use RAW format, then you will need some sort of physical back-up. If you don't travel with a laptop or tablet, then you can buy a backup drive that will copy directly from memory cards.

Available in both digital and print formats, Footprint's Travel Photography by Steve Davey covers everything you need to know about travelling with a camera, including simple post-processing. More information is available at www.footprinttravelguides.com

Where to stay

from hammocks to hotels and everything in between

In Colombia there are a number of quite exceptional hotels that are well worth seeking out. They are usually in colonial towns and not necessarily very expensive. There is also a small network of youth hostels of varying quality; they are used extensively by Colombian groups, but international members are welcome. Increasingly, more budget hotels and backpackers' hostels are opening up, as well as chic boutique hotels, often in restored colonial buildings.

Hotels

Colombia has many names for hotels, including *posada, pensión, residencia, hostal, hostería, hospedaje, hospedería, mesón* and *hotelito*. Ignore them all and simply look at the price range as a guide to what to expect. *Motels* are almost always pay-by-the hour 'love hotels' (see box, opposite). Some *residencias* also double up as *acostaderos*, or love hotels, so it's best to avoid these.

Prices The Colombian hotel federation, **COTELCO** ⓘ *www.cotelco.org*, has lists of authorized prices for all member hotels, which can be consulted at tourist offices. In theory, new laws require all hotels to be registered, but to date many cheaper hotels remain unregistered. The more expensive hotels add 19% IVA (VAT) to bills. Strictly speaking foreigners should be exempt from this, but there seems to be some confusion about the application of this law;

Price codes

Where to stay	
$$$$	over US$150
$$$	US$66-150
$$	US$30-65
$	under US$30

Price for a double room in high season, including taxes.

Restaurants	
$$$	over US$12
$$	US$7-12
$	US$6 and under

Price for a two-course meal for one person, excluding drinks or service charge.

ON THE ROAD

Love hotels

Every town has one but they are not what they seem. Colombia's motels are not cheap hotels for the weary motorist, but rather love hotels – convenient hideouts for lovers sneaking off for some alone-time that provide rates by the hour and the ultimate in discreet service.

You can recognize them by their suggestive nomenclature – names such as 'Hotel Seed' or 'Passion Hotel' – and by their lurid paintjobs, a mixture of electric blues or Pepto Bismol pinks, like sorry cast-offs from Miami's South Beach. Most have drive-in garages so that customers never have to show their faces at reception. Inside, a revolving dumb waiter allows the client to receive food, drinks, condoms and sex toys without ever having to meet the staff face-to-face. Some have jacuzzis, mirrored ceilings and pornography on TV, while others have special Saturday-night discounts.

Who goes there? Mainly teenagers and twenty-year-olds still living at home, but also adulterous couples and, of course, prostitutes with their clients. Colombia is a highly sexualized nation but also a predominantly Catholic country with strict moral codes. Motels are a convenient way of satisfying these conflicting desires and standards. You can measure how traditional a town is by the number of motels it has. For example, Armenia, in the heart of coffee country, has so many on its outskirts that the area has been nicknamed the Bermuda Triangle – no doubt because it's an easy place in which to lose yourself in passion.

raise the matter with your hotel and you may well get a discount. Some hotels also add a small insurance charge.

Prices are normally displayed at reception, but in quiet periods it is always worth negotiating and ask to see the room before committing. From 15 December to mid- or late January, and 15 June to 31 August, some hotels in holiday centres may increase their prices by as much as 50%. Outside the main cities hotels may offer (very cheap) *en pensión* (full board) rates, but there will be no reduction if you choose to miss a meal. Most hotels in Colombia charge US$3 to US$10 for extra beds for children, up to a maximum (usually) of four beds per room.

Safety and security In cheaper hotels, beware of electric shower heaters, which can be dangerous through faulty wiring. Toilets may suffer from inadequate water supplies. In all cases, do not flush paper down the toilet bowl but use the receptacle provided.

Hotels are sometimes checked by the police for drugs. Make sure they do not remove any of your belongings. You do not need to show them any money. Cooperate but be firm about your rights. For further information on drugs and the police, see Essentials A-Z, page 328 and page 333.

Camping

Local tourist authorities have lists of official campsites, but they are seldom signposted on main roads, so can be hard to find. Some hostels, particularly in rural areas, offer camping and often provide tents and other equipment at an additional cost that is still cheaper than a dorm bed. Permission to camp with tent, campervan or car may be granted by landowners in less populated areas; some haciendas have armed guards protecting their property, which will improve your safety. Never camp on private land without authorization. Those in vehicles can camp by the roadside, but it is not particularly safe and it can be difficult to find a secluded spot; the best option may be truck drivers' restaurants or sometimes at police or army posts. In all cases, check very carefully before deciding to camp: you may be exposing yourself to significant danger.

Youth hostels

La Federación Colombiana de Albergues Juveniles ① *Cra 7, No 6-10, Torre B, Oficina 201, Bogotá, T1-280 3232*, is affiliated to the International Youth Hostel Federation (IYHF) and has 12 hostels around the country, in Bogotá, Armenia, Cartagena, Medellín, Montenegro, Paipa, Santa Marta and Manizales. Hostels are often full in December and January and again from June to mid-July; it's best to telephone in advance at these times. Otherwise, it's usually possible to arrive without a reservation. Membership can be obtained in Colombia: Hostelling International Cards are recognized and qualify for discounts. An alternative is the Colombian Hostel Association ① *www.colombianhostels.com*, which has hostels in Bogotá, Bucaramanga, Cartagena, Cali, Manizales, Medellín, Mompós, San Gil, Salento, San Agustín, Taganga, Valledupar and Villa de Leiva. Hostel Trail Latin America ① *Cra 11, No 4-16, Popayán, T2-831 7871, www.hosteltrail.com*, is an online network of hostels and tour companies in South America providing information on locally run businesses for backpackers and independent travellers.

Homestays

In many places, it is possible to stay with a local family; check with the local tourist office to see what is available. This is a good option for those interested in learning Spanish informally in a family environment. For a uniquely Colombian experience, you can also stay on a coffee finca; see box, page 228.

Food
& drink

ants, coffee and wonderful fruit juice

Colombia has yet to achieve international renown for its cuisine, but as tourism in the country grows, the word is getting out about the nation's culinary treats, which involve so much more than the hearty *sancocho* and the formidable *bandeja paisa*. There are gastronomy festivals in various cities and towns showcasing the best the country has to offer, but the foodie adventurer will need to travel far and wide to sample the many local specialities found in the different regions. Standard menu items are listed on page 34. See also Spanish words and phrases, page 345.

Regional food

Bogotá and Cundinamarca *Ajiaco de pollo* (or *ajiaco santafereño*) is a delicious chicken stew with maize, manioc (yuca), three types of potato, herbs (including *guascas*) and other vegetables, served with cream, capers and pieces of avocado. It is a Bogotá speciality. *Chunchullo* (tripe) and *morcilla* (blood sausage) are also popular dishes. *Cuajada con melado (melao)* is a dessert of fresh cheese served with cane syrup, or *natas* (based on the skin of boiled milk).

Boyacá *Mazamorra* is a meat and vegetable soup with broad and black beans, peas, varieties of potato and cornflour. *Puchero* is a stew based on chicken with potatoes, yuca, cabbage, turnips, corn (on the cob) and herbs. *Cuchuco* is another soup with pork and sweet potato. *Masato* is a slightly fermented rice beverage. *Longaniza* (long pork sausage) is also very popular.

Santander and Norte de Santander *Hormigas culonas* (large black ants) are the most famous culinary delight of this area, served toasted and particularly popular in Bucaramanga and Barichara at Easter time. Locals claim they have aphrodisiac qualities. *Mute* is a traditional soup made with meat, vegetables and various cereals, including corn. Goat, often served with its *pepitoria* (tripe and intestines), and pigeon appear in several local dishes. *Rampuchada* is a north Santander stew based on the fish of the Zulia river, which flows into Venezuela. *Hallacas* are cornmeal turnovers, like oversized *tamales*, filled with different meats and whatever else is to hand; they're typical of neighbouring Venezuela. *Carne oreada* is salted dried meat marinated in a *panela* (unrefined sugarcane) and pineapple sauce; it has the consistency of beef jerky. Dishes featuring chickpeas and goat's milk are also popular. *Bocadillo veleño* is similar to quince jelly but made from guava. It takes its name from Vélez, but can be found elsewhere in Colombia.

Caribbean Colombia Fish is naturally a speciality in the coastal regions. In *arroz con coco*, rice is prepared with coconut. *Cazuela de mariscos*, a soup/stew of shellfish and white fish, sometimes including octopus and squid, is especially good. *Sancocho de pescado* is a fish stew with vegetables, usually simpler and cheaper than *cazuela*. *Chipichipi*, a small clam found along the coast in Barranquilla and Santa Marta, is a standard local dish served with rice. *Empanada* (or *arepa*) *de huevo*, is deep fried with eggs in the middle and is a good light meal. *Canasta de coco* is a local sweet pastry containing coconut custard flavoured with wine and topped with meringue.

Northwest Colombia *Bandeja paisa* consists of various types of gut-busting pork cuts or other grilled meats, plus *chorizo* (sausage), *chicharrón* (pork crackling) and sometimes an egg, served with rice, beans, potato, manioc and a green salad; originally from Antioquia, this has now been adopted in other parts of the country. *Natilla*, a sponge cake made from cornflour, and *salpicón*, a tropical fruit salad, are popular desserts. *Lechona*, suckling pig with herbs, is a speciality of Ibagué (Tolima). *Viudo de pescado* is a dish based on small shellfish from the local Opía river. *Achira* is a kind of hot biscuit.

Southern Colombia In contrast to most of Colombia, menus here tend not to include potato (in its many forms). Instead, emphasis is on corn, plantain, rice and avocado with the usual pork and chicken dishes. *Tamales* are a speciality of Cali, and *manjar blanco*, made from milk and sugar or molasses, served with biscuit, is a favourite dessert. *Cuy, curí* or *conejillo de Indias* (guinea pig) is typical of the southern department of Nariño. *Mazorcas* (baked corn-on-the-cob) can be found at roadside stalls throughout southern Colombia.

Tinto – the national small cup of black coffee rather than a glass of red wine – is taken at all hours; a *tinto doble* is a large cup. Colombian coffee tends to be mild, unless you're on a coffee finca, so if you want it strong, ask for *café cargado*. Coffee with milk is called *café perico*; *café con leche* is a mug of milk with coffee added. If you want a coffee with less milk, order *tinto y leche aparte* and they will bring the milk separately. For more on coffee in Colombia, see box, page 228.

Herbal tea, known as (*bebida*) *aromática*, is popular; flavours include *limonaria* (lemon grass), *orquídea* (orchid) and *manzanilla* (chamomile). *Té de menta* (mint tea) may only be available in an upmarket café or *casa de té* in one of the bigger cities. If you want Indian tea, *té Lipton en agua* should do the trick. Chocolate is also drunk: *chocolate Santafereño* is often taken during the afternoon in Bogotá with snacks and cheese. A milk and maize drink is widely available; it is known as *care* in Boyacá, *mazamorro* in Antioquia and elsewhere, and *peto* in Cundinamarca. *Agua de panela* (hot water with unrefined sugar) is another common beverage, also served with limes, milk or cheese.

Bottled soft drinks, commonly called *gaseosas*, are available throughout the country. If you want non-carbonated, ask for *sin gas*. You will find that many of the country's special fruits (see below) are used for bottled drinks. Water comes in bottles, cartons and even plastic bags. Tap water is considered safe to drink in Bogotá and Medellín; however, you are advised to buy bottled water in rural areas and along the Caribbean coast.

Many acceptable brands of beer are available, although until recently they were almost all produced by the Bavaria group. Each region has a preference for different brands. The most popular are **Aguila**, the award-winning **Club Colombia**, **Costeño** and **Poker**. The **Bogotá Beer Company** (BBC) has its own small brewery in Chapinero and has several bars around the city serving delicious draught beer modelled on British and German ales. It has increased in popularity over the years, so much so that bottles are available at many supermarkets, bars and hostels throughout the country.

A traditional drink in Colombia is *chicha*. It is corn-based with sugar and/ or *panela* added. The boiled liquid is served as a non-alcoholic beverage, but becomes very potent if it is allowed to ferment over several days, and especially if it is kept in the fridge for a while.

The local rum (*ron*) is good and cheap; two of the best are **Ron Viejo de Caldas** and **Ron Medellín** (dark). Try *canelazo*: cold or hot rum with water, sugar, lime and cinnamon. As common as rum is *aguardiente* (literally 'fire water'), a white spirit distilled from sugar cane. There are two types, with *anís* (aniseed) or without. Wine is very expensive in Colombia: as much as US$15 in restaurants for an acceptable bottle of Chilean or Argentine wine, more for European and other wines. Local table wines include **Isabella**, but none of them is very good.

Fruit and juices

Colombia has an exceptional range and quality of fruit – another result of the diversity of altitude and climate. Fruits familiar in northern and Mediterranean climates grow here, though with some differences, including: *manzanas* (apples); *bananos* (bananas); *uvas* (grapes); *limones* (limes; lemons are rarely seen); *mangos*; *melones* (melons); *naranjas* (oranges; usually green or yellow in Colombia); *duraznos* (peaches) and *peras* (pears).

Then there are the local fruits: *chirimoyas* (a green fruit, white inside with pips); *curuba* (banana passion-fruit); *feijoa* (a green fruit with white flesh, high in vitamin C); *guayaba* (guava); *guanábana* (soursop); *lulo* (a small orange fruit); *maracuyá* (passion-fruit); *mora* (literally 'blackberry' but actually more like a loganberry); papaya; the delicious *pitahaya* (taken either as an appetizer or dessert); *sandía* (watermelon); *tomate de árbol* (tree tomato, several varieties normally used as a fruit), and many more.

All of these fruits can be served as juices, or with milk (hopefully fresh) or water (hopefully bottled or sterilized). Watch the drinks being prepared on street stalls and experiment to find your favourite. There are few better ways to beat the coastal heat than with an icy cup of *mandarina* or *limonada* from a street vendor.

Fruit yoghurts are nourishing and cheap; **Alpina** brand is good, especially *crema* style. **Kumis** is a type of liquid yoghurt.

> **Tip...**
> Fresh fruit ice cream and frozen yoghurt are also delicious; either sold on street stalls – with the usual health warnings – or from more expensive but safer, in ice-cream bars, particularly good and refreshing along the Caribbean coast.

Eating out

Restaurant food in Colombia is generally good and, occasionally, very good; this guide tries to list a tested choice at all available price levels. Note that more expensive restaurants may add a discretionary 19% IVA/VAT to the bill. In the main cities (Bogotá, Cartagena, Medellín and Cali) you will find a limitless choice of menu and price. The other departmental capitals have a decent

SIX OF THE BEST
Gastronomic experiences

Feast on a tuna steak with culona ant crust in **Leo**, culinary home of Leonor Espinoza, one of Bogotá's star chefs, page 57.

Take a Caribbean cookery course in **Ohlala Bistrot**, Cartagena, page 121.

Browse the open-air bars and bistros in Medellín's buzzing Parque Lleras, pages 200 and 201.

Enjoy a high-octane cup of coffee at **Hacienda Venecia**, page 225.

Sample tropical fruit smoothies at the Mora Castilla café in Popayán, page 260.

Munch on a mojojo palm-tree worm, Amazonian speciality, in Leticia, page 280.

range of specialist restaurants and all the usual national and international fast-food outlets. Only in the smaller towns and villages, not catering for tourists, will you struggle to find a choice of places to eat. Most of the bigger cities have vegetarian restaurants, which are listed in the text; the **Govinda** chain is widely represented. In other towns and villages vegetarians will have to ask for special food to be prepared. Watch out for opening times in the evenings and at weekends, as some restaurants still close around 1800. On Sundays in smaller towns it can be particularly difficult to find an open restaurant and even hotel dining rooms may be closed.

Lunch (*almuerzo*) is the main Colombian meal of the day, when restaurants will serve a *menú ejecutivo/del día*, with soup, main course and fruit juice or *gaseosa* (soft drink) included; many restaurants will display the menu and cost in the window. If you are economizing, ask for the *plato del día*, *bandeja* or *plato corriente* (just the main dish).

The cheapest food can be found in markets (when they are open), on street stalls in most downtown areas and at transport terminals, but bear in mind that standards of hygiene and food safety may not be good. Watch what the locals are eating as a guide to the best choice and follow these general rules: keep away from uncooked food and salads; eat fruit you have peeled yourself; take it easy with unfamiliar dishes, especially if you have arrived from a different climate or altitude, and only drink from sealed bottles. Having said that, you may find that fresh fruit drinks are irresistible, in which case you will have to take your chance! See also Health, page 328.

Menu reader

Regional specialities are described on page 29. Some of the standard items on the menu are:

Ajiaco a thick soup made with potatoes, chicken and cream. Especially popular in Bogotá.

Almojábanas sour milk/cheese bread roll, great for breakfast when freshly made.

Arepas flat maize griddle cakes found throughout the country and often served as an alternative to bread.

Arequipe sugar-based brown syrup used for desserts and confectionary, universally loved by Colombians.

Arroz con pollo chicken and rice, one of the standard Latin American dishes, is excellent in Colombia.

Brevas figs. They are served with *arequipe* as a popular dessert.

Buñuelos 4-6 cm balls of wheat flour and egg dough, deep-fried and best when still warm.

Carne asada grilled beefsteak, usually an inexpensive cut, served with *papas fritas* (chips) or rice and a vegetable of the day.

Chicha corn-based drink with sugar and/or *panela* added.

Champús corn-based drink with fruit, *panela*, cloves and cinnamon.

Empanadas maize pasties, filled with chicken, meat or vegetables and deep fried in oil. A popular snack.

Huevos pericos eggs scrambled with onions and tomatoes. A popular, cheap and nourishing snack available almost everywhere, especially for breakfast.

Pan de bono cheese-flavoured bread.

Patacones cakes of mashed and baked *platano* (large green banana).

Sancocho a meat stock (may be fish on the coast) with potato, corn (on the cob), yuca, sweet potato and plantain.

Sobrebarriga belly of beef served with varieties of potato in a tomato and onion sauce.

Tamales meat pies made from chopped pork, potato, rice, peas, onions and eggs in a maize dough. They are wrapped in banana leaves (which you don't eat) and steamed. Other ingredients may include olives, garlic, cloves and paprika. In certain areas Colombians eat *tamales* for breakfast with hot chocolate.

Bogotá & around

leave your preconceptions at the airport

Set high in a valley surrounded by the mountains of the Cordillera Oriental, Bogotá is vast and sprawling, but is also a highly cultured metropolis. It has undergone a renaissance in the past 20 years, overcoming much of the blight caused by drugs, crime and corruption, and is now one of the most exciting capital cities in Latin America.

However, although its nightlife, dining and cultural scene may now match anything that Buenos Aires or Rio de Janeiro can offer, Bogotá still suffers from extremes of wealth and poverty. But, despite these extremes, it is a very pleasant city to explore. The old centre, La Candelaria, has countless well-preserved colonial buildings and important museums along cobbled, hilly streets. Emerald sellers do deals on street corners, but for a safer view of all that glitters, visit the Gold Museum, one of the most stunning collections of pre-Columbian treasures in the Americas.

Beyond Bogotá are the Llanos, vast plains that stretch all the way to the Orinoco, in Venezuela. This staunchly traditional cattle country has also been opening up its fincas to visitors in recent years, offering abundant flora and fauna and adventurous wildlife safaris.

Best for
Museums ▪ Churches ▪ Nightlife

Footprint
picks

★ **La Candelaria**, page 42

Stroll the cobbled streets of the historic centre.

★ **Museo Botero**, page 46

Browse the distinctively voluminous artworks by one of Colombia's best-known modern artists.

★ **Museo del Oro**, page 49

Discover pre-Columbian treasures at the outstanding Gold Museum.

★ **Jardín Botánico José Celestino Mutis**, page 51

See native species of orchid and other plants without leaving the city.

★ **Monserrate**, page 51

Climb to this hilltop sanctuary for unrivalled views.

★ **Mercado de Paloquemao**, page 61

Revel in the sights, sounds and smells of Bogotá's central market.

★ **Zipaquirá**, page 66

Head into the ancient salt mine to see its awe-inspiring cathedral.

★ **Los Llanos**, page 73

Discover the abundant wildlife of the vast eastern plains and experience working life on a traditional cattle ranch.

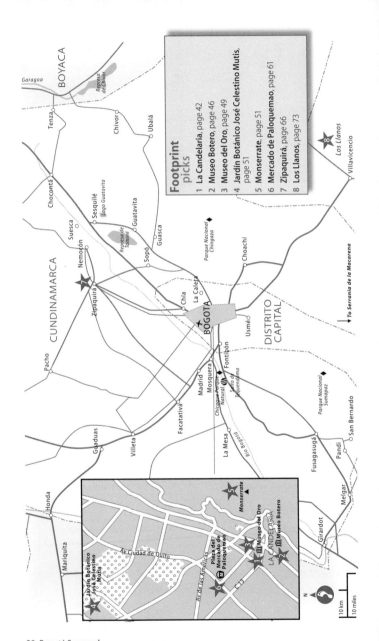

Footprint picks

1 La Candelaria, page 42
2 Museo Botero, page 46
3 Museo del Oro, page 49
4 Jardín Botánico José Celestino Mutis, page 51
5 Monserrate, page 51
6 Mercado de Paloquemao, page 61
7 Zipaquirá, page 66
8 Los Llanos, page 73

BOYACA

Garagoa
Represa de Chivor

Tenza
Chivor
Ubalá

CUNDINAMARCA

Chocontá
Sesquilé
Lago Guatavita
Suesca
Nemocón
Guatavita
Sopó
Guasca
Zipaquirá
Chia
La Calera
Pacho

Parque Nacional Chingaza

Choachí

BOGOTÁ
DISTRITO CAPITAL

Usmé

Mosquera
Fontibón
Madrid
Salto del Tequendama
Chicaque Parque Natural

Parque Nacional Sumapaz

To Serranía de la Macarena

Facatativá
La Mesa
Río Bogotá

San Bernardo

Villeta

Gaduas

Honda

Mariquita

Fusagasugá
Pandi
Melgar
Girardot

Los Llanos
Villavicencio

N

10 km
10 miles

Jardín Botánico José Celestino Mutis
Av Ciudad de Quito
Av de las Américas
Plaza del Mercado de Paloquemao
Monserrate
Museo del Oro
LA CANDELARIA
Museo Botero

Bogotá
city

The old centre is La Candelaria, a rabbit warren of colonial buildings, narrow, cobbled streets, theatres, universities and countless cafés buzzing with intellectual debate. La Candelaria is home to one of Latin America's most impressive cultural attractions, the Gold Museum, a dazzling display of pre-Columbian treasures. Beyond the noisy, polluted Downtown area, the northern suburbs are effectively a new city, characterized by the opulent restaurants, bars and nightclubs of the Zona G, Zona T and Parque 93. Further afield there are numerous attractions and pretty towns to visit, perfect for day or weekend excursions; the most impressive of these is the extraordinary salt cathedral at Zipaquirá.

Essential Bogotá

Finding your feet

Bogotá is bounded to the east by the mountains of the Eastern Cordillera, a useful landmark for getting your bearings. Most of the interesting parts of the city follow the foot of the cordillera in a north–south line. La Candelaria, full of character, occupies the area bordered by Avenida Jiménez de Quesada, Calle 6, Carrera 3 and Carrera 10. There is some modern infill but many of the houses here are well preserved in colonial style, one or two storeys high with tiled roofs, projecting eaves, wrought ironwork and carved balconies. The main colonial churches, palaces and museums are concentrated around and above the Plaza Bolívar. Some hotels are also found in this area, especially along the margins. Downtown Bogotá runs in a band northeast along Carrera 7 from Avenida Jiménez de Quesada to Calle 26. It is a thorough mix of styles including modern towers and run-down colonial buildings. The streets are full of life, but can be paralysed by traffic at busy times. The bohemian area of La Macarena (also known as Zona M), along Carrera 4 between Calle 25 and Calle 27, was formerly inhabited by struggling artists but is now becoming increasingly fashionable with many good restaurants and bars.

From Calle 50 to Calle 68 is El Chapinero, once the outskirts of the city and now a commercial district with a sprinkling of old, large mansions. It also doubles up as the epicentre of Bogotá's thriving gay scene, known as 'Chapigay', with many bars and clubs. Beyond Calle 60, the main city continues north to a comparatively new district,

North Bogotá, which is split into various points of interest. Most of the best hotels, restaurants and embassies are in this area, which is regarded as the safest in Bogotá. Between Carrera 4 and Carrera 5 and Calle 68 and Calle 71 is what is known as the Zona G (for 'gourmet'), home to some of Bogotá best (and most expensive) restaurants. The T-shaped pedestrianized area made up of Calle 83 and Carrera 13 is Bogotá's Zona Rosa (also known as the Zona T) with many fashionable bars, clubs and restaurants. Further north the streets around Parque 93 have some of the most expensive bars and restaurants in the city, while at the very limits of the city, off Carrera 7 between Calle 117 and Calle 119, is Usaquen, formerly a satellite town of Bogotá and now a popular evening and weekend excursion for *rolos* (as Bogotanos are sometimes called), looking to get a break from the metropolis.

Best restaurants

St Just, page 57
Criterion, page 57
Leo, page 57
Tábula, page 57
Castanyoles, page 58
La Puerta Falsa, page 58

Getting around

Walking is the best way to explore the downtown area and La Candelaria, as distances are short and the traffic is heavy. North Bogotá is more spacious, so buses and taxis are a more convenient option here. The TransMilenio bus service is good for crossing the city from north to south, but if you are short of time or have luggage or valuables, take a licensed taxi.

Tip...

Bogotá's altitude (2640 m) means that visitors should take it easy for the first 24 hours and should be careful what they eat and drink for a day or two.

These are relatively cheap and plentiful, and the service is generally good. At night, always travel by licensed taxi.

Addresses

It is easy enough to find a place once the Colombian address system is understood. The *Calles* (abbreviated as 'C', or 'Cll') run at right angles across the *Carreras* ('Cra' or 'K'). The address C 13, No 12-45 is the building on Calle 13 between Carreras 12 and 13 at 45 paces from Carrera 12; however *Transversales* (Tra) and *Diagonales* (Diag) can complicate the system. *Avenidas* (Av), broad and important streets, may be either *Calles* or *Carreras* or both (19 is Calle 19 in the centre and Carrera 19 in the north). The *Calles* in the south of the city are marked 'Sur' or 'S'; this is an integral part of the address and must be quoted.

Safety

As in any city of this size, take care not to tempt thieves by careless displays of money or valuables. Beware anyone approaching you in the street, as they may well be a thief or a con-artist. This is a particular problem around Plaza de Bolívar. Note that they may be well dressed and plausible, may pose as plain-clothes officials and often work in pairs. La Candelaria district is relatively safe by day, but there have been several reports of muggings and robberies by night. Begging is also common in this area as well as in the city centre. You are strongly advised to take registered taxis, preferably radio taxis, if travelling in the city at night; keep the doors locked. If you are the victim of theft or other crime, contact a **Centro de Atención Inmediata** (CAI) office or call T156. For further advice, read the Safety section in Practicalities carefully (see page 334) and take note of safety comments throughout the text.

When to go

Bogotá is an all-year-round city thanks to its temperate climate: cool to warm in the middle of the day but normally much cooler at night, when a light sweater or even a coat may be required. There can be showers at any time of year. The surrounding countryside is noticeably warmer. Holiday times such as Easter and Christmas are quiet, but attractions are often closed. You'll need three to four days to explore the city, or a week if you want to venture further afield.

Weather Bogotá

Month	High	Low	Rainfall
January	18°C	6°C	40mm
February	18°C	7°C	50mm
March	19°C	8°C	80mm
April	18°C	8°C	110mm
May	18°C	8°C	100mm
June	17°C	8°C	60mm
July	17°C	8°C	40mm
August	17°C	7°C	40mm
September	18°C	7°C	50mm
October	18°C	8°C	140mm
November	18°C	8°C	110mm
December	18°C	7°C	60mm

When the conquistadors first arrived in the 16th century, the area was inhabited by the Chibcha people. The district, named after Nuestra Señora de la Candelaria, is where the conquistador Gonzalo Jiménez de Quesada founded Santafé (later renamed Bogotá) in 1538. Events in 1810 made La Candelaria synonymous with the Independence movement (see below), while the Franciscans and Jesuits founded schools and monasteries giving La Candelaria a reputation as a centre of learning. Among the oldest educational establishments is the Colegio Nacional de San Bartolomé on Calle 10, No 6-57, founded 1573, now a prestigious school. The narrow, cobbled streets and mansions of the Barrio La Candelaria cluster around Plaza Bolívar. There is some modern infill but many of the houses are well preserved in colonial style, one or two storeys high with tiled roofs, projecting eaves, wrought ironwork and carved balconies.

Plaza Bolívar

The heart of the city and government is Plaza Bolívar, a good starting point for exploring the colonial district. It is claimed that the first ever statue of South America's liberator, Simón Bolívar, stands here. On the northern side of the plaza is the **Corte Suprema de Justicia** (the Supreme Court of Justice) destroyed by fire in 1985 after the now-defunct M-19 guerrilla group stormed in. The court was wrecked and the present building was completed in 1999. On the west side of the plaza is the **Alcaldía Mayor de Bogotá** (the office of Bogotá's influential mayor and City Hall). On the south side is the **Capitolio Nacional** (Congress), an imposing classical-style structure with fine colonnades (1847-1925).

The **Catedral** ⓘ *Tue-Sun 0900-1700,* was rebuilt 1807-1823 in classical style. It has a notable choir loft of carved walnut and wrought silver on the altar of the Chapel of El Topo. The banner brought by Jiménez de Quesada to Bogotá is now in the sacristy and there is a monument to Jiménez inside the cathedral. Gregorio Vásquez de Arce y Ceballos (1638-1711), the most famous painter in colonial Colombia, is buried in one of the chapels and many of his paintings can be seen in the cathedral. Next door is the beautiful **Capilla del Sagrario** ⓘ *Mon-Fri 0730-1200, 1300-1800, Sun 1500-1800, US$2.20,* built in the late 17th century, with several paintings by Vásquez de Arce.

Also on the east side of the plaza, visit the **Casa del Florero** or **Museo de la Independencia** ⓘ *Cra 7, No 11-28, T1-334 4150, museoindependencia@mincultura. gov.co, Tue-Fri 0900-1700, Sat-Sun 1000-1600, US$1, Sun free, seniors and children under 5 free, guided tours Tue-Fri 1100, 1500, Sat 1100, 1400, Wed 1500 in English.* It was here that the first rumblings of independence began and it houses the famous flower vase that featured in the 1810 revolution. Its 10 rooms display the history of Colombia's independence campaigns and their heroes. It still has original early 17th-century Spanish-Moorish balconies.

BACKGROUND

Bogotá

The city of Santa Fe de Bogotá (also written Santafé and with or without accent) was founded by Gonzalo Jiménez de Quesada on 6 August 1538 in territory inhabited by the indigenous Muisca. The name of the king, Bacatá, was adopted for the new city. In 1575, Felipe II of Spain confirmed the city's title as the "very noble and very loyal city of Santafé de Bogotá", adopting the name of Jiménez de Quesada's birthplace of Santa Fe in Andalucía. It was the capital of the Viceroyalty of Nueva Granada in 1740. After Independence in 1819, Bogotá became the capital of Gran Colombia, a confederation of what is today Venezuela, Ecuador, Panama and Colombia, and remained capital of Colombia as the other republics separated.

For much of the 19th century, Bogotá suffered from isolation in economic terms mainly due to distance and lack of good transport. The population in 1850 was no more than 50,000. By 1900, however, a tram system unified the city and railways connected it to the Río Magdalena. Migrants from the Colombian countryside flocked to the city; by 1950, the population was 500,000, and the move to develop the north of the city accelerated. Bogotá's population today exceeds eight million, consolidating its position as the dominant city of Colombia.

The official name of the city is now simply Bogotá, the urban area of the metropolis is known as the Distrito Capital (DC), and it is also the capital of the surrounding Department of Cundinamarca.

East of Plaza Bolívar

At the southeastern corner of the plaza is the **Palacio Arzobispal**, with splendid bronze doors. In the block behind it is the colonial **Plazuela de Rufino Cuervo**. Located here is the house of Manuela Sáenz, who was the mistress of Simón Bolívar. Inside is the **Museo de Trajes Regionales** ① *C 10, No 6-18, http:// museodetrajesregionales.com, Mon-Fri 0900-1600, Sat 0900-1400, US$1, reductions for seniors, children and on Sat,* a small collection of traditional costumes from indigenous groups of Colombia. Beside it is the house in which Antonio Nariño printed in 1794 his translation of Thomas Paine's *The Rights of Man* which had a profound influence on the movement for independence. You can read an extract of the text in Spanish on the wall of the building. Across from Plazuela de Rufino Cuervo is **San Ignacio**, a Jesuit church built in 1605. Emeralds from the Muzo mines in Boyacá were used in the monstrance and it has more paintings by Gregorio Vásquez de Arce. The **Museo de Arte Colonial** ① *Cra 6, No 9-77, www.museocolonial.gov.co, Tue-Fri 0900-1700, Sat-Sun 1000-1600, US$1, reductions for students and children, seniors free,* is a fine colonial brick building. It belonged originally to the Society of Jesus, and was once the seat of the oldest university in Colombia and of the National Library. It has a splendid collection of colonial art and paintings by Gregorio Vásquez de Arce, all kinds of utensils, and two charming patios. Across Carrera 6 is the **Palacio de San Carlos** ① *C 10, No 5-51, T1-381 4000 (restricted access, book appointment,* *www.cancilleria.gov.co)*, where Bolívar once lived and which now houses the Foreign Ministry. Bolívar is said to have planted the huge walnut tree in the courtyard. On 25 September 1828, there was an attempt on his life. His mistress, Manuela, thrust him out of the window and he hid for two hours under the stone arches of the bridge across the Río San Agustín (now Calle 7). General Santander (see page 285), suspected of complicity, was arrested and banished.

Almost opposite the Palacio de San Carlos is the **Teatro Colón** ⓘ *C 10, No 5-32, T1-381 6380, http://teatrocolon.gov.co.* It is considered Colombia's most prestigious

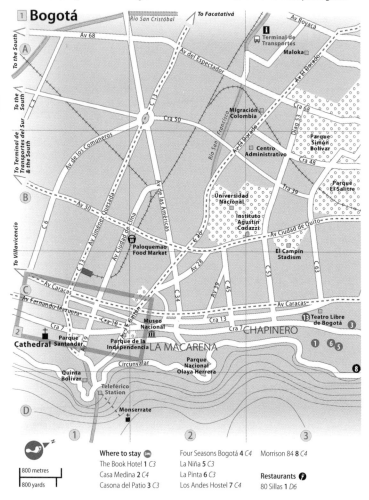

1 Bogotá

Where to stay 🛏
The Book Hotel 1 *C3*
Casa Medina 2 *C4*
Casona del Patio 3 *C3*

Four Seasons Bogotá 4 *C4*
La Niña 5 *C3*
La Pinta 6 *C3*
Los Andes Hostel 7 *C4*

Morrison 84 8 *C4*

Restaurants 🍴
80 Sillas 1 *D6*

800 metres
800 yards

theatre. Its opulent style is typical of late 19th-century Italian architecture. South of the Palacio de San Carlos is the **Iglesia de María del Carmen** ⓘ *Cra 5, No 8-36*, the most striking church building in Bogotá, in neo-Gothic style, with excellent stained glass and walls in bands of red and white.

One block northeast of here is the **Casa de la Moneda (Mint)** ⓘ *C 11, No 4-93, www.banrepcultural.org, Mon-Sat 0900-1900, Sun and holidays, 1000-1700, closed Tue, free*. The building dates back to 1620 when Felipe III of Spain ordered its construction, making this the first mint in South America to produce gold coins.

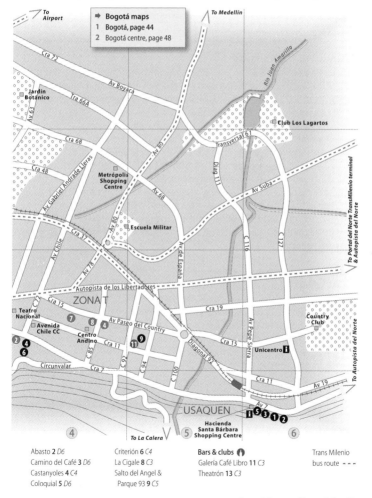

Abasto **2** *D6*	Criterión **6** *C4*	**Bars & clubs** 🎵	Trans Milenio
Camino del Café **3** *D6*	La Cigale **8** *C3*	Galería Café Libro **11** *C3*	bus route - - -
Castanyoles **4** *C4*	Salto del Angel &	Theatrón **13** *C3*	
Coloquial **5** *D6*	Parque 93 **9** *C5*		

It houses Colombian and European art and sculptures and the machines used to produce gold and silver coins. The courtyard is worth seeing. In the same block is the ★ **Museo Botero** ⓘ *No 4-41, same website and hours*. A well-displayed, excellent collection of Fernando Botero's own sculptures and paintings, as well as works by the likes of Picasso, Miró, Dalí and Monet. It's well worth a visit. Also in this block is the Botero shop, the **Colección de Arte del Banco de la República** ⓘ *No 4-21*, and **La Manzana Café**. In the same street is the modern **Biblioteca Luis Angel Arango** ⓘ *No 4-14, Mon and Wed-Sat 0800-2000, Sun and holidays 0800-1600, closed Tue, free*, one of the best-endowed and arranged libraries in South America, with three heavily used reading rooms (free Wi-Fi), research rooms, art galleries, a splendid concert hall, arthouse cinema and a musical instrument collection.

Northeast of Plaza Bolívar

Casa de Poesía Silva ⓘ *C 12C, No 3-41, T1-286 5710, http://casadepoesiasilva.com, Mon-Fri 0900-1300, 1400-1800, free*, was the house of the poet José Asunción Silva until his death in 1895. The restored colonial house has a museum, bookshop and a fine library with taped readings of almost every Spanish-speaking author. CDs are sold in the bookshop. There are also lectures and poetry readings.

Up from the Casa de Poesía to Calle 12C/Carrera 2, turn right up a delightful narrow alleyway (Callejón del Embudo) to the **Plaza del Chorro de Quevedo** ⓘ *C 12B y Cra 2*, which is believed to be the centre of the Muisca village of Teusaquillo and was certainly where Jiménez de Quesada took possession of the territory in the name of King Charles of Spain to form the kingdom of New Granada on 6 August 1538. The name dates from around 1800 when Father Francisco Quevedo provided a *chorro* (well) for the local people. Students take a break from their studies in the bars and cafés here, adding to the activity (and safety) of the area until about 2000.

South of Plaza Bolívar

The **Palacio de Nariño** ⓘ *open to the public with free guided tours, Mon-Fri 0900, 1030, 1430 and 1800, Sat 1430 and 1600, Sun 1500 and 1600* (1906), the presidential palace and offices, occupies a large space due south of Plaza Bolívar. It has a spectacular interior and a fine collection of modern Colombian paintings. The guard ceremonially changes Wednesday and Friday at 1430 and Sunday at 1500, and can be seen during the relevant tours. To the south is the elaborately ornate **Church of San Agustín** (1637) ⓘ *daily 0800-2000*. It, too, has fine paintings by Vásquez Arce and the Image of Jesus, which was proclaimed Generalísimo of the army in 1812.

Up Calle 7 from the Palacio Nariño is the **Museo Arqueológico** ⓘ *Cra 6, No 7-43, T1-243 1690, www.musarq.org.co, Mon-Fri 0830-1700, Sat 0900-1600, Sun 1000-1600 US$1.35, ISIC discount*, a fine and extensive collection of pottery from the early Colombian cultures, in the beautiful restored 17th-century mansion of the Marqués de San Jorge. Below the Palacio Nariño, the colonial **Santa Clara church and museum** ⓘ *Cra 8, No 8-91, www.museocolonial.gov.co, Tue-Fri 0900-1700, Sat-Sun 1000-1600, US$1, reductions for students and children, seniors free*, has a fine

ON THE ROAD

Antanas Mockus

In the early 1990s, Bogotá had a reputation as a world capital of anarchic disorder: it was choked with traffic and pollution; kidnappings, murders and car bombings were rife, and much of the population suffered abject poverty.

Enter 'anti-politician' Antanas Mockus, the son of Lithuanian immigrants and a former mathematics professor at the Universidad Nacional de Colombia who served as Mayor of Bogotá for two terms (1995-1997 and 2001-2003) and oversaw the city's transformation into a place where citizens felt safe to walk the streets.

Mockus first came to public attention when he dropped his pants and mooned a class of students. His time in office would be full of equally imaginative stunts.

Many felt that it would take a superhero to restore a sense of moral fibre to a society apparently falling apart at the seams, and Mockus took them at their word, often dressing up in spandex and a cape, taking on the character of 'Supercitizen'.

To combat Bogotanos' disregard for the highway code, he employed 420 mime artists to mock and shame motorists into heeding stoplights and pedestrian crossings, believing that Colombians were more afraid of ridicule than being fined. When there was a water shortage in the city, he starred in an ad on TV in which he was shown turning off the water while he soaped in the shower.

To tackle gun crime, he offered an amnesty on guns in exchange for food and had the melted metal from the weapons recast as spoons for babies. He also encouraged a 'Ladies' Night' in which men were asked to stay at home while their wives went out on the town.

While there were those who mocked Mockus, labelling him little more than a clown, many of his initiatives were effective. Homicide rates fell from 80 per 100,000 to 23 per 100,000 during his tenure, while traffic accidents decreased by 50% and water usage by 40%. His government managed to provide a sewage system that reached 100% of the population, up from 78%. He even managed to leave a US$700 million surplus to his successor, partly aided by his success in persuading 63,000 people to pay a voluntary extra 10% tax. Diagnosed with Parkinson's disease in 2010, he became the Partido Verde Colombiano (Colombian Green Party) candidate for president the same year, finishing second in the polling and only losing to current president Juan Manuel Santos in the run-off election. He left the Green Party in 2011, but remains a powerful presence in politics and the media today.

interior. It is now a religious museum and concert hall. A block north of Santa Clara is the **Escuela de Artes y Oficios Santo Domingo** ① *C 10, No 8-73, T1-282 0534, www.eaosd.org, Mon-Fri 1000-1300, 1400-1700, guided tours Mon-Fri 0900, 1000, 1100 and 1500,* a school for traditional teaching trades and arts in a beautiful colonial building. Expensive craft items and furniture are sold.

Avenida Jiménez de Quesada marks the La Candelaria and Downtown boundary. This is one of Bogotá's best-known streets and owes its lack of straightness to having been built over a river bed; a water feature now runs along it called Eje Ambiental. At the junction of Carrera 7 is the Plazoleta del Rosario with, on its southern side, the Colegio Mayo de Nuestra Señora del Rosario (1651), a beautiful colonial building, now a university.

Around Parque Santander

Across Avenida Jiménez de Quesada is the **Banco de la República** and the **Parque Santander**, with a bronze statue of Santander, who helped Bolívar to free Colombia

② Bogotá centre

Where to stay
Abadia Colonial **1** *C3*
Botánico Hostel **2** *C2*
Casa Deco **3** *C2*
Casa Platypus **4** *C4*
The Cranky Croc **5** *C3*
Hostal Fátima **6** *C3*
Hostal Sue Candelaria **7** *C3*
Hotel de la Opera **8** *B2*
Iku Hostel **9** *C4*
Masaya **10** *C3*
Swiss Hostal Martinik **11** *C3*
Tequendama **12** *B5*

Restaurants ❼
Artesano Gourmet **2** *C6*
Asadero Capachos **3** *B4*
Boulevard Sésamo **4** *C3*
Kutral **5** *C3*
La Puerta Falsa **6** *B3*
La Totuma Corrida **7** *C3*
Leo **8** *A6*
Moros y Cristianos **9** *C2*

Panadería Pastelería
  La Vieja Suiza **10** *C3*
St Just **11** *C3*
Tábula **12** *C6*

Bars & clubs ❼
Bogotá Beer Company **14** *C3*
Quiebra Canto **15** *B4*

200 metres
200 yards

and was later its president. There is a handicraft market most days. Around the park are three of the city's finest churches.

San Francisco ⓘ *C 6, No 7-35, www.templodesanfrancisco.com, open daily for Mass 0700-1800, Sun 0800-1900, holidays 0900-1200*, dates from the mid-16th century, with paintings of famous Franciscans, choir stalls, an ornate gold high altar (1622), and a fine Lady Chapel with blue and gold ornamentation. The remarkable ceiling is in *mudéjar* style. Try to visit when it is fully illuminated.

The church of **La Veracruz** was first built five years after the founding of Bogotá, rebuilt in 1631, and again after the 1827 earthquake. José de Caldas, the famous scientist, was buried along with many other victims of the 'Reign of Terror' under the church. It has a bright white and red interior and a fine ceiling.

La Tercera Orden is a colonial church famous for its carved woodwork along the nave and a high balcony, massive wooden altar reredos, and confessionals, built by the Third Franciscan Order in the 17th century.

★ Museo del Oro (Gold Museum)

Parque Santander, C 16, No 5-41, T1-343 2222, www.banrepcultural.org/museo-del-oro, Tue-Sat 0900-1800 (leave by 1900), Sun and holidays 1000-1600 (leave by 1700), closed every Mon, 1 Jan, Good Fri, 1 May, 20 Jul, 24, 25, 31 Dec; US$1.30, free on Sun; audioguides in Spanish, English and French, also guided tours in Spanish and English.

This unique collection is a must and a poignant reminder of why the conquistadors found Colombia and the rest of the continent so appealing. There are more than 35,000 pieces of pre-Columbian gold work in the total collection, most of which is held here; superbly lit and displayed, with some explanations in English. The rest are in other Museos de Oro sponsored by the Banco de la República throughout Colombia. The ancient gold objects discovered in Colombia were not made by primitive hammering alone, but show the use of virtually every technique known to modern goldsmiths. A tasteful light show in the **Salón Dorado** (Gold Room) highlights some 8000 pieces and should not be

Churches ⛪
Catedral **1** *B2*
Capilla del Sagrario &
  Palacio Arzobispal **2** *B2*
La Tercera Orden **3** *B4*
La Veracruz **4** *B3*
Mária del Carmen **5** *C2*
San Agustín **6** *B2*
San Diego **7** *B5*

San Francisco **8** *B3*
San Ignacio **9** *B2*
Santa Clara **10** *B2*

Trans Milenio
bus route ------

ON THE ROAD

Emeralds

Thinking about buying a diamond? Think again. A fine emerald is a much rarer gemstone, and the finest emeralds in the world hail from Colombia. Like diamonds, emeralds are evaluated according to the four 'C's – Colour, Clarity, Cut and Carat weight – although colour, not clarity, is considered the most important attribute. A dark green emerald is considered the most precious variety, although they vary in colour. Unlike other gemstones, all emeralds have flaws or 'inclusions'. However, rather than detracting from their value, inclusions are said to give an emerald its personality.

If you are in the market for a stone, go to Avenida Jiménez in Bogotá, which is the heart of Colombia's unofficial emerald exchange, and visit the Emerald Trade Center, among other vendors. The emeralds sold in this area come from Colombia's three most prolific mines – Muzo, Coscuez and Chivor – all located in the cloudforests of Boyacá, just a few hours to the north. These mines have a long history that dates back to AD 1000, long before the Spanish invasion. To catch a glimpse of some exquisite examples of emerald jewellery from pre-Hispanic times, check out the Museo del Oro, see page 49.

missed. Opposite the Gold Museum is the **Galería Artesanal de Colombia** ① *C 16, block 5, Mon-Sun 0900-1900*, an arts and crafts market.

Parque de la Independencia and around

Continuing north along Carrera 7, at Calle 26 you reach **Parque de la Independencia**, adorned with wax palms. In the park is the **Planetarium/Museo del Espacio** ① *C 26 B, No 5-93, T1-281 4150, www.planetariodebogota.gov.co, Tue-Sun 1000-1700, US$13.30 including dome and museum, reductions for students, children and seniors.* Behind is the impressive Moorish-style brick bullring, **La Santamaria**, see under What to do, page 61.

Also at this junction (Carrera 7 and Calle 26) are the church and monastery of **San Diego**, a picturesque, restored old building. The Franciscan monastery with fine *mudéjar* ceiling was built in 1560 and the church in 1607 as its chapel. Local craft items are sold in the old monastery. Across the street is the **Tequendama Hotel**, one of the city's finest. Near the park is the **Biblioteca Nacional** ① *entrance at Calle 24, No 5-60, www.bibliotecanacional.gov.co, Mon-Fri 0800-1800, Sat 0900-1600.* On the corner is the **Museo de Arte Moderno (Mambo)** ① *C 24, No 6-00, www.mambogota.com, Tue-Sat 1000-1800, Sun-holidays 1200-1630, US$3.70, students and seniors half price,* with a well-displayed collection of Colombia's modern artists as well as foreign artists including Picasso, Dalí and Ernst. There is also a good shop. **Museo Nacional** ① *Cra 7, No 28-66, T1-381 6470, www.museonacional.gov.co, Tue-Sat 1000-1800, Sun 1000-1700, permanent collections free, various tours available (in English by request),* is in a converted old prison, founded by Santander in 1823. There is an excellent archaeological collection. Its top floor houses a fine art section, comprising national paintings and sculptures. Allow at least two hours to look round. There is also a gourmet restaurant, El Panóptico.

Beyond the centre

shopping, eating, nightlife – and a great view

El Chapinero and around

In the link between Central and North Bogotá is Colombia's main state university, **Universidad Nacional**, housed in the Ciudad Universitaria. Be aware that the university's main entrance on Carrera 30 is periodically the focal point of protests (sometimes violent) between students and riot police. Avoid the area during these times. Instead, escape to the ★ **Jardín Botánico José Celestino Mutis** ⓘ *Av 63, No 68-95, T1-437 7060, Mon-Fri 0800-1700, Sat-Sun and holidays 0900-1700, US$, US$1, children US$50 guided tours at weekends*, which is interesting, peaceful and well organized. It has a large collection of orchids, plus roses, gladioli and trees from all over the country.

Maloka ⓘ *Cra 68D, No 24A-51, near the bus terminal, www.maloka.org, Tue-Fri 0800-1700, weekends and holidays 0900-1800, US$10 including everything*, is a complex of science and technology exhibits, multi-screen cinema (including 3-D) and ice rink, all under a dome. Entry is cheaper without cinema ticket.

★ Monserrate

T1-284 5700 (answer service in English too), www.cerromonserrate.com. The main site is open Mon-Sat 0630-2400; Sun 0630-2100; closed the week after Semana Santa and with shorter opening times during other religious holidays. Funicular every 15 mins Mon-Fri 0630-1145, 1730-2100, Sat-Sun 0630-2100; Mon-Sat US$3.50 one way US$7 return; approximately half price on Sun, reductions for over-62s on all fares. The cable car runs Mon-Sat 1200-2400, Sun 1030-1830; fares are the same as the funicular. Times and fares change frequently.

There is a very good view of the city from the top of Monserrate (3152 m), the lower of the two peaks rising sharply to the east. It is reached by a funicular railway, a cable car and, formerly, a path. The new convent at the top is a popular shrine and pilgrimage site. At the summit, near the church, a platform gives a bird's-eye view of the city's tiled roofs, modern suburbs and of the plains beyond stretching to the rim of the Sabana. Sunrise and sunset can be spectacular, with beautiful birdsong. There are two upmarket restaurants at the top, **Casa Santa Clara**, which also has a cheaper café with covered terrace, and **Casa San Isidro** (closed Sunday); both offering superb views. The bottom station is not far from the top end of Avenida Jiménez de Quesada and Las Aguas terminus of the **TransMilenio**; you can walk there in daylight with the same precautions you would take anywhere else in the city. If you prefer, you can take a taxi to or from the entrance. There is a health centre at the top should you need it.

As of 2016 the path, which was comfortably graded all the way up, was closed indefinitely. The walk up to **Guadalupe**, the higher peak opposite Monserrate, is not recommended.

Good Kopp

The tomb of Leo S Kopp in Bogotá's Cementerio Central has something of a cult following. Kopp, of German origin, founded Bavaria Beer, Colombia's largest brewery. Famously generous, he was known to find employment for anyone who came and asked him.

It appears that his capacity for giving continues after his death. On any given day it's not uncommon to see the poor and the unemployed laying flowers at his grave or kissing the magnificent bronze statue that guards it. Rumour has it that the statue retains its radiance thanks to a civil servant who, having prayed at the feet of Kopp's statute, was rewarded with a job and now shows his gratitude by secretly cleaning and shining the effigy.

At the foot of Monserrate is the **Quinta de Bolívar** ① *C 21, No 4A-31 Este, T1-336 6410, www.quintadebolivar.gov.co, Tue-Fri 0900-1700, Sat-Sun 1000-1600, US$1, reductions for students and children, free on Sun, guided tours 1100 and 1400, in English on Wed 1100*. This is a fine colonial mansion, with splendid gardens and lawns. There are several cannons captured at the battle of Boyacá. The elegant house, once Bolívar's home, is now a museum showing some of his personal possessions and paintings of events in his career.

North Bogotá

North of Calle 68 are expanding wealthy suburbs, shopping malls and classy restaurants, an area regarded as having the best hotels. Between Carrera 4 and Carrerra 5 and Calle 68 and Calle 71 is the **Zona G** (for 'gourmet'), home to some of Bogotá's best (and most expensive) restaurants. The T-shaped pedestrianized area made up by Calle 83 and Carrerra 13 is Bogotá's **Zona Rosa** (also known as the Zona T) with many fashionable bars, clubs and restaurants. Further north the streets around Parque 93 have more expensive bars and restaurants, while at the very limits of the city, off Carrera 7 between Calle 117 and Calle 119, is **Usaquén**, formerly a satellite town with a pleasant plaza, a popular evening and weekend excursion for Bogotanos wishing to escape the metropolis.

North Bogotá is also noted for its huge, lavish shopping malls, which are worth a visit even if the prices don't grab you. One of the largest, the **Hacienda Santa Bárbara** ① *Cra 7 115-60, T1-6120388*, has some 350 shopping outlets within a large country mansion, and parts of the colonial architecture, even some of the old gardens, have been retained.

Tourist information

Instituto Distrital de Turismo (Cra 24, No 40-66, La Soledad, T1-217 0711, www.bogotaturismo.gov.co, open 0700-1630, in Spanish and English) has 12 detailed tourist routes and 7 permanent tourist information kiosks dotted around the city. They are: **La Candelaria** (Cra 8, No 9-83, T1-555 7627/8, Mon-Sat 0800-1800, Sun and holidays 0800-1600), 2-hr tourist walks leave from here daily 1000 and 1400 (Tue and Thu in English); **El Dorado airport** (at international arrivals, T1-746 9636, daily 0700-2200); **bus station** (Módulo 5, local 127, T1-410 0929, daily 24 hrs); **southern bus terminal** (C 57 Q Sur 65F-68, T1-555 7696/7, daily 0700-1300); **western bus terminal** (Diagonal 23 No 69-60, Modulo 5, local 127, T1-555 7692/3); **Parque de la Independencia** (Quiosco de la Luz, Cra 7, No 26-07, T1-555 7700/1 Mon-Sat 0900-1700); **Unicentro shopping centre** (Entrada Principal, T1-555 7694/5, Mon-Sat 1100-1900, Sun1100-1600); **Centro Internacional** (Cra 13, No 26-62, T1-555 7700/1, Mon-Sat 0900-1700. There is also a **Cundinamarca tourist office** (C 26, No 51-53, T1-749 1844, www.cundinamarca.gov.co; Mon-Fri 0830-1600).

Guía del Ocio (known as GO, www. goguiadelocio.com.co, also for Cartagena) and *Vive.in* (www.vive.in) have listings on events, restaurants and clubs in Spanish.

Where to stay

IVA/VAT of 16% is charged by mid-range and more expensive hotels in Bogotá. It is additional to the bill but included in our price classification. Always insist that taxi drivers at the airport or bus station take you to the address we quote. There are many small, cheap, unregistered hotels and *hostales* in parts of the city which may be unsafe for tourists and are far from the sights.

La Candelaria

Several hostels and hotels are members of the **Asociación de Alojamiento de la Candelaria** (ASACAN), T311-530 2677, Facebook: asacan.

$$$ Abadia Colonial
C 11, No 2-32, T1-341 1884,
www.abadiacolonial.com.
Fine colonial building in the heart of this area. Comfortable rooms if a bit small, ask for a street-facing room, safe, Italian and Colombian dishes in restaurant. Recommended.

$$$ Hotel Casa Deco
C 12C, No 2-36, T1-283 7262,
www.hotelcasadeco.com.
A handsome art deco-style hotel on a quiet side street; colourful rooms and suites, TV, Wi-Fi and safe; plus large roof terrace and bar, transport and laundry services available.

$$$ Hotel de la Opera
C 10, No 5-72, T1-336 2066,
www.hotelopera.com.co.
Once the residence of Simón Bolívar's personal guard. Opulent, exquisite rooms in colonial, republican and deco style,

2 rooftop restaurants with superb views, spa facilities.

$$ Casa Platypus
Cra 3, No 12F-28, T1-286 1643,
www.casaplatypusbogota.com.
Beautiful colonial building overlooking the Parque de los Periodistas. Rooms (including a 4-bed dorm) are cosy and spotlessly clean, with chunky wooden furniture and stripped floorboards, TV, free Wi-Fi, pretty courtyard with hammocks and roof terrace with great views over the neighbourhood. Laundry service, use of kitchen, excellent breakfast included; quiet, well-run and helpful, welcome drink and free coffee, PCs and safety boxes in reception. Highly recommended.

$$-$ The Cranky Croc
C 12D, No 3-46, T1-342 2438,
www.crankycroc.com.
Aussie-run hostel in a beautiful 300-year-old building, carefully restored to retain many of the original features. Excellent facilities, lounge with a fireplace. Several private rooms with and without bath and dorms with bunks, US$12-15 pp.

$$-$ Masaya
Cra 2, No 12-48, T1-747 1848,
www.masaya-experience.com.

French-owned hostel with dorms for 4 to 6 (US$12-13.30), also private rooms with breakfast (**$$**), tapas bar, games, excursions and cultural events. Has other branches in Santa Marta and Medellín (**$$-$**).

$$-$ Swiss Hostal Martinik
Cra 4, No 11-88, T1-283 3180,
www.hostalbogota.com.
Swiss management, good location, from US$10 pp in 4- to 10-bed dorms, also private rooms, good facilities, information and activities.

$ Botánico Hostel
Cra 2, No 9-87, T1-745 7572,
www.botanicohostel.com.
Newly opened (Jul 2017), this highly recommended hostel has a superb location at the top of La Candelaria, with great views from its garden. Spotlessly clean, with private rooms and dorms, breakfast included.

$ Hostal Fátima
C 12C, No 2-24, T1-281 6389,
www.hostalfatima.com.
A maze of brightly coloured rooms and sunny patios with lots of stained-glass windows and potted plants. Sauna, jacuzzi, weekly programme of events and its own travel agency. Several

private rooms with and without bath as well as dorms with bunks (US$8). Long stays available. Also has another branch, **Fátima Suites**, in La Candelaria.

$ Hostal Sue Candelaria
Cra 3, No 12C-18, T1-341 2647, www.suecandelaria.com.
Excellent facilities, including hot water and places to relax in hammocks. Attracts a young crowd, with a party atmosphere. Dorms with bunks (from US$10).

$ Iku Hostel
C 12F, No 2-55, T1-334 8894, http://ikuhostel.com.
This small hostel has snug dorms and private rooms, with good facilities including Wi-Fi, laundry, and PCs for guests; breakfast available (extra). Arranges activities from dance to gastronomy, has a tour company, good for students and groups.

Downtown and El Chapinero

$$$ Tequendama
Cra 10, No 26-21, T1-382 0300, www.hotelestequendama.com/nuestros-hoteles/.
One of Bogotá's traditional grand hotels, witness to some of Colombia's most important political events since its inauguration in 1953. With 4 restaurants, a spa, pool and large rooms it is well equipped for the conferences it hosts.

$$ The Book Hotel
Cra 5, No 57-79, Chapinero Alto, T1-745 9988, www.thebookhotel.co.
In an 'English-style' house, quiet, well appointed, with restaurant and café, good reports, also has a bookshop on the premises, **La Madriguera del Conejo**.

$ La Pinta and La Niña
La Pinta, C 65, No 5-67, T1-211 9526, www.lapinta.com.co, and La Niña, C 66, No 4a-07, T1-704 4323, www.lanina.com.co.
2 popular, welcoming hostels with private rooms, with and without bath, and dorms (US$7.50-11.25), Colombian-run, with gardens, tours and Spanish classes offered, lots of activities. Also has hostels and apartments on the Caribbean coast and in Cali.

North Bogotá
Many international hotel chains are well represented here, such as **Sonesta**, www.sonesta.com (opposite Unicentro), as are local groups such as **Estelar**, www.hotelesestelar.com.

$$$$-$$$ Casa Medina
Cra 7 No 69-22, T1-325 7900, www.fourseasons.com/bogotacm/.

One of Bogotá's grandest and most distinguished old hotels, now part of the Four Seasons chain, the Casa Medina oozes traditional comfort and style, with sumptuously furnished rooms; also excellent Spanish restaurant, **Castanyoles** (see Restaurants, page 58).

$$$$-$$$ Four Seasons Bogotá
Cra 13, No 85-46, T1-325-7930,
www.fourseasons.com/bogota.
Smart and luxurious business-style hotel in upmarket Zona T, with modern suites, gym and spa, highly recommended; also features a glitzy new restaurant **Nemo** (opened Sep 2017), run by Colombian celebrity chef Harry Sasson.

$$$$-$$$ Morrison 84
C 84 Bis, No 13-54, T1-622 3111,
www.hotelmorrison.com.
Handily located near the Zona T, contemporary British design, large rooms with thermo-acoustic windows. It looks out onto the beautiful Parque León de Greiff.

$$ Casona del Patio
Cra 8, No 69-24, T1-212 8805,
http://casonadelpatio.com.
With 24 immaculate rooms set around a sunny patio and well situated near the Zona G, this is one of the best mid-range options. Recommended.

$$-$ Los Andes Hostel
Cra 13A, No 79-07, El Lago, T1-482 9554,
www.losandeshostel.com.
1 block from Zona T and its nightlife, with and without bath, safe, quiet, laundry facilities, airport pick-up, Spanish and salsa classes arranged.

Restaurants

The more exotic and fashionable places to eat are in North Bogotá, but Candelaria has its bistros and good-value, typical Colombian food. Take local advice if you want to eat really cheaply in markets or from street stalls; *panaderías* are also good for early-morning breakfasts.

Throughout the city there are a number of chains with several outlets. Don't miss **Crepes & Waffles** (www.crepesywaffles. com, see website for branches in Colombia and elsewhere), serving very good salads, pittas, crêpes, soups, vegetarian choices, plus lots of desserts, and **Wok** (www.wok.com.co), for Asian cuisine. Also **El Corral** (www. elcorral.com), for hamburgers, pizzas, etc, with regular and **Gourmet** branches; **La Hamburguesería** (www. lahamburgueseria.com), for steaks and sandwiches as well as burgers; the popular coffee shop chains **Juan Valdez** (www.juanvaldezcafe.com) and **Oma** (www.cafeoma.com) are both good for snacks too (**$$-$**).

La Candelaria

$$ Kutral
C 17, No 2-60, T1-459 0455,
www.kutral.wixsite.com/kutral.
Just off the Parque de los Periodistas, serving delicious Italian/Argentine cuisine, including steaks, freshly made pasta, juices and veggie options; small and cosy with rustic gaucho-style decor.

$$ Moros y Cristianos
C 7, No 5-30, T1-342 6273, Facebook:
Restaurante-Moros-y-Cristianos-
Cocina-Cubana. Mon-Fri 1200-1600,
Sat-Sun 1200-1800.

Cuban restaurant with Colombian and other touches. Live music Fri-Sat nights and Sun.

$$ St Just
C16A, No 2-73, T4-777 555,
www.santjustbogota.com
Excellent-value French cuisine at this arty little bistro with funky decor and upbeat music; locally sourced ingredients beautifully presented; sumptuous desserts include amaranto crème caramel with tonka bean glaze.

$$-$ La Totuma Corrida
Cra 2, No 12B-90, T1-284 9462,
Facebook: La-Totuma-Corrida.
On C del Embudo, economic sushi and other Japanese and Colombian fusion dishes. Colourful surroundings.

$ Boulevard Sésamo
Av Jiménez de Quesada 4-64.
Busy vegetarian lunch spot; pay first and find a table; give ticket to waitress; extensive menu includes veggie burgers, vegan *empanadas* and mixed fruit smoothies.

$ Panadería Pastelería La Vieja Suiza
Cra 3 at C 12C 3-07. Closed Sun.
Tiny Swiss place selling coffee, *pasteles*, vegetables, bread and cakes. Has hotel above.

Downtown Bogotá
Many restaurants and cafés along Cra 4A in Barrio La Macarena (behind the Bull Ring), as well as Zona G nearby.

$$$ Criterión
C 69A, No 5-75, T1-310 1377,
www.criterion.com.co.
Chic minimalist decor, expensive French-influenced menu from highly acclaimed chefs, Jorge Rauch and his brother Mark, with shellfish, steak and artistically

presented desserts; large wine list. It also has a booming chain of gastro-restaurants, with branches around Bogotá and the rest of the country.

$$$ Leo
C27B, No 6-75, Pasaje Mompox,
La Macarena, T1 283 8659/286 7091,
www.restauranteleo.com.
A sensational gastronomic experience: star chef Leonor Espinoza takes diners on a culinary tour of Colombia. The tasting menu features 9 courses, based on indigenous recipes from around the country. Standout dishes include raw tuna with ant crust, and *pirarucu* (Amazonian fish) in fermented yuca with *ojo de pez* pepper. Excellent service. Formal, dress smart; advance booking essential (around the corner is partner restaurant **Misia**, more casual, but similarly superb cuisine).

$$$-$$ ArteSano Gourmet
Cra 4A, No 27-12, T1-337 6853,
www.artesanogourmet.com.
Specializes in 'woodfire cooking': fish and meat dishes, as well as pizzas, plus pastas, sandwiches, etc. Also has a high-class *pastelería*, and a new branch in Chapinero (Alto, Cra 6, No 58-63).

$$$-$$ La Cigale
C 69A, No 4-93, T1-249 6839,
www.lacigale.com.co.
French gourmet restaurant, run by Belgian-born François Cornelis, serving a variety of Gallic specialities, with steaks and risottos.

$$$-$$ Tábula
C 29 bis, No 5-90, T1-287 7228, http://
elorigendelacomida.co/tabula. Daily
1200-1600, also Thu-Sat 1900-2300.
Gourmet international menu, serving imaginative and adventurous cuisine in stylish surroundings a couple of blocks

from La Macarena; also has large chain of gastro-sandwich bars, **Sr Ostia**, dotted around the city.

$$ Asadero Capachos
C 18, No 4-68, T1-243 4607, www.asaderocapachos.com. Lunchtimes only, closed Mon.
Not for vegetarians, meat from the Llanos, simple menu, good food, live music Thu-Sun, busy; diners eat in a huge barn-like building with thatch-roofed cubicles to complete the rustic vibe.

$$-$ La Puerta Falsa
C 11, No 6-50, T1-286 5091.
One of Bogotá's longest-standing restaurants, serving excellent-value traditional dishes and Spanish-style tapas in a lively, bustling setting.

North Bogotá
North of C 76 there are 3 popular areas for eating and drinking: Zona T, also known as the Zona Rosa, C 83 and Cra 13; further north is Parque 93, surrounded by eating places, most of which have queues at lunchtime; and C 117 with Cra 6A and Cra 7 in Usaquén.

$$$ Abasto
Cra 6, No 119b-52, Usaquén, T1-215 1286, http://abasto.com.co. Mon-Thu 0700-2200, Fri 0700-2300, Sat 0900-2230, Sun 0900-1700.
Described as "honest" food with the best organic local ingredients, gourmet coffees and teas. Many good reports.

$$$ Castanyoles
Cra 7, No 69A-22, T1-325 7918, in Casa Medina, see page 55.
Spanish tapas restaurant, in a pretty conservatory inside Bogotá's grandest old hotel; with creative modern takes on Spanish classics, such as salmon tartare and yuca/cassava wafer, and crispy suckling pig with coconut cream; good wine list too.

$$$-$$ 80 Sillas
C 118, No 6A-05, Usaquén, T1-644 7766, www.80sillas.com. Lunch and dinner daily from 1200 (closed Sun 1800).
All kinds of ceviches and other seafood served in wooden elevated patios with encroaching ferns.

$$$-$$ Coloquial
Cra 6A, No 116-17 in Usaquén, T1-853 8385. Tue-Sat 1600-0300.
Traditional Colombian cuisine with imaginative twists, plus rich desserts and local cheese, in a stylish modern setting.

$$$-$$ Salto del Angel
Cra 13, No 93A-45, T1-654 5455, Facebook: Salto-del-Angel-Bogota.
This huge restaurant on Parque 93 has a large, varied menu including steaks, ceviches and international options, including fish and chips. On Sat-Sun, after dinner, the tables are cleared and it becomes a popular upmarket disco, plus occasional live music.

$$ Camino del Café
Cra 6A, No 117-26, Usaquén, T1-637 5152,Facebook: Camino-Del-Café.
Pleasant café with outdoor terrace and Wi-Fi. Good coffees, sandwiches, ice creams and cocktails.

Bars and clubs

The 3 liveliest districts are **La Candelaria** (lots of students and backpackers), **Chapinero** and **La Zona T** (aka Zona Rosa – both of these more upmarket). Club admission charges – often called 'cover' – get higher the further north you go, and usually include 1 drink.

Keep your receipt as you might need to show it when you leave.

Gay bars are clustered in **Chapinero**, around C60; the biggest is **Theatron**, with 13 rooms. **Doña Ceci** is the legendary dive-bar drinking hole in La Candelaria; for a more sophisticated vibe, go to **Usaquén**, for its chilled cocktail bars. For a more edgy, local atmosphere, try **Cuadra Picha** near the Primera de Mayo, or **Normandía**, which is cosier and more suburban.

Bogotá Beer Company
C 12D, No 4-02, www.bogotabeer company.com.
The La Candelaria branch of this expanding chain of good pubs (throughout Bogotá, also in Medellín and on the Caribbean coast), belonging to a microbrewery with 11 types of craft beer, plus snacks and pizzas.

Quiebra Canto
Cra 5, No 17-76, T1-243 1630, www.quiebracanto.com.
In a stripped-down colonial house, playing a varied musical range, including world, funk, reggae, soul, rap, Afro-Caribbean, jazz and salsa; friendly crowd, the best nights are Wed and Thu. Also has another branch in Getsemaní, Cartagena.

Downtown to North Bogotá
Most bars and clubs are concentrated in the Cra 11-13, C 80-86 region, known as the Zona Rosa. Some of these have live entertainment. Further south along Cra 7, from C 32 up to C 59 draws an edgier crowd of filmmakers, artists and students.

Galería Café Libro
Cra 11A, No 93-42, T1-218 3435, www. galeriacafelibro.com.co. Tue-Sat.

Restaurant, bar, karaoke and dancing, with 2 other branches in Palermo, Tr 15B, No 46-38, and **Salón Café Bohemia**, Tr 15B, No 46-32, and 1 in Parque 93, C 11A 93-42

Theatrón
C 58, No 10-32, T1-235 6879, www.portal theatron.co. Fri-Sat 2100-0500, or later.
In old large theatre, claiming to be the biggest nightclub in Latin America; gay and mixed crowd, attracts international DJs, good atmosphere with 10 different zones, from low-lit bars to heaving dance floors. Be careful leaving the club at night, use a taxi.

Entertainment

Cinema
Consult *El Espectador*, or www.vive.in for programmes. There are cinema complexes in the principal shopping centres; see for instance *CineColombia*, www.cinecolombia.com. Foreign films, old and new, are shown on weekend mornings in some commercial cinemas and there are many small screening rooms running features.
Cine Paraíso, *C 120A, No 5-69, Usaquén, T1-213 3756, www.cinemaparaiso.com.co.* Foreign art films and independent mainstream productions.
Cinemanía, *Cra 14, No 93A-85, T1-621 0122, www.cinemania.com.co.* Mainstream and foreign art films.

There's an international film festival in mid-Oct (**Festival de Cine de Bogotá**, www.bogocine.com), founded in 1984, and a European film festival (**Eurocine**, www.festivaleurocine.com) in Apr/May.

Dance classes
Punta y Taco, *Salón de Baile, C 85, No 19A-25, of 201B, T300-218 7199, www. puntaytaco.com.* Tango and salsa classes

Mon-Fri 0700-2200, Sat 0800-1800, Sun 0800-1200. Lessons, workshops and shows. Flexible class times, professional.

Theatre

Many of the theatres are in the Candelaria area. For **Teatro Colón** (see details on page 44). Bogotá hosts the biennial **Ibero American Theatre Festival** (www.festivaldeteatro.com. co). The **Temporadas de Opera** and **de Zarzuela** are held annually, the former in Sep, the latter in May-Jun, with international artists (http:// www.primerafila.com.co, www. operadecolombia.com). In the city centre, **Centro Cultural Gabriel García Márquez** (C 11, entre Cras 5 y 6, *T1-283 2200*, www.fce.com.co/CCGGM), has activities, concerts, dance classes and exhibitions; it also has a large **FCE** bookshop, **El Corral Gourmet** restaurant and **Banco de Bogotá**.

Festivals

There are many local religious festivals and parades at Easter and Christmas.
Jan Fiesta de Reyes Magos (Three Kings) in the suburb of Egipto (up the hill to the east of Candelaria) has traditional processions and is one of the best.
Apr/May Feria Internacional del Libro (book fair) is held in **Corferias** (see below), www.feriadellibro.com.
Jun/Jul Rock al Parque is the biggest annual rock festival in Latin America (www.rockalparque.gov.co).
Sep Festival Internacional de Jazz (www.teatrolibre.com).
Dec Expoartesanía, at Corferias, www.expoartesanias.com, offers an excellent selection of arts and crafts and regional food from across Colombia. Highly recommended.

There are events throughout the year at **Corferias** (Cra 37, No 24-67, www. corferias.com), a vast modern exhibition and entertainment complex.

Shopping

In Barrio Gaitán, Cra 30 y C 65, are rows of leather shops. This is an excellent area to buy made-to-measure leather jackets, good value; not safe at night, go during the day.

Camping equipment

Monodedo, *Cra 16, No 82-22, T1-616 3467, www.monodedo.com*. Good selection of camping and climbing equipment. Enquire here for information about climbing in Colombia.
Tatoo, *C 122, No 18-30, T1-629 9949, and Cra 14A, No 82-56, T1-300 2140, https://tatoo. ws*. Complete outdoor gear suppliers.

Handicrafts

See also markets, below.
Artesanías de Colombia, *Claustro de Las Aguas, next to the Iglesia de las Aguas, Cra 2, No 18A-58, see http://artesaniasde colombia.com.co for other outlets*. Beautiful but expensive designer crafts.
Centro Colombiano de Artesanos, *Cra 7, No 22-66*, and **Colombia Linda**, *Cra 7, No 23-49*, are 2 central craft galleries.
Galería Cano, *Ed Bavaria, Cra 13, No 27-98 (Torre B, Int 119), also at Unicentro, Airport and elsewhere, www.galeriacano.com.co*. Sell textiles, pottery, and gold and gold-plated replicas of some of the jewellery on display in the Gold Museum.
Pasaje Rivas, *C10 y Cra 10*. Persian-style bazaar. Hammocks, basketware and ceramics; cheap.

Jewellery

The pavements and cafés along Av Jiménez, below Cra 7, and on Plazoleta del Rosario are used on weekdays (especially Fri) by emerald dealers. Rows of jewellers and emerald shops also along C 12 with Cra 6. Great buying expertise is needed: you can get bargains, but synthetics and forgeries abound.

Emerald Trade Centre, *Av Jiménez, No 5-43, p 1 y 2*. Has a collection of outlets in one place.

GMC Galería Minas de Colombia, *Diag 20A, No 0-12, T1-281 6523, www. galeriaminasdecolombia.com, at foot of Monserrate diagonal from Quinta de Bolívar*. Great choice of gold and emerald jewellery at good prices.

Markets

Mercado de Pulgas (fleamarket) *on Cra 7/C 24, on Sun morning and holidays*. A better fleamarket can be found at the Usaquén market around the plaza, Cra 6 y C 119B, on Sun, also a good arts and crafts market at the top of the hill in Usaquén.

★ **Paloquemao food market**, *C 19, No 25-04, www.plazadepaloquemao.com. Mon-Sat 0430-1630, Sun 0500-1430*. Bogotá's huge central market, good to visit just to see the sheer abundance of Colombia's tropical fruits and flowers. Cheap stalls serving *comida corriente*. Safe.

San Andresito de la 38, *Cra 38 entre C 8 y C 12*. Popular market, cheap alcohol, designer sports labels, electrical goods, football shirts.

What to do

Bullfighting

A ban on bullfighting in 2012 was overturned in 2014. Nevertheless, since then the debate has rumbled on which makes trying to predict future legality of the sport a dubious proposition. When bullfighting is allowed, there are *corridas* on Sat and Sun during the season (Jan-Feb), and occasionally for the rest of the year, at the municipally owned **Plaza de Toros de Santamaría** (Cra 6, No 26-50, T1-334 1482, near Parque Independencia). Local bullfighting museum at bullring, door No 6.

Cycling

The *Ciclovía* is a set of streets leading from Cra 7 to the west, closed to motor traffic every Sun and bank holidays, 0700-1400 for cyclists, joggers, rollerskaters etc. There are also the extensive *Cicloruta* paths.

Bogotá Bike Tours, *Cra 3, No 12-72, La Candelaria, T1-281 9924, T312-502 0554, www.bogotabiketours.com*. Bike tours (US$15pp) at 1030, 1330, rentals (US$4 per hr, US$17 per day), walking tours, cooking classes and more besides; many good reports.

Bogotravel Tours, *C 12F, No 2-52, T1-282 6313, T313-368 0441, www.bogotravel tours.com*. Bike tours (US$20) and rentals, emeralds tours, walking tours, party bus tour, Zipaquirá and Guatavita, and other tours in Bogotá and beyond; Spanish classes; enthusiastic, local guides.

Football

Tickets for matches at El Campín stadium can be bought in advance at **Federación Colombiana de Futbol** (Cra 45A, No 94-06, http://fcf.com.co) or from online ticketing agencies such as **Tuboleta** (www.vivetuboleta.com). It is not normally necessary to book in advance, except for the local Santa Fe-Millonarios derby, and internationals. Take a cushion, matches Sun at 1545, Wed at 2000. Big matches can be rowdy and sometimes violent.

Horse riding

Cabalgatas San Francisco, *47 km from the city near La Vega, T310-265 2706, Facebook: Cabalgatas-San-Francisco.* Daily rides around coffee farms, in the mountains, by rivers and lakes, from US$16 per hr.

Riding Colombia, *www.ridingcolombia. com.* Small ecotourism company offering day-long and multi-day horse rides.

Language courses

You need a student visa, not a tourist visa, to study. Some of the best Spanish courses are in the **Universidad Nacional** (see map, page 44, B2, T1-316 5000, www.unal.edu.co), about US$586 for intensive courses, group discount available, or at the **Universidad de los Andes** (T1-339 4949, https:// ele.uniandes.edu.co/index.php/en/ ocourses/modes-of-study, summer/ semester courses US$460, 45/90 hrs), and **Pontificia Universidad Javeriana** (T1-320 8320 ext 4563, www.javeriana. edu.co). Good-value Spanish courses at the **Universidad Pedagógica** (C 79, No 16-32, T1-610 8000 ext 211, http:// spanishcourse.pedagogica.edu.co). Good reports. Language exchanges with students wishing to learn English are also popular. **Spanish World Institute** (Cra 4A, No 56-56, T1-248 3399, www.spanishworldinstitute.com). Personalized courses from beginner to advanced, activities and events organized, 30 hrs US$290.

Trekking

Camina por Colombia, *Cra 7, No 22-31, of 226, T1-286 7487, www. caminaporcolombia.com.* Walks in different parts of Colombia. There are several other groups and operators.

Caminantes del Retorno, *T1-457 0716, or 315-249 0090, www.caminantesdelretorno. com.* A group of guides with 25 years' experience of treks in out-of-the-way places in the country.

Corporación Clorofila Urbana, *Cra 49B, No 91-41, T1-616 8711, Facebook: Corporación Clorofila Urbana.* Offers walking opportunities with an emphasis on environmental awareness.

Sal Si Puedes, *Cra 7, No 17-01, of 640, T1-283 3765, www.salsipuedes.org. Mon-Fri 0800-1700.* Hiking group arranges walks every weekend and sometimes midweek on trails in Cundinamarca, and further afield at national holiday periods; very friendly, welcomes visitors. Hikes are graded for every ability, from 6 km to 4-day excursions of 70 km or more, camping overnight. Groups are often big (30-60), but it's possible to stray from the main group. Reservations should be made and paid for a week or so in advance.

Tour operators

Aventure Colombia, *Av Jiménez No 4-49, of 204, T1-702 7069, http://aventure colombia.com.* Specializes in classic (Caribbean coast, coffee region, the Andes) and alternative (Guajira, Sierra Nevada, Cocuy, Amazon) tours and expeditions across Colombia, focusing on trekking, eco- and rural tourism. Head office is in Cartagena. Highly recommended.

Aventureros, *Cra 15, No 79-70, of 403, T1-467 3837, www.aventureros.co. Mon-Fri 0900-1700, Sat 0900-1300.* Arranges a variety of tours and adventure sports throughout the country.

Colombia Oculta, *Cra 29, No 74-19, T1-301 0213, www.colombiaoculta.org.* Adventure tours throughout Colombia, ecotourism, programmed or personalized tours.

De Una Colombia Tours, *Cra 24 (Parkway), No 39b-25, of 501, La Soledad, T1-368 1915, www.deunacolombia.com.* Dutch-run tour agency with tailor-made trips throughout Colombia and an emphasis on introducing tourists to the country's people as well as its landscapes; very proficient and professional.

Eco-Guías, *Cra 7, No 57-39, of 501, T1-347 5736 or T1-212 1423, www.ecoguias.com.* Colombian/English team specializes in tailor-made trips, ecotourism, adventure sports, trekking, riding and tourism on coffee fincas, efficient, knowledgeable and well organized. Highly recommended.

Universal Tourism, *T313-352 9355, http://universaltourismcolo.wix.com/mbia/inicio.* Individual and small-group tours with bilingual guides (several languages), focus on Colombia from a local's perspective.

Air

El Dorado airport, on Av El Dorado, has 2 terminals: Terminal 1 for all international and most domestic flights. Some **Avianca** domestic flights and smaller airlines use Puente Aéreo (Terminal 2). T1-266 2000 for the airport call centre, or visit http://eldorado.aero/ for information in Spanish, Portuguese, French and English. Allow at least 2 hrs for checking in and security for all flights. The terminals have *casas de cambio* and ATMs which accept international credit cards. Use only uniformed porters; trolleys US$1.50 (typical charge throughout Colombia). There are tourist offices in international arrivals and in domestic arrivals, see Tourist information, above. An expansion programme is under way and an

additional airport, El Dorado II, is planned for 2021, in the east of Bogotá.

The taxi fare from airport to city is roughly US$10. Only take a yellow, registered taxi by getting a ticket from the official booth at international, or domestic arrivals. There are *colectivos* (US$1-1.50 plus luggage pp) from airport to centre. A *bus satélite* connects the terminals and the bus stop for the city, 0500-2300. The **TransMilenio** extends almost to the airport on a route starting at C 100 on Cra 7, then taking C 26. A feeder bus on Level 2 links the airport with the **TransMilenio** terminus, Portal Eldorado (5 mins, US$1.40, Mon-Fri 0430-2245, Sat 0600-2245, Sun and hols 0600-2145; buy top-up card from there for buses into city centre, ie Bus 1, marked Universidades, to La Candelaria, Las Aguas station (marked on map), and 5 mins' walk to Parque de los Periodistas).

For internal flights, which serve all parts of the country, see page 323. Reconfirmation is not necessary if booking online. Otherwise reconfirm all flights 48 hrs before departure.

Bus

Local Fares start at US$0.60, depending on length of route and time of day. Most buses have day/night tariff advertised in the window. **Busetas** (green) charge a little more and can be dirty. Fares are a little higher on Sun and holidays. The **TransMilenio** (www.transmilenio. gov.co), an articulated bus system running on dedicated lanes connects North, Central and South Bogotá. **Corriente** services stop at all principal road intersections, *expresos* limited stops only. Journeys cost US$0.60-0.80; charge cards are available for frequent use. Using the **TransMilenio** is a good way of getting around, but it can be crowded and confusing, and sometimes even slower than main traffic because of the many buses blocking up the lanes; make sure you know which bus stops at your destination. Taking luggage onto the **TransMilenio** is not recommended during rush hour.

Long distance The main **Terminal de Transportes** is at Diagonal 23, No 69-60, near Av Boyacá (Cra 72) between El Dorado (Av 26) and Av Centenario (C 13), sometimes referred to as Terminal El Salitre, T1-423 3630, www.terminal de transporte.gov.co. There is also access from Cra 68. It is divided into 5 modules; modules 1-3 have several bus companies serving similar destinations, with luggage deposits at the entrance to each module. Module 4 is for interdepartmental taxis and has a first aid centre beside it (open 24 hrs) and module 5 is for arrivals. If possible, buy tickets at the ticket office before travelling to avoid overcharging and to guarantee a seat, especially during bank holidays. Fares and journey times are given under destinations below. If you are travelling to or from the north or northwest, you can significantly cut down on the journey time by taking the **TransMilenio** to Portal del Norte, or Portal de la 80 on C 80, thus avoiding an arduous journey through Bogotá's traffic. If you are travelling to or from the south, many buses use the **Terminal de Transportes del Sur**, C 57 Q Sur, No 75F-82, by Autopista Sur, near the Portal del Sur **TransMilenio** terminus. This is as convenient for the centre of the city as the main terminal if you don't have large bags. To get to the main terminal take a bus marked '**Terminal terrestre**' from the centre or a *buseta* on Cra 10. A taxi costs around US$5 from or to the centre, with a surcharge at night. Give your desired address at the kiosk in module 5, which will print out a slip with the address and price. At airport and bus terminals, unofficial taxis are dangerous and should be avoided. To get into town from the terminal take buses marked 'Centro' or 'Germania'; ask the driver where to get off (the 'Germania' bus goes up to the centre). To get to North Bogotá from the terminal, take a bus heading in that direction on Cra 68.

International Ormeño, bus terminal modelo 2, T1-410 7522, has a Lima–Caracas service 3 days a week via Cúcuta; there is also a weekly Bogotá–Lima service. International tickets with Ormeño can only be bought at the bus terminal. Much better (and cheaper) is to do the trip in stages and enjoy the countries you are travelling through.

Car hire
There are lots of agencies at the airport. **Colombiana Rent a Car**, Av Boyacá, No 63-12, T1-473 8694, www.colombianarentacar.com.

Taxi
Taxis are relatively cheap, with fares priced in units displayed on a meter, starting at 29. The minimum fare is about US$1.30. Average fare from North Bogotá to the centre US$6. Check for additional charges above what the meter states eg: night charge and rides to the airport, and check that the meter is set at 29 when you get in. At busy times, empty taxis flagged down on the street may refuse to take you to less popular places. If you are going to an address out of the city centre, it is helpful to know the neighbourhood (barrio) you are going to as well as the complete street address, eg Chicó, Chapinero (ask at your hotel). Radio taxis are recommended for safety and reliability, though slightly more expensive; when you call, the dispatcher gives you a cab number, confirm this when it arrives. Try these numbers and websites: T434 2000, www.autotaxiejecutivo.com; T250 3670, or www.coopteletaxi.com. Also the taxi apps such as http://tappsi.co and www.easytaxi.com/co/. Note also that there are plans to replace meters with Uber-style tablets, by the end of 2017, allowing passengers to track progress from back seats.

Around
Bogotá

The basin on which Bogotá stands, with high ranges of the Cordillera to the east, is known as La Sabana de Bogotá and is the centre of Colombia's important cut-flower industry. Around La Sabana are many places of interest in nearby towns for weekend excursions out of the city, including the Salt Cathedral at Zipaquirá and the Laguna de Guatavita, perhaps the nearest place the Spaniards came to finding their El Dorado.

North of the city

a unique salt cathedral and the original El Dorado

★ **Zipaquirá** *Colour map 2, C5.*

Zipaquirá's famous rock salt mine is still producing salt after centuries. Within the mines, the **Salt Cathedral** ⓘ *www.catedraldesal.gov.co, daily 0900-1740 (last entry 1640), various ticket combinations available starting at US$11.30; guided tour (in English and Spanish) US$17, well worth it, including sound-and-light show, emerald exhibition and 3D film; discounts for children and seniors*, is one of the major attractions of Colombia. The entrance is in hills about 20 minutes' walk west of the town from Parque Villaveces. At the site, there is an information centre, shops, restaurants, and the **Museo de la Salmuera (Brine)** ⓘ *US$1*, which explains how salt is produced. The original underground cathedral was dedicated in 1954 to Nuestra Señora del Rosario (patron saint of miners). Continuing deterioration made the whole cave unsafe and it was closed.

A remarkable, new Salt Cathedral, minimalist in style but vast in scale, was opened on 16 December 1995. Inside, near the entrance, are the 14 Stations of the Cross, each sculpted by a different artist. Other sections of the cathedral follow to the nave, 180 m below the surface, with huge pillars 'growing' out of the salt, and ongoing work on further wall friezes. All is discreetly illuminated and gives an austere impression.

Zipaquirá has two pleasant colonial plazas lined with restaurants; the main plaza is dominated by a brick cathedral (see www.zipaquira-cundinamarca.gov.co) and shaded by tall palm trees. Tuesday is market day. In the town is the **Museo Quevedo Zornoza** ⓘ *C 3, No 7-69, Mon-Fri 0830-1200, 1400-1700, Sat-Sun 0900-1600, US$1*, which displays musical instruments and paraphernalia including the piano of

ON THE ROAD

The Gilded Man

The basis of the El Dorado (Gilded Man) story is established fact. It was the custom of the Chibcha king to be coated annually with resin, on which gold dust was stuck, and then to be taken out on Laguna de Guatavita on a ceremonial raft. He then plunged into the lake and emerged with the resin and gold dust washed off. The lake was also the repository of precious objects thrown in as offerings; there have been several attempts to drain it (the first, by the Spaniards in colonial times, caused the sharp cut in the crater rim) and many items have been recovered over the years. The factual basis of the El Dorado story was confirmed by the discovery of a miniature raft with ceremonial figures on it, made from gold wire, which is now one of the most prized treasures of the Museo del Oro in Bogotá. Part of the raft is missing; the story is that the gold from it ended up in one of the finder's teeth! (Read John Hemming's *The Search for El Dorado* on the subject.)

General Santander. The **Museo Arqueológico** ⓘ *C 1, No 6-21, T1-852 3499, next to the Parque Villaveces entrance, Tue-Sun 1000-1800, US$1.60,* houses more than 1500 pieces of pre-Columbian pottery at the **station** ⓘ *C 4, No 11-01, T1-593 9150 ext 138.*

Around Zipaquirá

Nemocón, 15 km northeast of Zipaquirá, also has **salt mines** ⓘ *C 2, No 0-05, T1-854 4120, www.minadesal.gov.co, tours daily 0900-1700, US$8, children US$5.50, 10 mins' walk from centre.* It's a more down-to-earth experience than Zipaquirá, colourfully lit, with a small museum, and a church with original 17th-century frescos. (ATM on the main plaza.) A side road connects with the Bogotá–Cúcuta highway. Some 8 km beyond Nemocón, with its own access to the main Tunja road, is **Suesca**, a centre of rock climbing on sandstone cliffs overlooking the Río Bogotá.

Guatavita *Colour map 2, C5.*

The modern town of Guatavita Nueva, 75 km from Bogotá at 2650 m, is a popular haunt for Bogotanos. It was rebuilt in replica colonial style when the old town of Guatavita was submerged by the Embalse de Tominé. There is a small bullring, cathedral and two small museums, one devoted to the Muisca people and the other to relics of the old Guatavita church. There are many artisan shops, which sell *ruanas*. Market day is Sunday. The tourist information booth can find accommodation.

Laguna de Guatavita, a sacred lake of the Muisca, is where the legend of El Dorado (see box, above) originated. Access to the Laguna del Cacique Guatavita y Cuchilla de Peñas Blancas park is only allowed with a permit from the **Corporación Autónoma Regional de Cundinamarca** (CAR) ⓘ *Cra 7, No 36-45, Bogotá, T1-320 9000, lake open Tue-Sun 0900-1600 (closed Tue when Mon is a holiday) but you can stay in the park till 1800, US$5 for foreigners, children and locals pay less.* The lake is a quiet, beautiful place; you can walk right round it, 1½ hours, or climb to the rim of the crater. From the park entrance there are guided walks and interpreted

Río Magdalena

Colombia's most famous and iconic river, the Magdalena flows for 1540 km (949 miles) from its source, the Laguna de Magdalena, high on the *páramo* in the southern Huila department, to Barranquilla on the Caribbean coast. It crosses most of the country, through deep ravines and flooding out into vast lagoons and tropical swamps.

The river has played a vital role throughout Colombia's history. Originally called the Yuma by the Muisca people who lived by its banks, the Magdalena was given its present name by the Spanish explorer Rodrigo de Bastidas on April 1, 1501. Gold-crazed conquistadors navigated deep river valleys and treacherous rapids in search of the fabled ore. Instead of gold, however, the river led them to hostile tribes and impenetrable swamps teeming with mosquitoes, caiman and anacondas. In their exhausted frustration, the Spaniards named the estuary Bocas de Ceniza – Mouths of Ashes.

Nevertheless, pioneering early travellers were undeterred by the Spaniards' travails. Naturalists, such as German Alexander von Humboldt, and Colombian botanist José Celestino de Mutis recognized the river's greater scientific value and travelled up the Magdalena and deep into the interior, collecting priceless specimens of unique flora and fauna.

And, for three centuries, before the advent of road and rail, the Magdalena provided the main access to inland Colombia for passengers and cargo, transporting coffee, rubber, cotton and other goods from Bogotá to the coast. Riverside towns, such as Honda and Mompós, grew rich from the booming traffic. Honda, between Bogotá and Medellín, was developed as a major river port by the Spanish, with Mississippi-style steamboats conveying wealthy

trails; guides speak English and Spanish. Opinions differ on whether the crater is volcanic or the result of a meteorite impact, but from the rim at 3100 m there are extensive views over the countryside.

Towards Honda

The Sabana de Bogotá is dotted with farms and groves of eucalyptus. Two routes go to Honda (see Transport, page 72). The older road passes through the small towns of **Fontibón**, **Madrid** and **Facatativá**, 40 km from Bogotá. Some 3 km from Facatativá, on the road to the west, is the park of Piedras de Tunja, a natural rock amphitheatre with enormous stones, numerous indigenous pictographs and an artificial lake. The roads meet at **Villeta**, 71 km from Facatativá, a popular weekend resort. The road continues to the interesting historical town of **Guaduas**. In the main plaza is a statue of the heroine of independence (Policarpa Salavarrieta), the cathedral and one of several museums in the town; also the **tourist office** ⓘ *C3, No 3-45, T1-846 6052, Mon-Fri 0800-1200/1400-1700, Sat 0800-1200.* Market day is Sunday. Nearby La Piedra Capira offers great views of Río Magdalena. From here, a bus to Honda is US$1.75, one hour.

passengers to and from the coast in the utmost comfort, albeit on a week-long journey. Eventually, however, Honda was bypassed when faster roads were built to the Caribbean. As a result, the town has retained its colonial splendour, as well as its attachment to the river. The population swells each year during the *subida* fish festival: when thousands of migrating fish swim up its rapids, attracting similar numbers of anglers to scoop them out of the water.

Mompós, further downstream, has also enjoyed the ebb and flow of the river's fortunes. This steamy town deep inland south of Cartagena, was built on a huge island in the middle of the Magdalena. Until the river silted up in the 19th century it was one of Colombia's leading ports and its third-largest city, with sumptuous villas and magnificent churches built along the waterfront. Again, with the advent of road and rail, Mompós was sidelined and forgotten for centuries, until adventure tourists rediscovered the town's unique tranquillity, and the abundant birdlife of the river's vast lagoons, the *ciénegas*.

Besides its natural and man-made features, the Magdalena has also long been a rich source of indigenous folklore. The pre-Columbian inhabitants of the Tolima region, around present-day Honda, told stories of mythical riverine creatures, including El Mohán, La Patasola, La Llorona and El Hombre Caimán. El Mohán is a hairy monster who capsizes fishing boats and bewitches young girls; one-legged, siren-like La Patasola entices lascivious men before sucking their blood and revealing herself as a hideous hag; La Llorona is a wailing woman who curses anyone that tries to help her babe in arms; and El Hombre Caimán was turned into half-man, half-caiman by a witch who caught him spying on women bathing in the Magdalena.

To see graphic illustrations of these monsters, as well as a fine exhibition of the Magdalena's colourful past, visit Honda's Museo del Río Magdalena (see below).

Honda and beyond *Colour map 2, B4.*

On the west bank of the Río Magdalena, Honda is an impressive old town, brimming with character. Founded in 1539 and in a stunning riverside setting with narrow cobblestoned streets, painted wooden balconies, and a gentler pace of life, it attracts weekender Bogotanos. It was once a major port for cargo and passengers from the centre of the country to the Caribbean. Paddle steamers plied the river to and from the Caribbean, but with the advent of first rail then roadbuilding in the 1950s, it fell into decline. In recent years, however, Honda has undergone a revival, as colonial mansions are being restored to their former glory and its historical significance is being rediscovered. The town lies at the confluence of the Ríos Magdalena and Guali, and is well known for its many bridges, most notably the Puente Navarro, the first metal bridge over the Magdalena, built in 1898 by the San Francisco Bridge Company (cross the bridge at sunset for superb views and for watching egrets and other birds). The historic centre has narrow, picturesque streets and the lively indoor market in a grand, early 20th-century building. There are two museums: **Museo del Río Magdalena** ⓘ *at end of C del Retiro, Tue-Sun* and bank holiday Mon 1000-1200, 1400-1800, a great little collection in a restored former army barracks, with artefacts, photos and artworks charting the changing fortunes of the Magdalena, its riverine inhabitants, wildlife and riverboat history, with a small shop; and **Casa Museo Alfonso López Pumarejo** ① *C13, No 11-75, Plaza América, Tue-Sat 0800-1200, 1400-1800, Sun 0900-1300, free*, dedicated to the ex-president (1934-1938, 1942-1945), who died in 1959 in London, where he was the ambassador. Exhibits include photographs, costumes, memorabilia and an overview of Colombia's modern history (in Spanish only).

El Salto de Honda (the rapids that separate the Lower from the Upper Magdalena) is below the town. In February/March, the Magdalena rises and fishing is especially good as fish swim upstream en masse to lay their eggs, attracting fishermen in their droves and celebrated in Honda as the Festival de la Subienda.

Beyond Honda the road passes cattle fincas and eroded outcrops on its way to La Dorada and, across the river, Puerto Salgar with a huge military base. The highway to Medellín leaves the south–north road to Santa Marta just before Puerto Triunfo. The other main road from Honda heads west to Manizales (see page 221).

Listings North of the city

Tourist information

Zipaquirá

Tourist office
C4 and Cra 12, T1-593 9150, www.zipaquiratravel.co. Mon-Fri 0800-1230, 1400-1700.
Very helpful, with maps and leaflets.

Around Zipaquirá

Nemocón tourist office
Cra 6, No 6-11, T1-854 4123.

Suesca Tourist office
Cra 4, No 2-20, T1-856 3565.

Where to stay

Zipaquirá

$$ Cacique Real
Cra 6, No 2-36, on road to salt mine, T1-851 0209 or 311-532 1251, www.hotelcaciquereal.com.
Listed as 'Patrimonio Cultural', this fine colonial-style hotel has a lovely courtyard with hanging baskets, good rooms, restaurant (breakfast only) and car park.

$$-$ Casa Virrey
C 3, No 6-21, T1-852 3720, casavirreyorani@hotmail.com.
Housed in a new building with comfortable rooms.

$ Torre Real
C 8, No 5-92, T1-851 1901, hoteltorrereal@yahoo.es.
Light and airy rooms with large beds.

Around Zipaquirá

$$$ La Esperanza
Cra 71C, No 98A-44, Vereda Cuaya, Km 1 along railway from Suesca, T1-637 3753 (Bogotá), 320-277 0011 (Suesca), www.hotellaesperanza.com.co.
With restaurant, conference centre, sauna, camping at Campamento Zhay, or house or room to rent sleeping 3-5, good for groups.

$ Caminos de Suesca
Vereda Cacicazgo, Entrada a las Rocas, Suesca, T310-341 8941, http://caminosdesuesca.wix.com/hostal.
Hostal and restaurant offering packages that include adventure sports or just B&B, very helpful. Rooms are cheaper midweek and without bath, also has dorm accommodation. Arranges all sorts of outdoor sports, climbing, riding, rafting, parapenting, in various combinations. Recommended.

Honda

$$$ Posada Las Trampas
Cra 10A, No 11-05, T310-343 5151, www.posadalastrampas.com.
Boutique hotel in a converted 16th-century mansion on C Las Trampas, suites and standard rooms, pool on the terrace, spa, bar and business centre, with safe parking.

$$$-$$ Casa Belle Epoque
C 12, No 12A-21, Cuesta de San Francisco, T8-251 1176/310-481 4090, www.casabelleepoque.com.
A lovely old house overlooking the market, with spacious, tastefully furnished rooms, all with fan or a/c, 1 small dorm (**$** pp), beautiful roof terrace with jacuzzi, pool and period touches. British/Colombian-run, very helpful, advance booking preferred. Arranges horse riding, boat and fishing trips, with *tambo* lodge by the riverside. Recommended.

$$-$ Riviera Plaza
C 14, No 12-19, T312-745 1446, hotelrivieraplaza@hotmail.com.
Cheaper with fan, rooms around a large pool, which is open till 2200. End rooms have views over the Río Gualí and the colonial part of town. All meals extra, in restaurant 0700-2100.

$ Calle Real
Cra 11, No 14-40, T8-251 7737, opposite Teatro Honda.
Central, safe, cheaper with fan, parking, restaurant, small rooftop pool.

$ Tolima Plaza
Cra 11, No 15-75, T8-251 7216.
Large, rambling hotel, pool, large car park. Rooms are a bit spartan but OK, with fan, cheaper in shared room. Helpful management.

Festivals

Honda
Feb Subienda Festival. People come from all over the country for the festival, which marks the end of the fishing season.
Mar/Apr Semana Santa. Celebrations are good.

What to do

Around Zipaquirá
Rock climbing
For information call **Monodedo** climbing centre, T311-577 6008, www.monodedo.com (shop open at weekends). In Suesca turn right at the entrance to Las Rocas, past Rica Pizza restaurant. **Ricardo Cortés**, the owner of Rica Pizza, also arranges climbing trips and local accommodation. See also **Caminos de Suesca**, Where to stay, above.

Transport

Zipaquirá
Bus
The Zipaquirá bus station is on Cra 7, about 6 blocks/15 mins' walk from the mines and cathedral; frequent buses to Bogotá, about every 15 mins, US$2-

3. Many buses leave from **Bogotá**'s Terminal de Transporte; take a bus from Módulo 3, otherwise from the Intermunicipio terminal at the Portal del Norte terminus of the **TransMilenio** in North Bogotá, US$2-3 each way on either route, 1½ hrs from Terminal de Transport, 45 mins from Portal Norte. Zipaquirá can also be reached from Tunja (see page 80), by taking a Bogotá-bound bus and getting off at La Caro for connection to Zipaquirá, US$2.50. Note when arriving to C174 terminus from Zipaquirá you need to buy a **TransMilenio** bus ticket to leave the station. To avoid this, ask the driver to drop you off before the bus station. Frequent buses from Zipaquirá to Nemocón, 30 mins, US$1, or from Bogotá, 1½ hrs, US$2-3.

Train
La Sabana station is at C 13, No 18-24, Bogotá. A slow tourist steam train runs on Sat, Sun and holidays at 0815, calling at **Usaquén** in the north of Bogotá, going north to **Zipaquirá** (1105) and **Cajicá**, back in Bogotá, **La Sabana** at 1730. Trains leave from Usaquén at 0915, arriving back at 1630. Cost: adult US$20, child up to 12, US$17.75. Tickets should be bought in advance at La Sabana station, T1-316 1300, or Usaquén station, Trv 10, No 100-08, Mon-Fri 0830-1730, Sat 0800-1700, www.turistren.com.co, or from travel agents.

Guatavita
Bus
Bogotá–Guatavita Nueva via Autopista del Norte and Sesquilé, from Portal del Norte on the **TransMilenio**, US$2.75, 2 hrs, several departures morning; last return bus at 1730. A 2nd route goes from C 72 y Cra 13 opposite Universidad Pedagógica via La Calera, Tres Esquinas, Guasca and Guatavita Nueva, US$2.30. The routes meet at the entrance to the park, but from Guatavita Nueva it's a 1½-hr walk to the park entrance, or you can share vehicle, about US$5 pp.

Honda
Bus
The bus terminal is on the outskirts, where Diagonal 17 meets the main road heading north to La Dorada. Buses to **Bogotá** take 2 routes, via Facatativá ('Faca') which is slower but has cheaper tolls and is used by most companies, and via La Vega and C 80 to the north. The roads diverge at Villeta. Several companies go to Bogotá via Faca, from US$9.30, 4-5 hrs; **Cundinamarca** go via La Vega, 3 a day, US$10 (also to **Zipaquirá**, US$12), also **Tax La Feria** *camioneta*, 9 a day on Manizales–Bogotá route, 3½ hrs, US$13 (for La Feria, T1-263 8678, or 320-696 6016). To **Manizales**, US$14. Several daily buses to **Medellín**, **Bolivariano**, **Flota Magdalena**, US$15-18, 6 hrs.

Parque Natural Chicaque
Contact in Bogotá, Tr 26B, No 41-51, La Soledad, T1-3683114, www.chicaque.com. Park open daily 0800-1500, US$5.15, with separate prices for lodging, guides and riding. To get there, take the Transmilenio from Bogotá to Terreros/Hospital in Soacha. At weekends the park runs transport from there for US$2 each way at set times. See www. chicaque.com for details of how to arrive on weekdays and how to get there by car.

The picturesque Simón Bolívar Highway runs 132 km from Bogotá to **Girardot**, the former main river port for Bogotá. About 20 km along this road from the centre of Bogotá is Soacha, the end of the built-up area. A right fork here leads to the Parque Natural Chicaque, a 300-ha privately owned park, principally cloudforest between 2100 m and 2700 m on the edge of the Sabana de Bogotá. It is a popular spot for walkers and riders at weekends with good facilities for day visitors and a Swiss-style *refugio*, cabins, camping and restaurant, about 45 minutes down the trail from the entrance (full board price from US$70 double, camping from US$21).

★ **Villavicencio and Los Llanos** *Colour map 2, C5.*
Through Colombia's longest tunnel, the impressive Buenavista, and along an 85-km road running southeast from Bogotá lies **Villavicencio**, capital of Meta Department.

Villavicencio (known as 'Villavo') is a modern town and is a good base for visiting Los Llanos (the plains), which stretch more than 800 km east from the foot of the Eastern Cordillera as far as Puerto Carreño, on the Orinoco in Venezuela. Los Llanos is cowboy country and the never-ending expanse of fertile plains makes it ideal for raising cattle, the area's main industry. The area is also rich in oil and the flames from distant oil refineries can be seen flickering on the horizon. Some ranches welcome visitors and tour operators are beginning to offer trips to destinations such as San José de Guaviare, southeast of Villavicencio, the **Ecolodge Juan Solito** (www.juansolito.com) in Casanare, Parque Nacional Tuparro, reached from Puerto Carreño, and Los Cerros de Mavecure, reached from Puerto Inírida (both near the Venezuelan border). Consult tour operators such as **De Una**, **Colombia Oculta** and **Aventure Colombia** in Bogotá (see pages 62-63).

There are three popular routes from Villavicencio into Los Llanos:

Ruta del Piedemonte Llanero Heading northwards from Villavicencio, this route has parks, indigenous communities and hot springs to visit. Around 3 km northeast is the **Bioparque Los Ocarros** ① *Km 3 via Restrepo, T300-815 6222, www.bioparquelosocarros.com.co, US$5, children US$3.50, Mon-Fri 0900-1600, Sat and Sun 0900-1630*, a thematic park set among lakes and forests, with nearly 200 species endemic to Los Llanos, and with nature guides, educational talks and workshops on offer. Further along the road is the pleasant town of **Restrepo**, famous for its salt mines and its pretty twin-towered church on the main square. Beyond is **Cumaral**, which has palm-tree plantations and is known as the best place to eat meat in Los Llanos. A few kilometres north of Cumaral, near Barranca de Upía, are **Las Termales Aguas Calientes** ① *T310-751 8226, www.lastermales. com/, Sat, Sun and holidays, 0900-1800, US$8, children US$5*, which has a natural pool set in exuberant forest, as well as thermal swimming pool, Turkish baths, nature trail and a restaurant.

Ruta del Amanecer Llanero Running east on the R40 towards Puerto López, this route, after about 62 km, passes near the **Resguardo Indígena Maguare** ① *office at Cra 33 No 34A-46 Lc 1, Villavicencio, T8-682 4325, www.facebook.com/ EcoEtnoturismoMaguare/*, a community project set up and managed by the Uitoto,

Tatuyo and Bora people. The community puts on ancestral dances in a traditional *maloca* as well as talks about Colombia's indigenous people and workshops on how to use some of their traditional tools and weapons. Some of the proceeds go towards supporting displaced and marginalized indigenous groups.

The road east passes through the Apiay oil field before reaching Puerto López, on the Río Meta. A few kilometres beyond Puerto López is the 21-m-high **El Obelisco** at Alto Menegua, built in 1993 to mark the geographic centre of Colombia. This colourful monument displays elements of prehistory, cultural heritage and a relief map of Colombia; there are also wonderful views of the Llanos from here. A further 150 km east is **Puerto Gaitán**, with more stunning views and excellent sunsets to be seen from the bridge across the Río Manacacías. North of town, the Manacacías reaches the Río Meta, where there are some beautiful white-sand beaches.

Ruta del Embrujo Llanero Heading south from Villavicencio the road passes through Acacias, Guamal and **San Martín**, a staunch cattle town, that hosts a horse show in November, the **Cuadrillas de San Martín** (claimed to be the biggest of its kind in the world). From Guamal, a road leads southwest to the village of Cubarral and the Río Ariari, on the edge of the **Parque Nacional Natural Sumapaz**. This area is increasingly popular for adventure sports, including paragliding and abseiling. Whitewater rafting is particularly recommended, as well as *balsaje* (floating downriver on bamboo rafts); contact El Meta regional tourist office in Villavicencio (see below), Km 7 Vía Camino Ganadero, T8-683 0848, www. turismometa.gov.co, Monday-Friday 0730-1600. The road, meanwhile, eventually leads to San Juan de Arama, gateway to the **Parque Nacional Natural Serrranía de la Macarena** (see below).

Serranía de la Macarena *Colour map 3, A6.*
Caño Cristales is a river in which *Macarenia clavigera* plants bloom deep red for a brief period and, together with other natural colours – red, blue, green and black – create an amazing spectacle. It is often called "the most beautiful river in the world". The river, in the south of the Serranía de la Macarena, is reached from the town of **La Macarena**, to which there are three weekly flights from Bogotá between June and December with **Satena**, and local air taxi flights from Villavicencio. Check in advance as the phenomenon can occur anytime between June and November. The site is closed January to May. The area is protected and policed, and you cannot camp or go independently. Several agencies run tours and there are two- to five-day packages available, all controlled by **Cormacarena** ⓘ *www.cormacarena.gov.co*. At weekends and on bank holidays it is usually packed. Two sources of information are: www.cano-cristales.com (also at Calle 5, No 7-35, La Macarena, T321-842 2728) and the private portal of local photographer Mario Carvajal, www.canocristales.co. At the time of writing, the area of La Macarena near Río Caño is safe to visit, but don't venture outside the organized tour routes and check with local authorities before setting out.

Tourist information

Villavicencio

Instituto de Turismo de Villavicencio
*C 33A, No 39-43, p 2, Centro, T8-683 3681
or 8-673 3681, www.turismovillavicencio.
gov.co. Mon-Sat 0900-1200, 1400-1800,
with offices at the airport and bus terminal.*

Instituto de Turismo del Meta
*Km 7 Vía Camino Ganadero, T8-683
0848, www.turismometa.gov.co.
Mon-Fri 0730-1600.*

Where to stay

Villavicencio

$$$ Hotel del Llano
*Cra 30, No 49-77, T311-562 5040,
www.hoteldelllano.com.*
Tucked under the forested hills of the
Cordillera Oriental, a smart modern
option with good rooms, spa, sauna,
pool, restaurant and tour agency.

$$$-$$ María Gloria
*Cra 38, No 20-26, T8-672 0197,
www.hotelmariagloria.com.*
Large rooms in a featureless building,
with a good pool area with sauna and
Turkish bath.

$$ Savoy
C 41, No 31-02, T8-662 2666.
Simple rooms with a/c. Vegetarian
restaurant downstairs.

$ Mochilero's Hostel
*C 18, No 39-08-10, Barrio Balatá,
T8-667 6723/320-488 5046, Facebook:
mochileroshostelvillavicencio.*
Hostel with private rooms and dorms,
restaurant, also offers salsa and yoga
classes, adventure tours.

Los Llanos
One of the best ways to get to know
Los Llanos is by staying on a cattle ranch
(finca), where you'll have the chance to
go hiking, wildlife spotting and horse
riding. **Ecolodge Juan Solito** (www.
juansolito.co, near Yopal), has been
highly recommended, or visit www.
alquilerfincasenlosllanos.com, which
has multiple listings.

Festivals

Villavicencio and Los Llanos
**Jun-Jul Torneo Internacional del
Joropo**, involving parades, singers and
over 3000 couples dancing the *joropo*
in the street.
Mid-Oct Encuentro Mundial de Coleo,
similar to rodeo, in which cowboys
tumble young calves by grabbing their
tails and twisting them until they lose
their balance.
Dec Festival Llanero, www.turismo
villavicencio.gov.co, with *joropo* and
other music, *coleo* and other cowboy
skills and gastronomy from the Llanos.

Transport

Villavicencio and Los Llanos
Air
Avianca, **LATAM** and **Satena** to **Bogotá**
daily (it is much more convenient to go
by bus to Villavicencio than by plane).
Satena flies to **Puerto Carreño** and to
destinations in the Llanos.

Bus
Station outside town, taxi US$1.50.
To/from **Bogotá**, **Flota Magdalena**,
Bolivariano minivans and others
leave frequently, US$7.15, 1½ hrs.

North of Bogotá

the colonial heart of the country

Heading north from Bogotá towards the border with Venezuela or the Caribbean coast, the road takes you on a historical journey through the heart of Colombia, passing picturesque valleys, canyons and spectacular high mountain passes.

Set on a high plateau is Tunja, capital of the Department of Boyacá and formerly the seat of power of the indigenous Muisca. The area also played its part in the liberation of Colombia from the Spanish, particularly at Puente de Boyacá, where Simón Bolívar and his troops fought a decisive battle. Boyacá is dotted with dozens of colonial towns and villages, notably Villa de Leiva and Monguí.

From the Andean foothills of Boyacá, the road swoops down to the turbulent Río Fonce and the Department of Santander. Here too the Spanish colonial legacy is very much intact, particularly in Barichara, Guane and Girón. In recent years the area's countless tumbling rivers, caves and deep canyons have made it the capital of Colombia's burgeoning adventure sports scene, centred around the pretty town of San Gil. From the Department capital of Bucaramanga, a road climbs northeast over moorland for more lessons in Independence history around Pamplona and Cúcuta in Norte de Santander. Another road heads north towards the Sierra Nevada de Santa Marta and the Caribbean coast.

Best for
Adventure sports ▪ Colonial heritage ▪ Independence history

Footprint
picks

★ **Villa de Leiva and Barichara**, pages 82 and 91

Stroll around these beautiful and well-preserved colonial towns.

★ **Paipa mudbaths and thermal springs**, page 88

Pamper yourself at the therapeutic spa, perhaps to recover from the rigours of hiking in the Sierra Nevada del Cocuy.

★ **Sierra Nevada del Cocuy**, page 88

Trek among dazzling snow-capped peaks.

★ **San Gil**, page 90

Go abseiling, caving, kayaking and rafting in the country's adventure capital.

★ **Chicamocha Canyon**, page 92

Marvel at the steep cliffs carved by the Río Chicamocha.

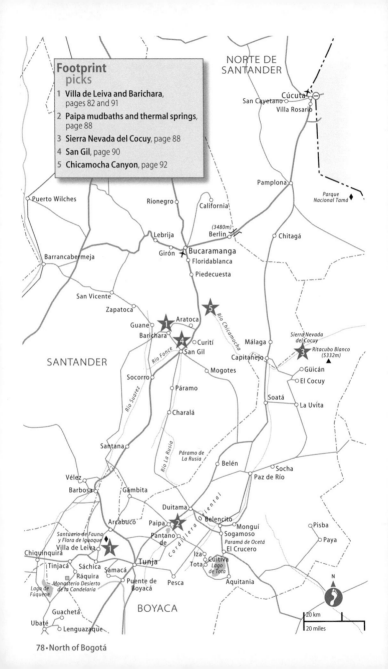

Footprint
picks

1 **Villa de Leiva and Barichara,**
   pages 82 and 91

2 **Paipa mudbaths and thermal springs,**
   page 88

3 **Sierra Nevada del Cocuy,** page 88

4 **San Gil,** page 90

5 **Chicamocha Canyon,** page 92

Essential North of Bogotá

Finding your feet

The transport hubs are Tunja in Boyacá Department, Bucaramanga in Santander Department and Cúcuta on the border with Venezuela. All are served by regular buses to and from Bogotá. The main road north from Bogotá passes through Tunja and San Gil; at Bucaramanga it divides: north to the Caribbean coast and northeast to Cúcuta. There are regular flights from Bogotá to both Bucaramanga and Cúcuta.

Getting around

Walking is the best way to explore colonial town centres, but you'll need buses, taxis and *colectivos* to explore outlying regions.

When to go

The mountainous regions around Tunja and El Cocuy are cool and can be rainy or foggy even in the dry seasons (December to April and July to August). The weather becomes increasingly hot as you head north into Santander. Cúcuta is very warm year-round.

It is best to avoid Cocuy in the peak holiday times, as campsites can get very busy.

Time required

Two weeks will allow you to explore some of the towns and villages; add another week for trekking.

Weather North of Bogotá (Tunja)

January	February	March	April	May	June
19°C 7°C 16mm	19°C 8°C 29mm	19°C 9°C 55mm	18°C 10°C 77mm	17°C 10°C 84mm	16°C 9°C 58mm

July	August	September	October	November	December
16°C 8°C 46mm	17°C 8°C 42mm	17°C 8°C 54mm	18°C 9°C 85mm	18°C 9°C 69mm	18°C 8°C 31mm

Tunja, Villa de Leiva and around

colonial towns with historic and prehistoric sites nearby

The department of Boyacá is the cultural and historical heart of Colombia. Its green valleys and colonial villages were the centre of the Muisca empire, whose gold was so coveted by the Spanish. The empire's capital was at Tunja, which at the time rivalled Bogotá in size and importance. Today, tourists mostly flock to nearby Villa de Leiva, with its whitewashed colonial mansions and cobbled streets, which is becoming a popular weekend retreat for affluent Bogotanos. In the northeast of the department is the Sierra Nevada del Cocuy, a mountain range of jagged ice peaks and breathtaking lakes to rival any in South America.

Tunja *Colour map 2, B5.*

Tunja, capital of Boyacá Department and 137 km from Bogotá, has some of the finest and best-preserved colonial churches in Colombia. When the Spaniards arrived in what is now Boyacá, Tunja was already an indigenous city, the seat of the Zipa, one of the two Chibcha kings. It was refounded as a Spanish city by Gonzalo Suárez Rendón in 1539 and has been declared a national monument. The **cathedral** and five other churches are all worth visiting, particularly for their colonial woodwork and lavish decoration.

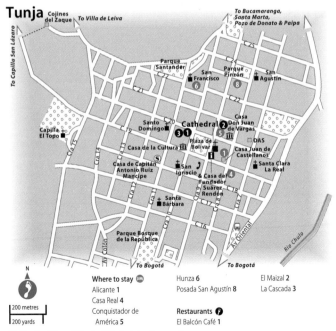

Tunja

Where to stay
Alicante 1
Casa Real 4
Conquistador de
  América 5
Hunza 6
Posada San Agustín 8
El Maizal 2
La Cascada 3

Restaurants
El Balcón Café 1

ON THE ROAD
Simón Bolívar

Aside from Columbus, no single man has had a greater influence on South American history than Simón Bolívar. This Venezuelan aristocrat galvanized the many factions of the continent into a united army that succeeded in expelling the Spanish from present-day Colombia, Venezuela, Panama, Ecuador, Peru and Bolivia.

His campaign through the Departments of Norte de Santander, Santander and Boyacá remains one of his greatest achievements.

In May 1819, Bolívar marched into Colombia from Venezuela with a force of 2000 men, meeting with General Francisco de Paula Santander's forces at Tame. He proposed to cross the Andes by the rarely used route across the Páramo de Pisba, a barren, windswept section of the Cordillera Oriental, the lowest pass of which was over 3200 m. There were many deaths and few of his 800 horses survived, but the audacious manoeuvre outwitted the Spanish. The armies met near Paipa and Bolívar's troops inflicted a surprise defeat.

On 6 August, Bolívar marched into Tunja, but his route to the capital was blocked by the royalists at a bridge crossing the Río Boyacá, 16 km to the south. Despite the strength of their position, the Spanish were routed at the first attack and disintegrated. Over 1600 prisoners were taken, and, four days later, Bolívar entered Bogotá as the liberator of Colombia.

Two years later, on 6 May 1821, the First Congress of Gran Colombia met at Cúcuta. It was at this meeting that the plan to unite Venezuela, Colombia and Ecuador was ratified, the pinnacle of Bolívar's career.

The **Casa del Fundador Suárez Rendón** ⓘ *Plaza de Bolívar (Cra 9, No 19-56, next door to the cathedral), daily 0830-1230, 1400-1800, US$1*, is one of Colombia's few mansions of a Spanish conquistador (1539-1543) and has a peaceful courtyard with fine views of the valley; see the unique series of plateresque paintings on the ceilings.

The market, near Plaza de Toros on the outskirts of town, is open every day (good for *ruanas* and blankets). Friday is the main market day. During the week before Christmas (16-22 December), there is a lively festival with local music, traditional dancing and fireworks.

The battle of Boyacá was fought about 16 km south of Tunja, on the road to Bogotá. Overlooking the bridge at Boyacá is a large **monument to Bolívar** ⓘ *daily 0800-1800, entrance free*. There are several other monuments, an exhibition hall and restaurant at the site. Bus from Tunja, US$1, ask for 'El Puente'. Bolívar took Tunja on 6 August 1819, and next day his troops, fortified by a British Legion, the only professional soldiers among them, fought the Spaniards on the banks of the swollen Río Teatinos. With the loss of only 13 killed and 53 wounded they captured 1600 men and 39 officers. Only 50 men escaped, and when these told their tale in Bogotá the Viceroy Samao fled in such haste that he left half a million pesos of the royal funds.

★ **Villa de Leiva** *Colour map 2, B5.*

About 40 km west is the beautiful and unmissable colonial town of Villa de Leiva (also spelt Leyva) which has one of the largest plazas in the Americas. It is surrounded by cobbled streets, a charming, peaceful place. The town dates back to the early days of Spanish rule (1572) and, like Tunja, it has been declared a national monument so will not be modernized. The first president of Nueva Granada, Andrés Días Venero de Leiva, lived in the town. Many of the **colonial houses** are now hotels, others are museums, such as the restored birthplace of the independence hero, **Casa de Antonio Ricaurte** ⓘ *Cra 8 y C 15, Wed-Fri 0900-1200, 1400-1700, Sat-Sun 0900-1300, 1400-1800, US$0.75.* Ricaurte was born in Villa de Leiva and died in 1814 at San Mateo, Venezuela, fighting with Bolívar's army. The house has a nice courtyard and garden. The **Museo Antonio Nariño** ⓘ *Cra 9, No 10-25, Mon-Tue, Thu-Sat 0900-1230, 1400-1800, Sun 0830-1230, 1430-1700, free,* displays documents from the Independence period. The **Casa del Primer Congreso** ⓘ *Cra 9, No 13-25, on the corner of the Plaza Mayor, daily 0800-1200, 1400-1700, free,* in which the first Convention of the United Provinces of New Granada was held,

Villa de Leiva

To ⑧ ② & Museo Paleontológico

Monasterio de las Carmelitas Descalzas

Plazuela de San Agustín

Casa de Antonio Ricaurte

Museo Luis Alberto Acuña

Alcaldía

Casa del Primer Congreso

Plaza Mayor

Iglesia Parroquial

Parque Nariño

Casa de Antonio Nariño

Plaza de Mercado

San Francisco

To Bogotá, via Tunja or Chiquinquirá

To Santa Sofía, Ecce-Homo & El Fósil

Av Circunvalar

200 metres
200 yards

Where to stay 🛏
Candelaria 1
Casa Viena 2
Colombian Highlands &
  Hostal Renacer 3

El Marqués de San Jorge 5
El Molino
  la Mesopotamia 6
Hostal Sinduly 7
Plaza Mayor 8

Posada de los Angeles 9
Posada Don Blas 10

Restaurants 🍴
Casa Blanca 1

Casa Quintero (La Cocina de
  la Gata, Savia, Zarina) 2
Olivas & Especias and
  Carnes & Olivas 3

is worth a visit if the local authority is not in session. On the Plaza Mayor the **Casa-Museo Luis Alberto Acuña** ⓘ *http://casamuseoacuna8.wix. com/casamuseoacuna, US$2.50, daily 1000-1200, 1400-1800, guided tours at weekends*, houses fascinating examples of Acuña's work.

Tip...
Some colonial houses close Monday to Friday out of season, but the trip to the town is worthwhile for the views and for long, peaceful walks in the hills.

The **Monasterio de las Carmelitas Descalzas** ⓘ *C 14 y Cra 10, Sat, Sun and holidays 1000-1300, 1400-1700, US$0.75*, has one of the best museums of religious art in Colombia. Part of the monastery is the **Iglesia del Carmen** and the **Convento**, all worth a visit. The shops in the plaza and adjoining streets have a great selection of Colombian handicrafts.

Many places, particularly restaurants, are closed Monday and Tuesday. Market day is Saturday, held in the Plaza de Mercado 0400-1300. During weekends and public holidays, the town is very crowded with Bogotanos. The helpful **tourist office** ⓘ *Cra 9, No 13-11 just off the plaza, T8-732 0232, http://villadeleyva-boyaca.gov.co, Tue-Fri 0800-1230, 1400-1800, Sat 0800-1500*, has local maps, gives advice on cheaper accommodation and bus schedules. Useful websites include www.envilladeleyva. com, and www.villaleyvanos.com. There is an ATM on the Plaza Mayor.

West of Villa de Leiva

The wide valley to the west of Villa de Leiva abounds in fossils. A **palaeontological museum** ⓘ *Cra 9, No 11-42, US$1.10, Tue-Sat 0900-1200, 1400-1700, Sun 0900-1500*, 15 minutes' walk north of the town, is part of the Universidad Nacional de Colombia, and has some 440 well-displayed exhibits. About 5 km along the road to Santa Sofía is the fossil of a dinosaur (possibly a kronosaurus) found in 1977, now with a museum built around it. Further fossils discovered in the area have been added to the collection, including the remains of another pliosaur, found in 2010. Look for road signs to **El Fósil** ⓘ *daily 0800-1800, US$2*. About 2 km from El Fósil along this road is the turning for (1 km) the archaeological site of **Parque Arqueológico de Monquirá** or **El Infiernito** ⓘ *Tue-Sun 0900-1200, 1400-1700, US$1.75 with guide*, where there are several carved stones believed to be giant phalli and a solar calendar. About 1 km beyond El Infiernito is the **Fibas Jardín del Desierto** ⓘ *T311-222 2399, US$5, Wed-Sun 0830-1730, Mon and Tue with forewarning*, which sells cactus and desert plants. It features two mazes, based on indigenous designs, in which meditation exercises and spiritual workshops are held.

Some 6 km after the Infiernito turning is the **Monasterio del Santo Ecce-Homo** ⓘ *museum open Mon-Fri 0900-1700, US$1.50* (founded 1620); note the fossils on the floor at the entrance. It was built by the Dominicans between 1650 and 1695. It was reclaimed from the military in 1920, since when it has been repeatedly robbed; some of the religious art is now in the Chiquinquirá museum. What can be seen of the monastery is impressive, but the fabric and roof are in a poor state. There are buses from Villa de Leiva (0800-1745) to Santa Sofía, US$3; it is 30 minutes to the crossing, then a 1-km walk to the monastery. About 12 km north of Villa de Leiva is a right turn for the **Santuario de Fauna y Flora de Iguaque** ① *www.parquesnacionales. gov.co, or Naturar Iguaque, T312-585 9892, http://naturariguaquesp.weebly.com, the Laguna Sagrada section is open (2016), but other parts are closed, 0800-1000 for access to the 4.6-km trail, US$14 (US$5.30 for Colombians).* The 6750-ha park is mainly high cloudforest of oak, fig and other temperate trees, many covered with epiphytes, lichens and bromeliads. There is also *páramo* (moorland) and a series of lakes at over 3400 m, and the mountains rise to 3800 m. At the **Furachiogua visitor centre** ① *entry 0800-1700,* there is accommodation in lodge dorms ($ per person), camping and a restaurant.

Ráquira *Colour map 2, B5.*

In the Chibcha language, *Ráquira* means 'city of pots' and with over 100 *artesanía* shops selling earthenware pottery in a village of just a dozen blocks, it is rightly considered the capital of Colombian handicrafts (see http://raquira.turismo.co). In recent years, however, there has been an influx of cheap products from Ecuador, somewhat diluting its appeal. The village itself, 25 km from Villa de Leiva, has been painted in an array of primary colours and has a picturesque plaza embellished with terracotta statues. You can find accommodation ($$-$) and places to eat on or near the plaza.

About 7 km along a very rough road, which winds up above Ráquira affording spectacular views, is the beautiful 16th-century **Monasterio Desierto de La Candelaria** ① *daily 0900-1200, 1300-1700, US$2.50 includes Hermit's Cave.* On the altar of the fine church is the painting of the Virgen de La Candelaria, dating from 1597, by Francisco del Pozo of Tunja. The painting's anniversary is celebrated on 1 February and 28 August, the saint's day of San Agustín. The convent has two beautiful cloisters, one with a 170-year-old dwarf orange tree, the other virtually untouched since the 17th century. They are lined with anonymous 17th-century paintings of the life of San Agustín.

Chiquinquirá *Colour map 2, B5.*

On the west side of the valley of the Río Suárez, 134 km from Bogotá and 80 km from Tunja, this is a busy market town for this large coffee and cattle region. In December thousands of pilgrims honour a painting of the Virgin whose fading colours were restored by the prayers of a woman, María Ramos. The picture is housed in the imposing **Basílica**, but the miracle took place in what is now the **Iglesia de la Renovación** ① *Parque Julio Flores.* In 1816, when the town had enjoyed six years of independence and was besieged by the Royalists, this painting was carried through the streets by Dominican priests from the famous monastery, to rally the people. The town fell, all the same. There are special celebrations at Easter and on 26 December, the anniversary of the miracle. The town is known for making toys and musical instruments. See http://chiquinquira-boyaca.gov.co.

Tourist information

Tunja

Municipal tourist office
Cra 9, No 9-95, T8-740 5770,
www.tunja-boyaca.gov.co/turismo.
shtml. Mon-Fri 0800-1600.

Villa de Leiva
Useful websites include www.envillade
leyva.com, and www.villaleyvanos.com.

Tourist office
Cra 9, No 13-11 just off the plaza, T8-
732 0232, http://villadeleyva-boyaca.
gov.co. Tue-Fri 0800-1230, 1400-1800,
Sat 0800-1500.
This helpful office has local maps, and
gives advice on cheaper accommodation
and bus schedules.

Where to stay

Tunja
Hotel Hunza (C 21A, No 10-66, T8-742
4111, www.hotelhunza.com) is one of
several smart hotels in the **$$$-$$** range.

$$ Alicante
Cra 8, No 19-15, T310-852 1636,
www.hotelalicantetunja.com.
Minimalist design, sunny patio fringed
by varieties of cactus, bright rooms,
great value.

$$ Casa Real
C 19, No 7-65, T310-852 1636,
www.hotelcasarealtunja.com.
Sister hotel to **Alicante**. A real bargain,
comfortable rooms in a lovely colonial
building with varnished wooden
floorboards. Highly recommended.

$$ Posada San Agustín
C 23, No 8-63, T8-742 2986,
www.posadadesanagustin.co.
Beautiful colonial building on the Parque
Pinzón, balustraded courtyard, antiques
and old photos of Tunja, comfortable
rooms, "a bit of a gem".

$ Conquistador de América
C 20, No 8-92, T8-742 3534.
Lovely foyer with a bright skylight,
rooms are small but comfortable.

Villa de Leiva
The town tends to be full of visitors at
weekends and holidays when booking
is advisable. Book in advance for the
Festival of Light; see What to do, below.

$$$ Candelaria
C del Silencio (Cra 18), No 8-12, T8-732
0534, hotelcandelaria@hotmail.com.
Refurbished colonial building with
9 rooms of "monastic simplicity",
in delightful location.

$$$ El Marqués de San Jorge
C 14, No 9-20, T8-732 0480, www.
hospederiaelmarquesdesanjorge.com.
Simple little place with rooms around
a courtyard, cheaper Mon-Thu.

$$$ El Molino la Mesopotamia
Cra 8, 15A-265, T8-732 0235,
www.lamesopotamia.com
A beautifully restored colonial mill filled
with antiques, excellent home cooking,
beautiful gardens, freshwater pool
(US$2.50 for non-guests), memorable.
Recommended.

$$$ Plaza Mayor
Cra 10, No 12-31, T8-732 0425,
www.hotelplazamayor.com.co.

On the plaza, delightful octagonal courtyard with lemon trees, comfortable rooms and a good restaurant.

$$ Posada Don Blas
C 12, No 10-61, T8-732 0406, posada.donblas@hotmail.com.
Sweet, simple little place 1 block from the plaza, with just 10 rooms.

$$-$ Colombian Highlands and Hostal Renacer
Cra 10, No 21-Finca Renacer, T8-732 1201, or T311-308 3739, www.colombianhighlands.com.
15-min walk from town, this hostel, belonging to English-speaking biologist Oscar Gilède, has very comfortable dorm rooms, highly rated. Extensive gardens, wood-fired pizza oven, hammocks, bike hire, tour agency. Camping US$6-8.25, also tent rental.

$$-$ Posada de los Angeles
Cra 10, No 13-94, T8-732 0562.
Attractive, clean rooms in a fine building 2 blocks from the plaza, restaurant, ask for a room overlooking the Iglesia del Carmen.

$ Casa Viena
Cra 10, No 19-114, T8-732 0711, http://hostel-villadeleyva.com.
Austrian/Colombian-run, 10 mins from plaza, small, comfortable homestay with 4 rooms, kitchen and communal area, long-stays welcome. Also has Finca Puente Piedra outside Villa de Leiva, which takes working guests, minimum stay 20 days.

$ Hostal Sinduly
Cra 11, No 11-77, T8-732 0325, www.hostalsinduly.com.
Run by Austrian Manfred, 2 private rooms (1 with bath) and 2 dorms in a colonial house 1 block from the plaza. English and German spoken.

Chiquinquirá

$$ El Gran
C 16, No 7A-55, T1-726 3700, www.elgranhotel.amawebs.com.
Central, secure, comfortable, good restaurant.

$$ Sarabita
C 16, No 8-12, T316-330 8701, Facebook: HOTEL-Sarabita.
In a national monument, with pool and restaurant.

Restaurants

Tunja

$ El Balcón
Pasaje Vargas C 19A, No 10-16, T8-743 3954.
Expansive café overlooking the main plaza. Lovely wood interior, friendly service, free Wi-Fi, and a long list of excellent coffees.

$ El Maizal
Cra 9, No 20-30, T8-742 5876.
Good varied menu of local specialities.

$ La Cascada
Pasaje Vargas (C32), No 5-60, T8-744 5750.
Popular at lunchtime, good value for lunches and breakfasts. There are other places on this street.

Villa de Leiva
Villa de Leiva has dozens of good restaurants with international and local menus. Most are concentrated in the town's upmarket food courts, **Casa Quintero** (on the plaza) and **La Guaca** (on C Caliente). Some are closed Mon-Wed.

$$ La Cocina de la Gata
Cra 9, No 11-75 (Casa Quintero,
on the plaza; see map).
Pleasantly decorated fondue restaurant,
which also serves chicken and steak.

$$ Olivas & Especias
Cra 10, No 11-99.
On the corner of the plaza, pizzas and
pastas in homely surroundings. Next
door's **Carnes & Olivas ($$$)** is also
worth a try.

$$ Savia
Cra 9, No 11-75 (Casa Quintero, on the
plaza; see map).
Great range of organic starters and
interesting mains, including some tasty
veggie dishes.

$$ Zarina
Cra 9, No 11-75 (Casa Quintero, on the
plaza; see map).
Good Arabic, Mediterranean and
vegetarian cuisine, as well as the usual
chicken and steak.

$ Casa Blanca
C 13, No 7-06.
A simple little place, popular with locals,
for regional specialities, plus *ajiaco* and
other classics.

Festivals

Villa de Leiva
Jan-Feb Astronomical festival,
telescopes are set up in the Plaza for
public use.
Apr Encuentro de Música Antigua
celebrates historic music from all over
the world (Facebook: Encuentro de
Música Antigua en Villa de Leyva).
12 Jun Anniversary of founding of
town, with fireworks, market, music and
other arts events.

13-17 Jul Virgen del Carmen, with
street market, agricultural fair, music
and entertainment based in and around
the main plaza.
Mid-Aug International kite festival
is held in the Plaza Mayor (see www.
villadeleyva-boyaca.gov.co), for 3 days
usually over the 2nd weekend.
Early Dec Festival of Light is held every
year, for the Immaculate Conception,
with balconies and streets decorated
with candles and lanterns.

What to do

Villa de Leiva
Horse riding
Raul Oswaldo, *T310-757 5327.* Offers
horse-riding trips, group discounts when
booking with **Colombian Highlands**,
see page 86.

Tour operators
Alpine Colombia, *5 km outside town,*
http://alpinecolombia.weebly.com. Hiking
trip for individuals and small groups,
also homestay in our **$$-$** range, owner
Christian speaks German and English.
Colombian Highlands, *see Where to*
stay, above. Tours of the local area and
throughout Colombia, specifically
geared towards botanists, ornithologists
and enthusiasts of adventure sports.
Zebra Trips, *C Caliente, Cra 9 No 14-80,*
T098-732 0016/311-870 1749, www.
zebratrip.com. With its zebra-striped
fleet of Land Rovers, this company
provides a fun way to explore the desert
area outside Villa de Leiva. A variety
of different tours starting at US$15,
including a gourmet outing.

Transport

Tunja
Bus

Bus station is 400 m steeply down from city centre. From **Bogotá** several companies, 3-3½ hrs, 4½-5 hrs weekends and holidays, US$8. To **Villa de Leiva**, *colectivos* every 15 mins 0600-1900, US$3, 45-60 mins. To **Bucaramanga**, frequent services, 7 hrs, US$20.

Villa de Leiva
Bus

The bus station is on Cra 9 between C 11 and C 12. Advisable to book the return journey on arrival at weekends. Buses to/from **Tunja**, 45-60 mins, US$3, every 15 mins from 0600 to 1800. To **Bogotá**, either go via Tunja, or 5 direct buses a day, 3½-4 hrs with **Valle Flota de Tenza**, at main bus terminal, T1-428 1008 (T320-337 6585 in Villa de Leiva), www.flotavalledetenza.com, US$8, or 2 a day with **Libertadores**. To/from **Chiquinquirá**, 1½ hrs, US$3, 6 a day. To **Ráquira** see below.

Ráquira
Bus

Buses from **Villa de Leiva** 4 a day, 0600-1730, 30 mins, US$2. For the return, check if you have to change at Ramal. There are also buses to **Tunja** (3 a day) and **Bogotá**, US$7.50.

Chiquinquirá
Bus

To **Tunja**, 3 hrs, US$7. To **Zipaquirá**, US$5.50. To **Bogotá**, 2½ hrs, US$4.

★ Sierra Nevada del Cocuy   *Colour map 2, B6.*

a must-visit national park for high-altitude climbing and trekking

The breathtaking Sierra Nevada del Cocuy in the Eastern Cordillera is the best range in Colombia for mountaineering and rock climbing. The sierra consists of two parallel north–south ranges about 30 km long, offering peaks of rare beauty (more than 22 are snow covered), lakes and waterfalls. The flora is particularly interesting, notably the thousands of frailejones.

Tunja to El Cocuy

A road runs northeast of Tunja to ★ **Paipa** (41 km; bus from Bogotá, US$8), noted for the **Aguas Termales complex** ① *3 km southeast of Paipa, T321-209 5655, www. termalespaipa.co, Mon-Fri 1000-1900, Sat 1000-2030, entrance US$4.50*, with a range of massage and mud therapies at extra cost, hydrotherapy US$22, and on for 15 km to Duitama. From here it is 85 km to Soatá, one of the junctions for reaching the Parque Nacional Natural El Cocuy. The other route to the park is 20 km further north, by the bridge over the Río Chicamocha at Capitanejo.

Parque Nacional Natural El Cocuy

The park is accessible from the small towns of **El Cocuy** or, further north, **Güicán**. Either town is a perfect start or end point for hiking or climbing in the park. On the central plaza of El Cocuy is a model of the mountain area. One of the most spectacular hikes is from south to north (or vice versa), during which you will see

Essential Parque Nacional Natural El Cocuy

Park information

Park offices Calle 5, No 4-22, T098-789 0359, El Cocuy, or Transversal 4A, No 6-60, T098-789 7280, Güicán, both open 0700-1145, 1300-1645. It is obligatory to visit a park office, here, in Bucaramanga (Avenida Quebrada Seca, No 30-12, T7-645 4868), Tame (Carrera 22, No 15-04, T097-888 6054), or in Bogotá (www.parquesnacionales.gov.co) to get a permit to enter the park and to receive the rules of conduct within the park.

Guiding association Aseguicoc, T311-236 4275, aseguicoc@gmail.com.

Park admission Entry to the park 0500-0900, exit 1300-1800, with numbers of visitors strictly limited. Check the latest situation locally, as the park is still undergoing an environmental impact study.

Entrance fee US$18 for foreigners, payable at the park offices, where you must also obtain rescue insurance, which costs US$2.50 per day, and a walking map.

Be aware...

The park has recently reopened, with limited access, following protests by the U'wa people and local campesinos, against a perceived threat from tourism to the park's fragile environment and against the disrespectful actions of some visitors at U'wa sacred sites. At the time of research, no overnight stays were allowed and only the following paths are currently open to visitors: Ritacuba to the edge of the Ritacuba Blanco glacier; Laguna Grande de la Sierra, from La Cuchumba to the edge of the Pico Cóncavo glacier; and Lagunillas Pulpito, from the shelter above Sisuma to the lower levels of the Pico Púlpito del Diablo.

When to go

The peak holiday periods (the last week in December, the first two weeks of January and Easter week) can get very busy. The best season for trekking is December to March but even in those months it can rain or be very foggy.

---

a great part of what the park has to offer. It might appear an easy marked trail, but it is highly recommended to go with a guide as sudden changes in weather can cause visibility to drop to less than 10 m.

La Laguna de La Plaza is probably the most beautiful lake in the Sierra Nevada del Cocuy, surrounded by the snow tops of **Pan de Azúcar** and **Toti** in the west and **Picos Negro** and **Blanco** to the east. Just below Pan de Azúcar is **Cerro El Diamante**. At sunrise, this rock can change from grey to yellow, gold, red and orange if you are lucky with the weather. **Laguna Grande de la Sierra** is surrounded by the Pan de Azúcar, Toti, Portales, Concavo and Concavito peaks. **El Púlpito de Diablo** is an enormous, altar-shaped rock at 5000 m. **Valle de los Cojines** is an enormous valley surrounded by snow peaks, filled with *cojines* (pillow plants). The views at the top over the Valle de Cojines and many other parts of the park are stunning. Currently off limits are the climb from El Púlpito to the top pf **Pan de Azúcar** (5100 m), overlooking Laguna de la Plaza on one side and Laguna Grande de la Sierra on the other, and **Ritacuba Blanco** (5322 m), the highest mountain of all.

Listings Sierra Nevada del Cocuy

Where to stay

There are places to stay in El Cocuy and Güicán and *cabañas* on some of the trails into the park (although no overnight stays are currently allowed inside the national park – see note, page 89).

$$ Hotel Pinares del Carrizalito
2.45 km from El Cocuy, T300 776 7529, Facebook: Pinares del Carrizalito.
Country lodge B&B in leafy grounds, friendly hosts will pick up and drop off guests at bus station.

$ Casa Muñoz
Cra 5, No 7-28, El Cocuy, on the main plaza, T098-789 0328, T313-829 1073, https://sites.google.com/site/ hotelcasamunoz/Home.
With private and shared rooms, *comedor*.

$ La Posada del Molino
Cra 3, No 7-51, El Cocuy, T8-789 0377, 312-352 9121, http://elcocuycasamuseo. blogspot.co.uk.
In a historic building, with private rooms, restaurant and information on tours to the national park. Highly recommended.

Transport

Bus
El Cocuy and Güicán can be reached by direct bus (0650 departure) from **Bogotá**, 10-12 hrs, US$17; buses also from **Tunja**. Around 0600 a milk truck leaves the main plaza of El Cocuy, taking you to the southern park entrance, about US$4. Or take an *expreso* (private transport), US$28, from El Cocuy main plaza.

Tunja to Bucaramanga and the border with Venezuela *Colour map 2, B5-A6.*
visit San Gil for thrills, then recover your composure in beautiful Barichara

Socorro *Colour map 2, B6.*
The main road from Tunja heads northeast and then roughly follows the Río Suárez to Socorro, with steep streets and single-storey houses set among graceful palms. It has a singularly large stone cathedral. The **Casa de Cultura museum** ⓘ *opening hours vary*, covers the local history and the interesting part played by Socorro in the fight for Independence. It is well worth a visit. There is a daily market.

★ San Gil *Colour map 2, B6.*
About 21 km beyond Socorro, northeast on the main road to Bucaramanga, is San Gil, an attractive colonial town with a good climate. It's a friendly, relaxed place and its main square is lively at night. San Gil is a centre for adventure sports (rafting, kayaking, parapenting, paragliding and caving) and is also a good place for biking, horse riding and walking. See What to do, page 101.

Parque Gallineral ⓘ *www.gallineral.sangil.com.co, daily 0800-1700, US$3, guides, some English-speaking, tip them as they are not paid,* a delightful riverside park, covers 4 ha where the Quebrada Curití runs through a delta to the Río Fonce. It has a superb freshwater swimming pool and beautiful trees covered with moss-like tillandsia. There's a good view from **La Gruta**, the shrine overlooking the town (look for the cross). Visit **Juan Curi waterfalls** ⓘ *T311-489 3272, www.lascascadasdejuancuri.com, entry US$2.50,* for abseiling or hiking; there are also *cabañas* ($$), camping ($) and restaurant. To get there, take a bus towards Charalá from the main bridge on the edge of town, US$3 return, 45 minutes; buses every 30 minutes (ask to be dropped off at the entrance). A return taxi fare is US$19. There are two approaches to the Cascadas, approximately 20 minutes' walk, passing through private fincas.

★ **Barichara and around** *Colour map 2, B6. See also map, page 92.*

From San Gil a paved road leads 22 km to Barichara, a beautiful, quiet colonial town founded in 1741 and designated as a national monument. Among Barichara's places of historical interest are the cathedral and three churches, the cemetery and the house of the former president **Aquileo Parra Gómez** ⓘ *Cra 2 y C 6, daily 0900-1700, free.* There is a superb wide-ranging view from the mirador at the top of Carrera 10 across the Río Suárez to the Cordillera de los Cobardes, the last section of the Cordillera Oriental before the valley of the Magdalena.

An interesting excursion is to **Guane**, 9 km away by road (bus US$1), or two hours' delightful walk by *camino real* (historic trail), where there are many colonial houses and an archaeological museum in the **Parroquia San Isidro** ⓘ *daily 0800-1200, 1300-1800 (but times can be erratic), US$1.* It has an enormous collection of fossils found in the local area (which is constantly being added to), as well as Guane textiles and a mummified woman. Three good restaurants on the plaza serve regional food.

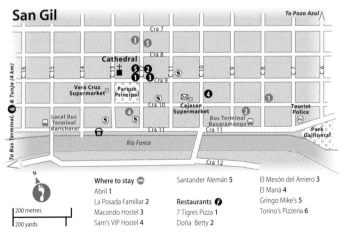

San Gil

Where to stay 🛏
Abril 1
La Posada Familiar 2
Macondo Hostel 3
Sam's VIP Hostel 4

Santander Alemán 5

Restaurants 🍴
7 Tigres Pizza 1
Doña Betty 2

El Mesón del Arriero 3
El Maná 4
Gringo Mike's 5
Torino's Pizzeria 6

★ Chicamocha Canyon *Colour map 2, B6.*

Between San Gil and Bucamaranga is the spectacular Río Chicamocha Canyon, with the best views to the right of the road. The **Parque Nacional** ① *T7-639 4444, www.parquenacionaldelchicamocha.com, Mon-Fri 0900-1800, Sat, Sun and holidays 0800-1900, US$9.50, range of prices up to US$22.00 for extra options, including cable car and Aqua Park, children under 2 free,* has a visitor centre with panoramic views, activities, parking, snack bars and toilets and a 6.3-km **cable car** across the canyon. Another way to experience the canyon is on a three-day walk from San Gil to the villages of Barichara, Guane, Villanueva, Los Santos, and the ghost town of Jordán. The walk involves a spectacular descent of the canyon. Speak to the staff at the **Macondo Hostal** in San Gil for more details of *hostales* and eating places on the way.

Bucaramanga *Colour map 2, A6.*

The capital of Santander Department, 420 km from Bogotá, was founded in 1622 but was little more than a village until the latter half of the 19th century. The metropolitan area of this modern, commercial city has grown rapidly because of

Barichara

Where to stay 🛏	La Mansión de Virginia 4	Restaurants 🍴
Coratá 1	La Posada de Pablo 2 5	Al Cuoco 1
Hicasua 2	Tinto Hostel 6	El Compá 2
Hostel Color de Hormiga 3		Las Cruces 3

the success of coffee, tobacco and staple crops, but the city's great problem is the lack of space for expansion. Erosion on the lower, western side topples buildings over the edge after heavy rain, leaving behind spectacular deep ravines.

Bucaramanga is known as the 'city of parks' for its fine green spaces, such as **Mejoras Públicas**, **de los Niños**, **San Pío** and **Las Palmas**, but some areas, particularly Parque Centenario, are not very safe even in daylight. The **Parque Santander** is the heart of the modern city, while the **Parque García Rovira** is the centre of the colonial area. On it stands the city's oldest church, **Capilla de Los Dolores** ⓘ *C 35/Cra 10*, a national monument. Just off Parque García Rovira is the **Casa de Cultura** ⓘ *C 37, No 12-46, T7-642 0163, Mon-Fri 0800-1200, 1400-1800*, in a fine colonial building with exhibitions, films and an *artesanía* display. The **Casa de Bolívar** ⓘ *C 37, No 12-15, T7-630 4258, Mon-Fri 0800-1800, Sat 0800-1200, US$1*, where Bolívar stayed in 1828, is interesting for its connections with Bolívar's campaign in 1813.

Around Bucaramanga *Colour map 2, A6.*
In **Floridablanca**, 8 km southwest, is the **Jardín Botánico Eloy Valenzuela** ⓘ *T7-634 6100, daily 0800-1600, US$1.70, take a Florida Villabel bus from Cra 33, US$1, or Florida Autopista to the plaza and walk 1 km; taxi from centre, US$4*, belonging to the national tobacco agency, with a collection of more than 7500 plants from the Santander Department, as well as birds and animals including squirrels, tortoises and, if you're lucky, sloths.

Girón, a tobacco centre 9 km southwest of Bucaramanga on the Río de Oro, is a quiet and attractive colonial town. Its white buildings, beautiful church, bridges and cobbled streets are well preserved and the historic part of town is unspoilt by

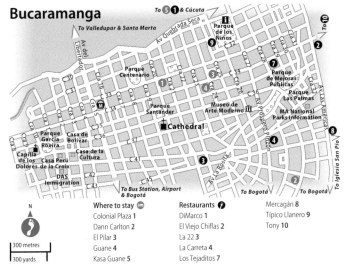

Bucaramanga

Where to stay	Restaurants	
Colonial Plaza 1	DiMarco 1	Mercagán 8
Dann Carlton 2	El Viejo Chiflas 2	Típico Llanero 9
El Pilar 3	La 22 3	Tony 10
Guane 4	La Carreta 4	
Kasa Guane 5	Los Tejaditos 7	

300 metres
300 yards

modernization. Girón can be easily reached from Bucaramanga and makes a good day trip. By the river are *tejo* courts and open-air restaurants with cumbia and salsa bands. Take a bus from Carrera 15 or 22 in Bucaramanga, US$1, taxi US$4.

Piedecuesta is 18 km southeast of Bucaramanga. Here you can see cigars being handmade, furniture carving and jute weaving. Cheap, hand-decorated *fique* rugs can also be bought. There are frequent buses to all the surrounding towns; a taxi costs US$8. Corpus Christi processions in these towns in June are hugely popular, involving hundreds of costumed participants filling the streets. Take a bus from Carrera 22, 45 minutes.

Berlín to Pamplona *Colour map 2, A6.*

The road (paved but narrow) runs east to Berlín, and then northeast (a very scenic run over the Eastern Cordillera) to Pamplona, about 130 km from Bucaramanga. Berlín is an ideal place to appreciate the grandeur of the Eastern Cordillera and the hardiness of the people who live on the *páramo*. The village lies in a valley at 3100 m, the peaks surrounding it rise to 4350 m and the temperature is constantly around 10°C, although on the infrequent sunny days it may seem much warmer. There is a tourist complex with cabins and there are several basic eating places.

Pamplona *Colour map 2, A6.*

Founded in 1548 in the mountains, Pamplona became important as a mining town but is now better known for its university. It is renowned for its Easter celebrations. The climate is chilly at this altitude: 2342 m. Pamplona is a good place to buy *ruanas* and has a good indoor market. The **cathedral** in the spacious central plaza is the most attractive feature of this otherwise unprepossessing city. The **Iglesia del Humilladero**, adjoining the cemetery, is very picturesque and allows a fine view of the city. Museums include the **Casa Colonial archaeological museum** ⓘ *C 6, No 2-56, T7-568 2043, Mon-Fri 0800-1200, 1400-1800*, a little gem, and the **Museo de Arte Moderno** ⓘ *C 5, No 5-75, Tue-Sun 0900-1200, 1400-1700, US$0.50*.

Cúcuta *Colour map 2, A6.*

Some 72 km from Pamplona is the city of Cúcuta, capital of the Department of Norte de Santander, 16 km from the Venezuelan border at San Antonio. Founded in 1733, destroyed by earthquake 1875, and then rebuilt, its tree-lined streets offer welcome respite from the searing heat, as does the **cathedral** ⓘ *Av 5 between C 10 and 11*. The **Casa de Cultura** ⓘ *C13, No 3-67* (also known as Torre de Reloj) houses art exhibitions and the **Museo de la Ciudad** which covers the city's history and its part in the Independence Movement. For a border town, it is a surprisingly pleasant place to visit, with plenty of green spaces and a busy but non-threatening centre, but see Warning, page 102. The international bridge between Colombia and Venezuela is southeast of the city.

Border with Venezuela *Colour map 2, A6.*

If you do not obtain an exit stamp, you will be turned back by Venezuelan officials and the next time you enter Colombia, you will be fined. At the time of writing, the border was closed to vehicle traffic, but open to pedestrians from 0800 daily. However, the crossing is severely congested with many thousands of Venezuelans leaving the country on foot daily, seeking exodus from the economic and political crisis, with regular reports of cross-border gun-fire and casualties.

Colombian immigration ⓘ *Migración Colombia (CFSM), Av 1, No 28-57, T7-573 5210, Mon-Fri 0800-1200, 1400-1700*. Take a bus from the city centre to Barrio San Rafael, south towards the road to Pamplona. Shared taxi from border is US$6, then US$1.50 to bus station. Exit and entry formalities are also handled at the Migración Colombia office the white building on the left-hand side of road just before the international border bridge (Puesto Terrestre CENAF Villa del Rosario, Puente Internacional Simón Bolívar). There is no authorized charge at the border.

Venezuelan consulate ⓘ *Av Aeropuerto Camilo Daza y C 17, Zona Industrial, T7-579 1954, http://cucuta.consulado.gob.ve, near airport, Mon-Thu 0800-1000, 1400-1500, Fri 0800-1000*. Nationals not requiring a visa are issued an automatic free tourist card by the Venezuelan immigration officers at the border. Overland visitors requiring a visa to Venezuela can get one here, or at the Venezuelan Embassy in Bogotá, although they may send you to Cúcuta. As requirements change frequently, it is recommended that all overland visitors check with a Venezuelan consulate in advance. Apply for visa at 0800 to get it by 1400. If you know when you will arrive at the border, get your visa in your home country.

Leaving and entering Colombia by private vehicle At the time of writing the border is closed to vehicles. Should it reopen, passports must be stamped with an exit stamp at the white Migración Colombia building before the crossing. If not you will have to return later. Expect very long queues. Car papers must be stamped at the SENIAT office in Venezuela.

Exchange For the best exchange rates, it is best to change pesos to bolívares in Cúcuta and not in Venezuela. Exchange rates fluctuate throughout the day. There is an ATM tucked away on the left side of the international bridge in Venezuela. Good rates of exchange at the airport, or on the border. It is difficult to change pesos beyond San Antonio in Venezuela; likewise, bolívares are rarely accepted elsewhere in Colombia. Money changers on the street all around the main plaza and many shops advertise bolívares exchange. There are also plenty of *casas de cambio*, and new ones were opened in San Antonio in 2017.

Time There is a 30-minute time difference between Colombia and Venezuela, or 1½ hours during Daylight Saving Time.

Tourist information

Barichara

Tourist office
*Cra 5 y C 9, www.barichara-santander.
gov.co. Daily 0730-1200, 1400-1800.*

Bucamaranga

Tourist office
*Instituto Municipal de Cultura, C 30,
No 26-117, T7-634 1132, www.imcut.
gov.co. Mon-Fri 0745-1145, 1415-1745,
Sat 0800-1630.*
Friendly and knowledgeable.

Migración Colombia
*Cra 1,No 41-13, T7-633 9426.
Mon-Fri 0800-1200, 1400-1700.*

Pamplona

Instituto de Cultura y Turismo
*Casa Colonial, C 6, No 2-56, T7-568 2043,
www.ictpamplona.gov.co.*
Very helpful, organizes tours and guides.

Cúcuta
There are tourist police at the bus station
and airport.

Corporación Mixta de Promoción de
Norte de Santander
C 10, No 0-30, T7-571 8981.
Helpful.

Where to stay

San Gil

$$ Abril
*C 8, No 9-63, T7-724 8795,
Facebook: hotelabrilcomco.*
Rambling old hotel, austere façade,
but with comfortable and spacious
rooms with fan; good lounge area
with TV and PCs with Wi-Fi, laundry
service, recommended.

$$-$ La Posada Familiar
Cra 10, No 8-55, T7-724 8136.
Small, 6 rooms set around a sunny, plant-
filled courtyard, very clean and cosy;
super friendly and helpful owners, use
of kitchen and clothes-washing facilities.
Recommended.

$$-$ Sam's VIP Hostel
*Cr 10, No 12-33, p 2, main plaza,
T7-724 2746/249 7400.*
Good reports on value and services,
dorms and private rooms, breakfast
included, rooftop pool, adventure
activities, bar, sauna, English spoken.
Recommended.

$ Macondo Hostel
*Cra 8, No 10-35, T7-724 8001,
www.macondohostel.com.*
Australian Shaun Clohesy has created
more of a home-from-home than
a hostel. Social area decked out
with hammocks, garden, jacuzzi,
board games, free coffee and Wi-Fi,
regular barbecues and other events,
comfortable dorms (US$9.50-11.50),
and a wealth of information on local
activities. Recommended.

$ Santander Alemán
*C 10, No 15-07, T7-724 0329,
www.hostelsantanderaleman.com.*
Private and shared rooms, nice
communal areas including a roof terrace,
hammocks, book exchange, bicycle hire,
and adventure sports arranged.

Barichara

$$$-$$ Coratá
Cra 7, No 4-08, T7-726 7110, www.
hotelcoratabarichara.inf.travel.
Delightful colonial building with a fine
courtyard, no fan or a/c but high ceilings
keep you cool.

$$$-$$ Hicasua
C 7, No 3-85, T7-726 7700,
www.hicasua.com.
If you have the cash to splash this is the
place to stay. Located at the edge of
town, Hicasua offers tastefully decorated
rooms with fans and TVs. There is a
restaurant and a stunning swimming
pool in the courtyard, as well as a spa
and sauna.

$$$-$$ Hostel Color de Hormiga
C 6, No 5-35, T7-726 7156/312-558 1256,
Facebook: ColordeHormigaHostel.
Good budget option in a charming
colonial building just off the plaza. Offers
dorms and privates with en suite bath,
but no hot water or fan. Hammock-filled,
grapevine-covered courtyard. With same
owner is **Color de Hormiga Reserva
Natural** (T315-297 1621/314-455 8268),
a finca 1 km outside town. Immense
rooms with high ceilings, owner Jorge
often cooks dinner for guests in the
large, open-air kitchen (which is also
available for guests to cook their own
meals). Tours of the grounds include
visiting ant colonies, turtles and natural
fish farms.

$$ La Mansión de Virginia
C 8, No 7-26, T7-726 7170, www.
lamansiondevirginia.com.
Impeccable colonial house with rooms
(for up to 5) around a lovely courtyard,
comfortable beds, en suite, hot water,
TV in rooms, and Wi-Fi. Recommended.

$$-$ La Posada de Pablo 2
C 3, No 7-30, T317-659 0888, www.
posadadepablobarichara2.com.
One of several places belonging to Pablo.
This one is next to the Iglesia de Jesús
Resucitado and a gorgeous park. Good
beds, rooms 10 and 11 have fine views,
breakfast included, laundry service, with
shady little inner courtyard garden.

$$-$ Tinto Hostel
Cra 4, No 5-39, T7-726 7725,
www.tintohostel.com.
Excellent hostel in lovely colonial
building on a hill overlooking the
surrounding countryside. There are
4- and 6-bed dorms, as well as large
private rooms, pool, terrace bar,
spacious lounge areas.

Camping
In Barichara, at **Baralomas campsites**
(T311-828 0062, Facebook: Camping-
Baraloma-en-Barichara), ask for Rodrigo,
US$5 pp, with bathroom and showers.
On the road to San Gil is **La Chorrera**
(T318-832 7327, US$2 to camp), clean,
attractive with a natural swimming pool
and meals by arrangement.

Around Barichara
Guane

$$-$ Hotel Santa Lucia de Mucuruva
Cra 5 y C 7, T7-724 2761, 318-459 2474.
1 block off the plaza, this option offers
rooms at affordable rates.

$ Posada Mi Tierra Guane
Cra 7, No 7-45, Parque Principal,
opposite museum, T311-566 0402.
Same owner as the *artesanía* shop on the
plaza, comfortable and charming small
hostel with a pleasant courtyard. Some
rooms have bunk beds. Recommended.

Bucaramanga

$$$$-$$$ Dann Carlton
C 47, No 28-83, T7-697 3266,
www.hotelesdann.com.
Part of the Dann hotel chain, top
of the range, business class, in city
centre, with rooftop bar and restaurant
with panoramic view, gym and usual
5-star service.

$$$ El Pilar
C 34, No 24-09, T7-634 7207,
Facebook: hotelelpilarbucaramanga.
Business-style hotel with good rooms
and lots of extras, parking, restaurant,
close to Parque Santander.

$$$ Guane
C 34, No 22-72, T7-634 7014,
www.hotelguane.com.
Smart hotel with large rooms, pool,
gym and spa.

$$ Colonial Plaza
C 33, No 20-46, T7-645 4125, www.
hotelcolonialplaza.inf.travel.
Pseudo-colonial façade, but rooms are
good, a/c, TV, cheaper with fan.
Has a restaurant.

$$-$ Kasa Guane
C 11, No 26-506, T7-657 6960, Facebook:
kasaguanehostelbucaramanga.
The best budget option in town. Owned
by paragliding instructor Richi of
Colombia Paragliding and British expats
Milo and Tim, it's decorated with Guane
artefacts, has private rooms and dorms
(US$10), pool table, kitchen, lively bar,
dance classes and good local information.
Also runs volunteer programmes.

Around Bucaramanga

$$$ Girón Chill Out
Cra 25, No 32-06, Girón, T7-646 1119/
315-475 3001, www.gironchillout.com.

Suites and studios in a colonial house,
boutique style, with restaurant.

$$ Las Nieves
C 30, No 25-71, Girón, T7-681 2951,
http://hotellasnievesgiron.com/.
Characterful colonial building on
the main plaza, large rooms, simply
furnished but clean. Street-facing rooms
have balconies, good-value restaurant.
Much cheaper with fan.

Pamplona

$$$-$$ 1549 Hostal
C 8B, No 5-84, T7-568 0451 or 317-699
6578, http://1549hostal.com.
Another lovingly restored colonial
building. Rooms and suites are light
and airy and decorated with great taste.
Restaurant and bar in a large covered
courtyard. Highly recommended.

$$$-$$ El Solar
C 5, No 8-10, T7-568 2010,
www.elsolarhotel.com.
Beautifully restored colonial building.
Rooms upstairs are enormous and
have kitchen and balconies. Rooms
downstairs, without kitchen, are cheaper.
Also has probably the best restaurant in
town, especially for grilled meats.

Cúcuta

$$$-$$ Arizona Suites
Av 0, No 7-62, T7-572 6020,
www.hotelarizonasuites.com.
Central, modern business-style hotel,
well-equipped rooms with all mod
cons including safety boxes, restaurant
serving Mediterranean and international
food, pool, gym and sauna.

$$ Casa Blanca
Av 6, No 14-55, T7-582 1600,
www.hotelcasablanca.com.co.

Modern block, business-style, with large pool, restaurant serving regional and international food.

$$ Hotel de la Paz
C 6, No 3-48, T7-571 8002.
Basic rooms, but has a pool. 10% discount for stays longer than 5 days.

$$ Zaraya
C 11, No 2-46, T7-571 0829,
www.hotelzaraya.com.
Central, with restaurant, pool and sauna.

$$-$ Lady Di
Av 7, No 13-76, T7-583 1922.
A huge photo of Princess Diana above the doorway and more photos throughout. Rooms are clean but basic.

Restaurants

San Gil
Few places open in the evening. The **market** (Cra 11 entre C13/14), is good for breakfast, fruit salads and juices.

$$ El Mesón del Arriero
C 12, No 8-39, T7-243 954.
Highly rated little restaurant for excellent traditional cuisine, huge portions and very tasty meats.

$$-$ Gringo Mike's
C 12, No 8-35, T7-724 1695, www.
gringomikes.net. Open 0800-2300.
US/British-run restaurant and bar, with West Coast specialities and lovely Mexican influences, excellent sandwiches. Friendly staff, good nosh and cocktails. Recommended.

$ 7 Tigres Pizza
C 12, No 8-40, Facebook: 7-Tigres-
Pizza-1374818486121483.
Basic place but serves delicious pizzas and good veggie dishes.

$ Doña Betty
Cra 9 y C 12, Parque Principal,
T7-724 6297.
Good for breakfast, *arepas*, scrambled eggs, fruit juices and people-watching.

$ El Maná
C 10, No 9-12, www.elmanasangil.inf.
travel. Tue-Sun lunchtime and evenings.
Filling set meals for US$7.50-9, plus local soups and à la carte menu.

$ Torino's Pizzeria
C 9, No 11-68, local 210, T7-724 7496,
Centro Comercial Camino Real.
Open evenings.
Popular pizzeria with a brick oven. Home delivery.

Barichara

$$ Al Cuoco
Cra 4, No 3B-15, T312-527 3628.
Across from Parque Cementerio, in a cosy dining room and large patio. Owner Máximo serves handmade pastas with recipes that have been passed down through generations in Rome.

$$ Las Cruces
Cra 5, No 4-26, San Antonio, T7-726 7577,
http://tallerdeoficiosbarichara.com.
Fri 1900-2130, Sat-Sun 1200-1600, 1900-
2130, holidays 1200-1600, open every day
in high season. Café Mon-Fri 1200-2100,
weekends 0900-2130.
In the Escuela Taller, with a plant and tree-filled courtyard, offers cooking and ceramics classes as well as an upscale restaurant. Those who want to try a local speciality should ask for the roast goat in ant sauce (yes, those ants.)

$ El Compá
C 5, No 4-48, T7-726 7492.
Family-run restaurant serving regional dishes, including *sobre barriga* and *arepa*

santandereana, and good-value set lunch (around US$3).

Bucaramanga

Try the *hormigas culonas* (a large, winged ant often eaten deep-fried as a crunchy snack), a local delicacy available Mar-May (mostly sold in shops, not restaurants).

$$$ La Carreta
Cra 27, No 42-27, T7-643 6680, www.lacarreta.com.co.
Established by football legend Roberto Pablo Janiot, tastefully restored, swish colonial building, meat-based international food, *parrillas* and seafood.

$$$ Mercagán
Cra 33 y C42, T7-632 4949.
Steaks and hamburgers in a *parrilla* restaurant near the beautiful Parque San Pío. Several other locations in the city.

$$ DiMarco
C 28, No 54-21, T7-643 2626, www.dimarcoparrilla.com. Tue-Sat lunch and dinner, Sun-Mon 1100-1600.
Argentine-style *parrilla*, excellent meat, since the 1960s.

$$ El Viejo Chiflas
Cra 33, No 34-10, T7-632 0640, www.elviejochiflasrestaurante.inf.travel.
Well-established, since 1957, good, typical food from the region, generous portions. Recommended.

$$ La 22
Cra 22, No 45-18, T7-630 4503, www.restaurantela22.com.
This local restaurant is so popular that at weekends (when they serve the regional speciality *mute*, a hearty, meaty soup) you will struggle to be seated; also good for trout, paella and other rice dishes.

$$ Los Tejaditos
C 34, No 27-82, T7-634 6028, www.restaurantelostejaditos.com.
Popular for its varied menu of meat, seafood, pastas and salads.

$$ Tony
Cra 33A, No 33-67, http://desayunostony.com. Daily 24 hrs.
Typical food, popular. Good *tamales* and *arepas*, breakfasts are their speciality.

$ Típico Llanero
C 31, No 25-07, T7-634 5586.
Just off Parque Los Niños, corner restaurant serving regional food hot off a coal-fired grill, popular, set-price *almuerzos* and refreshing iced juices for US$4.

Pamplona

Pamplona is famous for its bread. Particularly well-known *panaderías* are **Chávez** (Cra 6, No 7-30), and **Araque** (Cra 5, No 8B-15). Try *pastel de horno*, *queso de hoja*, *pan de agua* or *cuca*, a kind of black ginger biscuit often topped with cheese. Pamplona even has a *cuca* festival in Sep/Oct of each year.

$$ La Casona
C 6, No 7-58, T7-568 3555.
Local favourite serving meats and seafood.

$$-$ Delicias del Mar
C 6, No 7-60, T7-568 4558.
Popular lunchtime venue specializing in fish.

Cúcuta

Lots of fast food outlets on the 3rd level of **Centro Comercial Ventura Plaza** (C 10 y 11 Diagonal Santander), also cinema and shops.

$$ Rodizio
Av Libertadores, No 10-121, Malecón II Etapa, T7-575 0095, www.rodiziocucuta.com.

Elegant, good service, big choice of meat dishes, seafood, salad bar.

$ Venezia
C 13, No 6AE-46, Edif La Riviera, local 5, T7-575 0006.
Oven-fired pizzas and other Italian specialities.

Festivals

San Gil
Nov Festival San Gil, during the 1st weekend of the month the town celebrates with dancers, music, local gastronomy, horse parades and even bullfighting.

Bucaramanga
Sep Feria Bucaramanga, 2 weeks of music, dancing, food and theatre.

What to do

San Gil
Activities include **abseiling** (rappel) at Juan Curi waterfall (US$20); a 3-day beginner's **kayaking** course on Río Fonce (US$150, minimum 2 persons); **parapenting** over the Chicamocha Canyon (US$65 for 30-60 mins). For rafting, the Río Fonce is best for beginners, US$13.50; Río Suárez, for more advanced, 1-2 hrs from US$47. The area also offers bungee jumping (US$14), caving (US$12), mountain biking, hiking, horse riding (said to be better in Barichara) and swimming.
Aventura Total, *C 7, No 10-27, T7-723 8888, www.aventuratotal.com.co.* Biggest tour company in town, specializes in parapenting, rafting, abseiling and caving.
Colombia Rafting Expeditions, *Cra 10, No 7-83, T311-283 8647, www.colombia rafting.com.* The best for rafting, with

International Rafting Federation-qualified guides. Also hydrospeed.
Páramo Santander Extremo, *Parque Principal, Cra 4, No 4-57, Páramo, T7-725 8944, www.paramosantanderextremo. com.* Based in nearby Páramo, this company is best for abseiling and canyoning. But it also has caving, rafting and horse riding.

Bucaramanga
Parapenting At Mesa del Ruitoque and Cañón de Chicamocha. Good schools are **Las Aguilas** (Km 2 vía Mesa de Ruitoque, Floridablanca, T300-762 2662, www.voladerolasaguilas.com), and **Colombia Paragliding** (T312-432 6266, www.colombiaparagliding.com).

Transport

San Gil
Bus
Station 5 mins out of town by taxi on road to Tunja. To **Bogotá**, US$15, 7-8 hrs; **Bucaramanga**, US$7, 2½ hrs, sit on right for lovely views of the Chicamocha Canyon; **Barichara** from C 12, US$2, 45 mins, every 30 mins.

Bucaramanga
Air
Palonegro, on 3 flattened hilltops south of city. Taxi US$10.50, *colectivo* US$3.50. Spectacular views on take-off and landing. Daily flights to **Bogotá**, **Cúcuta**, **Medellín**, **Cartagena** and **Barranquilla**.

Bus
Local buses cost US$0.65. The long-distance terminal is on the Girón road, T7-637 1000, with cafés, shops and showers. Taxi to centre, US$3; bus US$0.65. To **Bogotá**, 9 hrs, US$16-32 with **Berlinas del Fonce**

(C 53, No 20-40, T7-630 4468, www.
berlinasdelfonce.com, or at bus terminal),
and Copetran, 9½-10½ hrs, US$18-31.
To **Cartagena**, **Copetran**, US$34-47,
12-14 hrs. **Barranquilla**, 13 hrs, US$30-
43, **Copetran**, **Berlinas** or **Brasilia**.
Santa Marta, **Copetran**, 11-13 hrs,
US$26-37. To **Valledupar**, 9 hrs, US$25-31
with **Copetran**. To/from **Pamplona**,
US$9-12, 4-5 hrs. To/from **Cúcuta**,
6-8 hrs, US$12-17, many companies,
including **Copetran** and **Motilones**. The
trip to Cúcuta is spectacular and passes
through cloudforests and *páramos*. Best
to start the journey early morning as
thick fog usually covers the mountains
by afternoon. To **Medellín**, US$22-34,
8 hrs. **Barrancabermeja**, 2½ hrs, US$9,
paved road, scenic journey. To **El Banco**
on the Río Magdalena, US$18-23, 9 hrs,
several companies, direct or change
at Aguachica. Hourly buses to **San Gil**,
see above. Other companies with local
services to nearby villages on back roads,
eg the folk-art buses of **Flota Cáchira**
(C 32, Cra 33-34).

Taxi
Most have meters, minimum
fare US$1.75.

Pamplona
Bus
To **Bogotá**, Berlinas del Fonce and
Copetran, US$30-35, 13 hrs. To **Cúcuta**,
US$7, 2½ hrs. *Colectivos* or shared taxis to
Bucaramanga (US$12-18) and **Cúcuta**
(US$6.50) usually cut the journey by 1 hr,
with door-to-door pick-up and delivery.
To **Berlín**, US$5. Buses leave from Cra 5 y
C 4, minibuses to Cúcuta from Cra 5 y C 5.

Cúcuta
Air
The airport is 5 km north of the town
centre, T7-587 9797, 15 mins by taxi in
normal traffic from the town and border,
US$3, US$10 to border. Daily flights to
Bogotá, **Bucaramanga** and **Medellín**.
It's cheaper to buy tickets in Colombia
for these than in advance in Venezuela.

Bus
Bus station: Av 7, No 1-50 (a really
rough area). **Copetran**'s private terminal
is at Av 7, No 16N-33, Zona Industrial, T7-
587 4205 (also at municipal terminal);
taxi to town centre, US$3. The **Berlinas
de Fonce** terminal is at Av 7, No 0-05,
opposite the airport, T7-587 5105 (also
at the main terminal). To **Bogotá**,
14½ hrs, US$30-33, frequent with
Berlinas del Fonce and **Copetran**.
To **Cartagena**, 16-19 hrs, **Copetran**
and **Berlinas del Fonce**, US$30-50.
Reliable taxi service at the bus terminal,
Cotranol, T776-565 0512.

> **Warning...**
> To avoid theft at Cúcuta bus terminal,
> go straight to the **Berlinas del Fonce**
> and **Copetran** terminals. Otherwise,
> on the first floor of the main terminal
> there is a tourist office for help and
> information and a café/snack bar
> where you can wait in comparative
> safety. Do not allow anyone to divert
> you from the service you want and
> don't let your belongings out of your
> sight. Report any theft to the police,
> or Migración Colombia.

Border with Venezuela
Bus

San Cristóbal, US$2 (**Bolivariano**), *colectivo* US$3; **San Antonio**, taxi US$12, bus and *colectivo* from C 7, Av 4/5, US$1 to Migración Colombia, then US$0.75 to SAIME in San Antonio. From Cúcuta to **Mérida** or beyond, go to San Antonio or (better) San Cristóbal and change. Make sure that the driver knows that you need to stop to obtain exit/entry stamps etc. You will have to alight and flag down a later *colectivo*.

Caribbean
Colombia

life's a beach

Reaching Colombia's Caribbean coast is like entering another world, quite different in spirit from the highlands. Steamy, colourful and lively, the entire area pulses to the seductive rhythms of *vallenato*, heard at festivals throughout the region.

Cartagena, the emerald in the crown of Colombia, is a stunning colonial city positively bursting with colour and history, and with various sparkling coral islands within easy reach. South of Cartagena the shoreline stretches towards the virgin jungles of the Darién Gap. To the east, Santa Marta is the gateway to the spectacular Tayrona and Sierra Nevada de Santa Marta national parks. The latter conceals the Ciudad Perdida, the culmination of an unforgettable trek. Further east is the arid Guajira Peninsula.

Best for
Beaches ▪ Fiestas ▪ Trekking

Footprint
picks

★ **Cartagena's ramparts**,
page 108
Walk the perimeter of the colonial city and then watch the sun set over
the bay.

★ **Islas de Rosario and San Bernardo**, pages 127 and 134
Soak up the sun, sea and sand on these quintessential Caribbean islands.

★ **Mompós**, page 130
Come to this beautifully preserved riverside town for its extraordinary
Easter celebrations.

★ **Arboletes**, page 134
Wallow in the area's best mud volcano.

★ **Ciudad Perdida**, page 161
Trek through rainforest to the lost city of the Tayrona.

★ **La Guajira**, page 170
Learn about the Wayúu culture on this remote desert peninsula.

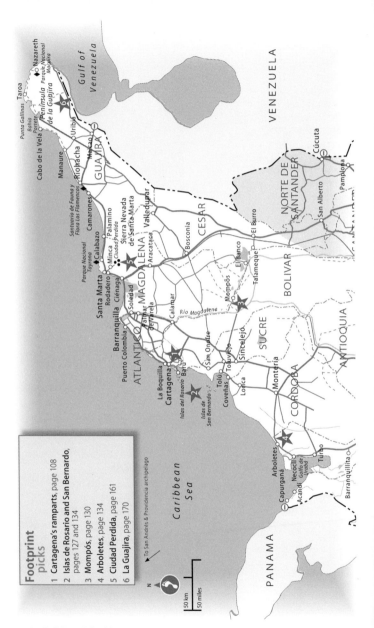

Caribbean Sea

Gulf of Venezuela

VENEZUELA

PANAMA

To San Andrés & Providencia archipelago

50 km
50 miles
N

Essential Caribbean Colombia

Finding your feet

Cartagena's Rafael Núñez Airport is served by direct daily flights to/from major Colombian cities and other smaller places in the north of the country, as well as by direct international flights to/from Lauderdale, Miami, New York and Panama City. From December to March flights can be overbooked, so turn up at the airport early. Santa Marta's Simón Bolívar Airport also gets very crowded in tourist season, when you will need to book flights well in advance. Barranquilla's Ernesto Cortissoz Airport is a cheaper and less busy alternative. There are also regional airports at Corozal (near Sincelejo), at Valledupar and Riohacha in the northeast and at Acandí in Darién. Daily buses run from Bogotá to Cartagena, Barranquilla and Santa Marta, and there are also very frequent services to/from Medellín.

Getting around

Boats are available all along the coast for trips to local beaches and offshore islands. Most other destinations can be reached by bus or *colectivo*, although services are limited southwest of Monterría and are non-existent in the Darién and parts of the Península de la Guajira.

When to go

The climate on the Caribbean coast varies little during the year. Temperatures rise marginally between August and November when there is more frequent rain and there can be flooding. This area is relatively humid, but trade winds between December and February provide relief from the heat. Fiestas are taken seriously in this region, and if you want a quiet time you might want to avoid certain periods, especially between Christmas and Easter. If you want to join in, be sure to plan in advance or be prepared to struggle for accommodation and expect higher prices.

Time required

You'll need two to three weeks to visit Cartagena and Santa Marta, relax on the coast and explore the rainforest.

Weather Caribbean Colombia (Cartagena)

January	February	March	April	May	June
29°C	29°C	30°C	30°C	30°C	30°C
23°C	24°C	25°C	25°C	26°C	26°C
4mm	3mm	2mm	22mm	90mm	100mm

July	August	September	October	November	December
30°C	30°C	30°C	30°C	30°C	30°C
26°C	26°C	25°C	25°C	25°C	24°C
80mm	110mm	130mm	220mm	130mm	30mm

Cartagena
& around

Cartagena should not be missed. Besides being Colombia's top tourist destination and a World Heritage Site, it is one of the most vibrant and beautiful cities in South America. It's an eclectic mix of Caribbean, African and Spanish tastes and sounds. During the high season the city becomes a playground for the rich and famous, while cruise liners dock at its port.

Old city Colour map 1, B2.

colonial splendour meets Caribbean spirit

The colonial heart of Cartagena lies within 12 km of ramparts. Inside the walled city, El Centro is a labyrinth of colourful squares, churches, mansions of former nobles and pastel-coloured houses along narrow cobbled streets. Most of the upmarket hotels and restaurants are found here. The San Diego quarter, once home to the middle classes, and Plaza Santo Domingo, next to the city's oldest church, perhaps best capture the lure of colonial Cartagena; don't miss a drink at night in the cafés here. On the opposite side of Parque del Centenario is the less touristy but up-and-coming Getsemaní neighbourhood, where colonial buildings of former artisans are being rapidly restored. Here are most of the budget hotels along with a few boutique hotels. Immediately adjoining Getsemaní is the downtown sector known as La Matuna, where vendors and fruit-juice sellers crowd the pavements and alleys between the modern commercial buildings and banks.

★ The ramparts
http://fortificacionescartagena.com/en.

The city walls make a great walk and are an excellent way to visit many of the attractions inside the old city (see below). A good place to start is the **Baluarte San Francisco Javier** from where, with a few ups and downs, the circuit is continuous to **La India Catalina**. From this point, there are two further

Tip...
One of the best places to view the sunset is from Baluarte de Santo Domingo. Get there from 1730 to enjoy the views.

sections along the lagoons to the **Puente Román** and then a final section along the Calle del Arsenal. The entire walk takes about 1½ hours. It is spectacular in the morning around 0600 and equally at sunset.

Historic centre: outer city

The **Puente Román** leads from the island of Manga into Getsemaní. North of the bridge, in an interesting plaza, is the church of **Santísima Trinidad**, built 1643 but not consecrated until 1839. North of the church, at Calle Guerrero 10, lived Pedro Romero, who set the revolution of 1811 going with his cry of "Long Live Liberty". The chapel of **San Roque** (early 17th century), near the hospital of Espíritu Santo, is by the junction of Calles Media Luna and Espíritu Santo.

If you take Calle Larga from Puente Román, you come to the two churches and monastery of **San Francisco**. The oldest church (now a cinema) was built in 1590 after the pirate Martin Côte had destroyed an earlier church built in 1559. The first Inquisitors lodged at the monastery. From its courtyard a crowd surged into the streets claiming independence from Spain on 11 November 1811. The monastery is now used by the Corporación Universitaria Rafael Núñez. Originally part of the Franciscan complex, the **Iglesia de la Tercera Orden** on the corner of Calle Larga is worth a visit.

Past the San Francisco complex is **Plaza de la Independencia**, with the landscaped **Parque del Centenario** beyond. Alongside the plaza, by the water, runs the **Paseo de los Mártires**, flanked by the busts of nine patriots executed in the square on 24 February 1816 by the royalist Morillo when he retook the city. At its western end, the **Torre del Reloj** (clocktower) is one of Cartagena's most prominent landmarks and the main entrance to the inner walled city.

Historic centre: inner city

Slaves from Africa were brought under the arches of the clocktower to the **Plaza de los Coches**, which served as a slave market. Around almost all the plazas of Cartagena arcades offer refuge from the tropical sun. On the west side of this plaza is the **Portal de los Dulces**, a favourite meeting place, where sweets are still sold. At night, the area becomes a popular place for an evening drink.

The **Plaza de la Aduana**, which has a statue of Columbus, is flanked by the **Palacio Municipal** and the old Customs House. The **Museo de Arte Moderno** ① *Plaza San Pedro Claver, C 30 No.4-08, www.mamcartagena.org, Mon-Fri 0900-1200, 1500-1900, Sat 1000-1300, Sun 1600-2100, US$2.60*, exhibits modern Colombian and other South American artists. Continue southwest to the **Church and Monastery of San Pedro Claver** ① *Mon-Fri 0800-1730, Sat-Sun 0800-1630, US$3.50*. Built by Jesuits in 1603, it was later dedicated to San Pedro Claver, a monk in the monastery, who was canonized 235 years after his death in 1654. Known as the Slave of the Slaves (El Apóstol de los Negros), he used to beg from door to door for money to give to the black slaves brought to the city. His body is in a glass coffin on the high altar and his cell and the balcony from which he sighted slave ships are shown to visitors. The monastery has a pleasant courtyard filled with flowers and trees in which Pedro Claver baptised slaves.

Cartagena historic centre

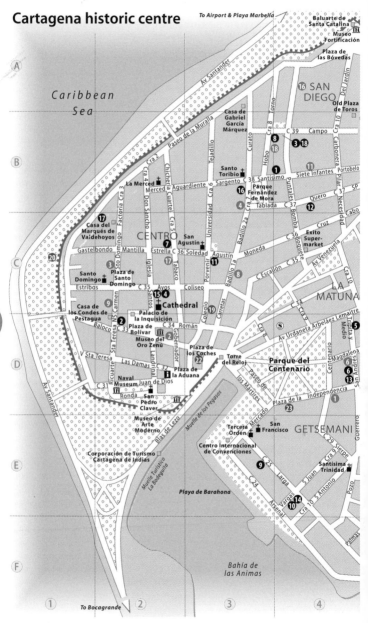

To Airport & Playa Marbella

Baluarte de Santa Catalina
Museo Fortificación
Plaza de las Bóvedas

SAN DIEGO
Old Plaza de Toros

Caribbean Sea

Casa de Gabriel García Márquez

Av Santander
Paseo de la Muralla
Curato
Campo
Carbonera

Santo Toríbio
Parque Fernández de Mora

La Merced
Chichén Iza
Santísimo
Siete Infantes
Portobelo

Casa del Marqués de Valdehoyos

CENTRO
San Agustín
Santo Domingo
Plaza de Santo Domingo
Casa de los Condes de Pestagua

Éxito Supermarket

LA MATUNA

Cathedral
Palacio de la Inquisición
Plaza de Bolívar
Museo del Oro Zenú

Av Urdaneta Arbeláez Lemaitre

Plaza de los Coches
Torre del Reloj
Plaza de la Aduana

Parque del Centenario

Naval Museum Juan de Dios
San Pedro Claver
Museo de Arte Moderno

Plaza de la Independencia

Tercera Orden
San Francisco
GETSEMANÍ

Corporación de Turismo Cartagena de Indias

Centro Internacional de Convenciones

Santísima Trinidad

Muelle Turístico La Bodeguita
Playa de Barahona

Bahía de las Ánimas

To Bocagrande

To Casa
de Núñez

Fuerte
de La
Tenaza

Lago del
Cabrero

Av del Mar

CHAMBACÚ

Mártir

La India
Catalina

Instituto
Agustín
Codazzi

Laguna de
Chambacú

C 34

Av Luis C López

C 32

Tortugas

C 31 Solar Concolon

Maravillas

Puente
Heredia

Media Luna

San
Roque

Espíritu Santo

To Castillo San Felipe de Barajas, La Popa & Bus Terminals

Carretero

Ancho

Lomba

ngosto

Tranchas

Playa del Pedrega

Laguna de
San Lázaro

Puente
Román

To Manga &
Club de Pesca

N

100 metres
100 yards

The church and convent of **Santa Teresa** on the corner of Calle Ricaurte, was founded in 1609. It is now a hotel, renamed the **Charleston Santa Teresa** (Carrera 3, No 31-23, www. hotelcharlestonsantateresa.com). Opposite is the **Museo Naval del Caribe** ⓘ *C San Juan de Dios No 3-62, T5-664 2440, www.museonavaldelcaribe.com, daily 1000-1730, US$5, discount for children*, displaying the detailed naval history of Cartagena and the Caribbean. Models and dioramas help bring the history to life, although most exhibits are described in Spanish only.

The **Plaza de Bolívar** (the old Plaza de la Inquisición) has a statue of Bolívar. On its west side is the **Palacio de la Inquisición** ⓘ *www.muhca. gov.co, Mon-Sat 0900-1800, Sun 1000-1600, US$6.50*. It was first established in 1610 and the present building dates from 1706. The stone entrance with its coats of arms and ornate wooden door is well preserved. The whole building, with its balconies, cloisters and patios, is a fine example of colonial baroque. It has been restored with air-conditioned rooms. The small museum contains photographs of Cartagena from the 20th century, paintings of historical figures, models of colonial houses and a torture chamber (with reproductions of actual instruments). On the opposite side of the Plaza de Bolívar is the **Museo del Oro Zenú** ⓘ *T5-660 0778, www. banrepcultural.org/Cartagena, Tue-Sat 0900-1800, Sun 1000-1600, free*. It has well-displayed pre-Columbian gold and pottery.

The **cathedral**, in the northeast corner of Plaza de Bolívar, was begun in 1575 and partially destroyed by Francis Drake. Reconstruction was finished by 1610. Great alterations were

BACKGROUND
Fortifying Cartagena

The full name of Cartagena is Cartagena de Indias, a reminder that the early Spanish navigators believed they had reached the Far East. The city was founded by Pedro de Heredia on 13 January 1533 and was built by the Spaniards on an island separated from the mainland by marshes and lagoons, close to a prominent hill. It was near to the mouth of the Río Magdalena, the route to the interior of the continent, and thus became one of the most important depots for merchandise arriving from Spain and for treasure collected from the Americas to be sent back. The Bahía de Cartagena, which is 15 km long and 5 km wide, was protected by several low, sandy islands, which formed natural sea defences. There were originally just two approaches to the bay – Bocagrande, at the northern end of Tierrabomba island, and Bocachica, a narrow channel to the south – thus making it a perfect place for a harbour and, more importantly at the time, easy to defend against attack. The city's wealth made it a prize target for French and English privateers operating in the Caribbean, including Sir Francis Drake who took the city in 1586. In response, a series of forts were built to protect Cartagena from raids from the sea, and formidable walls were constructed around the city, making it almost impregnable.

The harbour was protected by fortifications on Tierrabomba, Barú, Bocagrande and on the mainland, while the Puente Román, which connected the old city with Manga island to the southeast, was defended by three forts:

made between 1912 and 1923. It has a severe exterior, with a fine doorway and a simply decorated interior. See the gilded 18th-century altar, the Carrara marble pulpit, and the elegant arcades which sustain the central nave.

The church and monastery of **Santo Domingo** ① *Santo Domingo y Estribos*, was built 1570 to 1579 and is now a seminary. Inside, a miracle-making image of Christ, carved towards the end of the 16th century, is set on a baroque 19th-century altar. There is also a statue of the Virgin with a crown of gold and emeralds. Opposite the church is a fine bronze sculpture by Fernando Botero, the *Gertrudis*, presenting an interesting juxtaposition between the colonial and the modern.

Plaza Santo Domingo and Calle Santo Domingo have lots of pavement cafés, restaurants and wandering musicians, an excellent place to go in the evening. In Calle Santo Domingo, No 33-29, is one of the great patrician houses of Cartagena, the **Casa de los Condes de Pestagua** (now restored with great care as a hotel, www.hotelboutiquecasapestagua.com). North of Santo Domingo is the magnificent **Casa del Marqués de Valdehoyos** ① *C de la Factoría 36-57*, home of some of the best woodcarving in Cartagena and used for cultural events and conferences.

The monastery of **San Agustín** (1580) is now the **Universidad de Cartagena** ① *Universidad y La Soledad*. From its chapel the pirate Baron de Pointis stole

San Sebastián del Pastelillo, built between 1558 and 1567 (now occupied by the Club de Pesca), San Lorenzo and the very powerful Castillo San Felipe de Barajas inland to the east. Yet another fort, La Tenaza, protected the northern point of the walled city from a direct attack from the open sea. In 1650, the Spaniards built the 145-km-long Canal del Dique connecting the city to the Río Magdalena and allowing free access for ships from the upriver ports. The city suffered a devastating raid by the French, led by Baron de Pointis and Jean Baptiste Ducasse, in 1697, but returned to prosperity during the 18th century as one of the most important cities in the newly formed Viceroyalty of New Granada. Following an unsuccessful but sustained attack by Admiral Edward Vernon in 1741, Bocagrande was blocked by an underwater wall, thus leaving only one entrance to the harbour.

The huge walls that encircle the old city were started early in the 17th century and finished by 1735. They were on average 12 m high and 17 m thick, with six gates. Besides barracks, they contained a water reservoir. The old city was in two sections, outer and inner, divided by a wall. The artisan classes lived in one-storey houses in the outer city, in an area known as Getsemaní where many colonial buildings survive. The inner city, or El Centro, was originally occupied by the high officials and nobility, with the clerks, merchants, priests and military living in San Diego at the northern end.

Cartagena declared its Independence from Spain in 1811. A year later Bolívar used the city as a jumping-off point for his Magdalena campaign. After heroic resistance, Cartagena was retaken by the royalists under General Pablo Morillo in 1815. It was finally freed by the patriots in 1821.

a 500-pound silver sepulchre. It was returned by the King of France, but the citizens melted it down to pay their troops during the siege by Morillo in 1815. Nearby is the luxury hotel Casa San Agustín ① C de la Universidad No 36-44, www. hotelcasasanagustin.com. The church and convent of La Merced ① Merced y Chichería, was founded 1618. The convent was a prison during Morillos' reign of terror and its church is now the beautifully restored Teatro Heredia. Building of the church of Santo Toribio ① Badillo y Sargento, open for Mass only Mon-Fri 0630, 1200 and 1815, Sat 0630, 1200 and 1800, Sun 0800, 1000, 1800 and 1900, closed at other times, began in 1729. In 1741, during Admiral Vernon's siege, a cannon ball fell into the church during Mass and lodged in one of the central columns; the ball is now in a recess in the west wall. The font of Carrara marble in the Sacristy is a masterpiece. There is a beautiful carved *mudéjar*-style ceiling above the main altar. The church and monastery of Santa Clara de Assisi ① Santa Clara, C del Torno, No 39-29, built 1617-1621, have been converted into a fine hotel (www.sofitel.com). Near the hotel is the orange Casa de Gabriel García Márquez, for former Cartagena home of Colombia's most famous author, on the corner of Calle del Curato. Nearby, the Casa Museo Arte y Cultura-La Presentación ① C Estanco del Aguardiente, No 5-63, T5-76685902, Mon-Sat 0900-2000, free, is in a beautiful colonial building housing both a university and a modern art gallery. They programme temporary exhibitions and musical events and there's a modern air-conditioned café serving seven different coffee preparations.

North of Santa Clara is the **Plaza de las Bóvedas**. The walls of Las Bóvedas, built 1799, are some 12 m high and 15 to 18 m thick. From the rampart there is a grand view. At the base of the wall are 23 dungeons, now containing tourist shops. Both a lighted underground passage and a drawbridge lead from Las Bóvedas to the fortress of La Tenaza at the water's edge. In the neighbouring Baluarte de Santa Catalina is the **Museo Fortificación de Santa Catalina** ⓘ *daily 0800-1700, US$2.50, children US$1.35,* inside the city walls.

Casa de Rafael Núñez ⓘ *just outside the walls of La Tenaza in El Cabrero district, Cra 2 No 41-89, Tue-Fri 0900-1700, Sat-Sun 1000-1600, free,* was the home of Rafael Núñez, president (four times) and poet (he wrote Colombia's national anthem). His grandiose marble tomb is in the adjoining church. It's worth getting a guided tour.

East of the centre
excellent city views from the fortress and a ruined convent

Castillo San Felipe de Barajas
Cra 17, daily 0800-1800, US$8, guides and audiotour available.

Located 41 m above sea level on San Lázaro hill across the **Puente Heredia** from the old city (about a 25-minute walk), this is the largest Spanish fort built in the Americas. The site offers excellent views of both the old and new cities. Under the huge structure is a network of tunnels cut into the rock, lined with living rooms and offices. Visitors pass through these and on to the top of the fortress. Good footwear is advisable in the damp sloping tunnels, and although some are open and illuminated, a flashlight is handy in the others. In the **Almacén de Pólvora** (gunpowder store), there is a reproduction of Admiral Vernon's map, dating from his abortive attempt to take the city in 1741. A statue of Don Blas de Lezo below the fortress has a plaque displaying the medal prematurely struck celebrating Vernon's 'victory'.

Convento La Popa
Daily 0830-1730, US$1.50, children and students US$1.

On La Popa hill (named after its imagined likeness to a ship's poop) is the church and monastery of **Santa Cruz** and the restored ruins of the convent dating from 1608. The only reason to visit is for good views of the harbour and the city from this height (nearly 150 m). In the church is the beautiful little image of the Virgin of La Candelaria, reputed to be a deliverer from plague and a protector against pirates. Every year, nine days before 2 February, thousands of pilgrims go up the hill and on the day itself carry lighted candles in her honour. It can be unsafe to walk up on your own; seek local advice first. There are guided tours, or take a public bus to Teatro Miramar at the foot of the hill (US$0.75), then negotiate with a taxi up; they charge about US$20 with waiting time. If driving, take Carretera 21 off Avenida Pedro de Heredia and follow the winding road to the top.

Cartagena is also a popular beach resort and along Bocagrande and El Laguito are modern high-rise hotels on the seafront. Beyond Crespo on the road to Barranquilla is a fast-growing beach resort lined with luxury apartments.

Bocagrande
Take a bus south from the Torre del Reloj (10 minutes), taxi US$2.50, or walk to Bocagrande, a spit of land crowded with hotels and apartment blocks. Sand and sea can be dirty and you will be hassled by vendors. But do not ignore the *palenqueras*, the black women who elegantly carry bowls of fruits on their heads, serving excellent fruit salads on the beach. The **Hilton** hotel beach (www3.hilton.com) at the end of the peninsula is cleaner and has fewer vendors.

Marbella and the northern beaches
Northeast of the city is Marbella, just north of Las Bóvedas. The city continues beyond Marbella, with beaches along a spit of land between the sea and the Ciénaga de la Virgen. During the week, they are quiet and are decent for swimming, though sometimes there are dangerous currents. The promontory beyond the airport is built up with high rises, including many well-known hotels which have their own access to the beach. City buses run to Los Morros and Las Américas conference centre, carrying on towards La Boquilla and Manzanillo, which is a sparsely populated stretch of beach still close to the city. There are upscale dining options (including a gourmet supermarket) at the turn-off to Manzanillo.

Bocachica
The Bocachica beach, on Tierrabomba island, is also none too clean. Boats leave from the Muelle Turístico. The round trip can take up to two hours each way and costs about US$5 with regular services. *Ferry Dancing*, about half the price of the faster, luxury boats, carries dancing passengers. Boats taking in Bocachica and the San Fernando fortress include *Alcatraz*, which runs a daily trip from the Muelle Turístico. Recommended.

Playa Blanca and Isla Barú
Boats to the Islas del Rosario (see below) may stop at the San Fernando fortress and Playa Blanca on the Isla Barú for two to 2½ hours. Many consider this long stretch of white sand with shady palm groves to be the best beach in the region. Food and drinks are expensive on the island and you have to pay for umbrellas and chairs. Playa Blanca can be very crowded with armies of hawkers, apart from early morning and after 1530 when the tour boats have left (one way US$9 per person). If snorkelling, beware

> **Tip...**
> From the car park at Playa Blanca, take the steps down to the beach, then walk to your right as far as you can to find the least-crowded spots.

drunken jet ski drivers. There are several fish restaurants on the beach, a growing number of upmarket places to stay and a few hammock and camping places (take repellent against sand flies if sleeping in a tent or *cabaña*). You can arrange to be left and collected later, or you can try to catch an earlier boat on to Islas del Rosario or back to Cartagena with a boat that has dropped off people at the beach. Isla Barú is now connected to the mainland by a new bridge; you can hire a private or shared taxi, or book a bus tour through hotels and tour operators in Cartagena. A worthwhile excursion can be made to the **Aviario Nacional** ① *daily 0900-1700. last entry 1600, shows at 1100 and 1530, US$13 pp.* Situated at Km 14.5 after crossing the Barú bridge, or a five-minute taxi ride from Playa Blanca, this privately owned park is split into six different environments and offers the opportunity to observe a wide variety of birds (there are 135 different species here) from across Colombia and beyond. The birds mostly have a lot of space and many fly about freely. There are occasional iguanas and tortoises ambling along too. Allow two to three hours and take mosquito repellent. There's a café on site.

Listings Cartagena and around *map page 110.*

Tourist information

Useful websites include www.ticartagena.com and www.cartagenacaribe.com.

Corporación Turismo Cartagena de Indias (Corpoturismo)
Casa del Marqués del Premio Real, Plaza de la Aduana, T5-660 1583, www.cartagenadeindias.travel. Mon-Sat 0900-1200, 1300-1800, Sun and holidays 0900-1700.
This is the main tourist office and has very helpful and knowledgeable staff. Useful free maps available.

There are also kiosks in **Plaza de la Paz** (same hours as above), at the **airport** (daily 0700-2300, reduced hours on Sun), **Bocagrande**, Av del Malecón, opposite Parque Flanagan (Mon-Sat 0800-1200, 1300-1700, Sun 0900-1700) and at the **Sociedad Portuaria Regional de Cartagena** (open for cruise ship arrivals).

Instituto Agustín Codazzi
C 34, No 3A-31, Edif Inurbe, T5-664 4171, www.igac.gov.co. Mon-Fri 0800-1200, 1300-1700.
Contact for maps.

Instituto de Patrimonio y Cultura de Cartagena
C Larga No 9A-37, T5-664 9443, www.ipcc. gov.co. Mon-Fri 0800-1200, 1400-1800.
May also provide information.

Where to stay

Hotel prices rise for the high seasons, Nov-Mar and Jun-Jul. From 15 Dec to 31 Jan they can increase by as much as 50% (dates are not fixed and vary at each hotel). Hotels tend to be heavily booked right through to Mar. Bargain in low season.

Historic centre
There is a growing number of attractive boutique hotels in Cartagena. Most budget hostels are in **Getsemaní**. This area is very popular with travellers and

has been smartened up, with many places to stay, eat and drink (lots of happy hour offers). Do not, however, walk alone late at night.

See the description of the historic centre for descriptions and websites of colonial buildings converted to luxury hotels: **Charleston Santa Teresa** (see page 111), **Casa de los Condes de Pestagua** (see page 112), **Casa San Agustín** (see page 113) and **Santa Clara** (see page 113) are all special places to stay.

$$$$ Cartagena de Indias
C Vélez Daníes 33, No 4-39, T5-660 0133, www.movichhotels.com.
Small, friendly boutique hotel in a colonial building, comfortable, luxury accommodation, infinity pool and terrace with spectacular views of the old city.

$$$$ Casa Pestagua
C Santo Domingo, No 33-63, T5-664 9510, www.hotelboutiquecasapestagua.com.
Formerly home to the Conde de Pestagua, this historic house has been restored by architect Alvaro Barrera Herrera with great care. From the street it opens up into a magnificent colonnaded courtyard lined with enormous palm trees. Beyond is a swimming pool and spa, and on the top floor a sun terrace with jacuzzi and sea views. Exceptional service.

$$$$ El Marqués
C Nuestra Señora del Carmen, No 33-41, T5-664 4438, www. elmarqueshotelboutique.com.
A house belonging to the Pestagua family, famous in the 1970s for its celebrity guests. The central courtyard has giant birdcages, hanging bells and

large palm trees. The rooms are crisp and white. Excellent Peruvian restaurant, wine cellar and a spa. Exquisite.

$$$$ Hotel Capellán de Getsemaní
Sector Getsemaní, Cra 9 No 29-52, T5-660 9562, www.hotelcapellan degetsemani.com.
Opened in 2017, this chic boutique hotel offers 30 designer rooms and suites. A stylish blend of traditional and modern with glass-floored terraces, wonderful rooftop area with pool, jacuzzi, bar and great views. Impeccable service, spa and treatments available, eco-bikes for hire. Highly recommended.

$$$$ La Passion
C Estanco del Tabaco, No 35-81, T5-664 8605, www.lapassionhotel.com.
Moroccan-style chic, elegant and discreet comfort, helpful staff, breakfast served by the roof-top pool, very pleasant. Some rooms have balconies. Massage treatments and boat trips to Islas del Rosario organized. Highly recommended.

$$$$-$$$ Casa La Fe
Parque Fernández de Madrid, C 2a de Badillo, No 36-125, T5-664 0306, http://kalihotels.com.
Discreet sign (pink building), run by British/Colombian team. Very pleasant converted colonial house, quiet, jacuzzi on roof, free bicycle use. Recommended. Also has new sister hotel, **$$$ Posada la Fe**, in Getsemaní district (same website).

$$$ Kartaxa LifeStyle
C de las Bóvedas, No 39-120, T5-645 5300, http://hotelkartaxacartagena.com.
Near the delightful Plaza San Diego, this colonial building has modern rooms with an art and literature theme, courtyard, **La Comunión** restaurant.

$$$ Las Tres Banderas
C Cochera de Hobo, No 38-66, T5-660 0160, www.hotel3banderas.com.
Off Plaza San Diego, popular, helpful owner, very pleasant, safe, quiet, good beds, spacious rooms, massage treatments, small patio. Price depends on standard of room and season. Free ferry transport to sister hotel on Isla de la Bomba; has another hotel in Manzanillo.

$$ Don Pedro de Heredia
Cra 7, No 35-74, T5-664 7270, T316-2539875, www.hoteldonpedrodeheredia.com.
This colonial-style hotel is located in the heart of the historic centre. Rooms are spacious and comfortable with good a/c, minibar and safe. Roof terrace with views, pool, excellent buffet breakfast served on the top floor, friendly staff, good Wi-Fi, great value. Highly recommended.

$$-$ Mamallena
C de la Media Luna, No 10-47, T5-670 0499, www.hostelmamallenacartagena.com.
Rooms and dorms (US$12, some a/c), in same group as Mamallena hostels in Panama, www.mamallena. com. Thorough info on boat travel to Panama and on local activities and day tours, including the shuttle to Playa Blanca. There's a small kitchen, some comfortable common areas, café, breakfast, tea and coffee included.

$$-$ Villa Colonial
C de las Maravillas, No 30-60, Getsemaní, T5-664 5421, www.hotelvillacolonial.com.
Safe, well-kept hostel run by friendly family, English spoken, cheaper with fan, tours to Islas del Rosario. Its sister hotels, **Casa Villa Colonial** (C de la Media Luna No 10-89), and **Casa Mara** (C del Espíritu No 29-139, same phone, www.

casavillacolonial.com), are more upmarket ($$$-$$) and are also recommended.

$ Casa Viena
C San Andrés, No 30-53 Getsemaní, T5-668 5048, T320-538 3619, www.casaviena.com.
Popular traveller hostel with very helpful staff who provide lots of information and sell tours and **Brasilia** bus tickets. Cooking facilities, washing machine, TV room, range of dorms (US$10-13) and rooms: more expensive with private bath and a/c. Enquire here for information about boats to Panama.

$ El Viajero Hostel Cartagena
C Siete Infantes, No 9-45, T318-257 5354, www.hostelcartagena.com.
Member of the South American chain of hostels, with a/c in private rooms and dorms (average dorm bed price US$15 pp), busy and popular party hostel with bar, daily activities including salsa lessons and games nights.

$ Marlin
C de la Media Luna, No 10-35, T5-664 3507, http://hotelmarlincartagena.com.
Aquatic-themed hostel run by a friendly Colombian. Private rooms and dorms (US$10 pp). Has a fine balcony overlooking the busy C de la Media Luna, free coffee, laundry service, lockers, tours and bus tickets organized.

Bocagrande

$$$$-$$$ Hotel Caribe by Faranda
Cra 1, No 2-87, T5-650 1160, www.hotelcaribe.com.
Enormous Caribbean-style hotel, the first to be built in Cartagena, retaining some splendour of bygone years, with 2 newer annexes, a/c, beautiful grounds and a swimming pool. Expensive restaurant,

has several bars overlooking the sea, various tour agencies and a dive shop.

$$$ Playa Club
Av San Martín, No 4-87, T5-665 0552, www.hotelplayaclubcartagena.com.
Good rooms, inviting pool and direct access to the beach. TV, a/c and breakfast included. Restaurant serving good-quality food at reasonable prices.

$$$-$$ Bahía
Cra 4 with C 4, T5-665 0316, www.hotelbahiacartagena.com.
Retains the feel of a 1950s hotel – it was opened in 1958 – but with mod cons such as Wi-Fi and safes in rooms. Discreet and quiet, with 2 fine pools, children's play area and 3 restaurants, excellent breakfasts.

$$$-$$ Cartagena Millennium
Av San Martín, No 7-135, T5-665 8711, www.hotelcartagenamillennium.com.
A range of different suites and spacious rooms at various prices. Chic and trendy, with minimalist decor, a long pool which is half indoors, good restaurant serving typical and international food, a terrace bar and a lobby bar, friendly service, recommended.

$$$-$$ Charlotte
Av San Martín, No 7-126, T5-665 9365, www.hotelescharlotte.com.
Comfortable rooms stylishly designed in cool whites. Has a small pool, and Wi-Fi by the pool. Smart restaurant serving regional food. Recommended.

Marbella and the northern beaches

$$$ Hotel Kohsamui
Anillo Vial, Entrada Km 9.7 a Manzanillo del Mar, T317-648 9303, www.kohsamuicartagena.com.

Situated 20 km north of Cartagena, this is an ideal beachside spot for relaxation and rejuvenation. Owner María Fernanda runs the hotel and has information on mangrove tours, excursions and trips to Islas del Rosario and Volcán del Totumo. Amenities include a/c and fans, security box, Wi-Fi, minibar, restaurant, spa with massage, and a 2nd-floor terrace with hammocks. 10% discount for paying in advance. Highly recommended.

Playa Blanca and Isla Barú
Playa Blanca has several basic hostels right on the beach. Because of Wi-Fi connection being problematic here, they can be difficult to book in advance. Of those you can book, try **La Cabaña de Gerónimo ($$)**, which has clean cabins with or without sea view, or **Hostal Playa Blanca ($)**. Cash only as there are no ATMs on Isla Barú.

$$$ Playa Manglares
Km 12, Isla Barú Ararca, T311-403 9391, www.playamanglares.com.
Ecolodge with tranquil private beachfront, and beautifully decorated rooms (there are hammocks on the beach as well as in the rooms). Charming owner Olga is friendly and welcoming and can organize transport to and from Cartagena (private taxi US$26) as well as to Playa Blanca (5-10 mins away by taxi US$2), the aviary (taxi US$3) and day trips to Islas Rosario, which include a tour round the islands and snorkelling (prices vary depending on numbers). Breakfast included, delicious lunches and evening meals are extra. Attentive service, delightful.

Restaurants

There is a wide range of excellent restaurants. Reservations are recommended during high season.

At cafés try *patacón*, a round flat 'cake' made of green banana, mashed and baked; it's also available from street stalls in Parque del Centenario in the early morning. At restaurants ask for *sancocho*, the local soup of the day made from vegetables and fish or meat. Stands serving tasty shrimp cocktails can be found just outside of El Centro. Also try *obleas* for a snack: biscuits with jam, cream cheese or caramel fudge (*arequipe*); and *buñuelos*, deep-fried cheese dough balls. Fruit juices are fresh, tasty and cheap in Cartagena. Try *corozo*, a small red fruit with a flavour similar to cranberry: a good place is on the Paseo de los Pegasos (Av Blas de Lezo) from the many stalls alongside the boats. **Crepes y Waffles**, **Jeno's Pizza** and **Juan Valdez** have outlets in the centre, Bocagrande and elsewhere.

Historic centre

$$$ Carmen
C 38, No 8-19, T5-664 5116, www.carmencartagena.com.
Contemporary Colombian cuisine, beautifully presented in top-class restaurant. Delightful and inventive combinations of ingredients such as fish of the day with compressed cucumber and coconut smoke (released from under a glass). There are tasting menus with wine pairings, which are expensive but absolutely worth it. This is a true gastronomic experience. Always busy, so make sure you reserve a table.

$$$ Donde Olano
C Santo Domingo, No 33-81, T5-664 7099, www.dondeolano.com.
Tucked away, art deco style, intimate atmosphere, with romantic outdoor courtyard or a/c dining room. Smooth

jazz and French café music adds to the sophisticated mood. Excellent seafood with French and Creole influences. Try their seafood platter with coconut rice, Tentaciones de Zeus, well worth the price. Recommended.

$$$ Salou
Cra 2, No 36-86, Playa de la Artillería, T5-664 1693, T311-413 0831, www.salourestaurante.com.
Fine dining is offered at this family-run modern restaurant. Offers Asian/Latin American fusion cuisine with lots of innovative combinations, fresh local ingredients with a modern twist, and all beautifully presented. Ceviches, seafood and meat dishes. Try the Tour Colombia or Tour Salou, 2 different tasting menus. Highly recommended.

$$ El Balcón
C de Tumbamuertos, No 38-85, T5-643 4393.
Small restaurant with a nice balcony overlooking the Plaza de San Diego. Good atmosphere and good views.

$$ El Bistro
C de los Ayos, No 4-46, T5-660 2065, www.el-bistro.com. Closed Sun.
German-run restaurant with a relaxed atmosphere. Sofas, music, Colombian and European menu at reasonable prices, German bakery. Try the passion-fruit mojitos. Recommended.

$$ Juan del Mar
Plaza San Diego, No 8-21, T5-664 2782, www.juandelmar.com.
2 restaurants in 1: inside for expensive seafood, outside for tasty thin-crust pizzas. Fun atmosphere, and often has live music and dancing.

$$ Lunarossa
C Media Luna No 9-91 y San Andrés.

Italian place, with pastas, thin-crust pizzas and other dishes, also has a cocktail bar and open-air terrace at the back.

$$ Ohlala Bistrot
C 35 (C Larga) No 4-48, Getsemaní sector, T5-664 4321, see Facebook.
French/Colombian-owned café and restaurant serving excellent meals, including breakfasts. Delicious and unusual juices such as tangy tamarindo and local fruit *corozo*. They offer half-day cooking courses in small groups using fresh Colombian and Caribbean ingredients (US$60pp including cocktails and dinner, reservations necessary). Recommended.

$$ Perú Fusión
C de los Ayos, No 4-36, T5-660 5243, http://perufusionrestaurante.com
Good quality Peruvian-style food, including ceviches and Japanese sushi. Some unusual pairings of ingredients can be tried here.

$$ Teriyaki
Plaza San Diego, No 8-28, T5-664 8651, www.teriyaki.com.co.
Serves sushi and Thai food in smart surroundings; part of the chain with outlets in Bogota and Barranquilla.

$$-$ La Casa de Socorro
C Larga, No 8B-112, Getsemaní, T315-718 6666.
A busy restaurant, popular with locals and tourists, serving seafood and Caribbean dishes. Try the *sancocho de pargo*, a delicious fish soup. There are 2 restaurants of the same name on the street and this is the original.

$$-$ La Cocina de Pepina
C Vargas, No 9A-6, T5-664 2944.
Serving Colombian/Caribbean fare, established by the late chef and cookbook author María Josefina Yances Guerra. It's a small restaurant so get there early.

$ El Coroncoro
C Tripita y Media, No 31-22.
Typical local restaurant which is popular at lunchtime and serves good, inexpensive food.

$ Este es el Punto
C San Andrés, No 30-35.
Another popular restaurant, *comida corriente* at lunchtime, big portions, also serves breakfast.

$ La Esquina del Pan de Bono
C San Agustín Chiquito, No 35-78, opposite Plazoleta San Agustín. Daily from 0600.
Breads, *empanadas* with savoury and sweet fillings, *pasteles* and a wide selection of delicious juices, popular for a quick snack.

$ La Mulata
C Quero, No 9-58.
A popular lunchtime venue with locals, you get a selection of set-menu dishes. Also open in evenings from 1900. Try the excellent seafood casserole and coconut lemonade. Large portions and reasonable prices.

$ Pizza en el Parque
C 2a de Badillo, No 36-153.
This small restaurant serves delicious pizzas with some interesting flavours (pear and apple) which you can enjoy in the delightful atmosphere of Parque Fernández de Madrid.

Cafés and ice cream parlours

Gelateria Paradiso
C Estrella con Cuartel, T5-6604945. Daily 0900-2300.

Delightful ice-cream parlour with home-made ice cream, unusual flavours such as coconut lemonade, hibiscus, basil and many tropical fruit flavours. Free Wi-Fi.

East of the historic centre

$$$ Club de Pesca
San Sebastián de Pastelillo fort, Manga island, T5-651 7400, www.clubdepesca.com.
Wonderful setting, try to get there for sunset. Excellent fish and seafood. Recommended.

Bocagrande

$$$-$$ Arabe
Cra 3, No 8-83, T5-665 4365, www. restaurantearabeinternacional.com.
Upmarket Arab restaurant serving tagines, etc. A/c, indoor seating or pleasant outdoor garden. Excellent authentic food and service. Recommended.

$$$-$$ Carbón de Palo
Av San Martín, No 6-40, T5-665 6004.
Steak heaven (and other dishes, including great pasta), cooked on an outdoor *parrilla*.

$ La Fonda Antioqueña
Cra 2, No 6-164, T5-665 5805.
Traditional Colombian food from Antioquia served in a pleasant outdoor setting.

Marbella and the northern beaches
There are good fish dishes in La Boquilla and upscale dining options (including a gourmet supermarket) at the turn-off to Manzanillo.

$$ Archie's Trattoria
Km 9 via Manzanillo, local 601, T5-643 7070, www.archies.com.

Chain Italian restaurant serving delicious thin-crust pizzas and a large selection of pastas.

$$ Hotel Kohsamui
Trans 2, No 3-51, Manzanillo, T317-648 9303.
Chef Elbert runs the restaurant in the hotel, serving up a variety of seafood dishes, including fresh ceviches, *arroz con mariscos* and fried fish. Probably the best seafood on the beach.

Bars and clubs

Most nightlife is found in the historic centre. Many of the hotels have evening entertainment and can arrange *chiva* tours, usually with free drinks and live music on the bus.

Most places don't get going until after 2400, though the Cuban bars **Donde Fidel** (Portal de los Dulces) and **Café Havana** (see below) start a bit earlier and are recommended for Cuban salsa. The former is open daytime, with good atmosphere. Many clubs are on C del Arsenal. Most bars play crossover music.

Historic centre

Alquímico
C del Colegio No 34-24, T318-845 0433.
Trendy club with a rooftop bar, great atmosphere.

Café del Mar
Baluarte de Santo Domingo, El Centro.
The place to go for a drink at sundown.

Café Havana
C de la Media Luna y C del Guerrero, T314-556 3905, www.cafehavana cartagena.com. Wed-Sat 2030-0400.
A fantastic Cuban bar/restaurant, which feels like it has been transported from Havana brick by brick. The walls

are festooned with black-and-white portraits of Cuban salsa stars and live bands play most nights. No credit cards. Highly recommended.

Donde Fidel
Portal de los Dulces, T314-526 1892.
Loud, crowded bar with salsa music. Popular with locals and tourists alike.

Quiebra Canto
Cra 8B, No 25-119 at Parque Centenario, next to Hotel Monterrey and above Café Bar Caponero, Getsemaní, www. quiebracanto.com. Free admission.
Good for salsa, nice atmosphere.

Bocagrande
There are good local nightclubs in Bocagrande, eg **Club Cartagena**, C 4, No 3-80, with other places nearby, including spontaneous musical groups on or near the beach most evenings.

Entertainment

Cinema
There are many cinemas in Cartagena. In Bocagrande there is one in the **Centro Comercial Bocagrande** (Cra 2, No 8-142, T5-665 5024). Others are in the **Centro Comercial Paseo de la Castellana** (C 30, No 30-31, www. paseodelacastellana.com), and in **Centro Comercial La Plazuela** (Diagonal 31, No 71-130, www. multicentrolaplazuela.com).

Dance
El Colegio del Cuerpo, *Campus Universidad Jorge Tadeo Lozano, Módulo 6, Km 15-200, Anillo Vial Zona Norte, T5-665 4081, www.elcolegiodelcuerpo.org.*
A classical dance studio that works with children from Cartagena's slums. They perform internationally and occasionally in Cartagena.

Festivals

Mid-Jan Festival Internacional de Música, www.cartagenamusicfestival. com. Classical music festival with associated education programme for young musicians.
End-Jan Hay Festival Cartagena, www. hayfestival.com. Franchise of the famous UK literary festival, with internationally renowned writers.
Jan-Feb Nuestra Señora de la Candelaria, religious processions, horse parades, typical dances and regional cuisine (see La Popa, page 114).
Early Mar International Film Festival, www.ficcifestival.com. The longest running festival of its kind in Latin America. Although mainly Spanish American films are featured, the US, Canada and European countries are represented in the week-long showings.
1 Jun Foundation of Cartagena, celebrations to commemorate the founding of the city, in 1533.
2nd week of Nov Independence celebrations: masked people in fancy dress dance to the sound of *maracas* and drums. There are beauty contests, battles of flowers and general mayhem.

Shopping

Pricey antiques can be bought in C Santo Domingo and there are a number of jewellery shops near Plaza de Bolívar in Centro, which specialize in emeralds. The handicraft shops in the Plaza de las Bóvedas (see page 114) have the best selection in town but tend to be expensive – cruise ship passengers are brought here. Woollen *blusas* are good value; try the **Tropicano** in Pierino Gallo building in Bocagrande. Also in this building are reputable jewellery shops.

Abaco, *C de la Iglesia with C Mantilla, No 3-86, T5-664 8338, www.abacolibros. com*. A bookshop and popular hangout for local writers and poets. Delightful atmosphere and a café serving juices and snacks.

Centro Comercial Getsemaní, *C Larga between San Juan and Plaza de la Independencia*. A large shopping centre. Good *artesanías* in the grounds of the convent.

El Centavo Menos, *C Román, No 5-08, Plaza de la Proclamación*. Good selection of Colombian handicrafts.

Exito, *Escallón y del Boquete*. A supermarket, with a/c and cafeteria.

Galería Cano, *Plaza Bolívar No 33-20, www.lacano.co (and at the airport and Hotel Santa Clara)*. Has excellent reproductions of pre-Columbian designs.

Librería Nacional, *C 2 de Badillo, No 36-27, T5-664 1448, www.librerianacional. com*. A good bookshop with large stock.

The Shop, *C38, Cra7, No6-107, open Mon-Sat*. Locally sourced with a range of organic products such as fair trade coffee and chocolate and small gift items.

Upalema, *C San Juan de Dios, No 3-99*. A good selection of handicrafts.

Markets

The main market, **Mercado Bazurto** (open daily) is to the southeast of the old city near La Popa, off Av Pedro de Heredia. It's chaotic, hot and smelly, but a great way to see local life. You can buy almost anything here from fake designer clothing and electricals to fruit and veg. Leave your valuables behind. You can find good bargains in the **La Matuna** market (also open daily).

City tours

Many agencies, hotels and hostels offer city tours, US$15-25, depending on length of tour and what's included, etc. There are also hop-on, hop-off city sightseeing bus tours, www.city sightseeing.com.co and www.colombia trolley.com. A party tour on a *chiva* (brightly coloured local bus) costs US$12 pp. These are loud, include rum, and they finish with a free entry to a night club, where they'll pick you up after an hour, or you can make your own way home. Bookings can be made through **India Catalina Chiva** (T311-661 3972), departs from Bocagrande, eat before you go.

Horse-drawn carriages can be hired for a trip around the walled city from Puerta del Reloj, about US$15-20 for up to 4 people. Or from opposite Hotel El Dorado, Av San Martín, in Bocagrande, to ride into town at night (romantic but a rather short ride). You can also rent bicycles for riding the city streets from several places in the historic centre.

Diving

Discounts are sometimes available if you book via the hotels. There is a recompression chamber at the naval hospital in Bocagrande.

Cartagena Divers, *C de Jardín, No 39-190, T312-6199370, www.cartagenadivers.com*. PADI courses and diving trips, well-maintained equipment, professional, English spoken.

Club Isla del Pirata, *Islas del Rosario, T5-665 5622, www.hotelislapirata.com*. Has the best boats and is near the top end of the price range.

Diving Planet, *C Estanco del Aguardiente, No 5-09, T300-603 7284 (English), www.*

divingplanet.org. PADI training courses, PADI e-learning, snorkelling trips and various tours of the coral reefs and mangroves. English spoken.
La Tortuga Dive Shop, *Edif Marina del Rey, C 1, No 2-23, local 4, Av del Retorno, El Laguito, Bocagrande, T5-665 6994, www.tortugadive.com.* Fast boat, which allows for trips to Isla Barú as well as Salmedina and Los Rosarios.

Football
Estadio Jaime Morón León,
Villa Olímpica, south of the city.
Games are infrequent.

Language schools
Nueva Lengua School, *C 28, No 10b-52, sector Getsemaní, T315-855 9551, www. nuevalengua.com.* Offers courses ranging from ½-day schedules to a scheme that arranges volunteer jobs. There are even Spanish courses combined with dance, music, adventure, kitesurfing or diving.

Tour operators
Aventure Colombia, *C de la Factoría, No 36-04, T5-660 9721, T314-588 2378 www.aventurecolombia.com.* Also with branches in Bogotá and Santa Marta. The only tour organizer of its kind in Cartagena, French/Colombian-run, offering alternative tours across Colombia, local and national activities

and expeditions, working (wherever possible) with local and indigenous groups (eg their day tour to Palenque). The focus is on ecotourism and trekking. Also organizes boat trips (eg to Isla del Sol). Highly recommended.
Ocean & Land, *Cra 2, No 4-15, Edif Antillas, Bocagrande, T5-665 7772, 727, oceanlandtours_cartagena@hotmail.com.* Organizes city tours, rumbas in *chiva* buses and other local activities.

Yachting
Club Isla del Pirata, *T5-665 5622, www. hotelislapirata.com.* Has the best boats and is near the top end of the price range; or enquire at the quay.
Club Náutico, *Av Miramar No 19-50, Isla Manga (across the Puente Román), T5-660 4863, www.clubnauticocartagena. com.* Good for opportunities to charter, crew or for finding a lift to other parts of the Caribbean.

Transport

Air
Rafael Núñez Airport (www.sacsa.co) is 1.5 km from the city in the Crespo district and can be reached by local buses from Blas de Lezo, in the southwest corner of El Centro. A bus from the airport to Plaza San Francisco costs US$0.70; a taxi to San Diego or the centre is US$4 and to Bocagrande, US$7; agree the fare in advance as taxis here don't have meters. City buses can be very crowded so if you have a lot of luggage, a taxi is recommended. There is a *casa de cambio* (daily 0830-2000) at the airport, but rates are better in town. Travel agents have offices on the upper level. There are also a number of fast-food outlets.

There are direct flights daily to/from major Colombian cities, **San Andrés** and smaller places in the north of the country, as well as direct international flights to/from **Fort Lauderdale**, **Miami**, **New York**, **Panama** and **Lima**. From Dec to Mar flights can be overbooked, so arrive at the airport early. Airlines servicing the airport include **Avianca**, T5-664 7376, **Copa**, T1-800 011 2600; **EasyFly**, T5-693 0400; **LATAM**, T1-800 094 9490 and the good budget airline **Viva Colombia**, T5-693 7777.

Bus

The bus terminal, known as the 'Terminal de Transportes' (www.terminaldecartagena.com) is at least 35 mins away from town on the road to Barranquilla. A **Metrocar** city bus to the terminal from the centre costs US$0.75, or a taxi, US$6-8; agree your taxi fare before you get in.

Several bus companies run to **Barranquilla**, every 15 mins, 2-3 hrs, US$5-6; there's also a **Berlinastur** (www.berlinastur.com) minibus service from C 46C, No 3-80, Marbella, T5 693 0006, T318-724 2424, and *colectivos* from C 70, Crespo, every 2 hrs (centre-to-centre service). To **Santa Marta**, hourly, US$14, 4 hrs. Few buses go direct to Santa Marta from Cartagena, most stop in Barranquilla. To/from **Bogotá** via Barranquilla and Bucaramanga, daily, 21-28 hrs (depending on number of checkpoints), US$36-38, several companies. To **Medellín** 665 km, US$38-50, depending on the bus company, more or less hourly from 0530, 13-16 hrs; book early (2 days in advance at holiday times); the road is paved but in poor condition. To **Magangué** on the Río Magdalena (for connections to Mompós) with **Brasilia/Unitransco**, US$14-16, 4 hrs (www.expresobrasilia.com). For transport to **Mompós**, see

page 133. To **Riohacha**, US$18, 7-8 hrs, with **Expreso Brasilia**. To **Maicao** on Venezuelan border, in the evening, 8-9 hrs, US$21, with **Expreso Brasilia**.

Car hire

Several of the bigger hotels have car rental offices in their foyers, such as **S&M Rent a Car** at the Hotel Cartagena Plaza, Cra 1, N 6-154, T5-665 9047. There are also car rental companies in Edif Torremolinos, Av San Martín, including **International Car Rentals**, T5-665 5399, and **National**, T5-655 1215; also on Av San Martín: **Trans**, No 11-67, Edif Tulipana L-5, T5-665 2427. Multiple companies at the airport.

Sea

Boats go from Cartagena to the **San Blas Islands** (Panama); the journey takes 5 days in total, 2 sailing to the archipelago and 3 touring the San Blas islands. Trips usually end at Porvenir on the mainland, from where you can continue to Colón and thence to Panama City. The fare, about US$550, includes food, water and snorkelling gear. Some boats are cheaper, but you get what you pay for, so take your time before choosing a boat. Some captains are irresponsible and unreliable. The journey is cramped so it's best to get on with the captain. There are many notices

> **Tip...**
> On the street, do not be tempted by offers of jobs or passages on board a ship. Jobs should have full documentation from the Seamen's Union office and passages should only be bought at a recognized shipping agency.

in hostels in Getsemaní advertising this trip, for example in **Casa Viena** and **Mamallena**. Also **Sailing Koala**, T312-670 7863, www.sailingkoala.com, which offers a trip to San Blas and Panama. If entering Panama by boat, tourists pay a US$105 immigration fee, although this isn't consistently applied.

Taxi

There are no meters; journeys are calculated by zones and fixed by the Alcaldía with fares ranging from US$2-5. It is quite common to ask other people waiting if they would like to share, but, in any case, always agree the fare with the driver before getting in. By arrangement, taxis will wait for you if visiting more remote places. Fares go up at night.

★ Islas del Rosario

sparkling beaches with good snorkelling and diving

The Parque Nacional Corales del Rosario embraces the Rosario archipelago (a group of 30 low-lying, densely vegetated coral islets 45 km southwest of the Bay of Cartagena, with narrow strips of fine sand beaches and mangroves) and the Islas de San Bernardo, a further 50 km south (see page 134).

Isla Grande and some of the smaller islets are about an hour away, so easily accessible by day trippers. A day package to **Hotel Isla del Sol** on Isla Grande, for example, including buffet lunch and boat transport, costs US$60. There is a seawater pool, a clean, private beach

> **Tip...**
> When taking boat trips be certain that you and the operator understand what you are paying for.

and several activities on offer such as guided snorkelling (US$15, recommended), a walking tour of the village and canoeing in the mangroves. Other visitors who may need permits (US$2.55 entrance fee, park open 0800-1700) should contact the National Parks office in Bogotá or **Ecohotel La Cocotera** (T314-514 4067, Facebook: hotellacocoteracartagena). **Rosario** (the best conserved) and **Tesoro** both have small lakes, some of which connect to the sea. There is an incredible profusion of aquatic and birdlife. The **San Martín de Pajarales Aquarium** ⓘ *US$9, not included in boat fares (check that it's open before setting out)*, is an open sea aquarium; there are guides, but also shark and dolphin shows (Footprint does not endorse dolphins in captivity, see www.wdcs.org/captivity). Many of the smaller islets are privately owned. Apart from fish and coconuts, everything is imported from the mainland, fresh water included. Enquire in Bocagrande for other places to stay on the islands. Diving permits are organized by diving companies and are included in their tour prices (see page 124).

Where to stay

$$$$ San Pedro de Majagua
*Isla Grande; book at C del Torno,
No 39-29, Cartagena, T5-693 0987,
www.hotelmajagua.com.*
Everything from a 'pillow menu' to
Egyptian cotton bed sheets, this is a
lovely, luxurious place for utter relaxation.

$$$$-$$$ Ecohotel Isla del Sol
*Isla Grande, T5-665 1088,
www.ecohotelisladelsol.com.*
Pleasant clean beach resort offering
activities such as diving, snorkelling
and a visit by kayak to the mangroves.
There is also a seawater swimming pool.
The hotel's restaurant serves delicious
food and the rooms are simple, clean
and comfortable. It can get busy during
the day when a couple of tour boats
arrive with day-trippers, but otherwise
peaceful. Recommended.

$$$$-$$$ Isla del Pirata
*Isla del Pirata; T5-665 2952,
www.hotelislapirata.com.*
Simple, comfortable *cabañas*, activities
include diving, snorkelling, canoeing and
pétanque, good Caribbean restaurant.
Prices include transport to the island
from Cartagena, food and non-guided
activities. Highly recommended.

$$$ Ecohotel La Cocotera
*Comunidad de Orika, Isla Grande,
T376 474 0781, see Facebook.*
Rustic rooms with bath and solar
power, also has camping and
hammocks, restaurant, diving
school. Lovely isolated location.

North of Cartagena

take a mud bath in a volcanic crater

A good road continues beyond La Boquilla.

On the coast, 50 km northeast, is **Galerazamba**, no accommodation but good local
food. Nearby are the clay baths of **Volcán del Totumo** ⓘ *US$3.50, a bathe will cost
you US$3.50, masseurs available for a small extra fee*, in beautiful surroundings. The
crater is about 20 m high and the mud lake, at a comfortable temperature, 10 m
across, is reputed to be over 500 m deep.

South from
Cartagena

Just a few years ago, the area south of Cartagena was a no-go zone but today it's a different story and locals no longer sweat before making what was once a perilous journey. It is now even considered reasonably safe to travel between Cartagena and Medellín at night. That said, you should be aware that drug smuggling is still very active in the area near the Panama border.

The improvement in security means that this area, rich in culture and natural wonders, has opened up to tourism. Southeast is the colonial town of Mompós (also spelt Mompox), stranded in a time warp on an island in the Río Magdalena. Due south of Cartagena is Tolú, gateway to the coral islands of San Bernardo (part of the Parque Nacional Natural Corales de Rosario y San Bernardo), while further along the coast is Arboletes, location of the largest mud volcano in the area. Further still is Turbo, a rough frontier town from where boats can be caught to the emerald green coastline of the Darién.

Towards Mompós

After 24 km, the highway south towards Medellín goes through **Turbaco**, where the **Botanical Garden** ⓘ *1.5 km before the village on the left, www.jbgp.org.co, Tue-Sun 0800-1600*, has good birdwatching, with a café and restaurant. You can take a taxi from Cartagena there and back including four hours' waiting time for US$35-40. Next come **Malagana**, 60 km, **San Jacinto**, known for its cumbia music using *gaitas* and local craft work (handwoven hammocks), and **El Carmen de Bolívar**, 125 km. A road runs east from the highway at El Bongo to **Magangué** on the western loop of the Río Magdalena. It is the port for the savannahs of Bolívar. From here boats go to La Bodega where you pick up the road again for the small town of Mompós.

★ Mompós *Colour map 1, B3.*

time-warp town in a unique riverine setting

Also spelt Mompox, this town is a UNESCO World Heritage Site on the eastern arm of the river. Alfonso de Heredia (brother of the founder of Cartagena) founded the town in 1540, but due to the silting up of the Río Magdalena here, little has changed in this sweltering, humid town since the early 20th century. Simón Bolívar stayed here frequently and wrote, "If I owe my life to Caracas, I owe my glory to Mompós" (a monument outside the Alcaldía proclaims this).

Today, Mompós is one of Colombia's most beautiful colonial towns. Facing the river, on the Albarrada, is the old customs house and the mansions of Spanish merchants for whom this was an important stopping-off point on the Cartagena trade route. Rows of well-preserved buildings, some with balconies, have served as a backdrop in many Colombian films. Of its six churches, **Santa Bárbara**, **La Concepción** and **San Francisco** stand out. In the **Claustro de San Agustín** is a workshop where youngsters are taught local skills. The cemetery is of considerable historical interest. Mompós is packed during Easter week when visitors flock to see its ornate traditional processions. There is also a popular jazz festival, usually at the end of October, but check in advance (see also page 133). The town is known for its hand-worked filigree silver jewellery and its wicker rocking chairs. There are ATMs on Calle 18 by the junction with Calle del Medio. The town is safe and peaceful. Guided tours of the city on foot or motortaxi cost US$5-7 per hour (guides approach you on the street). Boat trips lasting three to four hours (US$11) can be taken along the Río Magdalena and into the surrounding wetlands. They provide excellent opportunities for birdwatching, And it's wonderful to swim in the middle of the wetlands. In the early morning or at dusk, you can walk along the river bank to look for birds, or in the afternoon, cross the river on the small ferry from beyond the Parque Santander, US$0.50, for a stroll on the opposite bank where birds can also be seen. Ferocious mosquitoes and the odd bat can be a nuisance after dusk; take insect repellent and wear long sleeves.

> **Tip...**
> Guides who approach you on the street can gain access to all the significant buildings and charge US$6 per hour for tours of the city on foot or by motortaxi.

Where to stay

It is essential to book in advance for Semana Santa, the jazz festival in Sep/Oct and other holiday periods, when prices go up.

$$$ Bioma
C Real del Medio (Cra 2), No 18-59, T5-685 6733, www.bioma.co.
Boutique style, cool and fresh, courtyard garden with running water, jacuzzi on roof terrace (lovely views of Mompós) and a small pool. Rooms are large, family rooms have 2 floors. There's a restaurant but reserve in advance.

$$$ Portal de la Marquesa
Cra 1, No 15-27, on the Albarrada, T5-664 3163, www.portaldelamarquesa.com.
Hotel in a converted colonial mansion, fronting the river, with gardens and patios, beautifully decorated throughout, suites and standard rooms with modern facilities. One of the suites has its own private plunge pool. Can arrange local guides and boat trips.

$$$-$$ La Casa Amarilla
Cra 1, No 13-59, T5-685 6326, www.lacasaamarillamompos.com.
A block up from the Iglesia Santa Bárbara near the riverfront. Master suites, suites

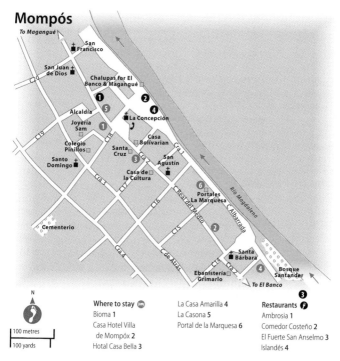

Mompós

To Magangué

San Francisco
San Juan de Dios
Chalupas for El Banco & Magangué
Alcaldía
Joyería Sam
La Concepción
Colegio Pinillos
Santa Cruz
Casa Bolívarian
Santo Domingo
San Agustín
Casa de la Cultura
Portales La Marquesa
Río Magdalena
Cementerio
Santa Bárbara
Ebanistería Grimarlo
Bosque Santander
To El Banco

N
100 metres
100 yards

Where to stay
Bioma 1
Casa Hotel Villa de Mompóx 2
Hotal Casa Bella 3

La Casa Amarilla 4
La Casona 5
Portal de la Marquesa 6

Restaurants
Ambrosia 1
Comedor Costeño 2
El Fuerte San Anselmo 3
Islandés 4

and cheaper 'colonial' rooms, all with a/c and beautifully decorated. All rooms open onto a cloister-style colonial garden. Tasty breakfast included. English owner Richard McColl is an excellent source of information on Colombia. Laundry, book exchange, use of kitchen, roof terrace, bicycle hire, tours arranged to silver filigree workshops and to wetlands for birdwatching and swimming (US$10 pp). Friendly and helpful staff. Highly recommended. The same family also own the new luxury hotel **San Rafael**, with 7 rooms and a pool.

$$ Casa Hotel La Casona
C Real del Medio (Cra 2), No 18-58, T5-685 5307, www.hotelmompos.com.
Fine colonial building with delightful courtyards and plants, all rooms with a/c and bathrooms, swimming pool and outdoor terrace.

$$-$ Casa Hotel Villa de Mompox
Cra 2, No 14-108, 500 m east of Parque Bolívar, T5-685 5208, http:// hotelvillademompox.blogspot.co.uk/.
Charming, family-run, decorated with antique bric-a-brac, private rooms with a/c plus dorms. Also arranges rooms for families during festivals.

$ Hostal Casa Bella
C Real del Medio (Cra 2) No 17-45, T322-654 9742.
Good, reasonably priced hostel in central location, set in attractive colonial building. Friendly staff.

Restaurants

Every night stallholders sell freshly cooked food and fresh juices in Plaza Santo Domingo.

$$$-$$ Ambrosia
C19, No1a-59.
Spacious restaurant offering a large choice, including local dishes. The *cazuela con camarones* (prawn soup) is delicious. Sometimes there is live music.

$$$-$$ Fuerte San Anselmo
C1, No 12-163, T314-564 0566, www. fuertemompox.com. Daily from 1830.
Opposite Parque Santander, this restaurant serves gourmet pizza in a restored colonial building. It is also the art gallery of Walter Maria Gurth and displays his paintings and wooden furniture. The pizzas are made in a wood-fired oven and there are other options to wash down with a jug of Walter's home-made ginger beer. Classical music, a/c and a delightful plant-filled garden combine to make a relaxing atmosphere Recommended.

$$-$ Comedor Costeño
On the riverfront between C 18 and C 19.
Good local food, popular for lunch.

$ Islandés
On the riverfront between C 18 and C 19.
In same vein as **Comedor Costeño** and almost next door, seating is outdoors and looks over the river, same owner as **Hotel San Andrés** (www. hotelsanandresmompox.com), which also offers river tours.

Shopping

Mompós is famous for its filigree gold and silver jewellery and its wicker rocking chairs. Several jewellers can be found on C del Medio (Cra 2). You can visit the workshops at the back of some of the shops.

Jewellery
The following jewellers have a good selection of beautifully worked gold and silver earrings, bracelets and necklaces.

Joyería Sam, *C 23 No 3-04, T311-403 5492*.
Santa Cruz, *Cra 2, No 201 132, T310-656 5568, tallersantacruz@yahoo.com*.
Tierra de Mompox, *Cra 2, No 18-91, T3015214560, www.filigranatierra demompox.blogspot.com.co*.

Festivals

Mar/Apr Easter week. Ornate traditional processions.
Sep/Oct Jazz festival (http://mompox colombia.blogspot.co.uk/p/eventos. html) with national and international artists, concerts and street music.

Transport

At the time of writing, a new bridge is under construction connecting Mompós with Magangué, which will cut journey times to Mompós. For now, cars are rare here: the main ways to get around are bicycle, moped, auto-rickshaw or on foot.

Air

The closest airport is **Corozal** (near Sincelejo), which has regular connections with **Medellín** and **Bogotá**. It's 1 hr by *colectivo* from Corozal Airport to Magangué, or 15 mins from Corozal to Sincelejo; then take a *colectivo* to Magangué, as below.

Bus

Buses from **Cartagena** and **Barranquilla** travel to Mompós either via Magangue for the river crossing (see below), or they take the new route El Carmen de Bolívar–Plato–La Gloria (on the road to Bosconia), then the new paved road to Santa Ana, where a bridge now crosses the Magdalena to Talaigua Nueva; transport from Santa Marta and Valledupar goes to Bosconia, then to La Gloria and Santa Ana. Buses from central Colombia travel via El Banco. **Note** Prices for public transport rise Dec-Jan and at Easter.

Direct services to/from **Cartagena** are run by **Brasilia/Unitransco**, 6½ hrs, US$17.65, depart 0445. **Toto Express**, T310-707 0838, totoexpress2@hotmail. com, runs a door-to-door *colectivo*, 6 hrs, US$27 pp. You can arrange door-to-door *colectivo* through hostels and hotels, US$27 pp (4 passengers), for an expreso, you pay for all 4 seats. There are additional services between Cartagena and Magangué. For transport between Mompós and **Santa Marta** and **Valledupar**, see the respective transport sections, below. From **Medellín**, **Copetran** runs an overnight service from Medellín to Mompós, or catch the overnight **Rápido Ochoa** or **Brasilia** bus to Magangué, 12 hrs, US$45-50, or travel to Magangué by *colectivo* from **Sincelejo**, US$9.50, 1½ hrs. From Montería to Magangué, there are *colectivos*, 3-4 hrs, US$13; they'll take you to the waterside if you are continuing to Mompós. From **Bogotá**, **Copetran** have a direct service at 1700, US$55, 14-15 hrs, otherwise **Copetran** and **Omega** have services to **El Banco** at 1700, 14 hrs, US$47, then take a 4WD to Mompós, US$10 (US$12 a/c), 1 hr.

Ferry

To get to Mompós from Magangué you have to travel to **La Bodega**, either by fast *chalupa* (motorized canoe, 20 mins, US$2.50, life jacket provided), or on the vehicle ferry (from 0600, 1 hr, food and drink on board), which leaves from Yati, about 2 km outside town. The last chalupa leaves Magangué at 1800. From La Bodega you continue by *colectivo* or taxi to Mompós (1¼ hrs, US$6).

On the coast, 35 km northwest of Sincelejo (the capital of Sucre Department) is Tolú, a fast-developing holiday town popular for its mud volcanoes, offshore islands and diving. Along the *malecón* (promenade), there are plenty of bars and restaurants and many lodges are opening. There are several banks with ATMs on the Parque Principal. Bicycle rickshaws armed with loud sound systems blast out *vallenato*, salsa and reggaeton. There are two mud volcanoes to visit. The nearer is in San Antero, 30 minutes' drive from Tolú, and further is in San Bernando del Viento, 1¼ hours (turn off the main road at Lorica). Both make good day trips; a six-hour trip to San Antero, including lunch and visits to other sights, costs US$55.

From Tolú, another good trip is by boat (three hours, US$17) to **Isla Múcura** or **Isla Tintipán** in the ★ **Islas de San Bernardo**; boats leave at 0800. With all tour boats converging on the island at the same time, it gets very crowded, attracting plenty of beach vendors. There is a charge for everything, including sitting at a table. To enjoy the islands at your leisure, it is better to stay overnight. If camping, take your own supplies. Trips to the mangrove lagoons are also recommended. On Isla Tintipán, **Juan Ríos Buceo y Mar** ① *T311-716 2418, www.juanrios.co*, is a peaceful and recommended diving centre with experienced instructor, accommodation and good food. Tolú and the islands are easy to combine with Cartagena; the road goes via Malagana, San Onofre and Toluviejo, 2½ to three hours by bus. Toluviejo is 20 km north of Sincelejo.

North of Tolú, about 10 km beyond Berrugas, is the **Reserva Natural Sanguaré** ① *T313-659 5707, www.reservanaturalsanguare.com*, where you'll find an upmarket eco-hotel and various activities, including diving, sailing and other water sports as well as being able to explore the reserve by horse or on foot. Manager Alavaro Roldán will pick you up from Berrugas if you are in a group of four people or more.

There are good beaches at **Coveñas**, 20 km further southwest (several hotels *cabañas* on the beach). This is the terminal of the oil pipeline from the oilfields in the Venezuelan border area. Buses and *colectivos* are available from Tolú.

The main road south from Tolú passes **Montería**, the capital of Córdoba Department, on the east bank of the Río Sinú. It can be reached from Cartagena by air, by boat, or from the main highway to Medellín (US$48, nine hours).

★ Arboletes

Southwest of Tolú is the unremarkable town of Arboletes, near which is the largest mud volcano in the area, the **Volcán de Lodo** ① *free entry*. Dipping into this swimming pool-sized mud bath is a surreal experience – like bathing in treacle. It's very good for your skin. You can wash the mud off using the freshwater showers (see below) or with a dip in the sea by walking down to the beach 100 m below. Arboletes is also a convenient stopover on the way to Turbo and the Darién coast. The mud volcano is a 15-minute walk from town on the road to Montería or a

Mud volcanoes

The Caribbean coast is peppered with several geological curiosities popularly known as 'mud volcanoes'. These large mud pools are believed to be the result of underground oil and gas deposits, which combine with water, forcing the mud to ooze to the surface. Often they form conical mounds, hence the name. Many of these pools can be found between the Gulf of Urabá and Santa Marta. Turbo has several in its proximity (Rodosalín, El Alto de Mulatos and Caucal), as does San Pedro de Urabá. The Volcán del Totumo is a popular day trip from Cartagena, but the pick of the bunch is Arboletes, where an enormous 30-m-wide lake has formed a stone's throw from the beach.

Wallowing in the grey-black mud is a strange experience: it's impossible to sink, and attempts to swim are about as worthwhile as trying to battle your way across a vat of treacle. When you have had enough, clamber out and join the line of mud-caked figures waddling down to the Caribbean for a wash and a swim. The stuff is reportedly an excellent exfoliant and does wonders for the skin and hair.

two-minute taxi ride (US$7 return – the driver will wait for you while you bathe). A mototaxi costs US$2. There is a small restaurant and changing rooms (US$ 0.50), plus a locker room (US$1 per bag) and showers (US$1).

Listings Tolú and around

Where to stay

$$$-$$ Soleira
Cra 11, No 4-12, T5-288 2288,
http://hotelsoleira.com.
Colourfully decorated modern hotel a couple of kilometres out of town, with pool, terrace, good restaurant and spacious rooms.

$$ Alcira
Av La Playa, No 21-151, T5-288 5016,
www.hotelalcira.amawebs.com.
Modern, a/c, on the promenade, with restaurant and parking.

$$ Hotel Pizzeria Opera Tolú
C 23, No 1-38, T317-4310565,
www.hotelpizzeriaoperatolu.com.
Italian-owned hotel with safe parking, a/c, laundry service and family rooms. Quiet location near the beach. Friendly and welcoming, also has restaurant serving excellent pizza and pasta. Recommended.

$ Hostel V&A
Cra 2, No 10-18, T301-597969.
Excellent hostel right near the beach, friendly and helpful owner who can help with tours, etc. Rooftop terrace, hammocks, good Wi-Fi, a/c, great value.

Islas de San Bernardo

$$$$ Punta Faro
Isla Múcura, T317-435 9583,
www.puntafaro.com.

Low-key luxury resort with 45 rooms in a gorgeous setting by the sea, inside Corales del Rosario National Park. Price includes all meals (buffet-style) and happy hour cocktails. Return boat transfer from Cartagena, 2 hrs, costs US$53 plus US$4.20 port tax (boats leave once a day), some boats also leave from Tolú. Massage treatments, hammocks on the beach, eco walks and bicycle tours around the island, on-site diving school, paddle-boarding and sailing. Has a good sustainability policy. Recommended.

$$ Hostal Isla Múcura
Isla Múcura, T316-620 8660.
Dorms and cabins are available at this beach-front hostel. It is clean and well-priced, and meals are excellent.

Transport

Bus
Rápido Ochoa and others from **Cartagena** from about 0615, 3 hrs, US$13. 7 a day to **Medellín** with **Brasilia** and **Rápido Ochoa**, US$43, via Montería except at night.

Turbo and the Darién Gap

blissful beaches backed by impenetrable jungle

On the Gulf of Urabá is the port of Turbo, an important centre of banana cultivation. It is a rough place, so it's best to move on quickly. There are various routes from Turbo involving sea and land crossings around or through the Darién Gap, which still lacks a road connection linking the Panamanian isthmus and South America. The trek across the Darién is held in high regard by adventurers but we strongly advise against it, not simply because it is easy and fatal to get lost, but also because it has a heavy guerrilla and drug-trafficking presence; it is virtually deserted by police and the military, and indigenous communities do not welcome tourists. The Caribbean coastline, however, heavily patrolled by Colombian and Panamanian forces, is safe.

Acandí
Acandí is a fishing village on the Caribbean side of the Darién (population about 9000). It has a spectacular, forest-fringed bay with turquoise waters. To the south are other bays and villages, such as **San Francisco**. In March-June, thousands of leatherback turtles come here to lay their eggs. There are several *residencias* in Acandí.

Capurganá *Colour map 2, A1.*
For many years, Capurganá and neighbouring **Sapzurro** have been one of the best-kept secrets in Colombia: a glistening, untouched shore of crystal waters, coral reefs and quiet villages. Capurganá has developed into a resort popular with Colombians, increasingly visited by foreigners. There are no

Tip...
To get to Capurganá by air from Medellín, it's best to fly to Acandí with ADA who have daily flights. The boats will wait for the flights to then take you to Aguacate, Capurganá or Sapzurro. Capurganá airport is mostly used for package holidays.

banks, ATMs or cars. Taxi rides are provided by horse and cart. The village has two beaches, **La Caleta** at the northern end, with golden sand, and **Playa de los Pescadores**, south of the village, fringed by palm and almond trees but with grey sand and pebbles. Ask the fishermen about fishing trips from here. Watch out for turtles bobbing their heads up when out on boats. The leatherback turtle hatching season is between July and December.

Several half- and full-day trips can be made by launch to neighbouring beaches, for example **Aguacate**, which has a small white-sand beach and good snorkelling; **La Piscina**, which is a hole in the reef next to the sea, where you can swim; and Playa Soledad, which has calm water for swimming and is perhaps the most attractive beach in the area. You can also walk to Aguacate, 1½ hours along the coast. Playa Soledad is another three hours' walk from Aguacate (or boat US$10 per person). Note that it can be difficult to obtain a return by launch if you walk, so make sure you organize it in advance. There are boat trips to the San Blas Islands (Panama) for about US$70 per person (minimum eight to 10 passengers); you can also arrange two-to three-day tours visiting several islands and staying with the indigenous Kuna people (US$110 per person); ask at lodges, *hostales* and tour operators.

A delightful half-day excursion is to **El Cielo** ① *open 0600-1700, entry US$2*, a small waterfall in the jungle; it's a (40-minute walk, take flip flops or waterproof boots for crossing a stream several times. To get there, take the path to the left of the airport and keep asking for directions. Just before the waterfall a small restaurant serves *patacones* and drinks. Alternatively, you can hire horses to take you there (US$9 per person for one hour without a guide – the horses know the way). Another horse ride is to **El Valle de Los Ríos**. The primary forest in this area is rich in wildlife, but you should take a guide. The trip includes lunch at a *ranchería*.

Sapzurro and the Panamanian border *Colour map 2, A1.*

Another trip is to **Sapzurro**, a few kilometres north and the last outpost before Panama and Central America. The houses of this village are linked by intersecting paths bursting with tropical flowers. It is set in a shallow horseshoe bay with a sandy beach and dotted with coral reefs, excellent for snorkelling, with a couple of underwater caves to explore. There are half a dozen or so hostels and restaurants in the village. A 10-minute walk inland takes you to **Cascada Diana**, signposted, only worth a visit in the wet season. An hour's steep walk (there are no cars here) takes you to the village of **La Miel** (in Panama), and on to its gorgeous white-sand beach. This could qualify as the most relaxed border crossing in the world. The Colombian and Panamanian immigration officers share a hut and copy each other's notes. Be sure to take your passport; if only going to La Miel they won't stamp it but they will take your details. There are breathtaking views of Panama and back into Sapzurro at the frontier on the brow of the hill. La Miel is one of the best beaches in the area, there are restaurants selling fresh fish and seafood dishes, but no hostels; snorkelling is possible from the beach (you can buy or hire a mask and snorkel in the large duty-free shop). Arrive early, especially at weekends and holidays, if you want to avoid the crowds. You can arrange for a launch to pick you up and take you back to Sapzurro or Capurganá.

Colombian immigration Ask Migración Colombia in Cartagena, Medellín or Montería (Calle 28, No 2-27, T4-781 0841, cf.monteria@migracioncolombia.gov.co, Monday-Friday 0800-1200, 1400-1700) whether the immigration office in Capurganá is open.

> **Tip...**
> Colombian pesos are impossible to change at fair rates in Panama.

Panamanian immigration Panamanian immigration at Puerto Obaldía will check all baggage for drugs. Requirements for entry are proof of US$500 in the bank and a yellow fever certificate. There is a **Panamanian consul** in Capurganá opposite the main square: T310-303 5285, nayi051991@hotmail.com. Check with the consul in Cartagena, Medellín, or the embassy in Bogotá (Calle 92, No 7A-40, T01-257 5067, www.panamaenelexterior.gob.pa/bogota) before setting out.

Listings Turbo and the Darién Gap

Where to stay

Turbo

$$$-$$ Simona del Mar
Km 13 Vía Turbo, T4-842 3729,
www.simonadelmar.com.
Turbo is not a safe place to walk around at night, so this option a few kilometres outside town is a safer choice. It has a number of *cabañas* (doubles as well as family units) with TV and fridge. Tranquil setting near the beach, popular with locals. Good restaurant and reasonably priced. A taxi to and from Turbo is US$10. You can also ask *colectivos* to drop you there.

$$ Castilla de Oro
C 100, No 14-07, T4-827 2185,
hotelcastilladeoro@hotmail.com.
The best option in town has a/c, safety box, minibar, a good restaurant and a swimming pool. Modern building with reliable water and electricity. Friendly staff.

Capurganá

Accommodation and food are generally more expensive than in other parts of Colombia. Upmarket options include **Tacarcuna Lodge** (www.hotelesdecostaacosta.com/capurgana).

$$$$ Bahía Lodge
Playa Aguacate, T314-812 2727,
www.bahia-lodge.com.
Price is for 2 people on a 2-night, 3-day package in simple, comfortable cabins next to the white-sand beach, with fan and bath, includes breakfast and dinner, lunch extra. Lothar, the helpful German owner can organize boats, horse riding and other excursions. Delicious meals, hammocks, peaceful location right on the beach and away from the towns. Recommended.

$$$ Finca El Regalo
1 km south of town.
Facing the beach, this finca offers a quieter location, with cabins and hammocks, restaurant and a pretty garden. Price includes breakfast.

$$ Cabaña Darius
10 mins' walk from town, T310-397 7768,
reservas@dariuscapurgana.com,
see Facebook.
In the grounds of Playa de Capurganá,
excellent value, simple, comfortable
rooms in tropical gardens, fan,
breakfast included.

$$ Marlin Hostal
Playa de los Pescadores, T310 593 6409,
http://hostalmarlin.com/.
The best mid-range option in town,
good rooms, also bunks ($), restaurant
serving excellent fish.

$$-$ Hostal Capurganá
C del Comercio, T318-206 4280,
www.hostalcapurgana.net.
Comfortable, pleasant patio, good
central location, English and German
spoken. Doubles, triples and dorms
available, price includes breakfast. Has
a restaurant and offers tours – can
also arrange bus tickets and flights.
Recommended.

$ Hostal Kachikine
El Aguacate, T316-359 1150, see Facebook.
Dorms and private rooms with shared
bath, breakfast included. Camping is
also available or you can hire a hammock
for US$5 pp. Airy wooden terrace and
comfortable lounge with DVDs and books.

$ Posada del Gecko
C del Comercio 2, T314-525 6037,
www.posadadelgecko.com.
Small place, 5 rooms with bath and
3 cabins, gardens, popular café/bar
that serves good Italian food. Also
tours to San Blas Islands.

Sapzurro and the Panamanian border

$$ El Chileno – Resort Paraíso
T313-685 9862, www.hosteltrail.com/
hostels/elchilenoresortparaiso.
Cabañas on the beach at the southern
end of the village, Chilean-run, higher
price includes half-board. Also has dorms
($) and space for camping.

$$-$ Hilltop Sapzurro
123 Lado de la Escuela Internacional.
Dorms or private rooms with a/c.
Comfortable, clean and friendly service.

$ Zingara Cabañas
Camino La Miel, T313-673 3291,
www.hospedajesapzurrozingara.com.
Almost the last building in Colombia,
2 lovely *cabañas* overlooking the bay.
The owners have a vegetable and
herb garden and sell home-made
chutneys. This also doubles up as
the village pharmacy.

Restaurants

Capurganá

$$ Donde Josefina
Playa La Caleta.
Josefina cooks exquisite seafood, served
to you under a shady tree on the beach.
Try the lobster cooked in garlic and
coconut sauce.

$$-$ Patacón Pisao
Playa La Caleta.
Outdoor tables on the beach, shady,
fresh seafood, excellent set lunch with
soup and salad for around
US$8, recommended.

$ Gecko
See Posada del Gecko, above.
Great value Italian food, especially
pizza, with a bar.

What to do

Capurganá
Diving and snorkelling
Dive and Green, *near the jetty, T311-578 4021, www.diveandgreen.com.*
Professionally run dive centre offering PADI and NAUI, lots of courses, snorkelling and diving in some pristine coral reefs. They also run excursions to San Blas. English spoken.

Transport

Turbo and the Darién Gap
Bus
To **Medellín**, buses every 90 mins, 8-10 hrs, US$20-24. To **Montería**, Rápido Ochoa, 4-5 hrs, US$12. Fewer to **Cartagena**. Check safety carefully before travelling by road to/from Turbo.

Sea
Turbo's port is known as El Waffe. Launches for **Capurganá**, T312-701 9839, leave daily at 0700-0900, 3 hrs, US$19. It's a spectacular journey that hugs the Caribbean shoreline of Darién. Rush for a seat at the back as the journey is bumpy and can be painful in seats at the front. There is a 10-kg limit on baggage (US$0.20 per extra kg). Make sure that all your belongings, especially valuables, are in watertight bags and be prepared to get wet. From mid-Dec to end Feb the sea is very choppy and dangerous. We advise you not to make the journey at this time.

Capurganá
Air
Daily flight from **Medellín** to Acandí, with **ADA**, www.ada-aero.com, T4-444 4232, flight times can change so best not to book on a tight schedule, US$75. From Acandí you take a horse-drawn cart to the port, 20 mins, US$1.50 pp. Boats go on to **Aguacate** or **Capurganá** (30 mins, US$7 pp) and **Sapzurro** (45 mins, US$11 pp).

There are charter flights directly to Capurganá airport from Medellín, mainly in high season and mostly used for package tours, www.colombia paraelmundo.com, T4-266 7822.

Sea
Launches to **Turbo**, T312-701 9839, daily 0800-0900, 2½ hrs, US$25, 10 kg limit on baggage (US$0.25 per extra kg). To **Necoclí**, boats leave daily at 1000, 90 mins US$25, book with **Caribe** agency opposite the pier, convenient for onward travel to Cartagena (6-8 hrs, US$30) via Montería and Magangué (7 hrs, US$35) by bus; we advise you not to make the journey across the Golfo de Urabá from mid-Dec to end Feb because of rough seas. Sometimes boats are unable to leave the ports. To **Acandí**, T314-614 0704, daily 1300, US$7. To **Sapzurro**, US$6, 30 mins. There are also launches to **Puerto Obaldía** in Panama, US$20. From here it's possible to catch an **Air Panamá** flight to **Panama City**, daily, cost US$110, www.flyairpanama.com. Essential to book in advance.

Sapzurro
Sea
Launch to **Capurganá**, US$6, 30 mins; to **La Miel**, US$4, 15 mins; to **Puerto Obaldía**, 45 mins, US$15.

Barranquilla
& around

Barranquilla (population 1,220,000) lies on the western bank of the Río Magdalena, about 18 km from its mouth. The deepening of the river and the clearing of silted sandbars has made the city a seaport as well as a river port, although its commercial and industrial importance has declined in recent years. Few colonial buildings remain, but its historic centre is being revived. In the northwest of the city are pleasant leafy residential areas and parks. Many people stay a night in Barranquilla because they can find better flight deals than to Cartagena or Santa Marta. The city is growing as a cultural centre and is worth a short stay; safety has improved; there are several things to do and see, and handicrafts, the same as can be found elsewhere, are cheaper.

The city is surrounded by a continuous ring road, which is called the 'Vía Cuarenta' from the north along the river to the centre; 'Avenida Boyacá' to the bridge (Puente Pumarejo) across the Río Magdalena for Santa Marta; and 'Circunvalación' round the south and west of the city. The long bridge over the Río Magdalena gives fine views.

The **Catedral Metropolitana** ⓘ *Cra 45, No 53-140, opposite Plaza de la Paz,* has an impressive statue of Christ inside by the Colombian sculptor, Arenas Betancur. The church of **San Nicolás**, formerly the cathedral, stands on Plaza San Nicolás, the central square, and before it is a small statue of Columbus. The commercial and shopping districts are round Paseo Bolívar, the main boulevard, a few blocks north of the old cathedral, and in Avenida Murillo (Calle 45). A cultural centre, **Parque Cultural del Caribe**, is on the Paseo Bolívar end of Avenida Olaya Herrera (Carretera 46). It contains the **Museo del Caribe** ⓘ *C36, No 46-66, T5-372 0581, www.culturacaribe.org, Mon-Fri 0800-1700, Sat-Sun 0900-1800, ticket office closes 1600 (1700 weekends), US$4.50,* an excellent introduction to the region, in Spanish only, but guided tours in English are available. Visits start on the top floor, at the Sala García Márquez, which has audiovisual displays and a library, then work your way down through floors dedicated to nature, indigenous people, cultures and languages, to a video musical presentation at the end. Outside is a large open space for theatre and children's games, and the **Cocina del Museo** restaurant. Not far away is the restored customs house, the **Antiguo**

1 Barranquilla centre

➡ **Barranquilla maps**
1 Barranquilla centre, page 142
2 Barranquilla – El Prado, page 144

200 metres	**Where to stay** 🛏	**Restaurants** 🍴	**Bars & clubs** 🍸
200 yards	Girasol **1**	La Cueva **1**	Guararé **2**

ON THE ROAD

Carnival in Barranquilla

The main reason people visit the city is for its famous annual Carnival, held 40 days before Easter week, end-February/beginning of March. It's one of the oldest in Latin America and less commercial and touristy than the Rio Carnival. It is a UNESCO "masterpiece of the oral and intangible heritage of humanity". Pre-carnival parades and dances last through January until an edict that everyone must party is read out. Carnival itself lasts from Saturday, with the Batalla de las Flores, through the Gran Parada on Sunday, to the funeral of Joselito Carnaval on Tuesday. The same families going back generations participate, keeping the traditions of the costumes and dances intact. Prepare for four days of intense revelry and dancing with friendly and enthusiastic crowds, spectacular float processions, parades and beauty queens. Tickets for the spectator stands are sold in major restaurants and bars. **La Casa de Carnaval**, Carretera 54, No 49B-39, T5-319 7616, www.carnavaldebarranquilla. org, is the official office and the best place for information.

Edificio de la Aduana ⓘ *Vía 40 y C 36*, (1919, which has historical archives. The **Museo Romántico** ⓘ *Cra 54, No 59-199, Mon-Fri 0800-1200, 1430-1700, US$2.50*, is a small, quirky museum covering the city's history with an interesting section on Carnival, including costumes. It too has a room dedicated to Gabriel García Márquez.

Barranquilla also attracts visitors because the most important national and international football matches are held here in Colombia's largest stadium, **Estadio Metropolitano** ⓘ *Av Murillo, south of the city*. The atmosphere is considered the best in the country. There is a good-value **handicrafts market** near the old stadium, which is at Carrera 46 y Calle 74 (at the end of Transmetro).

Around Barranquilla

Regular buses run from Paseo Bolívar and the church at Calle 33 y Carrera 41 to the attractive bathing resort of **Puerto Colombia** ⓘ *www.puertocolombia-atlantico. gov.co*, 20 minutes away. February to May is the best time to learn surfing here; the biggest waves are seen from November to January.

Heading south along the Magdalena, 5 km from Barranquilla, is **Soledad**; around its cathedral are narrow, colonial streets. **Parque Nacional Natural Isla de Salamanca** ⓘ *T312-577 7111, open 0800-1600, US$14 (US$5.30 for Colombians)*, across the Río Magdalena from the city, comprises the Magdalena delta and the narrow area of beaches, mangroves and woods that separate the Ciénaga Grande de Santa Marta (see page 155) from the Caribbean. It was designated a biosphere reserve by UNESCO in 2000. Its purpose is to restore the mangroves and other habitats lost when the highway to Santa Marta blocked off the channels that connect the fresh- and saltwater systems. There is abundant flora and fauna, some of which is endangered, and an interpretation centre and guided walking trails (US$7-9) and canoe trips with guides (US$50-130 for groups of 10).

Tourist information

La Casa de Carnaval
Cra 54, No 49B-39, T5-319 7616,
www.carnavaldebarranquilla.org.
The official carnival office and best place
for carnival information.

Secretaría de Cultura
Patrimonio y Turismo, C 34, No 43-31,
p 4, T5-339 9450, www.barranquilla.
gov.co/cultura.
The main tourist office. Information
is also available at the main hotels.

Tourist police
Plaza de San Nicolás. Open 0800-1200,
1500-1700.

Where to stay

Hotel prices rise significantly during
carnival; it's essential to book well
in advance. Most people stay in the
north zone, beyond the Catedral
Metropolitana, C 50. There are also
a few hotels in the business zone,
Cra 43-45, C 42-45.

② Barranquilla – El Prado

➡ **Barranquilla maps**
1 Barranquilla centre, page 142
2 Barranquilla – El Prado, page 144

Where to stay 🛏
Barranquilla Plaza **1**
El Prado **2**
Majestic **3**
Mamy Dorme **4**

Meeting Point Hostel **5**
N H Collection Barranquilla
  Smartsuites Royal **6**
Sonesta **7**

Restaurants 🍴
Arabe Gourmet **1**
Arabe International **2**
Firenze Pizza **3**
La Parilla Libanesa **4**

Los Helechos **5**

Bars & clubs 🍸
Frogg Club **6**
Henry's **7**

$$$ Barranquilla Plaza
Cra 51B, No 79-246, T5-361 0333,
www.hbp.com.co.
This deluxe hotel, popular with
Colombian businessmen, is worth
visiting just for the 360° view of the city
from its 26th-floor restaurant. It has all
the other amenities you would expect of
a hotel of this standard, including gym,
spa, sauna and Wi-Fi.

$$$ Sonesta
C 106, No 50-11, T5-385 6060,
www.sonesta.com.
Overlooking the Caribbean, a 1st-class
business hotel with fitness facilities and
restaurant to match. There is a shopping
centre and nightclub nearby.

$$$-$$ El Prado
Cra 54, No 70-10, T5-330 1530/40,
www.hotelelpradosa.com.
A landmark in Barranquilla, this
enormous hotel with 200 rooms has
been around since 1930 and still retains
some of its old-fashioned service. Rooms
are in need of updating, but the price
reflects this. Fantastic pool shaded by
palm trees, various restaurants, tennis
courts and a gym.

$$$-$$ NH Collection Barranquilla Smartsuites Royal
C 80, No 51b-25, T5-373 8080,
www.nh-hotels.co.
Well-located modern hotel with friendly
service. The rooms are comfortable and
quiet. Rooftop terrace with panoramic
views of the city and small pool, gym
and sauna.

$$ Girasol
C 44, No 44-103, T5-379 3191.
Safe, central, with a helpful manager,
and it has a restaurant.

$$ Majestic
Cra 53, No 54-41, T5-349 1010, www.
hotelmajesticbarranquilla.com.
An oasis of calm in the city, with large,
fresh rooms. It has a fine pool and a
restaurant serving the usual fish and
meat dishes and sandwiches.

$ Mamy Dorme
Cra 61, No 66-130, T5-344 0514.
Family-run hostel in a good location.
Small private rooms with shared bath or
dorms, laundry available, free parking.

$ Meeting Point Hostel
Cra 61, No 68-100, El Prado, T5-318 2599,
www.themeetingpoint.hostel.com.
Very helpful and congenial Italian/
Colombian-owned hostel – the best
choice for budget travellers. Mixed
dorms or women only, US$10-15, cheaper
with fan and shared bath, also has
private rooms. Eating places and cultural
centres nearby. Warmly recommended.

Restaurants

In Barranquilla you'll find places to
suit all tastes and budgets. Many
upmarket restaurants can be found
along Cras 52-54 from C 70 to 93. There
are numerous good Middle Eastern
restaurants, especially Lebanese,
in Barranquilla, due to waves of
immigration in the 20th century; also
Chinese restaurants and pizzerias.

$$$-$$ Arabe Gourmet
Cra 49C, No 76-181, T5-360 5930/
358 3805, http://arabegourmet
restaurante.co.
Excellent and authentic Middle Eastern
food. It is more formal than other Arabic
restaurants in the area and very popular
at lunchtimes.

$$$-$$ La Cueva
*Cra 43, No 59-03, T5-379 0342/340 9813,
www.fundacionlacueva.org. Closed Sun.*
This cultural centre was formerly a
high-class brothel and a favourite
haunt of Gabriel García Márquez and
his literati friends during the 1950s. Its
bohemian charm may have gone, but
its bar/restaurant is recommended for a
visit. Good typical food, live music and
other events.

$$$-$$ La Parrilla Libanesa
*Cra 61, No 68-02, near Meeting
Point Hostel, T5-360 6664, http://
parrillalibanesa.amawebs.com.*
Well-regarded Lebanese place, colourful,
indoor and terrace seating.

$$ Arabe Internacional
*C 93, No 47-73, T5-378 4700,
T302-412 0746.*
Good Arab cuisine in an informal,
cosy setting.

$$ Firenze Pizza
*C 68, No 62-12, El Prado, near Meeting Point
Hostel, T5-344 1067, T321-897 4535, www.
firenzepizza.com.co. Open 1500-2300.*
Excellent choice of pizza with generous
toppings (including some good
vegetarian options), to eat in or take away.

$$-$ Los Helechos de Carlos
*Cra 52, No 70-70, T5-345 1739, http://
restauranteshowloshelechos.com.
Daily from 1000 (closes 1700 on Sun).*
Offers *comida antioqueña* in a
good atmosphere.

Bars and clubs

Cra 8 is a popular nightlife area, but
you'll need to take a taxi there and back.

Frogg Club
*C 93, No 43-122, T5-304 8973,
www.frogg.co.*
Popular bar and restaurant with good
DJs and rumba music, lively atmosphere,
book in advance.

Guararé
*Cra 8 at C 35. T300-503 3303, Facebook:
GuarareSalsaDisco. Open until 0400.*
A good spot for salsa dancing.

Henry's Café
*C 80, No 53-18, CC Washington, T5-345
6431. See Facebook: Henryscafebaq.
Daily from 1600.*
Popular US-style bar and restaurant.

Festivals

Jan/Mar Carnaval. Carnaval is a long-
standing tradition in Barranquilla and
is comparable to the carnivals in Rio
de Janeiro and Trinidad. Pre-carnival
parades and dances throughout Jan
until an edict that everyone must
party is read out. Carnaval itself lasts
from Sat, with the Batalla de las Flores,
through the Gran Parada on Sun, to the
funeral of Joselito Carnaval on Tue. For
more information, contact **La Casa de
Carnaval**, www.carnavaldebarranquilla.
org. See box, page 143. Take special care
of your valuables.

Shopping

There is a good-value handicrafts
market near the old stadium, which is at
Cra 46 y C 74 (at the end of Transmetro).
Portal del Prado (C 53, No 46-92, www.
portaldelprado.com), is one of the larger
and more popular shopping complexes
in the city.

Transport

Air
Ernesto Cortissoz Airport, www.
aerocivil.gov.co, is 10 km from the city.

The airport has an ATM outside the terminal entrance, a *casa de cambio* in the hall (closed after 1900) and a tourist information desk. A city bus from the airport to town costs US$0.95 (more on Sun). Only take buses marked 'Centro'; you can catch them 200 m from the airport on the right. Taxis are booked at the central taxi kiosk; tell them your destination and you will be given a ticket with the price to pay the driver at end of ride. A taxi to the centre costs US$10 and takes about 30 mins. From town, the bus to the airport (marked Malambo) leaves from Cra 44, travels up C 32 to Cra 38, then along C 30 to the airport.

There are daily flights to **Bogotá**, **Cali** and **Medellín**. International flights go to **Miami**, **Curaçao** and **Panama City**. Airlines include: **Avianca**, C 53, No 46-38, T5-351 8344, and Cra 56, No 75-155, local 102, T5-353 4989, at airport T5-334 8396; **Copa**, C 72, No 54-49, local 1 y 2; **LATAM**, C 75 No 52-56 local 3; **EasyFly**, T5-385 0676; and **Viva Colombia**, T5-385 5555.

Bus

Local Within the city, the **Transmetro**, www.transmetro.gov.co, is a dedicated bus service with 2 routes: *Troncal Murillo* and *Troncal Olaya Herrera*. It takes prepaid cards; single journey US$0.95 (a little more on Sun and holidays). Taxis for trips within town should cost US$2-4.

Long distance The main long-distance bus terminal, Km 1.5 Prolongación Murillo, www.ttbaq. com.co, is south of the city near Circunvalación.

To **Santa Marta** with **Brasilia**, US$5, 2 hrs. To **Valledupar**, Copetran, 5-6 hrs, US$15. To **Bogotá**, 24 hrs, frequent, US$55-60, direct. To **Maicao**, US$15-20, 6 hrs (with **Brasilia** and others, frequent). To **Cartagena**, 2½-3 hrs, US$5-7, several companies. **Brasilia Van Tours** (Cra 35, No 44-63, T5-371 5226, as well as at the bus terminal) and **Berlinastur** (Cra 43, No 74-133, T318-396 9696, and other offices) have minibus services to **Cartagena** and **Santa Marta** (US$8).

Santa Marta
& around

Santa Marta (population 454,860) is Colombia's third-largest Caribbean port and capital of Magdalena Department. It lies on a deep bay at the mouth of the Río Manzanares, with high shelving cliffs to the north and south. The snow-clad peaks of the Sierra Nevada de Santa Marta are occasionally visible less than 50 km to the east. Nearby is the Tayrona National Park, with pre-Columbian remains. Santa Marta is the base for treks to La Ciudad Perdida.

Sights *Colour map 1, A3.*

this lively city is a gateway to stunning beaches and mountains

The city's fine promenade, Avenida R de Bastidas, offers good views of the bay and is lined with restaurants, accommodation and nightlife, though none is of a very high quality. At the southern end, where the main traffic turns inland on Calle 22, is a striking sculpture dedicated to the indigenous heritage of the region, La Herencia Tairona. Most shops and banks are on Carrera 5, which has many kerbside stalls, and Calle 15, which leads to Plaza Bolívar. Carrera 3 is the hub of nightlife in the centre and is largely pedestrianized, as is Calle 19.

The main promenade (Carrera 1) along the seafront is lined with hotels, restaurants and bars; the beach stretches as far as the port, although much more attractive beaches are to be found around Taganga and Parque Nacional Tayrona (see below). There has been much investment in new business, such as bars and restaurants on Carrera 3, the hub of nightlife in the centre. Much of Carrera 3 and Calle 19 are pedestrianized and Carrera 5 has many kerbside stalls. In the city centre, well-preserved colonial buildings and early churches still remain and more are currently being restored. On **Plaza de la Catedral** is the impressive white **cathedral** ⓘ *Cra 4, C 16/17, open for Mass Mon-Fri at 1200 and 1800 (Sun 0800, 1000, 1700, 1800, 1900)*, on the site of what is claimed to be Colombia's oldest church and one of the oldest in Latin America. **Casa de la Aduana/Museo del Oro Tairona** ⓘ *C 14, No 2-07 on Parque Bolívar, T5-421 0251, http://proyectos.banrepcultural.org/museo-*

del-oro-tairona, Tue-Sat 0900-1700, Sun 1000-1500, free, has an excellent archaeological collection, Tayrona culture exhibits and pre-Columbian gold artefacts; a visit is recommended before going to Ciudad Perdida. The **Convento de Santo Domingo** ① *Cra 2, No 16-44, open to the public Mon-Fri 0800-1800*, now serves as the Centro Cultural Universidad Magdalena and houses a library as well as the **Museo Etnográfico de la Universidad del Magdalena**, which has good displays tracing the history of Santa Marta, its port and the Tayrona culture.

Quinta de San Pedro Alejandrino ① *T5-433 1021, www.museobolivariano. org.co, daily 0900-1630 (1730 in high season), US$6, US$4.25 for Colombians, discounts for children*, a 17th-century villa surrounded by gardens, lies 5 km southeast of the city. Here is the simple room in which Simón Bolívar died, with a few of his belongings. Other paintings and memorabilia of the period are on display. This is an elegant memorial to Colombia's most revered man. To get there take a bus or *colectivo* from the waterfront, Carrera 1 C, in Santa Marta to Mamatoca and ask for the Quinta (US$0.75).

Beaches

Sandy beaches and headlands stretch all along this coast, surrounded by hills, green meadows and shady trees. The largest sandy bay is that of **Santa Marta**, with **Punta Betín**, a rocky promontory protecting the harbour to the north and a headland to the south. The rugged Isla El Morro lies 3 km off Santa Marta, topped by a lighthouse. **Playa El Rodadero**, 4 km south of the city (local bus service, taxi, US$5), has high-rise hotels of all standards, but it is attractive,

Essential Santa Marta and around

Getting around

Local bus services cost US$0.75 (this is a flat fee all the way to the airport and Rodadero); a taxi to Rodadero is US$5-6. Many of the buses coming from Barranquilla and Cartagena stop at Rodadero on their way to Santa Marta. There are also local minibuses to Taganga and Tayrona. Boats from Santa Marta, Rodadero and Taganga visit beaches along the coast.

When to go

Santa Marta is always hot, although it can be marginally cooler in August and September. The driest months are December to April. October is the low season for tourists, but it is also the wettest month.

Time required

You will need at least four days to see Santa Marta and Parque Tayrona; extend this to a week to trek to Ciudad Perdida.

Tip...

The north end of town near the port and the section beyond the old railway station are dangerous and travellers are advised not to go there alone, as it's rife with drugs, and prostitution is common. South of Rodadero Beach has also been reported unsafe.

tree lined, relatively clean and pleasant for bathing. Behind the promenade are restaurants, cheaper accommodation and other services. Beaches continue to the south. The bus from the airport passes by **Pleno Mar**, one of the more tranquil and recommended beaches in the area at the north end of **Playa Bello Horizonte**.

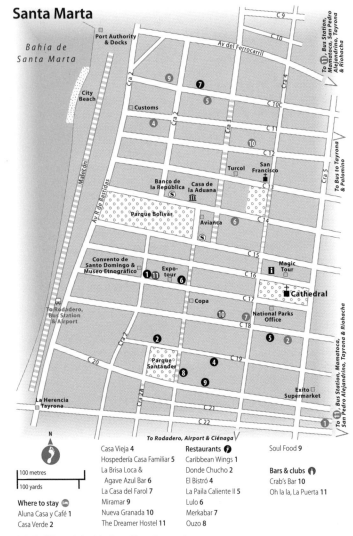

Santa Marta

Bahía de Santa Marta

Port Authority & Docks
Av del Ferrocarril
C 9
C 10
City Beach
Cra 2
Customs
Cra 3
C 10C
C 11
C 12
Turcol
San Francisco
Cra 5
Banco de la República
Casa de la Aduana
C 13
Parque Bolívar
Avianca
C 14
Malecón
Av de Bastidas
Convento de Santo Domingo & Museo Etnográfico
Expo-tour
C 15
C 16
Magic Tour
Cathedral
Copa
C 17
National Parks Office
C 18
To Rodadero, Bus Station & Airport
Cra 4
Parque Santander
C 19
Cra 3
Cra 2A
C 20
Éxito Supermarket
La Herencia Tayrona
C 21
C 22
To Rodadero, Airport & Ciénaga

To Bus Station, Mamatoca, San Pedro Alejandrino, Tayrona & Riohacha

To Bus to Tayrona & Palomino

To Bus Station, Mamatoca, San Pedro Alejandrino, Tayrona & Riohacha

N

100 metres
100 yards

Where to stay
Aluna Casa y Café **1**
Casa Verde **2**

Casa Vieja **4**
Hospedería Casa Familiar **5**
La Brisa Loca &
  Agave Azul Bar **6**
La Casa del Farol **7**
Miramar **9**
Nueva Granada **10**
The Dreamer Hostel **11**

Restaurants
Caribbean Wings **1**
Donde Chucho **2**
El Bistró **4**
La Paila Caliente II **5**
Lulo **6**
Merkabar **7**
Ouzo **8**

Soul Food **9**

Bars & clubs
Crab's Bar **10**
Oh la la, La Puerta **11**

BACKGROUND

Santa Marta

This part of the South American coastline was visited in the early years of the 16th century by Spanish settlers from Venezuela. At this time, many indigenous groups were living on and near the coast, trading with each other and with communities further inland. The dominant group were the Tayrona.

Santa Marta was founded in 1525 by Rodrigo de Bastidas, who chose it for its sheltered harbour and its proximity to the Río Magdelena and therefore its access to the hinterland. The *indígenas* represented a potential labour force, and the gold in their ornaments suggested fortunes could be made in the area. Within a few years, the Spanish settlement was consolidated and permanent buildings, such as the Casa de la Aduana, had been constructed. Things did not go well, however. The *indígenas* did not 'cooperate', and there was continual friction amongst the Spaniards, all of whom were expecting instant riches. Bastidas' successor, Rodrigo Alvarez Palomino, attempted to subdue the *indígenas* by force, with great loss of life and little success. The *indígenas* that survived took to the hills, where their successors, the Kogi, remain to this day.

By the middle of the 16th century, a new threat had appeared. Encouraged and often financed by Spain's enemies (England, France and Holland), pirates realized that rich pickings were to be had, not only from shipping, but also by attacking coastal settlements. The first raid took place around 1544, captained by the French pirate Robert Waal with three ships and 1000 men. He was followed by many privateers – the brothers Côte, Drake and Hawkins – who all ransacked the city. Forts were built on a small island at the entrance to the bay and on the mainland, but before the end of the century more than 20 attacks had been recorded; the pillage continued until as late as 1779, and the townsfolk lived in constant fear. Caches of treasure have been unearthed in old walls and floors around Santa Marta – testimony to the population's fear of looting during those troubled times. Cartagena, meanwhile, had become the main base for the conquistadors and much had been invested in its defences (see page 112). Santa Marta was never fortified in the same way and declined in importance.

Two important names connect Santa Marta with the history of Colombia. Gonzalo Jiménez de Quesada began the expedition here that led him up the Río Magdalena and into the highlands to found Santa Fe de Bogotá in 1538; and it was here that Simón Bolívar, his dream of Gran Colombia shattered, came to die. Almost penniless, he was given hospitality at the *quinta* of San Pedro Alejandrino, see below, where he died on 17 December 1830, at the age of 47.

Tourist information

National Parks office
Plaza de la Catedral, C 17, No 4-06, T5-423 0752, www.parquesnacionales.gov.co.
Has information for each of the 4 local parks.

Tourist office
Plaza de la Catedral, C 16, No 4-15, T5-420 9600, www.santamarta.gov.co. Mon-Fri 0800-1200, 1400-1800.
The main tourist office.

Where to stay

Do not stay at the north end of town near the port and beyond the old railway station. It's essential to book ahead during high season, particularly weekends, when some hotels increase their prices by 50%.

$$$ Casa Verde
C 18, No 4-70, T5-431 4122, www.casaverdesantamarta.com.
Only 5 suites, 'boutique' style, safe, small jacuzzi pool and juice bar. A *desayuno típico* is available.

$$$ La Casa del Farol
C 18, No 3-115, T5-423 1572, www.lacasadelfarol.com.
A luxury boutique hotel with 6 rooms, each with its own style, all modern conveniences, laundry service, beauty salon with massages and roof terrace with pool. Price includes breakfast.

$$-$ Aluna Casa y Café
C 21, No 5-72, T5-432 4916, www.alunahotel.com.
Pleasant and large Irish-run hostel in a converted 1920s villa, central and convenient. It has private rooms and

dorms (US$10-12 pp), with roof terrace. Breakfast is extra. There's a café, extensive book exchange, and a good noticeboard, excellent coffee available 24 hrs. Recommended. Under same ownership is **Finca Entre Ríos** (www. fincaentrerios.com), 15 km inland from Santa Marta, a working farm with outdoor pool, private chalets and dorm rooms (full board **$$** pp).

$$-$ Casa Vieja
C 12, No 1C-58, T5-431 1606, www.hotelcasavieja.com.
Has a Spanish feel about it with white tiling and simple, clean rooms and a/c. Cheaper with fan, welcoming.

$$-$ pp The Dreamer Hostel
Cra 51, No 26D-161 Diagonal, Los Trupillos, Mamatoco, T5-433 3264, or T300-251 6534, www.thedreamerhostel.com.
Travellers' hostel in a residential district 15 mins from the centre, on the way to Tayrona, 5 mins by taxi from the bus station. All rooms are set around a sunny garden and pool, dorms for 4-10 people and private rooms with and without bath, fan or a/c, bar, good Italian restaurant, tour information and activities, friendly staff and good atmosphere. All services close at hand, including a huge shopping mall, San Pedro Alejandrino and the bus stop for Tayrona. Recommended.

$$-$ La Brisa Loca
C 14, No 3-58, T5-431 6121, www.labrisaloca.com.
US-owned lively hostel, with a/c private rooms, all with shared bath. Meals extra. Rooftop party at the weekends, bar, swimming pool and billiard room.

$$-$ Nueva Granada
C 12, No 3-17, T5-421 1337.
This charming old building in the historic quarter has rooms round a pleasant courtyard, quiet. Shared rooms with fan are cheaper ($). Safety deposit boxes in rooms, small pool with jacuzzi, includes breakfast and welcome drink. Reductions in low season. Recommended.

$ Hospedería Casa Familiar
C 10C, No 2-14, T5-421 1697.
Facebook: casafamiliarSantaMarta.
Run by an extremely helpful family, rooms with fan, roof terrace, and laundry service. Has information on diving and other activities, and organizes trips to Tayrona, Sierra Nevada and Ciudad Perdida.

$ Miramar
2 blocks from malecón, C 10C, No 1C-59, T316-745 8947, www.hotelmiramar.com.co.
Very knowledgeable and helpful staff at this backpacker favourite. Can be crowded. Simple dorms and some nicer more expensive private rooms with a/c (US$15), motorbike parking, cheap restaurant. Often full. Reservations via the internet are held until 1500 on the day of arrival. Tours to the Ciudad Perdida, Tayrona, Guajira and local sites are available with the in-house operator. Airline tickets also sold here.

Restaurants

$$$-$$ El Bistró
C 19, No 3-68, T5-421 8080. Daily 1100-2300, happy hour 1730-1930.
Meat dishes, pastas, salads, burgers, sandwiches and set lunches, not a large place and the menu is limited, wine list, Argentine influence throughout.

$$$-$$ Soul Food
C20, No 3-51, T5-422 5297.
Fusion of Caribbean and Colombian food, ceviche, seafood, steaks. Excellent and friendly service. Recommended.

$$ Donde Chucho
C 19, No 2-17, T5-421 0861.
A little expensive but well situated in the corner of Parque Santander. Serves mostly seafood.

$$ La Paila Caliente II
C 18, No 4-60, T5-421 4954.
Delightful restaurant with good Colombian/Caribbean food, à la carte at night, excellent-value lunch.

$$ Ouzo
Cra 3, No 19-29, T5-423 0658, www.ouzosantamarta.com. Closed Sun.
Mediterranean, Italian, Greek restaurant and bar with seating on the street, popular.

$$-$ Caribbean Wings
C 17, No 2-53, T574-306 055.
Small *parrilla* near the water with a sports-bar vibe. Popular for American-style chicken wings. Great option on a budget.

$$-$ Lulo
Cra 3, No 16-34, www.lulocafebar.com.
Café and bar serving *arepas*, wraps, paninis, fresh juices, coffee and cocktails.

$ Merkabar
C 10C, No 2-11, T5-431 1568.
Opens early for breakfast.
Pastas, great pancakes, good juices and seafood. Family-run, good value and provides tourist information. Recommended.

Bars and clubs

Santa Marta is a party town; new clubs, discos and bars open every week. In the evening wander along Cra 3 and C 17 and 18 either side of it to see what's going on.

Crab's Bar
C18, No 3-69, T315-796 3636.
Bar with good atmosphere and live music, mainly rock and blues. There's a pool table and rock memorabilia.

Oh la la, La Puerta
C 17, No 2-29.
Excellent bar and atmosphere in a colonial house. Recommended.

Festivals

Jul Festival Patronal de Santa Marta. Celebrates the founding of the city with parades and musical performances. **Fiestas del Mar.** Aquatic events and a beauty contest.

Shopping

The **market** is at C 11/Cra 11, just off Av del Ferrocarril and has stalls with excellent selections of hammocks. There are several good **handicraft shops** on Parque Bolívar.

Artesanías Sisa, *Cra 4, No 16-42 on the Plaza Catedral, T5-421 4510.* Sells local handicrafts, including clothes, bags, hammocks and sombreros.

What to do

For trips to Ciudad Perdida and the Sierra Nevada, see under the relevant destination, below.

Tour operators
Aventure Colombia, *C 14, No 4-80, T5-430 5185, http://aventurecolombia. com.* Branch of the recommended Cartagena agency specializing in classic and alternative tours and expeditions across Colombia, focusing on trekking, eco- and rural tourism.
New Frontiers Adventures, *C 27, No 1C-74, close to Playa Los Cocos, T318-736 1565/317-648 6786, www.colombia. newfrontiersadventures.com.* Trekking to Ciudad Perdida, birdwatching, diving and other adventures and ecotours, with English-speaking guides.
Turcol, *C 13, No 3-13, Plaza San Francisco, local 115, T5-421 2256, http://turcoltravel. com.* Arranges trips to Ciudad Perdida, Tayrona, Pueblito, Guajira and provides a guide service.

Transport

Air
Simón Bolívar Airport is 20 km south of the city. A bus to town costs US$0.80; a taxi is US$15-20, less to Rodadero; beware of taxi drivers taking you to a hotel of their choice, not yours.

There are daily flights to **Bogotá**, **Bucaramanga**, **Cali** and **Medellín** for connections to other cities. During the tourist season, get to the airport early and book well ahead (the same goes for bus reservations). Airlines include **Avianca**, Cra 2A No 14-17, Edif de los Bancos, local 105, T5-421 4958, T5-432 0106 at airport; **Copa**, CC Rex, Cra 3, No 17-27, local 2; **EasyFly**, T5-435 1777; and **LATAM**, C 23, No 6-18, local 2.

Bus
The **bus terminal** is southeast of the city, towards Rodadero. A minibus to the centre of Santa Marta costs US$0.80; taxi to the centre US$3-4, or US$5 to Rodadero.

Local To **Aracataca**, US$5 with **Berlinas**. Buses to **Taganga** can be picked up on Cra 5; buses to **Rodadero** leave from the waterfront. Buses to **Tayrona** leave from the corner of C 11/Cra 11 in the market area, every 15 mins, US$3.

Long distance To **Bogotá**, 7 daily, 16 hrs, US$35-52, **Brasilia** or **Berlinas**

del Fonce. Berlinas and Brasilia to Bucaramanga about 9 hrs, US$33-37, frequent departures 0700-2200. Buses to Barranquilla, frequent, 2 hrs, US$5-6. To Cartagena, 5 hrs, US$14-16, with Brasilia. To Riohacha, 3 hrs, US$10-12. Frequent buses to Maicao, 4-5 hrs, US$15 a/c, cheaper non-a/c. Asotranstax runs a door-to-door *colectivo* service to Mompós, via Bosconia, which leaves Santa Marta 0300 and 1100, 6 hrs, US$25.50.

Around Santa Marta

abundant wildlife and a popular beach resort

Ciénaga Grande de Santa Marta

The paved coast road to Santa Marta from Barranquilla passes salt pans and skirts the Ciénaga Grande de Santa Marta, a huge marshy area and wildlife sanctuary, recognized by UNESCO and RAMSAR. It is not open to visitors, but all types of water birds, plants and animals may be seen on the large lake and its margins. Cutting off the egress from the lake to the sea to build the coast road killed large areas of mangrove and caused an ecological disaster, but a National Environment Programme is working to reopen the channels and restore the area. There are two villages built on stilts in the lake, Nueva Venecia and Buenavista. Ask at the Santuario de Flora y Fauna Ciénaga Grande de Santa Marta desk in the National Parks office in Santa Marta (T5-423 0752, see Tourist information, page 152) about guides and boatmen who take visitors to the lake from the community of Tasajera. On the east shore of the lagoon is Ciénaga, famous for its cumbia music.

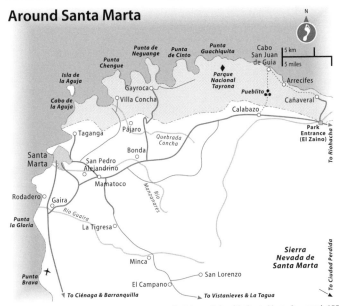

Around Santa Marta

Taganga

Close to Santa Marta is the popular former fishing village, turned beach resort of Taganga, set in a little bay with good views. It is laid back and welcoming, but beaches further east in Tayrona National Park are becoming more favoured on the backpacker circuit. Swimming is good, especially on **Playa Grande**, 25 minutes' walk round coast or US$3 by boat. Taganga is quieter midweek, but busy at weekends. Good fresh fish is served at places along the beach. Taganga is a popular place for diving and several well-established dive shops offer good-value PADI courses. There is also a good book exchange. An ATM that takes all major credit cards is next to the police station, half a block up from **Poseidon Dive Center**.

Listings Around Santa Marta

Where to stay

Taganga

$$$-$$ Bahía Taganga
C 8, No 1B-35, T5-421 0653,
www.bahiataganga.com.
Up on a hill at the north end of the bay with an unmissable sign on the cliff face. It has commanding views over the village and is tastefully decorated with clean rooms. Pool and jacuzzi, breakfast is served on a lovely terrace, hospitable, a/c, more expensive in the new building.

$$$-$$ Taganga Beach
Cra 1, No 18-49, T5-421 9058,
Great location on the beach. Rooms are quiet with a/c, friendly and helpful staff, beach can get noisy at weekends.

$$-$ La Casa de Felipe
Cra 5A, No 19-13, 500 m from beach behind football pitch, T316-318 9158 (mob), T5-421 9101, www.lacasadefelipe.com.
Cosy traveller place run by knowledgeable French team of Jean-Phillipe and Sandra Gibelin. Good kitchen facilities, excellent restaurant, breakfasts with delicious juices and crêpes, hospitable, relaxing hammock and expansive roof with terrace with sea views, studio apartments, dorms (US$8-

10.50 pp) and rooms. Good information on trips to Tayrona (maps provided), English spoken.

$$-$ Techos Azules
Sector Dunkarinca, Cabaña 1-100, T5-421 9141, www.techosazules.com.
Off the road leading into town, *cabañas* with good views over the bay, private rooms and dorm US$8 pp (low season prices), free coffee, laundry service.

$ Casa Blanca
Cra 1, No 18-161, T5-421 9232, at the southern end of the beach, Facebook: Hospedaje-Casa-Blanca.
Characterful. Each room has its own balcony with hammock, also has dorms. The roof terrace with its fabulous views is a fine place to pass the evening, drinking beer with fellow guests. Delicious fish meals served. Also has a tour desk.

$ pp Divanga B&B and Republika Divanga
Divanga B&B, C 12, No 4-07, T5-421 9092; Republika Divanga, C 11, No 3-05, T5-421 9217, www.divanga.com.
French-owned hostel, private rooms with or without bath or dorms (US$11-17), includes great breakfast in the B&B, breakfast not included at Republika,

but rooms are cheaper, comfortable, 5 mins' walk from the beach, nice views, attentive service, lovely atmosphere, good pool (at B&B). Also has **Diva Expe** tour operator and dive shop. Recommended.

$ Pelikan Hostal
Cra 2, No 17-04, T5-421 9057, www. hosteltrail.com/hostalpelikan.
Great location near the beach. Rooms with fan for 2-7 people, apartments, kitchen, laundry service, restaurant.

Restaurants

Taganga
Fresh fish is available in beach-side restaurants.

$$ Babaganoush
Cra 1C 18-22, 3rd floor next to the Tayrona Dive Center, T318-868 1476.
Serves up international dishes. Great steaks, veggie options and a generous half-price happy hour from 1700-2200, beautiful sea views from the rooftop setting. Recommended.

$$ Bitácora
Cra 1, No17-13, T316-796 3214.
Seafood, pastas, burgers, steaks and salads, has a good reputation.

Bars and clubs

Taganga

Mirador
C 1, No 18A-107, T301-638 8500, Facebook: Mirador-de-Taganga.
Rooftop bar and disco that strikes a nice balance between in- and outdoor fun. Also has a hostel.

Sensation
C 14, No 1-04, T314-220 2579,
Dance club that's open till 0300 at weekends.

What to do

Taganga
Adventure tours
Vergel Tours, *T304-571 1425, www. vergeltours.com.* The Vergel family organizes excursions from Taganga, including trips to Ciudad Perdida, scuba outings, snorkelling and cliff jumping.

Diving
There are several dive shops in Taganga.
Oceano Scuba, *Cra 2, No 17-46, T5-421 9004, www.oceanoscuba.com.co.* PADI, NAUI, TDI and other courses, 2, 3 and 4 days, professionally run.
Poseidon Dive Center, *C 18, No 1-69, T5-421 9224, www.poseidondivecenter.com.* PADI courses at all levels and the only place on the Colombian Caribbean coast to offer an instructor course. German owner, several European languages spoken. Own pool for beginners. Wi-Fi.

Transport

Taganga
Minibus from **Santa Marta**, US$0.75 (frequent, 0600-2130).

Taxi US$5, 15-20 mins.

Parque Nacional Natural Tayrona

palm-studded coves, forest trails and the Pueblito ruins

Stretching north of Taganga for some 85 km is the beautiful and mostly unspoilt coastline of Tayrona National Park, where the densely forested northern slopes of the Sierra Nevada fall into the Caribbean. Small, secluded bays with beaches of golden sand are guarded by giant boulders and islets. In the lush jungle vegetation and in the mangroves, you can see monkeys, iguanas, birds and maybe snakes. Of its 15,000 ha, 3000 are marine. There is accommodation at the eastern end, where the beaches and the accessible remnants of the Tayrona culture can only be reached on foot or horseback.

Essential Parque Nacional Natural Tayrona

Finding your feet

The park has three entrances: **Palangana** for day visits to Neguanje, Gayraca and Playa Cristal; **Calabazo** for Pueblito and Cabo San Juan de Guía, and **El Zaino**, at the eastern end of the park, 35 km from Santa Marta, for Cañaveral and Arrecifes; this last is the most commonly used

Tip...

There are food and drink stands in the park, or you can take your own food and water. If you are staying overnight in one of the campsites or hammock places, remember to take all supplies with you as there is only a small store in the park at Cañaveral. However, only take essential valuables, as robbery has been a problem. Littering was a big issue in the past, but there are now camouflaged litter bins along all the main trails and around the campsites. In the wet, the paths are very slippery, so hiking boots are recommended. Beware of falling coconuts and omnivorous donkeys in the campsites. Mosquitoes and other insects can also be a problem; take insect repellent.

Fact...

During high season, the park is very crowded. Sometimes it closes temporarily, but never for long. It's best to arrive early.

entrance. At El Zaino you sign in and buy a ticket. From the gate *colectivos* make a 10-minute ride to Cañaveral, US$2, where there is a gift shop, a car park, a museum (closed) and the trail of Nueve Piedras, to a mirador (about 30 minutes there and back). A few metres from the car park is a juice bar, campsite, the road to the **Ecohabs Minca** (see Where to stay, page 163) and horse hire at the start of the trail to Arrecifes (see below). It costs US$9 to ride to Arrecifes, US$14.50 to La Piscina, US$18 to Cabo San Juan, one way. See also Transport, page 160, for how to get to the park.

Park information

National Parks office www.parquesnacionales.gov.co. For the address of the National Parks office in Santa Marta, see page 152.
Entry Daily 0800-1700.
Fees US$14 foreigners, US$5.30 Colombians, US$3 children, parking extra.

Exploring the park

It is a one-hour walk through the forest from Cañaveral to **Arrecifes**. The trail is mostly level, apart from a couple of short, steep sections. At Arrecifes, beyond the cabins, campsites and eating places, is a long beach backed by mangroves. On no account be tempted to swim here as the tides and surf are treacherous. Every year, people drown because they do not heed the warnings. Walk on from Arrecifes to **La Piscina**, 40 minutes further, passing a little beach, **La Arenilla**, two-thirds of the way along, with a *cevichería* and juice stall. **La Piscina** also has a couple of places selling drinks and food. The beach is narrow, but the swimming after the walk is divine; excellent snorkelling, too. From La Piscina you can walk on to **Cabo San Juan de Guía**, 45 minutes, which also has excellent bathing, places to eat and a popular campsite/hammock place. From Cabo San Juan you can return the way you came, take the boat to Taganga (see Transport, page 160), or walk 1½ hours on a clear path up to the archaeological site of **Pueblito**. A guided tour around the site is free, every Saturday or as arranged with a park guard. Other Tayrona relics abound. Do not photograph the indigenous people at Pueblito. From Pueblito you can continue for a pleasant two-hour walk up to Calabazo on the Santa Marta–Riohacha road. A one-day circuit Santa Marta–Cañaveral–Arrecifes–Pueblito–Calabazo–Santa Marta needs a 0700 start at the latest. It is easier to do the circuit in reverse, although the first two hours from Calabazo is uphill (start walking before 0700); ask to be dropped at Calabazo. Tours can be arranged at several hotels and agencies in Santa Marta.

It is advisable to inform park guards when walking in the park. Wear hiking boots and beware of bloodsucking insects. Take food, water and only necessary valuables. If you are staying overnight in one of the campsites or hammock places, remember to take all supplies with you as there is only a small store in the park.

East of Tayrona

Beyond Cañaveral on the Santa Marta–Riohacha road is **Los Angeles**, with access to fine empty beaches, excellent for surfing. Ten minutes west of Los Angeles is the mouth of the **Río Piedras**, the border of Tayrona National Park, where you can bathe and enjoy sights to rival those in the park. At **Quebrada Valencia**, there are several natural swimming pools amid waterfalls, with good views. From the marked roadside entrance, it is a pleasant 20-minute walk along a clear path, or horse ride, to the waterfalls. It can get overcrowded during high season. Drinks and snacks are available along the way. The paved coastal road continues from Tayrona and crosses into Guajira Department at **Palomino**, 80 km from Santa Marta, which has a fine beach, a river running into the sea and good views of the Sierra Nevada, including snow-capped Pico Bolívar. There are hotels, hostels and *cabañas*, with more under construction.

Listings Parque Nacional Natural Tayrona

Tourist information

See above for the address of the National Parks office in Santa Marta.

Information can also be found at www.colombia.travel and www.parquesnacionales.gov.co.

Where to stay

Exploring the park

Comfortable cabins (**$**) with thatched roofs (*ecohabs*) for 1-4 people can be booked at **Cañaveral**, **Arrecifes** and other locations in or near the park, T311-600 1614, www.ecohabsanta marta.com. They offer privacy, great views over sea and jungle and they have decent restaurants.

Also at Arrecifes are various places to stay with double tents with mattress, US$5 pp (cheaper with own tent) and hammocks. These include **Bukaru** (T310-691 3626); and **Don Pedro** (T322-550 3933). Camping is also available at Cañaveral.

Centro Eco-turístico del Cabo de San Juan de Guía

www.cecabosanjuandelguia.com.co. A beautifully located campsite on a headland inside the park, with restaurant, hammocks for hire (US$10-12.50) and 2 *cabañas* (US$60). Pitching your own tent costs US$10; double tent hire, US$25.

East of Tayrona

There is an ecohostel called **Yuluka** about 2 km from El Zaino entrance on the main road.

$$$ Cabañas Los Angeles

Los Angeles, T321-522 1292, www. cabanasantamartalosangeles.com. Beachside apartments next to Tayrona National Park, with gorgeous sea views. Facilities include free breakfast, hammocks, large communal area and a restaurant. Choose from 4 different *cabañas*. The owner is Nohemi Ramos who also offers tours and hires out surfboards.

Restaurants

There are decent restaurants at both Cañaveral and Arrecifes, as well as smaller eateries at many of the beaches.

Transport

The beaches of Bahía Concha, Neguanje and Playa Cristal (a 10-min boat ride from Neguanje) can be reached from Santa Marta by tours, or in the case of Neguanje by *colectivos* from the market at 0700, return 1600. Hotels and hostels arrange tours, but there is no need to take guides (who charge US$20 pp or more for a day trip).

Boat

There is a boat service from **Taganga** at 1000-1100 to **Cabo San Juan**, 1-hr journey, US$25 pp one way (and you have to pay park entry); returns to Taganga 1500-1600.

Bus

To get to the park entrance in El Zaino, take a **Cootrans Oriente 'La Guajira'** bus from the market in Santa Marta, Cra 11 y C 11 outside the general store, or from in front of the **Buenavista** shopping centre in Mamatoca, near San Pedro Alejandrino and **The Dreamer**, US$2.25, every 15 mins from 0700, 1 hr, last back 1800-1830 (check on the day with the bus driver).

Taxi and colectivo

To return to Santa Marta (unless going to Pueblito and Calabazo, or taking the Taganga boat; see below), walk from Arrecifes to the car park and take the *colectivo* to the main road. At the carpark there may be taxis waiting: US$25 per car, US$20 for 1 person to Santa Marta, or you may get lucky and find a cheaper ride back to Santa Marta.

The Sierra Nevada (entry US$8, US$3.30 for Colombians, US$1.50 children. For the latest information check with the National Parks offices in Santa Marta (page 152) and Bogotá (page 22) and the Fundación Pro Sierra Nevada, Calle 17, No 3-83, Santa Marta, T5-431 5589), covering a triangular area of 16,000 sq km, rises abruptly from the Caribbean to 5800 m snow peaks in about 45 km, a gradient comparable with the south face of the Himalaya, and unequalled along the world's coasts. Pico Colón is the highest point in the country. Here can be found the most spectacular scenery and most interesting of Colombia's indigenous communities. The area has been a drugs-growing, processing and transporting region. For this reason, plus the presence of guerrilla and paramilitary groups, some local *indígenas* have been reluctant to welcome visitors. But the situation is improving and limited activities are now possible, such as the trek to Ciudad Perdida.

★ Ciudad Perdida *Colour map 1, A3.*
Trips of 4-6 days are organized by 4 authorized agencies in Santa Marta (see What to do, page 154). Going on your own is not allowed.

The Ciudad Perdida (Lost City) was called Teyuna by the Tayrona, meaning Mother Nature. The city covers 400 ha in the Sierra Nevada de Santa Marta and was built around AD 700. It was the political and trading centre of the Tayrona. The circular and oval stone terraces were once the living quarters for some 1400-3000 people. The city was also an important religious and burial site. The Tayrona built sophisticated irrigation systems and walls to prevent erosion. By around 1600, the Tayrona had been almost wiped out by the conquistadors and the few who survived were forced to flee. For the next four centuries, the city disappeared under the forest growth. In 1973, tomb looters searching for gold known to exist in burial urns and graves, rediscovered the city by chance. By 1975, the city was officially re-found, attracting local and international anthropologists and archaeologists who started to excavate, leading to the first tourist groups in 1984. Today the area is a protected indigenous reserve, where three main indigenous groups, the Koguis, Arhuacos and Arsarios (Wiwa), continue to live. For archaeological information, see **ICANH** ⓘ *C 12, No 2-41, Bogotá, T1-444 0544, www.icanh.gov.co.*

> **Tip...**
> There are many rivers to cross along the trail to the Lost City; take beach shoes or sandals to change into for the crossings, so your walking boots stay dry.

Trekking to the Ciudad Perdida The 45-km (round trip) trek to the Lost City is, at times, gruelling and challenging. The four-day trek involves walking seven or eight hours each day, but is well worth the effort for a rewarding and memorable experience. The trek is perhaps more spectacular than the archaeological site itself. Depending on the length of tour, it starts and ends at **Machete Pelao** or **El Mamey**.

The Lost City

From the first day we set out on the trail toward the mysterious Colombian Lost City, until day six when the remarkable adventure into the heart of the sierra came to an end, I was blown away by the crystal-clear rivers that cascaded down from the upper reaches of the mountains and treated us to amazing natural swimming pools, beautiful waterfalls and a much welcomed respite after hours of hiking amidst the endless jungle landscape. There are 18 or so river crossings en route to the Lost City, river pools to swim in each day and 1200 stone steps to climb at the very end of the third day that take you above the gorgeous river valleys to the high ridges blanketed in green. While the site alone is impressive, and its mysterious history and late discovery only add to its splendour, the surrounding mountain peaks dominate the endless landscape. What else lies undiscovered and hidden among such wild, rugged and beautiful terrain?

Craig Weigand

Along with lush tropical humid and dry forests, abundant flora and fauna, there are crystal-clear rivers, waterfalls and natural swimming pools. There are some 1200 steep slippery steps to climb to the summit of the site; the nearest campsite is below these steps. Watch out for snakes. Along the way, you will pass friendly Kogui villages. All tours include transport to the start of the trail and back (two hours from Santa Marta), sleeping in hammocks or basic bunk beds with mosquito nets, food, insurance, guides and entrance fees. The companies (see What to do, opposite) list the clothes and equipment you should take, such as sleeping bag, insect repellent, water bottle, etc. Bring your own binoculars. Accommodation is in organized camping or cabin sites. Don't forget that Ciudad Perdida is in a national park: it is strictly forbidden to damage trees and collect flowers or insects. Leave no rubbish behind and encourage the guides to ensure no one else does. Be prepared for heavy rain.

Fact...
Tours run all year apart from September when the park is closed for a spiritual cleansing ritual, which is performed annually by the indigenous Kogui and Wiwa people.

Minca and around *Colour map 1, A3.*

There are places to visit in the foothills of the Sierra Nevada, such as Minca, 20 km from Santa Marta. This village is surrounded by coffee fincas and begonia plantations, with several charming places to stay. Horse riding, birdwatching and tours further into the Sierra Nevada can be arranged from here. Buses run from Calle 11 between Carrera 11 and 12 in Santa Marta, and take 30 minutes (US$3, taxi US$18-20). About 45 minutes' walk beyond the village is **El Pozo Azul**, a local swimming spot under a waterfall, which is popular at weekends but almost always empty during the week. A 30-minute mototaxi ride away (US$7) is **Casa Elemento** (www.casaelemento.co), a *hostal* whose main attraction is its giant hammock with extensive views (entrance fee for non-residents). Beyond Minca, the partly paved road rises steeply to San Lorenzo which is surrounded by a forest of palm trees. On the way to San Lorenzo is **La Victoria**, a large coffee finca, which offers tours to demonstrate the coffee-making process. You can stay in *cabañas* run by the park authorities near San Lorenzo.

Listings Parque Nacional Natural Sierra Nevada de Santa Marta

Where to stay

Minca
There are many more places to stay in Minca.

$$$ Ecohabs Minca
T311-600 1614, www.ecohab santamarta.com.
Wood and thatch cabins for 2-8 people, with restaurant, bar, spa, activities and events organized, a good place for relaxation and birdwatching. Walking tours, transfers and packages can be arranged.

$$ Minca-La Casona
On the hill to the right as you enter, T315-519 3679, www.hotelminca.com.
Converted convent with views of the valley below, an easy short walk to town, tranquil setting, fully remodelled, with breakfast, bath, fan, hot water, comfortable beds, restaurant and bar. Various activities are on offer, including birdwatching.

$$ Sierra's Sound
C Principal, Minca, T321-522 1292, www.mincahotelsierrasound.com.
Italian owned, beautiful setting overlooking a rocky river, large patio with seating, hot water, home-made pasta, organizes tours into the Sierra Nevada.

$$-$ Finca Carpe Diem
Paso del Mango, Bonda, 50 mins from Santa Marta (see website for how to get there), T5-420 9610, www.fincacarpediem.com.

Breathtaking views at this Belgian-owned hostel on a farm and nature reserve, with private and dormitory accommodation (US$10 pp), camping, 2 pools, hammocks for relaxing, restaurant, home-produced vegetables, coffee and honey. Activities include treks, swimming and local visits. Recommended.

What to do

Ciudad Perdida
Trips of 4-6 days are organized by 4 authorized agencies in Santa Marta: **Turcol** (see above), **Magic Tour** (C 16, No 4-41, Santa Marta, T5-421 5820, and C 14, No 1b-50, T5-421 9429 (T317-679 2441, 24-hr number), Taganga, www.magictourcolombia.com), **Expotur** (Cra 3, No 17-27, T5-420 7739, www.expotur-eco.com) and **Wiwa Tour** (Cra 3, No 18-49, T5-420 3413, www.wiwatour.com). Other tour operators and hotels in Santa Marta or Taganga can make bookings for you. The cost starts at about US$290 pp and includes park permits. Under no circumstances should you deal with unauthorized guides; check with the tourist office if in doubt.

Minca
Semilla Tours, *Minca, T313-872 2434, www.hosteltrail.com/tour_companies/ semillatours.* Community tourism company offering tours in the region and elsewhere in Colombia. Also has volunteering opportunities.

Aracataca *Colour map 1, B3.*

Aracataca, 60 km south of Ciénaga (see page 155) and 7 km before Fundación, is the birthplace of **Gabriel García Márquez** and fictionalized as Macondo in some of his stories (notably *100 Years of Solitude*). His home is now a **Casa Museo** ① *Cra 5, No 6-35, T5-425 6588, (museum is next to La Hojarasca café, see page 167), open Tue-Sat 0800-1300, 1400-1700, Sun 0800-1400.* Different rooms have objects and quotations from his work in Spanish and English to provide an overview of his family life. You can also visit the **Casa del Telegrafista**, which houses a few dusty items. **Finca Macondo** (named after a type of tree) is 30 minutes from town. You can visit it in the afternoon, or take a tour in and around Macondo and to some outlying towns, such as **Sevilla**. The tour takes eight or nine hours and can be arranged through **Expotur** ① *T5-420 7739, US$32.* Other sites related to the stories are the river, where you can swim, and the railway station, through which coal trains pass.

Valledupar *Colour map 1, B4.*

South of Aracataca and Fundación is the important road junction of **Bosconia** (80 km). The main road continues to Bucaramanga; a road west heads to the Río Magdalena (with a turning at La Gloria towards Mompós – see Mompós Transport, page 133), while a road east goes towards Maicao, Valledupar (after 89 km) and **Cuestecitas**, where you can turn north to Riohacha, or carry on to Maicao on the Venezuelan border.

Valledupar, capital of César Department, lies on the plain between the Sierra Nevada de Santa Marta and the Sierra de Perijá. It is the home of *vallenato* music and culture (a UNESCO intangible cultural heritage). On the main Plaza Alfonso López Pumarejo, with a dramatic statue of La Revolución en Marcha, is the cultural centre **Fundación Festival de la Leyenda Vallenata: Compai Chipuco** ① *C 16, No 6-05, T5-738 393, www.festivalvallenato.com,* a good place for information. It sells handicrafts, books and music and has a bar, restaurant and photographic exhibition of La Cacica, Consuelo Araujonoguera, one of the founders of **El Festival de la Leyenda Vallenata** (see page 167). Also of interest are **La Academia de Música Vallenata Andrés Turco Gil** ① *C 31, No 4-265, http://static.losninosvallenatos.com,* with photos of events and famous personalities, and **Casa Beto Murgas/Museo del Acordeón** ① *Cra 17, No 9A-18, T5-573 7376, www.museodelacordeon.com, Mon-Fri 0900-1200, 1400-1700, Sat 0900-1200, US$7,* with an interesting collection of photographs, indigenous instruments and accordions. At the **Centro Artesanal Calle Grande** ① *C 16, block 7,* lots of stalls sell hats, bags, jewellery, hammocks and some musical instruments. (The **Exito** supermarket, Carreras 6 y 7, Calle 16 y 17, has ATMs.)

Around Valledupar

The Río Guatapurí runs cold and clear from the Sierra Nevada past the city. The **Balneario Hurtado** is a popular bathing spot, especially at weekends, with food, drink and music (the water is muddy after heavy rain). It is by the bridge just

ON THE ROAD

Gabriel García Márquez

More than any other Colombian, Gabriel García Márquez, or Gabo as he is affectionately known, shaped the outside world's understanding of Colombian culture. His books champion the genre of magical realism where the real and the fantastical blur so naturally that it is difficult to discern where one ends and the other begins.

But is this what life in Colombia is really like? Schoolteachers-turned-dictators who fashion a town's children into an oppressive army, a woman so beautiful she causes the death of anyone who courts her and a child born with his eyes open because he has been weeping in his mother's womb seem improbable, especially to sceptical Western sensibilities. Yet many of the places, events and characters are based on real life. Macondo, a place which features in so many of his stories, is modelled on his town of birth, Aracataca. Cartagena is easily recognizable as the unnamed port that is the setting for *Love in the Time of Cholera*, while Fermina Daza and Florentino Ariza's love affair is based on his own parents' marriage. Events in *Chronicle of a Death Foretold* and *The Story of a Shipwrecked Sailor* were inspired by real life stories lifted from newspaper articles.

Despite his death in April 2014, García Márquez's legacy of combining fantasy and reality continues to be a defining characteristic of Colombia's artistic identity. And who can challenge Gabo's interpretation of the truth when Colombia has produced real life characters such as Pablo Escobar? Where else in the world are there villages that host donkey beauty contests or elect a mayor who dresses up as a superhero? Sometimes Colombian reality is stranger than Gabo's fiction.

past the Parque de la Leyenda, the headquarters of the **Vallenato Festival** (see page 167). From the centre take Carrera 9, the main commercial avenue, or, if cycling, the quieter Carrera 4. Across the bridge is **Ecoparque Los Besotes** (9 km), a dry forest wildlife reserve, good for birdwatching.

From Valledupar, it is possible to enter the **Sierra Nevada de Santa Marta**, with permission from community leaders. The **Casa Indígena** ① *Av Simón Bolívar, just past the accordion statue at end of Cra 9*, is where the *indígenas* from the sierra gather; go here if you need permission to go to remote places. A full-day tour from the city is to **La Mina** (20 km), a natural swimming pool by magnificent rocks, also popular at weekends. The Arhuaco community of **Nabusímake** is one of the most important centres of indigenous culture in the sierra. It may be possible to visit, but tourism is sometimes not allowed by the Arhaucos. The nearest town is Pueblo Bello, 1½ hours by regular bus from Valledupar (from Carrera 7A, where it splits from Carrera 7, beyond 5 Esquinas, 0600). A jeep runs to Nabusímake (not daily), 2½ to three hours and comes straight back; as there are no hotels you cannot stay overnight. Ask at the Casa Indígena or at reputable tour operators about whether visits are possible.

Música tropical

No country in South America has a greater variety of musical genres than Colombia, and nowhere is music more abundant than in the fertile breeding grounds of the north coast. The diversity of musical expression comes from a mixture of African, indigenous and European influences.

On the coast, *música tropical* is an umbrella term used to encompass the many hybrids that have arisen over the years. Most popular among these is *vallenato*, a form of music that originated with farmers around Valledupar. Its primary instruments are the accordion; the *guacharaca* (a tube made from the trunk of a small palm tree, with ridges carved into it), which when scraped with a fork produces a beat, and the *caja vallenata* (a cylindrical drum brought over by African slaves).

Vallenato has its roots in a more ancient genre, *cumbia*, which is believed to derive from Guinean *cumbe* and began as a courtship dance practised among the slave population; it later mixed with European and indigenous instruments, such as the guitar, the accordion and the *gaita*, a type of flute used by the *indígenas* of the Sierra Nevada de Santa Marta. *Cumbia* is celebrated for bringing together Colombia's three main ethnic groups and was used as an expression of resistance during the campaign for Independence from the Spanish. *Cumbia* has many other derivatives, such as *porro*, *gaita*, *fandango* and *bullerengue*.

The newest genre to emerge is *champeta*. This is the most African of the genres; it takes its influence from *soukous* and *compas*, and is characterized by very sensual dancing. It gained popularity among the black population of Cartagena and San Basilio de Palenque in the 1980s.

Listings Inland from Santa Marta

Where to stay

Aracataca
Most people visiting the town stay in neighbouring Fundación, 10 mins by taxi, US$3.50. **Restaurant El Patio Mágico de Gabo y Leo Matiz** (see Restaurants, below) occasionally organizes rooms.

$$-$ Hotel Milán
C 7 No 8-24, Fundación, T301-707 9070.
Comfortable if functional hotel, clean rooms with a/c and fridge.

Valledupar

$$$ Sonesta
Diag 10, No 6N-15, T5-574 8686, www.sonesta.com.
Business-class hotel, next to CC Guatapurí Plaza and shopping mall, it has all the usual amenities including a pool, 24-hr gym, buffet breakfast and restaurant.

$$ Casa de Los Santos Reyes
C 13, No 4A-90, T5-580 1782, www. hotelboutiquevalledupar.com.

Centrally located, this restored colonial home has been turned into a boutique hotel. Its 2 spacious rooms and a suite have all mod cons and there's a small pool. Breakfast is served in a delightful garden. Run by the same people as **Hostal Provincia**.

$$ Vajamar
Cra 7, No 16A-30, T5-573 2010,
www.hotelvajamar.com.
Smart city centre hotel with pool and an expensive restaurant. Rooms are cheaper at weekends.

$$-$ Hostal Provincia
C 16A, No 5-25, T5-580 0558,
www.provinciavalledupar.com.
Private rooms with a/c and cheaper dorms for 6. A very good choice, with a nice atmosphere. Bike rental, Wi-Fi throughout, hammocks, large common areas, barbecue and bar, lots of information, helpful staff can organize tours and excursions to local indigenous communities. Warmly recommended.

$ Aqua Hostal
Cra 7 No 13A-42, T5-570 0439,
www.aquahostalvalledupar.com.
Hostel with private rooms as well as 12-bed dorms. Wi-Fi throughout.

Restaurants

Aracataca

$$ El Patio Mágico de Gabo y Leo Matiz
C 7 No 4-57.
Town centre restaurant offering Italian and local dishes in an open-air courtyard. Also has vegetarian options.

$ La Hojarasca
Next to the Casa Museo. Daily 1800-2200.
Local home-cooked meals, juices and snacks, clean and pleasant.

Valledupar
There are some cafés on the Plaza Alfonso López, but all types of restaurants on Cra 9 from C 15 down, heading towards Plaza del Acordeón.

$$ Varadero
C 12 No 6-56, T5-570 6175.
Simply put: the best seafood in town.

$$ Rider's Bike Bistro
C 13, No 6-45, T323-460 4230.
Good seafood and meat dishes, a reasonable wine list and cocktails.

Bars and clubs

Valledupar

Palenke Cultura Bar
Cra 5 No 13C 52, T315-235 4378.
A good bar with varied music, offering dance classes, free cinema nights and other cultural events.

Festivals

Valledupar
6 Jan The anniversary of the founding of Valledupar. There's dancing and accordion music in the streets.
Last week of Apr Festival de la Leyenda Vallenata. The festival celebrating *vallenato* music and culture draws thousands of visitors. It is focused around Parque de la Leyenda. Contact the cultural centre (C 16, No 6-05, T5-580 8710, www.festivalvallenato.com) for information.
Sep There are cultural events throughout Sep.

Shopping

Valledupar
Centro Artesanal Calle Grande,
C 16, block 7. Lots of stalls selling handicrafts and local artwork,

including distinctive hats (US$15-US$150), indigenous bags, jewellery, hammocks and some musical instruments.

Compai Chipuco, *on the plaza*. Sells books and music CDs of the region.

La Casa de la Música, *Cra 9, No 18-85*. Books, music and CDs.

What to do

Aracataca
Expotur, *Cra 3, No 17-27, Edif Rex, local 3, T5-420 7739, http://expotur-eco.com/*. Arranges 8- to 9-hr tours of the town and surroundings, US$37.

Valledupar
Paseo Vallenato Tour, *Diagonal 21, No 18-2 a 18-136, T313-571 9025, www.paseovallenato.com*. Offers cultural tours in and around Valledupar as well excursions to the river and indigenous communities. Recommended.

Transport

Aracataca
Bus
To **Santa Marta**, US$4-5. To **Barranquilla**, US$6. To **Valledupar**, 3 hrs 45 mins, US$7-9 with **Cootracosta**. There may be a long stop in Fundación, but you don't have to change bus. To go to **Bucuramanga** (US$25) or **Bogotá** (US$35), catch a bus coming from Santa Marta at the toll station (*peaje*) outside town 1½ hrs after the bus has left Santa Marta. Be at the toll 30 mins early. For information on all buses, go to the **Berlinas** office. **Bicycle taxi** from bus stop to centre US$0.65.

Valledupar
Air
The airport is 3 km southeast of the town, close to the bus station (taxi, US$5).

Flights to **Barranquilla** (30 mins) and **Bogotá** (1½ hrs) with **Avianca** (T01-8000-953434) and **LATAM** (Av Hurtado Diagonal 10N-6N, 15, CC Guatapuri, p 1, Plazoleta Juan Valdez). **Easyfly** (www.easyfly.com.co) also has flights from here.

Bus
The bus terminal is near the airport (taxi, US$3.55).

To **Aracataca**, US$7-9. To **Santa Marta**, 4 hrs, US$10-12. To **Barranquilla**, 5-6 hrs, US$13-15. To **Cartagena**, 7-8 hrs, US$17-21. To **Mompós** (via Bosconia) door-to-door service with local taxi/minibus driver Lalo Castro, T312-673 5226, US$22; if he isn't going, **CotraNorte**, **Cotracol** or **Cootracegua** buses leave every morning, or minibus from outside bus terminal to Santa Ana on the Río Magdalena, via Bosconia and La Gloria, US$27, then cross the Río Magdalena by bridge to Talaigua Nueva (if the bus isn't going to Mompós, take motorbike taxi to Mompós, US$6-9). There are also door-to-door services to **Riohacha**, US$15pp, and **Bucaramanga**, 8 hrs, US$25-28.

Riohacha & the
Guajira Peninsula

Roads head for the insalubrious border town of Maicao, but on the way is plenty of interest: lagoons where flamingos feed and the arid, empty Guajira Peninsula with its wildlife and special Wayúu culture.

Riohacha *Colour map 1, A5. See also map, page 173.*

The port of Riohacha, 160 km east of Santa Marta and capital of La Guajira Department, comes alive at the weekend, when it fills with party-goers and music (almost always *vallenato*). It was founded in 1545 by Nicolás Federmann, and in early years its pearling industry was large enough to tempt Drake to sack it (1596). Pearling almost ceased during the 18th century and the town was all but abandoned. Today, there is a pleasant stretch of beach with shady palms and a long wooden pier in the centre. A promenade along the beachfront (Calle 1) is lined with banks, hotels, restaurants and tour agencies. It is common to see Wayúus selling their wares and beautiful handmade *mochilas* (bags) along the seafront. There's a market 2 km from town on the Valledupar road where hammocks and bags woven by the Wayúu of the Guajira are also sold.

Riohacha is a useful base for exploring the semi-desert landscape of La Guajira. The **Dirección de Turismo de la Guajira** ① *C 1, Av de La Marina No 4-42, T5-727 1015*, has little information about the region, so it's better to ask tour operators and visit the University of the Guajira, which has an excellent resource centre related to the region and the Wayuú culture (ID is necessary to get in). The provincial website is www.laguajira.gov.co (T8-921 15015), and the municipal site is www.riohacha-laguajira.gov.co.

Santuario Los Flamencos
95 km east of Santa Marta and 25 km short of Riohacha.

There are several small and two large saline lagoons (Laguna Grande and Laguna de Navío Quebrado), separated from the Caribbean by sand bars. The latter is near Camarones (*colectivo* from Riohacha, roundabout between water tower and bus station, US$3) which is just off the main road. About 3 km beyond Camarones is 'La Playa', a popular beach to which some *colectivos* continue at weekends. Flamingos normally visit the large lagoons between October and December, during the wet season, though some birds are there all year. They are believed to migrate to and from the Dutch Antilles, Venezuela and Florida. Across Laguna de

Essential Riohacha and the Guajira Peninsula

Finding your feet

The Guajira Peninsula is bordered by the Gulf of Venezuela and the Caribbean Sea. Trips to the region are best arranged in Riohacha, but can also be organized in Bogotá, Cartagena and Santa Marta.

Getting around

Early morning is best for travel, as transport is scarce in the afternoon. Getting to Cabo de la Vela independently is a time-consuming and at times uncomfortable experience, particularly during the wet season, although it can be done: *colectivos* and taxis make the journey on the paved road to Uribia and Manaure, and from there on dirt tracks to Cabo de la Vela (two or three hours). Beyond Cabo de la Vela we advise you take a tour or at least contract your own jeep and guide. **Aventure Colombia** in Cartagena (see page 154) arranges trips here from time to time.

When to go

Rainy season is September to November; dirt tracks can become impassable at this time. To enjoy the deserted beaches around Cabo de la Vela, avoid Christmas and Easter when it is crowded and full of cars. The **Wayúu Indian Festival** in Uribia takes place in May.

Time required

Most tours of the peninsula last three days; add another couple of days' beach time to your itinerary.

Navío Quebrado is a community-run visitor centre called **Los Mangles**, with accommodation in *cabañas*, in hammocks ($) or camping. Meals are also available and the centre arranges birdwatching trips on foot or by boat (US$3 per person). For travel packages see http://ecoturismosantuario.weebly. com (T301-675 3862) and www.parques nacionales.gov.co. There are several bars and two stores on the beach.

★ **Guajira Peninsula** *Colour map 1, A6.*
Beyond Riohacha to the east is the arid and sparsely inhabited Guajira Peninsula. You'll see fields of cacti and fine views of flamingos and other brightly coloured birds. The sunsets and barren landscapes of the Guajira are magnificent. The indigenous Wayúu (or Guajiros) here collect dividivi (the curved pods of trees used in tanning and dyeing), tend goats and go fishing. Of special interest are the coloured robes worn by the women. Their language is Wayuunaiki; beyond Cabo de la Vela little Spanish is spoken.

Manaure is known for its salt flats southwest of the town. If you walk along the beach past the salt works, there are several lagoons where flamingos congregate year-round (take binoculars). Local children hire out bicycles to travel to the lagoons and salt flats. Take plenty of sunblock and water and a torch/flashlight for returning in the evening. Around 14 km from Manaure in this direction is **Musichi**, an important haunt of the flamingos, with the **Area Natural Protegida de los Flamencos Rosados**. From Manaure there are *busetas* to **Uribia** (US$4-5, 30 minutes), which has a Wayúu festival in June (no other reason to stop here), and thence to Maicao. You can get *busetas* from

ON THE ROAD

Hammocks

There's no better way to enjoy Colombia's beaches than to relax in a hammock, using conveniently located palm trees as supports. Plenty of places hire them out, but for true comfort it's best to buy your own.

The hammocks developed by the Wayúu are made up of intricately woven threads of cotton that form a crocheted net. These are known as *chinchorros* and are larger than the average hammock, with wrap-around sides that serve as a blanket and elaborate tassels. The best places to buy *chinchorros* are the market in Riohacha and Uribia's handicraft shops in La Guajira.

The other most common style uses brightly coloured woven cotton or wool to form a large stretch of material. These can be bought in San Jacinto, a couple of hours south of Cartagena, which is the capital of Colombia's hammock industry and the best place to find a bargain. The market in Santa Marta also has a good selection.

Increasingly hammocks are mass-produced and often not made out of natural fibres. Shop carefully and expect to pay US$75 or more for a cotton handwoven one.

Uribia to Puerto Bolívar (from where coal from El Cerrejón mine is exported) and from there transport to **Cabo de la Vela**, where the lagoons seasonally shelter vast flocks of flamingos, herons and sandpipers. It costs about US$7-11 from Uribia to Cabo de la Vela, *busetas* run until 1400, few on Sunday; all transport leaves from the market and the journey is slow. There are fine beaches, but very strong currents offshore. Good walks through desert scrubland, eg to Pan de Azúcar hill (one hour from beach) and El Faro, with superb views of the coastline and desert. To enjoy deserted beaches, avoid Christmas and Easter when the *cabañas* and beaches are crowded and full of cars.

Parque Nacional Macuira ⓘ *For information, C 8, No 5-73, T5-728 2636 in Riohacha. Mon-Fri 0800-1200, 1400-1600, entry US$11.25, Colombians US$3.75, children US$2.40, registration and 30-min compulsory induction at Nazareth park office, open Mon-Fri 0700-1200, 1400-1700, guides US$20.* Towards the northeast tip of the Guajira Peninsula is the Serranía de Macuira, a range of hills over 500 m which creates an oasis of tropical forest in the semi-desert. Moisture comes mainly from clouds that form in the evening and disperse in the

Warning...

The Guajira Peninsula is not a place to travel alone; if not taking an organized tour, parties of three or more are recommended. If going in your own transport, check on safety before setting out. Also remember it is hot, easy to get lost, and there is little cover and very little water. Locals, including police, are very helpful in giving lifts. Stock up with provisions and water in Riohacha or Maicao. Elsewhere, what little there is, is expensive.

early morning. Its remoteness gives it interesting flora and fauna and indigenous settlements little affected by outsiders. To reach the area, travel northeast from Uribia either round the coast past Bahía Portete, or direct across the semi-desert, to the Wayúu village of **Nazareth** on the east side of the park. Someone may let you stay the night in a hammock in Nazareth. Otherwise, there is camping beside the park office. Macuira can be seen on two-day trips from Nazareth. Beyond Cabo de la Vela take a tour, as there is no public transport.

Another worthwhile, but arduous trip is the journey to **Punta Gallinas**, the northernmost tip of the South American continent. It takes up to eight hours on unpaved roads, followed by a boat journey (three hours, shorter in dry season) that's not for the fainthearted, but the magic of the place makes it all worth it. Few people make it this far north, adding to the isolated feel and special atmosphere. The nearby sand dunes of Taroa are also spectacular. You can book two-night/three-day packages, including visits to **Cabo de la Vela** and the **Taroa dunes** through Kaí Ecotravel (see below), amongst others in Riohacha.

Maicao *Colour map 1, A5.*
The paved highway runs from Riohacha to the hot, dusty town of Maicao, 76 km (12 km from the Venezuelan border). Clothing and white goods make up much of the business, but the city has a reputation for black-market activities. Most commercial premises close early and after dark the streets are unsafe.

> **Warning…**
> At the time of writing, the Foreign Office advises against travel to Venezuelan border regions (see page 95).

Listings Riohacha and the Guajira Peninsula *map page 173.*

Where to stay

Riohacha

$$$ Hotel Taroa
Cra 1, No 44-77, T5-729 1122.
Modern hotel with comfortable rooms near the beach. Breakfast is served on the rooftop with stunning views of the bay.

$ Almirante Padilla
Cra 6, No 3-29, T5-727 3612/2328, hotel_almirante_padilla@yahoo.es.
Crumbling but with character. Has an inviting patio and a restaurant with cheap *almuerzo*. It's clean, friendly, large and very central. Some rooms with a/c.

$ Happiness Hostel
Av Los Estudiantes, Cra 15, No 14-51, T5-7273828, T315-613 2347, http://happinesshostelcol.wix.com/hostel.
With private rooms (**$$**) and dorms with bath (US$10 pp), all rooms have a/c or fan, bar, kitchen, great breakfast US$3, patio, helpful for information on the area and can arrange tours.

$ Internacional
Cra 7, No 13-37, T5-727 3483, hriohachainternacional@gmail.com.
A friendly option down an alleyway off the old market, with a pleasant restaurant on the patio. Free iced water. Recommended.

$ Yalconia del Mar
Cra 7, No 11-26, T5-727 3487,
hotelyalconiadelmar@hotmail.com.
Rooms with bath, cheaper with fan,
clean, safe, friendly, helpful, halfway
between the beach and the bus station.

Guajira Peninsula
Manaure

$$ Palaaima
Cr 6, No 7-25, T5-717 8455, T314-581 6789,
irisfaep@hotmail.com.

The best in town. Comfortable, cool,
simple rooms, central location, helpful
staff. There are always Wayúu locals
hanging around the hotel who are eager
to talk about their culture and traditions.

Uribia
Basic *hostales* (**$**, no running water);
most transport stops in Uribia.

$$ Juyasirain
Diag 2A, No 2B-04, T5-717 7284,
juyasirain2009@hotmail.com.

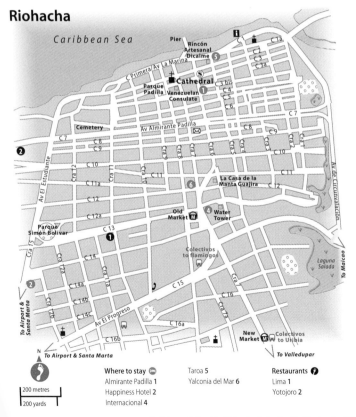

Riohacha

Caribbean Sea

Where to stay 🛏
Almirante Padilla 1
Happiness Hotel 2
Internacional 4

Taroa 5
Yalconia del Mar 6

Restaurants 🍴
Lima 1
Yotojoro 2

200 metres
200 yards

The only slightly upmarket accommodation in town. Large, light and airy, with simple rooms and a pleasant patio restaurant.

Cabo de la Vela

This area becomes very crowded during high season, but there are 60 hostels to choose from, mostly basic with hammocks, but some have TV, a/c. There is a telecom centre. Most places have hammock space on the beach, US$5-10. Fish meals cost US$4-6, including a large breakfast.

Maicao

$$$-$$ Hotel Maicao Internacional
C 12, No 10-90, T5-726 8186,
hotelmaicao2009@telecom.com.co.
Good rooms with a/c, rooftop pool and bar. A good option in Maicao, attentive staff.

$$ Maicao Plaza
C 10, No 10-28, T5-726 0310,
maicaoplazahotel@hotmail.com.
Modern and central, with spacious rooms.

Restaurants

Riohacha

Many ice cream and juice bars, and small *asados*, serving large, cheap selections of barbecued meat at the western end of the seafront. The western end also has a lovely row of brightly painted huts selling fresh seafood and ceviche. The eastern end has more restaurants for sit-down meals.

$$$ Yotojoro
C 7, No 15-81, T5-727 3919.
Modern interior, serving Caribbean-style food, especially seafood. Also recommended for cocktails.

$$ Lima
C 13, No 11-33, T5-728 1313.
Café/restaurant serving healthy meals and snacks at reasonable prices. Great salads and vegetarian and vegan options. Recommended.

What to do

Guajira Peninsula

Trips to the Guajira Peninsula are best arranged in Riohacha where there are several operators, but can also be organized with national operators and others in Cartagena and Santa Marta. Tours to Cabo de la Vela, 1-2 days, usually include Manaure (salt mines), Uribia, Pilón de Azúcar and El Faro. All operators organize tours to Wayúu *rancherías* in the afternoon (includes typical goat lunch).

Uribia

Kaí Ecotravel, *Diagonal 1B, No 8-68, T5-717 7173, or 311-436 2830, also at Hotel Castillo del Mar, C 9A, No 15-352 and at Av 1-A No 4-49, T05-727 0728, in Riohacha, and in Hotel Juyasirain, www.kaiecotravel.com.* Run by a network of Wayúu families. Organizes tours to Cabo de la Vela (for 2 days, US$130 pp for 2 people, discounts for larger groups), Parque Natural Nacional Macuira (for 5 days US$600 pp for 2 people), Punta Gallinas (for 3 days US$390 pp for 2 people), up to US$980 for a 8-day full circuit, including transport, accommodation and food. Recommended.
Kaishi, *Plaza Principal, T 311-429 6315, www.kaishitravel.com.* Andrés Delgado, the owner, organizes jeep tours around La Guajira, with lodging. Reliable and recommended.

Transport

Riohacha
Air
2 flights a day to **Bogotá**,
1 hr 35 mins, **Avianca**.

Bus
Main terminal is on C 15 (El Progreso).
Coopcaribe Taxis travel throughout
the region and can be picked up
almost anywhere in town, especially
close to the old market area near the
Hotel Internacional: daily to **Uribia**,
US$11, 1½ hrs, **Manaure** US$12, 1¾ hrs.
Leave when full (4 people), be prepared
to pay slightly more if there are no
travellers. Early morning best for travel,
transport is scarce in the afternoon.
No buses leave from Riohacha direct
to Cabo de la Vela: travel to Uribia
and wait for a jeep (leaves when full,
irregular service) to Cabo de la Vela,
long and uncomfortable, unpaved
road. Take plenty of water with you.

It is much easier and you are
recommended to take a tour from
Riohacha to Cabo de la Vela. To **Santa
Marta**, US$10-12, 3 hrs, and **Cartagena**,
US$18, 7-8 hrs, every 30 mins.

Maicao
Bus
Buses to/from **Riohacha**, US$4.50,
frequent, 1-1½ hr. **Santa Marta** 3 hrs,
US$14. **Barranquilla**, US$17. **Cartagena**,
US$21. Trucks leave regularly for **Cabo
de la Vela**, 2½-3 hrs, US$10 (can
be uncomfortably crowded). Take
water. **Fleta** is the local name for the
faster taxis. *Colectivos* (*por puestos* in
Venezuela), Maicao–**Maracaibo**, US$15,
or microbus, US$10, very few buses to
Venezuela after midday. Buses leave
from the bus terminal where you can
change money. Taxis from Maicao to
Maracaibo stop at both immigration
posts and take you to your hotel.
See the warning on page 172.

San Andrés
& Providencia

In 2000, the Archipelago of San Andrés, Old Providence and Santa Catalina was declared a World Natural Heritage Site called the Seaflower Biosphere Reserve. San Andrés is larger and more developed than Providencia and has lost much of its colonial Caribbean feel. Both are very expensive by South American standards. Nevertheless, their surrounding islets and cays, good diving, white-sand beaches and spectacular turquoise waters make them popular holiday resorts with Colombians and North Americans looking for winter sun. The original inhabitants, mostly descendants of Jamaican slaves, speak English, but the population has swollen with unrestricted immigration from Colombia. There are also Chinese and Middle Eastern communities.

The 11-km-long San Andrés island is made of coral and rises at its highest to 104 m. The town, commercial centre, resort hotel sector and airport are at the northern end. A picturesque road circles the island. The island's beaches are located in town and on the east coast; the best ones are at San Luis and Bahía Sonora/Sound Bay.

Places to see include the **Hoyo Soplador**, at the south end of the island, a geyser-like hole through which the sea spouts into the air when the wind is in the right direction. The west side is less developed, but there are no beaches. Instead there is **The Cove**, the island's deepest anchorage, and **Morgan's Cave** (Cueva de Morgan), reputed hiding place for the pirate's treasure, which is penetrated by the sea through an underwater passage. Next to Cueva de Morgan is a **museum** ⓘ *US$5*, with exhibitions telling the history of the coconut, paraphernalia from wrecks around the island and a replica pirate ship.

About 1 km south from Cueva de Morgan is **West View** ⓘ *daily 0900-1830, small restaurant opposite entrance*, an excellent place to see marine life as the sea is very clear. At The Cove, a road crosses up to the centre of the island and back to town over **La Loma**, on which is a Baptist church, built in 1847.

Cays

Boats leave from San Andrés in the morning for El Acuario (Rose Cay) and Haynes Cay, and continue to Johnny Cay in the afternoon, which has a white beach and parties all day Sunday (US$10

Essential San Andrés and Providencia

Finding your feet

The islands are 770 km north of continental Colombia, 849 km southwest of Jamaica and 240 km east of Nicaragua. A cheap way to visit San Andrés is on a package from Bogotá or another major city, with flights, accommodation and food included; look for supplements in the Colombian newspapers and adverts on the internet. Alternatively, you may wish to opt for a cheap airfare and choose where to stay when you get there. On arrival in San Andrés, you must buy a tourist card, US$22.50; it is also valid for Providencia, so don't lose it. You must also have an onward or return ticket. Visitors to Providencia can arrive by air from San Andrés (20 minutes) or by sea on launches and boats that ferry goods over. Beware that the sea can be choppy on this trip.

Getting around

Cars, motorbikes, bicycles and golf buggies can all be hired on San Andrés, but they may be in poor condition. Buses ply the route along the east coast and there are taxis, too. On Providencia, transport is provided by *chivas* and *colectivos* or by hiring a moped or golf buggy. Boats go to offshore cays.

When to visit

The islands have a typical Caribbean climate that includes hurricane season from roughly June to November. The best weather is from December to April, but these months also attract the largest crowds.

return). **El Acuario** has crystalline water and is a good place to snorkel. From here you can wade or swim across to **Haynes Cay**, a tiny cay with a couple of places to eat. The snorkelling here is good and there are iguanas living in the palm trees. If you want to avoid the crowds, hire a private boat and do the tour in reverse (US$150 for the day). Boats for the cays leave from **Tonino's Marina** between 0930 and 1100, US$10, returning at 1530, or from **Muelle Casa de la Cultura** on Avenida Newell.

Listings San Andrés *maps below and page 180.*

Tourist information

San Andrés Tourist Office
Av Newball, opposite Restaurante La Regatta, T8-512 5058, secturismosai@ yahoo.com. Mon-Fri 0800-1200, 1400-1800
Helpful, English spoken, maps and hotel lists. There is also a kiosk at the end of Av 20 de Julio, across from the sea (daily 0800-2000).

① **San Andrés Island**

Punta Norte
Johnny Cay
Bahía Sardinas
San Andrés
Punta Hansa
Roca del Pescador
Punta Paraíso
①
Bahía de San Andrés
Caribbean Sea
Baptist Church
Bahía Baja
Museo Casa Isleña
La Loma (120m)
El Acuario
La Laguna
Haynes Cay
Cueva de Morgan
Rocky Cay
San Luis
El Cove
Bahía Sonora
N
Monte Derecho
1 km
1 miles
La Piscinita
②
Where to stay
Casa Harb 1
Sunset 2
Hoyo Soplador
Punta Sur

➡ **San Andrés maps**
1 San Andrés island, page 178
2 San Andrés town, page 180

Where to stay

Hotels quote rates per person, but we list prices for double rooms. Prices include half board, but most can be booked without meals. Most raise prices by 20-30% mid-Dec to mid-Jan. The Decameron group has 5 hotels on San Andrés, www.decameron.com.

$$$$ Casa Harb
C 11, No 10-83, T8-512 6348, www.casaharb.com.
A 10-min drive from town, this boutique hotel takes its inspiration from the Far East and is the most stylish on the island. Each room is individually decorated with antique furniture, enormous granite baths, infinity pool and home-cooked meals.

$$$$ Portobelo
Av Colombia, No 5A-69, T8-512 7008, www.portobelohotel.com.
In a couple of buildings at the western end of the *malecón*, large beds.

$$$$ Sunset Hotel
Cra Circunvalar Km 13, T318-523 2286,
http://sunsethotelspa.com.
On the western side of the island across
the road from the sea, ideal for diving or
for getting away from the crowds. Bright,
fresh rooms set around a salt-water
swimming pool, helpful staff. Restaurant
with international and regional food in
a typical clapboard house, dive shop
next door.

$$ Hernando Henry
Av Las Américas, No 4-84,
T8-512 3416/T316-757 1433,
www.hotelhernandohenry.com.
At the back of town, shoddy but passable
rooms, cheaper with fan, laundry service.

$$ La Posada de Lulú
Av Antioquia, No 2-28, T8-512 2919/523
6308, www.laposadadelulu.com.
Brightly coloured hostel, comfortable
rooms and 2 apartments to rent for
longer stays, excellent restaurant.

$$ Posada Doña Rosa
Av Las Américas No 6-43,
con Aeropuerto, T8-512 3649,
http://posadarosa.blogspot.co.uk.
A 2-min walk from the airport, this is
a reasonable and economical option,
basic rooms with bath, use of kitchen,
TV room, a short walk from the beach.
Also has 2 apartments to rent.

$$-$ pp El Viajero Hostel
Av 20 de Julio No 3A-122, T8-512 7497,
www.elviajerohostels.com.
A member of the South American
El Viajero hostel chain. It has private
rooms including singles and dorms
(US$12-15 per bed) all with en suite bath,
a/c and safe boxes. Breakfast included in
the price, bicycles can be hired, weekly
activities such as dance and yoga, rooftop
bar and scuba certification courses.

There's a tourist office at reception that
books all tours and excursions. Like its
sister hostel in Cartagena, El Viajero is for
the party crowd.

Restaurants

Good fish and seafood meals at
San Luis beach.

$$$ La Regatta
Av Newball, next to Club Náutico,
T8-512 0437.
Seafood restaurant on a pier, excellent
lobster and ceviches, fine reputation,
reserve in advance. Recommended.

$$$-$$ Margherita e Carbonara
Av Colombia, No 1-93, T8-512 1050.
Good Italian, pizzas, pastas, juices
and coffee.

$$ Niko's
Av Colombia, No 1-93, T8-512 7535.
Bills itself as a seafood restaurant
though its steaks are good too. Varied
menu including Colombian dishes,
try the coconut rice. Lovely setting
by the water.

Entertainment

San Andrés is famous in Colombia for its
different styles of music, including the
local form of calypso, soca, reggae and
church music. Concerts are held at the
Old Coliseum (every Sat at 2100 in the
high season).

Festivals

Jun Jardín del Caribe. A folkloric festival.
20 Jul Independence celebrations on
San Andrés with various events.
Late Nov San Andrés de Apóstol,
patron saint of the island, celebrated
with 10 days of music, parades and
cultural events.

Dec Rainbow Festival. Reggae and calypso music.

What to do

Canopying
Canopy La Loma, *Vía La Loma-Barrack, T314-447 9868*. Site at the top of the hill in San Andrés. 3 'flights' over the trees at 450 m, 300 m and 200 m all with spectacular views out to sea. Safety precautions and equipment are good.

Diving
Diving off San Andrés is good; depth varies from 3 to 30 m, visibility from 10 to 30 m. There are 3 types of site: walls of seaweed and minor coral reefs, different types of coral, and underwater plateaux with much marine life. It is possible to dive in 70% of the insular platform. Diving trips to the reef:
Banda Dive Shop, *Hotel Lord Pierre, local 104, T8-513 1080, www.banda diveshop.com*. PADI qualified, various courses. Fast boat. Knowledgeable guides and good equipment.

Sharky Dive Shop, *Cra Circunvalar Km 13, T8-512 0651, www.sharkydiveshop.com*. Good equipment and excellent, English-speaking guides. PADI qualifications and a beginner's course held in the Sunset Hotel's saltwater pool.

Water sports and boat trips
Cooperativa Lancheros, *on the beach in San Andrés town*. Can arrange fishing trips, windsurfing, jet skiing and kite surfing. Snorkelling equipment can be hired for US$5.
Galeón Morgan, *Centro Comercial New Point Plaza, T8-512 8787*. Boat tours to El Acuario.

Transport

Air
Regular flights from **Bogotá**, **Cartagena**, **Cali** and **Medellín**. **Copa** once daily to **Panama City**. Sun flights are always heavily booked, similarly Jul-Aug, Dec-Jan. The airport at San Andrés is 15 mins' walk to town centre; buses to centre and San Luis leave from opposite the airport.

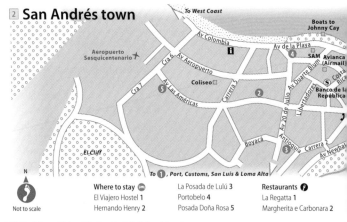

2 San Andrés town

Not to scale

Where to stay
El Viajero Hostel 1
Hernando Henry 2
La Posada de Lulú 3
Portobelo 4
Posada Doña Rosa 5

Restaurants
La Regatta 1
Margherita e Carbonara 2

Bus
Buses run every 15 mins on the eastern side of the island, US$1, and more often at night and during the holidays.

Taxi
Taxis around the island cost US$15-20, but in town fares double after 2200.

To airport US$7-9 (*colectivo* US$1). Cars can also be hired for 2 hrs or for a day. Passport may be required as deposit; you must have a driver's license. Bikes are easy to hire, but they may be in poor condition.

Providencia *Colour map 1 inset.*

unspoilt volcanic island

Parque Nacional Natural Old Providence McBean Lagoon

Located 80 km north-northeast of San Andrés, and commonly called **Old Providence**, Providencia is a mountainous island of volcanic origin. The barrier reef that surrounds it, the third largest in the world, is called **Old Providence McBean Lagoon**; it is easily visited (entry US$5.50). The official languages of its 5500 inhabitants are Spanish and Caribbean English. Musical influences are the mento from the Antilles, calypso from Trinidad and reggae from Jamaica. There are no high-rises, apartment blocks or shopping malls on Providencia and its quieter atmosphere than San Andrés attracts more European visitors.

Superb views can be had by climbing from Casabaja/Bottom House or Aguamansa/Smooth Water to the peak (about one hour, US$15 with a guide). There are relics of the fortifications built on the island during its disputed ownership. Horse riding is available, and boat trips can be made to Santa Catalina and to **Crab Cay** (good snorkelling – see What to do, page 184) to the northeast.

Santa Catalina (an old pirate lair) is separated from Providencia by a channel cut to improve defence of the island. This is crossed by the wooden Lover's Bridge (Malecón de los Enamorados). Go left after crossing this bridge (right is a dead end) and walk for about 500 m. Climb stairs to the Virgin statue for excellent views of Providencia. If you continue past the Virgin and go down the flight of stairs you will arrive at a very small beach (nice snorkelling). On the west side is a rock formation called Morgan's Head; from the side it looks like a profile.

Of the three main beaches, **Manzanillo** is the best preserved and wildest. There's not much space for lying out, but it's pleasant for walking. **Roland's Roots Bar** has excellent live, traditional island music at weekends. **South West Bay/Suroeste** has stunning

➡ **San Andrés maps**
1 San Andrés island, page 178
2 San Andrés town, page 180

Av Providencia

Punta Hansa

❸
❷

❶

Casa de la Cultura
Punta Paraíso

Niko's **3**

beaches and is the best for hanging out. There is access at each end. **Agua Dulce** is where most hotels and restaurants are.

Listings Providencia *map below.*

Tourist information

Providencia

Centro Administrativo Aury
Santa Isabel, T8-514 8054.
Provides information on Providencia.

Where to stay

Rooms can be rented at affordable prices in local houses or *posadas nativas.* Hotels in Agua Dulce are 10 mins by motor taxi (US$1) from

Providencia

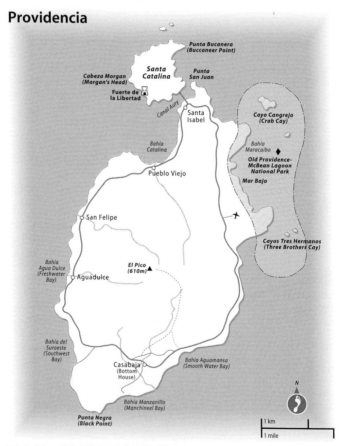

Punta Bucanera
(Buccaneer Point)

Cabeza Morgan
(Morgan's Head)

Santa Catalina

Punta San Juan

Fuerte de la Libertad

Canal Aury

Santa Isabel

Cayo Cangrejo
(Crab Cay)

Bahía Catalina

Bahía Maracaibo

Old Providence-McBean Lagoon National Park

Mar Bajo

Pueblo Viejo

San Felipe

El Pico
(610m)

Cayos Tres Hermanos
(Three Brothers Cay)

Bahía Agua Dulce
(Freshwater Bay)

Aguadulce

Bahía del Suroeste
(Southwest Bay)

Casabaja
(Bottom House)

Bahía Aguamansa
(Smooth Water Bay)

Bahía Manzanillo
(Manchineel Bay)

Punta Negra
(Black Point)

N

1 km
1 mile

centre or 1-hr walk. Suroeste is a 20-min walk from Agua Dulce.

The **Decameron** group (www.decameron.co), represents 5 properties on the island, including **Cabañas Miss Elma** (T8-514 8229), which also has a good restaurant.

$$$ Posada del Mar
Aguadulce, T8-514 8168, www.decameron.co.
Pink and purple clapboard house with comfortable rooms, each with a terrace and hammock facing the sea, hot water, pool, great service. Recommended.

$$$ Sol Caribe Providencia
Agua Dulce, www.solarhoteles.com.
Chain hotel with 2- to 5-night deals, pool, sea views, a/c, TV, fridge, bright.

$$$-$$ Sirius
Suroeste, T8-514 8213, www.siriushotel.net.
Large, colourful house set back from the beach. Large, light rooms, some with balconies, on the beach. Also dive centre, kayaks, wakeboarding, horse riding, massage. The owner speaks German, Italian and English. Half-board and diving packages available.

$$ Old Providence
Diagonal Alcaldía Municipal, Santa Isabel (centre), T318-788 0099, Facebook: Hotel-Old-Providence.
Above supermarket **Erika**, rooms are basic but clean with a/c and TV.

Restaurants

Typical dish is *rondón*, a mix of fish, conch, yuca and dumplings, cooked in coconut milk. Fish and crab are most common. Corn ice cream is also popular – it tastes a bit like vanilla but a little sweeter.

$$ Café Studio
Between Agua Dulce and Suroeste.
Great pies and spaghetti.

$$ Caribbean Place (Donde Martín)
Aguadulce, T311-287 7238.
Bogoteño chef Martín Quintero uses local ingredients.

$$ Roland's Roots bar
Playa Manzanillo, T8-514 8417, rolandsbeach@hotmail.com.
Parties at Roland's bar-restaurant are legendary. Live reggae music (cover charge US$3.50). The menu is mainly seafood. He also hires tents (**$**).

$ Arturo Newbell
On Suroeste beach, next to Miss Mary.
Palm-thatched shack right on the beach, highly recommended for its fish soup, lobster and other seafood.

Festivals

Late Jun Carnival.

What to do

Diving
Recommended diving spots on the Old McBean Lagoon reef are **Manta's Place**, a good place to see manta rays; **Felipe's Place**, where there is a submerged figure of Christ; and **Stairway to Heaven**, which has a large wall of coral and big fish.
Felipe Diving, *South West Bay, T8-514 8775, www.felipediving.com.* Mini and full courses with experienced instructors, also rents snorkel equipment, can arrange lodging. Owner Felipe Cabeza even has a diving spot on the reef named after him. Warmly recommended.
See also **Hotel Sirius**, above. PADI qualifications, mini courses.

Snorkelling and boat trips

Recommended snorkelling sites include the waters around **Santa Catalina**, where there are many caves to explore as well as **Morgan's Head** and lots of starfish; **Hippie's Place**, which has a little bit of everything; and **El Faro** (The Lighthouse), the end of the reef before it drops into deep sea.

Tour operators

Cabañas Agua Dulce, *Aguadulce, T8-514 8160, http://cabanasaguadulce.com.* Owner Jennifer Archbold organizes boat tours of the island and snorkelling, fishing and hiking trips, currency exchange, accommodation and more.

Walking

A good 1.5-km walk over Manchineel Hill, between Bottom House (Casa Baja) and South West Bay, through tropical forest, fine views, many types of bird, iguanas and blue lizards.

Transport

Air

Satena flies from San Andrés 3 times a day, US$90, also **Searca**, a charter airline, www.searca.com.co. Bookable only in San Andrés. Essential to confirm flights to guarantee a seat. Schedules change frequently. Taxi from airport to centre, US$10 (fixed).

Boat

Catamaran Sensation, www.catamaranelsensation.inf.travel, T310-222 5403, sails Mon, Wed, Thu, Fri, Sun 0800, returning at 1430, US$53 one way, US$100 return, 4 hrs. Cargo boat trips leave from San Andrés, taking 4 uncomfortable hrs, 3 times a week, US$65 return. They usually leave at 0600-0700. *Miss Isabel, Doña Olga* and *Raziman* make the trip regularly, about US$18 one way. Speak directly to the captain at the port in San Andrés, or enquire at the Port Authority (Capitanía del Puerto) in San Luis.

Motoped hire

US$40 per day from many hotels. No licence or deposit needed. Golf buggies are safer, and are also available for US$40-60 per day.

Medellín & west of Bogotá

an intoxicating mixture of diverse landscapes and people

Paisas, as people from Antioquia are known, are enterprising individuals, who have made this corner of Colombia the country's industrial heartland. They are known for their distinctive accent, gregarious nature and generous hospitality.

Their boundless optimism has seen Medellín, for so long associated with drugs and violence, undergo an extraordinary transformation into a city buzzing with new ideas, art and culture. Outside Medellín are delightful *paisa* villages, such as Santa Fe de Antioquia.

To the west, the department of Chocó could not be more different. This area's relentless rainfall and dense jungles have hampered attempts to build any significant roads, and, as a result, it is one of the poorest places economically but one of the richest culturally. The population is proud of its African heritage and distinctive music. Bahía Solano and Nuquí boast beautiful, untouched beaches, as well as a chance to see one of the great whale migrations.

South of Medellín, the Zona Cafetera is Colombia's main coffee-producing region. Surrounding the three main cities – Manizales, Pereira and Armenia – are delightful fincas, pretty villages, banana groves and coffee plantations. Moreover, the icy peaks of Los Nevados, the wax palms of the Valle de Cocora, and the birdlife at the Río Blanco reserve make this an excellent destination for nature lovers.

Best for
Coffee ▪ Landscapes ▪ Wildlife

Footprint
picks

⭐ **Nightlife in Medellín**, page 201
Learn to dance the tango in a back-street bar.

⭐ **Medellín's Flower Festival**, page 202
Soak up the sights and smells of this extraordinary floral event.

⭐ **Metrocable**, page 205
Ride Medellín's cable cars and discover their effect on the social
fabric of the city.

⭐ **El Peñol**, page 206
Climb the monolithic rock.

⭐ **Whale watching**, page 215
See humpback whales off the Pacific coast.

⭐ **Zona Cafetera**, page 219
Stay on a coffee finca to learn about Colombia's black gold.

⭐ **Los Nevados**, page 222
Trek among snow-covered volcanic peaks.

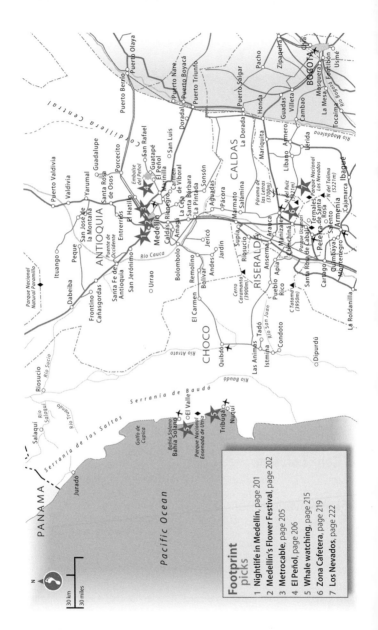

Footprint picks

1 Nightlife in Medellín, page 201
2 Medellín's Flower Festival, page 202
3 Metrocable, page 205
4 El Peñol, page 206
5 Whale watching, page 215
6 Zona Cafetera, page 219
7 Los Nevados, page 222

Medellín
& around

Encompassing the cordilleras Central and Occidental, Antioquia is the largest of the western departments. It is an important agricultural and commercial region, with the rejuvenated city of Medellín as its urban hub. The people of Antioquia are called 'paisas'.

modern art, tango clubs and cable cars

Medellín (population 2,700,000), capital of Antioquia, is considered by many to be the engine of Colombia; *paisas* are known for their canny business sense as well as their hospitality. Previously the home and headquarters of notorious narco-trafficker Pablo Escobar, Medellín has, since his death, shaken off its association with drugs and violence in what is one of the most remarkable turnarounds in Latin America. It is now a fresh, vibrant, prosperous city known for its progressive social politics and culture. In the centre, few colonial buildings remain, but many large new buildings incorporate modern works of art. Music, arts and gastronomy festivals attract many visitors, and the flower festival, the Feria de las Flores, in August, is the most spectacular parade in Colombia.

Central Medellín
Plaza Botero (or de las Esculturas) is dotted with 23 bronze sculptures by **Fernando Botero**, Colombia's leading contemporary artist, who was born in Medellín in 1932. One side of the plaza has **El Palacio de la Cultura Rafael Uribe**, formerly the governor's office, which is now a cultural centre and art gallery (free entry). Across the square is the **Museo de Antioquia** ⓘ *Cra 52, No 52-43, T4-251 3636, www.museodeantioquia.co, Mon-Sat 1000-1730, Sun and holidays, 1000-1630, US$6, metro stop: Parque Berrío*, which has well-displayed works by contemporary Colombian artists, including a large collection by Botero. More works by Botero can be seen in **Parque San Antonio** ⓘ *between C 44/46 and Cra 46*, including the 'Torso Masculino' (which complements the female version in Parque Berrío), and the 'Bird of Peace' which was severely damaged by a guerrilla bomb in 1996. At Botero's request, it has been left unrepaired as a symbol of the futility of violence, with a new sculpture placed alongside. Parque Berrío has the church of the Señora

Essential Medellín

Finding your feet

Note that maps of the city are not generally available in shops; try the tourist office or the **Instituto Geográfico Agustín Codazzi** in the basement of the Fundación Ferrocarril building, Carrera 52, No 42-43, T4-381 0561, www.igac.gov.co, Monday-Friday 0730-1545.

Streets

Medellín's central streets have names as well as numbers. Our maps show both numbers and names, but in addresses we give the Calle (C) and Carrera (Cra) numbers only for easy reference. Particularly important are: Carrera 46, part of the inner ring road, which has several names but is known popularly as 'Avenida Oriental'; Carrera 80/Carrera 81/Diagonal 79, the outer ring road to the west, which is called 'La Ochenta' throughout; Calle 51/52, east of the centre is 'La Playa'; and Calle 33, which crosses the Río Medellín to become Calle 37, is still called 'La Treinta y Tres'.

Getting around

The best way to get around the city is by metro, which serves the three main sectors of Medellín: centre, south and west. It is efficient and safe; most of the track in the centre is elevated and none of it is underground, so you can get a good overview of the city. A single ticket, US$1 is valid for the whole network, including the three Metrocable (cable car) lines. Town bus services are marginally cheaper and are smart and comfortable, but slower because of the volume of traffic. *Colectivos* operate on certain main routes, US$0.75-0.80. There are plenty of taxis. Pasaje Junín (Carrera 49) is pedestrianized from Parque de Bolívar to Parque San Antonio (Calle 46). This gives walkers pleasant relief from traffic in the busy heart of the city. If driving in Medellín, check for rules that restrict the use of hire cars.

When to go

Known as 'The City of Eternal Spring', Medellín has a pleasant, temperate climate: warm during the day and cool in the evening. It is often cloudy, however, and rain can come at any time over the Cauca Valley from Chocó, which is only 100 km to the west. The city's festivals draw many visitors from the rest of Colombia and abroad.

Time required

Three to four days is enough to see the best of the city and its surroundings.

Weather Medellín

January 26°C 17°C 50mm	**February** 26°C 18°C 60mm	**March** 26°C 18°C 100mm
April 26°C 18°C 180mm	**May** 26°C 18°C 190mm	**June** 26°C 18°C 130mm
July 26°C 17°C 110mm	**August** 26°C 17°C 130mm	**September** 26°C 17°C 150mm
October 25°C 17°C 200mm	**November** 25°C 17°C 140mm	**December** 25°C 17°C 80mm

BACKGROUND
Medellín

Though the Valle de Aburrá was discovered early on by the Spaniards (1541), there were few settlements here until early in the 17th century. The town is thought to have been founded in 1616 as 'San Lorenzo de Aburrá', on the site of what is now El Poblado. It was given the official title of town (*villa*) in 1675 by Queen Mariana of Austria and named after Don Pedro Portocarrero y Luna, Count of Medellín. The town established itself around the Basílica de La Candelaria (now known as the Old Cathedral), which was built at the end of the 17th century. Medellín was declared a city in 1813 and in 1826 became the capital of Antioquia.

The industrialization of Medellín followed the coffee boom. The first looms arrived in 1902, and the textile industry remains an integral part of Medellín and a major export to this day. Other major local industries are brick-making, leather goods and plastics. There has been limited immigration from overseas since the original settlement, but the natural growth in population has been extraordinary. A positive manifestation of this rapid expansion is the fine metro system, which connects all areas of the city including cable cars and escalators up to the isolated hillside barrios (see the Metrocable, page 205).

de la Candelaria on one side, formerly the city's cathedral. It was succeeded by the **Catedral Metropolitana** on Parque Bolívar. Built between 1875 and 1931, this is claimed to be the third-largest brick building in the world. Parque Bolívar has flowering trees and a fountain display. The **Mercado San Alejo** is held here on the first Saturday of every month (except January), selling handicrafts at good prices. Of the colonial churches near the centre, white **La Veracruz** ① *C 51, No 52-58, T4-512 5095, Mon-Sat 0730-1800, Sun Mass 0830-1000, 1200-1600*, is a national historical monument.

North of the centre

To the north, near the University of Antioquia campus, is the **Jardín Botánico de Medellín** ① *C 73, No 51D-14, T4-444 5500, www.botanicomedellin.org, daily 0900-1630, free, Metro Universidad,* the botanical gardens, with 5500 species of plant, orchid and trees, also a butterfly house. It's a beautiful and peaceful place, perfect for getting away from the noise of the city. There are two restaurants, one more economical than the other, a café and facilities for children. Opposite the botanical gardens is the **Parque Explora** ① *Cra 52, No 73-75, T4-516 8300, www.parque explora.org, Tue-Fri 0830-1730 (ticket office closes 1600), Sat, Sun and holiday Mondays, 1000-1830 (ticket office closes 1700), US$8,* a science and technology museum plus associated aquarium, planetarium (entry US$5, www.planetariomedellin.org) and other spaces. With more than 300 interactive scientific puzzles and games, this is fun for adults and heaven for kids. Nearby is **Museo Casa Gardeliana** ① *Cra 45, No 76-50, T4-444 2633, Mon-Sat 0900-1700, shows last Fri of month 1800-2200* *(free entry, donations welcome)*, commemorating the tango legend Carlos Gardel, who died in a plane crash in Medellín in 1935.

West of the centre

The **Museo de Arte Moderno** ⓘ *Cra 44N, No 19A-100, T4-444 2622, www.elmamm. org, Tue-Fri 0900-1800, Sat 1000-1800, Sun 1000-1700, US$3.50, children, students*

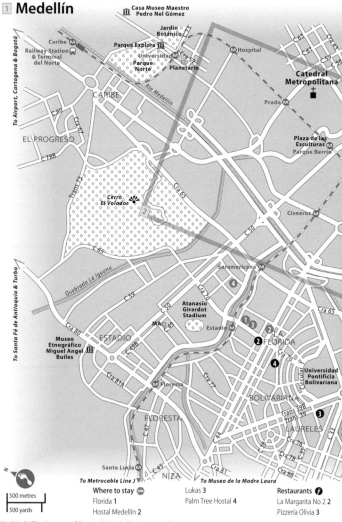

1 Medellín

Casa Museo Maestro Pedro Nel Gómez

Jardín Botánico

Caribe Ⓜ

Parque Explora 🏛

Railway Station & Terminal del Norte

Universidad Ⓜ

Parque Norte

Planetario

Ⓜ Hospital

To Airport, Cartagena & Bogotá

Río Medellín

CARIBE

Catedral Metropolitana ✝

Prado Ⓜ

EL PROGRESO

C 80

Cra 67

C 78B

Trans 78

Plaza de las Esculturas Ⓜ
Parque Berrío

Cerro El Volador

Cra 65

C 50

Cisneros Ⓜ

C 65

Quebrada La Iguana

C 59

Suramericana Ⓜ

Cra 70

To Santa Fé de Antioquia & Turbo

Cra 80

Atanasio Girardot Stadium

MAM 🏛

Estadio Ⓜ

1 3
2

LA FLORIDA

Cra 65

Museo Etnográfico Miguel Angel Builes 🏛

ESTADIO

C 49B

Cra 77

4

Universidad Pontificia Bolivariana

Cra 81A

Floresta

BOLIVARIANA

3

Trans 39B
Trans 39

FLORESTA

Cra 44

Circular

LAURELES

Cra 76

C 45

C 38

Santa Lucía Ⓜ

Cra 81

Cra 78

Cra 80

NIZA

To Metrocable Line J ▼

To Museo de la Madre Laura

N

500 metres
500 yards

Where to stay 🛏
Florida 1
Hostal Medellín 2

Lukas 3
Palm Tree Hostal 4

Restaurants 🍴
La Margarita No 2 2
Pizzería Olivia 3

with card and seniors US$2.50, has a small collection and a variety of special visits, it also shows films, and holds many events at other locations. The **Biblioteca Pública Piloto para América Latina** ⓘ *Cra 64, No 50-32, T4-460 0590, entrance at Cra 64 y C 52, www.bibliotecapiloto.gov.co, Mon-Sat 0830-1730,* is one of the best public libraries in the country, with art and photo exhibitions, readings and

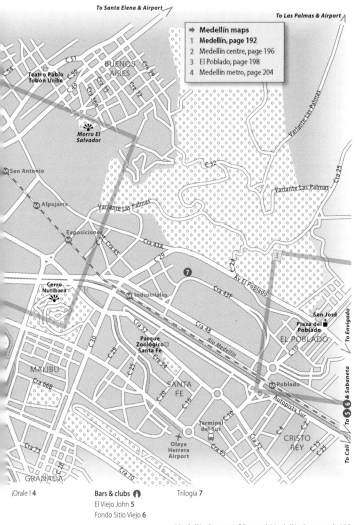

To Santa Elena & Airport

To Las Palmas & Airport

➡ **Medellín maps**
1 **Medellín, page 192**
2 Medellín centre, page 196
3 El Poblado, page 198
4 Medellín metro, page 204

Teatro Pablo
Tobón Uribe

BUENOS
AIRES

Morro El
Salvador

Ⓜ San Antonio

Ⓜ Alpujarra

Variante Las Palmas

Exposiciones

Cerro
Nutibara

Ⓜ Industriales

Av El Poblado

San José
Plaza del
Poblado

MALIBU

Parque
Zoológico
Santa Fe

EL POBLADO

To Envigado

SANTA
FE

Ⓜ Poblado

To 5 6 Sabaneta

Autopista Sur

Terminal
del Sur

CRISTO
REY

Olaya
Herrera
Airport

To Cali

GRANADA

¡Orale ! **4**

Bars & clubs 🎧
El Viejo John **5**
Fondo Sitio Viejo **6**

Trilogía **7**

ON THE ROAD
Pablo Escobar

Pablo Emilio Escobar Gaviria, Colombia's most notorious outlaw, was born in 1949 into a middle-class family in the Antioquian town of Rionegro. He began his criminal career allegedly stealing and re-selling tombstones. He progressed to car crime and then muscled his way into the drug business, eventually becoming the head of the most powerful drug cartel in the world. His trademark technique for dealing with the authorities became known as plata o plomo (cash or lead); any judge or official who refused his bribes was shot. By 1989, his lucrative drug organization afforded Escobar boats, planes, banks and properties throughout the world. *Forbes Magazine* listed him as the seventh richest man on the planet, with an estimated fortune of US$30 billion a year.

Despite his brutal methods, he was incredibly popular. He actively cultivated an image as the '*paisa* Robin Hood', raising money to build roads and even a housing development for the poor, known as Barrio Pablo Escobar. At the height of his popularity he successfully ran for Congress. But Escobar's forays into public life also brought attention to his nefarious activities. Following the assassination of presidential candidate Luis Carlos Galán (in which Escobar is believed to have been involved), President César Gaviria ordered his arrest. He went on the run for several years, before he eventually tired and negotiated very favourable terms of surrender.

He was allowed to design a luxurious new prison that was built for him outside Medellín, but when the government eventually tried to transfer him to a 'real' prison he slipped through the cordon of an entire army batallion and evaded arrest for a further 18 months. His business empire began to crumble, however, when a vigilante group known as Los Pepes (Los Perseguidos por Pablo Escobar – People Persecuted by Pablo Escobar) turned his own violent tactics against him: 300 of his business associates were assassinated, severely hampering his cash flow. He was eventually tracked down and shot dead by special forces in December 1993 while attempting to escape across the rooftops of a Medellín suburb.

During his three-decade career he is believed to have been responsible for the death of more than 4000 people, including 30 judges and 457 policemen. Today, however, despite the ubiquity of Escobar T-shirts in souvenir shops, many Colombians are tiring of constant reminders of this bloodthirsty figure from their past, and are keener to show their country as a transformed place of peace and progress.

films. **Puntocero** ⓘ *at the C 67 river bridge*, is an elegant steel double arch with a pendulum marking the centre of the city.

In Alpujarra district, southwest of the centre is **El Edificio Inteligente** ⓘ *Cra 58, No 42-125*, a highly energy-efficient building used jointly by Medellín's public services. Nearby is the **Parque de Los Pies Descalzos** (Barefoot Park), a relaxing

ON THE ROAD

Fernando Botero

If you visit Medellín, you'll be hard pushed to miss the enormous sculptures adorning several parts of the city, including one of the main squares, known as Plaza Botero. These imposing works were created by local-born Fernando Botero, one of Latin America's best-known living artists. Botero, who has spent many years living abroad, donated these works to the city of Medellín, perhaps, one might guess, because he found them too difficult to pack on his departure. His striking rotund figures tower impressively over the viewer in Botero's own characteristic style: disproportionately large, bulbous and voluptuous. Despite first leaving the country in 1952 and spending most of his time in Paris, Botero returns to his roots every year, spending a month in his native Colombia. His works have been exhibited worldwide, from Tokyo and New York, to Mexico, Athens, Armenia and Singapore. Besides Medellín, the Museo Botero in Bogotá (see page 46) has more than 120 of his artworks, including some of his more controversial paintings, such as those depicting torture victims in Abu-Ghraib, Iraq.

space with cafés, sandpits, Zen garden and fountains. Also here is the interactive **Museo del Agua EPM** ⓘ *Cra 57, No 42-139, T4-380 6966, www.epm.com.co, Tue-Fri 0830-1730, Sat-Sun, 1030-1830, US$2.50.*

As you ride the metro you will notice two prominent hills in the Aburrá valley. **Cerro Nutibara** ⓘ *C 30A y Cra 55, T4-235 8370,* in the southwest, has good views over the city. There is a stage for open-air concerts, a sculpture park, a miniature Antioquian village (known as **Pueblito Paisa**), souvenir and crafts shops and restaurants. **Cerro El Volador** (seen as the metro turns between Universidad and Caribe stations) is tree-covered and the site of an important indigenous burial ground.

Listings Medellín *maps pages 192, 196, 198 and 204.*

Tourist information

Information booth
Plaza Botero, Cra 51, No 52A-48, T4-511 1309, http://infolocal.comfenalco antioquia.com. Mon-Sat 0900-1700. English, French and Spanish spoken, very helpful staff.

Oficina de Turismo de Medellín
C 41, No 55-80, of 306, in the Centro de Convenciones, T4-261 7277, www.medellin.travel.

For information on the city. Helpful staff, English spoken. Has kiosks (PITs) at both **airports**, both **bus terminals**, at the **Pueblito Paisa** at the top of Cerro Nutibara, open daily, the **Arví cablecar station** (El Tambo) and in the main hall of **Plaza Mayor** (less regular hours).

Other sources of information include the **Subsecretaría de Turismo** (C 53A, No 42-101, p 11, Ala B, T4-385 6966, www.guiaturisticademedellin.com);

and the **National Parks office** (C 49, No 78A-67, T4-422 0883). The **tourist police** can be contacted on T4-265 5907 or, 4-437 6125.

Most of the city's better accommodation options are around Cra 70 and in El Poblado.

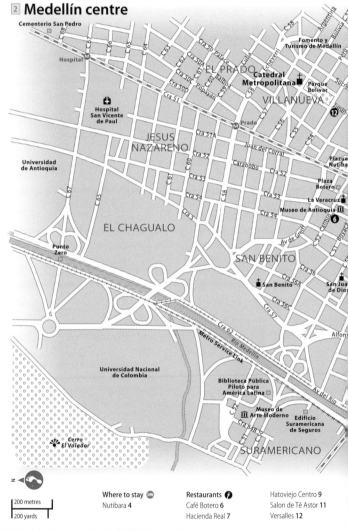

2 **Medellín centre**

Cementerio San Pedro

Hospital

Fomento y Turismo de Medellín

EL PRADO

Catedral Metropolitana

Parque Bolívar

VILLANUEVA

Hospital San Vicente de Paul

JESUS NAZARENO

Juan del Corral

Carabobo

Universidad de Antioquia

Prado

Plazuela Nutibara

Plaza Botero

La Veracruz

Museo de Antioquia 6

EL CHAGUALO

Punto Zero

Av de Greiff

SAN BENITO

San Benito

San Jua de Dios

Río Medellín

Metro Service Link

Alfons

Universidad Nacional de Colombia

Biblioteca Pública Piloto para América Latina

Av del Río

Museo de Arte Moderno

Edificio Suramericana de Seguros

Cerro El Volador

SURAMERICANO

200 metres
200 yards

Where to stay 🛏	Restaurants 🍴	Hatoviejo Centro **9**
Nutibara **4**	Café Botero **6**	Salon de Té Astor **11**
	Hacienda Real **7**	Versalles **12**

Central Medellín

Many of the cheaper hostels in this part of town are now *acostaderos* or pay-by-the-hour brothels with questionable security that we advise you to avoid.

$$$ Nutibara

C 52A, No 50-46, T4-511 5111, www.hotelnutibara.com).

This grand old lady of Medellín was the city's 1st major hotel, built in 1945. Its

Medellín maps
1 Medellín, page 192
2 **Medellín centre, page 196**
3 El Poblado, page 198
4 Medellín metro, page 204

Bars & clubs
La Boa **13**
La Papayera **14**

Salón Málaga **15**

best days may be behind it, but it retains a certain art deco charm, has all modern amenities, including a pool, sauna, Turkish bath, a food court with banks and Wi-Fi zone on the 1st floor and a wine bar in the tunnel that connected with the old Residencias Nutibara.

West of the centre
Cra 70 (Metro Estadio) is full of hotels in roughly the same price range. Although standards can vary they are good value. There are plenty of eateries, bars and discos as well.

El Poblado

➡ **Medellín maps**
1 Medellín, page 192
2 Medellín centre, page 196
3 **El Poblado, page 198**
4 Medellín metro, page 204

$$$-$$ Florida
Cra 70, No 44B-38, T4-260 4900, www.hotelfloridamedellin.com.
A bit more upmarket than others, well-equipped business-like rooms, with desk, a/c and cable TV, car park and restaurant.

$$ Lukas
Cra 70, No 44A-28, T4-260 1761, www.lukashotel.com.
Crisp rooms with safe and all facilities, weekend and long-stay rates available.

$ Hostal Medellín
C 44B, No 69-13, T4-260 0660, www.hostalmedellin.com.
Spacious hostel, private rooms and dorms (US$8.50), German/Colombian-run, popular with bikers. Garden with a hammock, pool table, organizes tours, close to Metro Estadio. Recommended.

$ Palm Tree Hostal
Cra 67, No 48D-63, T4-444 7256, www.hostalenmedellin.com. (Metro Suramericana, behind Exito supermarket on C 50).
Good backpackers' hostel, bike hire, book exchange and hammocks. Private rooms and dorms, free barbecue on Fri, dance classes on Mon.

El Poblado and around
There are many luxury and business-class hotels in El Poblado, such as **Diez** (C 10A, No 34-11, www.diezhotel.com) and the boutique-style **Art** (Cra 41, No 9-31, T4-369 7900, www.arthotel. com.co). Also many more hostels than we can list here.

$$$$ Estelar Milla de Oro
C3 Sur No 43A, T4-369 6300, www.estelarmilladeoro.com.
Tucked away in a quiet corner of El Poblado, this towering modern hotel has luxuriously appointed rooms with

all mod cons, amazing views from upper floors, excellent restaurant, including buffet breakfast, plus gym, sauna, spa and solarium terrace, business centre with PCs available. Highly recommended.

$$ La Habana Vieja
C 10 Sur 43A-7, T4: 321 2557, www. *hotellahabanaviejamedellin.com.*
This is probably the only colonial-style hotel in Medellín, with bags of homely charm and character, despite being dwarfed by surrounding modern towers and flyovers (some traffic noise at the front); cosy and quaintly old-fashioned rooms, comfy lounges with kitsch artwork; very friendly and helpful staff, good breakfast, about 10 mins' walk from Metro Aguacatala. Highly recommended.

$$-$ Black Sheep Hostel
Transversal 5A, No 45-133 (tell taxi drivers it's in Patio Bonito), T4-311 1589, T317-518 1369, www.blacksheepmedellin.com.
Run by welcoming Kiwi, Kelvin, homely feel, well organized, private rooms and dorms (US$10.50-12.50 pp), TV areas, popular weekly barbecue, washing machine, excellent service, Spanish lessons arranged. Information on paragliding. Recommended.

$$-$ Casa Blanca
Transversal 5A, No 45-256 *(Patio Bonito), T4-586 5149,* *www.casablancamedellin.com.*
Large hostel with dorms (US$8-10) and private rooms, quiet location, parking for cars or motorbikes, pool table, table tennis.

$$-$ Pitstop Hostel
Cra 43E, No5-110, T4-352 1176, *www.pitstophostel.com.*
A big hostel with party atmosphere, swimming pool, Irish bar, steam room,

gym, pool table and a huge outdoor area. Dorms US$9-11 pp, private rooms with and without bath for up to 4 people. Tours and events organized.

$ Casa Kiwi
Cra 36, No 7-10, T4-268 2668, *www.casakiwihostel.com.*
Private rooms with fan and safe, and dorms, US$10 pp. Good travellers' hostel, hammock terrace, roof-top pool, bar and TV room with theatre seating. Near Parque Lleras but on a quiet street, welcoming, paragliding and many other activities and tours arranged, good breakfast (US$3). Recommended.

$ Tiger Hostel
Cra 36, No 10-49, T4-311 6079, *www.tigerpawmedellin.com.*
A variety of rooms, some with bath, dorms US$8-9, remodelled in 2016, tourist packages, sports bar with microbrews and lots of activities.

Restaurants

Central Medellín

$$ Café Botero
Cra 52, No 52-43.
Excellent lunchtime venue in the Museo de Antioquia building. Fish, fine steaks and delicious puddings.

$$ Hacienda Real
Cra 49, No 52-98 (next door to *Salón de Té Astor).*
Pleasant restaurant with balcony seating, overlooking Pasaje Junín/Cra 49.

$$ Versalles
Pasaje Junín, No 53-59, T4-511-9146, *http://versallesmedellin.com.*
Famous Argentine-run *pastelería* and restaurant, with long-standing link to the city's bohemian set, as portrayed in black-and-white photos lining the

walls. Good-value set lunches, *parrillas* and *empanadas*, lovely coffees and breakfasts too. The cool upstairs room offers a peaceful retreat from the hubbub of the shopping street below. Highly recommended.

$$-$ El Unión Centro Comercial
Cra 49 (Junín), No 52-107, www. elunioncentrocomercial.com.
Many eateries on the **Balcón de Comidas** of this shopping mall, including **San Miguel Cazuelas**, for typical dishes; **Bistro Gourmet**, for French traditional cuisine, cakes and snacks; **Latin Coffee**, for combos, crêpes and sandwiches; all do breakfasts.

$$-$ Salón de Té Astor
Cra 49, No 52-84, www.elastor.com.
Delightful traditional tea and pastry house, famous for its chocolate delicacies, ice cream, and animal-themed *moros*, fondant fancies – the frog cake is delicious!

West of the centre
Several eateries on Cra 70, No 45E block, all serving *bandeja paisa* (**$$$**) and other cheaper lunches.

$$ La Margarita No 2
Cra 70, No 45E-11.
Antioquian dishes in a lively, friendly atmosphere.

$$ Pizzería Olivia
Cra 74B, No 39-46, Laureles, T4-250 7785, http://pizzeriaolivia.co.
Thin and crispy fresh-baked pizzas, pasta and main-course salads in this bustling Italian restaurant, attracting trendy young local crowd, with airy patio for people-watching. Several other branches around town, very good.

$ ¡Orale!
C 41, No 70-138.
Excellent little Mexican *cantina* with tables on the street. Another branch at Cra 43B, 10A-49, El Poblado, does Mexican and pizza. Recommended.

El Poblado and around
In Parque Lleras/Zona Rosa, there are so many places that it is impossible to mention them all. Those we do list have been found to be good, but recommendations change as places become fashionable. Just wander around and see what takes your fancy, but at weekends especially, don't leave it too late as places get very busy, with queues for tables.

$$$ Hatoviejo Las Palmas
C 16, No 28-60, opposite Hotel Intercontinental, T4-268 6811, http://hatoviejo.com.
Serving upmarket *paisa* cuisine in a giant thatch-roofed *cabaña* for 30+ years. Specialities include *bandeja paisa*, *mondongo*, *ajiaco* and *sancocho*, huge portions with equally tasty side dishes (such as coconut rice). Superb food, lively buzz and impeccable service, highly recommended, with several other branches around the city, including **Hatoviejo Centro**, Cra 47, No 52-17.

$$$ Triada
Cra 38, No 8 (Vía Primavera)-03, T4-311 5781.
Enormous restaurant/bar/club in the heart of the Zona Rosa, steaks, sushi, salads and Tex Mex, good atmosphere. Packed at weekends.

$$$-$$ Verdeo
Parque Explora, Cra 35, No 8A-3, T4-444 0934, www.ricoverdeo.com.

Excellent vegetarian on a pedestrian alley, open from 1200 daily (closes 1600 on Mon and holidays).

$$ Kuelap
C3 Sur 43A – 40 Milla de Oro, T574-311 5043/45.
Cosy and chic little Peruvian restaurant, down a (rare) quiet side street in Poblado, near the **Estelar Milla de Oro** hotel; not cheap but authentic Peruvian cuisine, including ceviche, *causa* and *chaufa* rice dishes, plus South American wines and cocktails.

$$ Le Bon
C 9, No 39-09, T57-266 7790.
French café with lovely atmosphere. Often has jazz in the evening.

$$-$ Poke Bowl
C34, No 7-43A, T574-499 8051, Facebook: Poke Bowl – Colombia.
Pick and mix Hawaiian sushi with rice, noodles and quinoa in this funky little café a few blocks above Parque Lleras; approximately US$9 for 2 protein dishes (ie meat and fish), or US$7 for 1; delicious fresh ingredients, filling and great value for money, takeaway too. Highly recommended.

★ Bars and clubs

In El Poblado, the best bars and clubs are in the Zona Rosa, around Parque Lleras; there are plenty of them. If the Zona Rosa prices get too much, an alternative after-hours location is **Sabaneta** (www.sabaneta.gov.co), 11 km from the centre, with an attractive plaza. It's popular with young and old alike. There are several excellent bars and restaurants with lots of local history. Take the metro to Sabaneta or La Estrella or a taxi

from El Poblado, US$10-15. Also check out Medellín's local brewery, **Tres Cordilleras** (C30 No 44-176, Barrio Colombia, www.3cordilleras.com, T4-444 2337), tours Thu 1730-2100, US$8, Fri 1830-2300, US$11, both including 5 free beers.

El Viejo John
Cra 45, No 70 Sur-42, Sabaneta, T4-288 7022.
A popular local spot with strings of chorizo hanging from the ceiling. Also serves typical dishes.

Fonda Sitio Viejo
C 70 Sur, No 44-25, Sabaneta, T4-288 1170.
Another bar full of character. This one has photographs of every church in Medellín.

La Papayera
C 53, No 42-55, Centro, T4-239 3400.
A local institution for salsa, popular with foreigners. Live salsa on Tue and Thu nights.

Trilogía
Cra 43G, No 24-08, Barrio San Diego, T4-204 0562/321-803 5387.
This long-standing bar attracts an older crowd, with resident live cover band playing a mix of rock and latino pop. Arrive before 2230 on Fri, Sat (also open Thu and Sun).

Entertainment

Cinema
Check the press for movies, music, theatre and other cultural events. **Centro Colombo Americano**, *Cra 45, No 53-24, T4-204 0404, www.colombo world.com*. Shows foreign art films, also holds cultural events, has a café and bookshop. The main malls have multiplexes.

Tango

Medellín is famous in Colombia for its love of tango. There are popular tango bars in El Envigado.

La Boa, *C 53, No 43-59, T4-239 3580*. This bar has been around for more than 40 years and is famous for its tango and jazz, open nightly until 0300.
Salón Málaga, *Cra 51, No 45-80, T4-231 2658, www.salonmalaga.com*. One of Medellín's oldest tango bars.

Theatre

Teatro Metropolitano, *C 41, No 57-30, T4-232 2858, www.teatrometropolitano. com*. Major artistic presentations, from classical concerts to modern dance.

★ Festivals

Mar/Apr Semana Santa (Holy Week) is celebrated with religious parades.
Jun Festival Internacional de Tango.
Jul International Poetry Festival, see www.festivaldepoesiademedellin.org.
1st week of Aug Flower Festival (Feria de las Flores/Desfile de Silleteros) (www.feriadelasfloresmedellin.gov.co) is held annually with spectacular parades and music, one of the finest shows in Colombia.
End Aug Otro Sabor gastronomy festival.
Sep-Nov International Jazz and World Music Festival, www.festivalmedejazz.com.

Expoartesano, held in the Plaza Mayor exhibition centre, is an annual handicrafts exhibition, http://artesanias decolombia.com.co; its date changes each year. There are many other music and cultural festivals throughout the year.

What to do

City tours

Comuna 13, *T311-347 3131, Facebook: LaCasaKolacho*. Walking tours, led by locals, of the formerly crime-ridden Comuna 13 hillside barrio, which has been transformed into a thriving neighbourhood. Its gleaming new escalators whisk residents down to the city centre, and bring visitors up to its winding streets, brightly painted with graffiti murals, providing amazing views over the city. Highly recommended.
Real City Tours, *www.realcitytours.com*. 4-hr walking tours in English. A great way to learn about the city and its history, culture and the *paisa* residents. Tours start from Poblado or Alpujarra metro stations, Mon-Fri, times vary. Insightful, enthusiastic and knowledgeable guides, booking is essential as numbers are strictly limited (don't be late as places are then given away), free (pay by tip), highly recommended. They also run an **Exotic Fruits** tour, visiting a market and tasting some of the produce (US$17). Recommended.

Dance classes

Academia Dance, *Cra 46, No 10 Sur-36, T4-444 8582/3*. Offers many dance lessons, including salsa, merengue and rumba.

Language classes

Eafit University, *Cra 49, No 7 Sur 50, Av Las Vegas, T4-261 9500, www.eafit.edu.co*. Popular, well-organized Spanish courses.

Sports complex

Estadio Atanasio Girardot, *Cras 70-73, C 48-50, T304-375 7149*. Football, baseball, velodrome, swimming, next to Metro Estadio. Just outside the station is **EnCicla** bicycle hire (www.encicla.gov.co).

Tour operators

Destino Colombia, *C 50, No 65-42, CC Contemporáneo, local 225, T4-260 6868, www.destinocolombia.com*. Tours to nearby attractions in Antioquia and nationwide. Very well-informed English-speaking guides. Can also arrange flights. Recommended.

Transport

Air

José María Córdova international airport (T4-444 2818, www.airplan.aero, also called Rionegro) is 28 km, 40 mins, from Medellín by road and 9 km from the town of Rionegro. Taxi to town from US$20-22. *Buseta* to centre, US$4, frequent service from 0330-1800, taking about 1 hr to the San Diego terminal on the small road (Cra 50A/C 53) behind **Hotel Nutibara**. To Rionegro from the airport US$2 bus, US$8 taxi. The airport has good shops and services, but no left luggage. Frequent services to **Bogotá**, **Cartagena** and all major Colombian cities.

Municipal airport: **Enrique Olaya Herrera**, airport information T4-365 6100, www.aeropuertoolayaherrera. gov.co, 10 mins by taxi from the centre, US$5.50, or you can take the metro to Poblado for all but the last 1.5 km. Taxi to/from Rionegro airport US$18. National flights only including to **Quibdó** (change here for **Nuquí**), **Acandí**, **Capurganá** and major cities.

The terminal for long-distance buses going north and east is **Terminal del Norte** at Cra 64 (Autopista del Norte) y Transversal 78 (Cra 64C, No 78-58), T4-444 8020, about 3 km north of the centre, with shops, cafés, left luggage, ATMs and other facilities. It is well policed. Walkway from Metro Caribe.

Taxi to/from the centre US$7. To/from **Bogotá**, 9-12 hrs, US$18-21, frequent with many companies. To **Cartagena**, 15 hrs, US$41. Same fare to **Barranquilla**, 18 hrs, and to **Santa Marta**. To **Turbo**, US$18-21 with **Gómez Hernández** (the best), 10 hrs. To **Magangué** (for Mompós), US$41, with **Rápido Ochoa**.

Bus

City buses charge US$0.65. *Busetas* charge US$0.70. For buses going south, **Terminal del Sur**, Cra 65, No 8B-91, T444 80 20, or T361 1499, alongside the Olaya Herrera airport. Similar services to Terminal del Norte plus a shopping centre. Take No 143 bus marked 'Terminal del Sur' from C 47 (in front of Edificio del Café) along Cra 46, or metro to Poblado, then a taxi for the remaining 1.5 km to the bus station, US$4 (US$6 to centre). To **Quibdó**, 7-8 hrs, US$23-26, with **Rápido Ochoa**. Frequent buses to **Manizales**, 4-7 hrs US$16-21, including **Empresa Arauca**. To **Pereira**, 6-8 hrs, US$15-22. Frequent buses for **Cali**, **Flota Magdalena** among others, US$19-24, 7-8 hrs. To **Popayán**, US$30-35, 12 hrs, **Flota Magadalena**. To **Ipiales**, US$50, 20 hrs.

Metro and cable car

The city's integrated transport system (metro, cable car, tram and bus detailed at www.metrodemedellin.gov.co) operates Mon-Sat 0430-2300, Sun and hols 0500-2200. A single journey, anywhere on the metro system, is US$0.65; cable car, about US$2. There are 2 metro lines: **A** from Niquía in the north to La Estrella in the south, **B** from San Javier east to San Antonio, where they intersect. A tramway line, **T-A**, continues from San Antonio to

Oriente and 2 rapid-transit bus lines join Parque Aranjuez and Universidad de Medellín, taking different routes around the centre. There are also 5 connecting cable cars, known as Metrocable:

H from Oriente to Villa Sierra; **J** from San Javier to La Aurora; **K** serving the areas on the mountain slopes from Acevedo up to Santo Domingo Savio; and **L** from Santo Domingo further

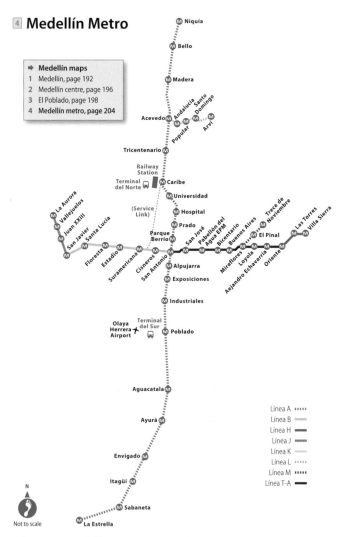

4 Medellín Metro

Niquía
Bello
Madera
Acevedo · Andalucía · Santo Domingo
Popular · Arví
Tricentenario
Railway Station
Terminal del Norte · Caribe
Universidad
(Service Link)
Hospital
La Aurora · Vallejuelos · Juan XXIII · Santa Lucía · San Javier
Prado
Parque Berrío · San José · Pabellón del Agua EPM · Bicentario · Buenos Aires · Trece de Noviembre · Las Torres · Villa Sierra
El Pinal
Floresta · Estadio · Suramericana · Cisneros · San Antonio · Miraflores · Loyola · Aejandro Echavarría · Oriente
Alpujarra
Exposiciones
Industriales
Olaya Herrera Airport · Terminal del Sur · Poblado
Aguacatala
Ayurá
Envigado
Itagüí
Sabaneta
La Estrella

N
Not to scale

Línea A ·····
Línea B ———
Línea H ━━━
Línea J ———
Línea K ———
Línea L ·····
Línea M ·····
Línea T-A ━━━

ON THE ROAD

★ The Metrocable

Medellín's cable car, the Metrocable, has become one of the symbols of this city's remarkable renaissance. It is the first cable car in the world designed primarily as a public transport system, although its success as a tool for social change has made it a popular tourist attraction.

The Metrocable connects the *comuna nororiental* (northeastern area), a slum full of brick and corrugated-iron shack communities constructed haphazardly on the side of the hill, with the metro station at Acevedo. During the 1980s and 1990s this was one of the most notorious slums in Latin America, the *zona de cultivo*, or cultivation area, for drug trafficker Pablo Escobar's army of *sicarios* (assassins).

In terms of transportation, it was a difficult place to leave. Narrow streets clogged with traffic meant that it could take up to two hours to get into town by bus. Back in the 1990s the area was highly segregated, with sectors at war with each other. The bridge between the communities of La Francia and Andalucía, for example, was a no-go area. Today, residents walk freely between the two neighbourhoods over what has been rechristened the 'Bridge of Reconciliation'.

Part of the local government's drive to propagate 'participatory democracy', the Metrocable's aim is to allow the city's very poorest to take an active role in society and to 'de-ghettoize' the area. Commuting time has been reduced to 45 minutes, allowing easier access for those looking for employment in the centre, and it has significantly improved congestion in the area. Most importantly, it has restored a sense of pride to the community.

The Metrocable is just one cog in a movement that has allowed the people of this neighbourhood to reclaim public space from criminals. Other initiatives include the Biblioteca de España, which brings books, computers and spaces for social and artistic activities to one of Latin America s most deprived communities.

The success is measurable. Violent deaths in the neighbourhood fell from 6349 in 1994 to 373 in 2005, while individual living space grew from less than half a square metre to between two and three square metres per person.

The cable car's success is being replicated across Colombia and the region. San Javier metro station, and there are now five cable car lines, to Arví, Trece de Noviembre, and Villa Sierra, in the east of the city. An escalator network also connects Comuna 13, once a no-go barrio, but now hosting popular walking tours of its graffiti-decorated streets (see City tours, page 202). There is even talk of building a connection with the airport in Rionegro. Elsewhere in Colombia, the villages of Guatapé near El Peñol and San Agustín in Huila have expressed an interest in building their own systems.

up the mountains to Arví, a stunning ride high over the treetops (Tue-Sun 0900-1800, closed Mon, or Tue if Mon is a holiday), change at Acevedo on line A for this cable car; and **M** from Miraflores to Trece de Noviembre.

Taxi

Meters are used (though Über-style system is planned for the future); minimum charge US$2.50. **Radio taxis**: **Cootransmede**, T4-265 6565, www.cootransmede.com, **Tax Andaluz**, T4-444 5555, http://taxandaluz.co. Many others. For airport service for up to 8 people, try **Iván Agudelo Gómez**, T313-744 0667, T315-509 9035.

Around Medellín

paisa villages and a very large rock

Southeast from Medellín *Colour map 2, B3-B4.*

Five kilometres from Medellín airport is **Rionegro** in a delightful valley of gardens and orchards. The **Casa de Convención** and the **cathedral** are worth a visit. There are colourful processions in Easter Week. There are various hotels and many places to eat in and near the plaza.

On the Medellín–Bogotá highway is **Marinilla**, 46 km from Medellín. A road north goes 25 km to ★ **El Peñol** ① *US$5*, a precipitous, bullet-shaped rock which towers above the surrounding hills and the Embalse del Peñol reservoir. It has been eroded smooth, but a spiral staircase has been built into a crack from the base to the summit (649 steps). The views from the top are spectacular. At the entrance and summit are snack bars. The rock and the nearby town of **Guatapé** are a popular excursion, especially at weekends. Ask the bus driver to drop you off at the small road leading to El Peñol, from where it's a 10-minute walk uphill to the entrance. Guatapé is 3 km further along the main road. All the houses are cheerfully painted, each with a distinctive frieze. The *malecón* is lined with restaurants and pleasure boats offering tours (US$15-25). There is also a zip-line.

Another popular trip is to **Reserva Natural Cañón del Río Claro** ① *T313-671 4459, www.rioclaroelrefugio.com, daily 0800-2000, free* (see box, page 208), clearly signed on the Medellín–Bogotá highway, 152 km/three hours from either Medellín or Honda. The crystal-clean Claro river is lined with limestone cliffs and is a beautiful, tranquil place to relax and take leisurely walks along its banks. The reserve is noted for its incredible biodiversity with over 50 new species of plant discovered and more than 370 different species of bird identified since its foundation. Oilbirds live in the caves. Take an early bus, from Terminal del Norte, spend a day and a night at the reserve and continue to Honda the next day (or vice versa). Accommodation is available ($$$-$$ full board).

South from Medellín *Colour map 2, B3.*

Santa Bárbara lies 57 km south of Medellín on the main road via the town of Caldas, with stunning views in every direction of coffee, banana and sugar plantations, orange-tiled roofs and folds of hills. A further 26 km is **La Pintada**. Here the main road crosses the Río Cauca and continues via Marmato to

Around Medellín

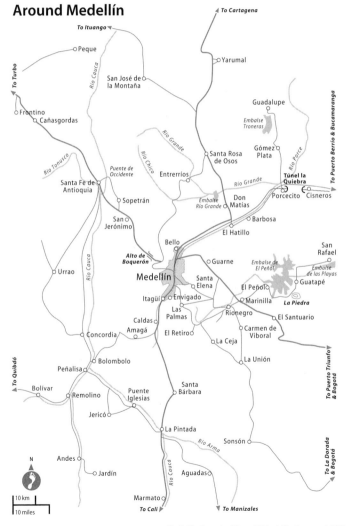

ON THE ROAD

Discovering Reserva Natural Cañón del Río Claro

Before the main Bogotá–Medellín trunk road was completed, this magnificent 150-m-deep limestone canyon was known only to jaguars and other animals of the forest.

Eduardo Betancourt, a *campesino* from a nearby finca, first discovered the gorge in 1964. Tracking a jaguar that had been killing his livestock, it took him six weeks to follow it back to the canyon. The animal eventually escaped him but not before leading him to the site, which locals refused to enter, believing it to be bewitched.

He returned home empty-handed but told his landowner, Juan Guillermo Garcés, about the canyon. Garcés was fascinated, but nothing was done for a further six years until, in 1970, a government engineer spotted it from a helicopter while searching for a suitable place to build a bridge across the river for the new road.

Garcés was inspired to see it for himself, so he set out with his brother and Betancourt. It took them two days to hack through the jungle, and they had to enter the canyon itself by pulling themselves upriver on a raft. They remained at the site for several months, building shelters in the caves under the steep walls of the canyon. The diversity of species Garcés discovered during his stay inspired him to develop it into a private nature reserve to ensure its protection.

The canyon gained some publicity from journalists who were staking out nearby Hacienda Nápoles belonging to Pablo Escobar, and on the first weekend after the completion of the new road, 1500 visitors descended on the reserve. Garcés decided that it would be impossible to keep people away and that the best way of protecting the canyon was to develop a sustainable tourism reserve. He named it 'El Refugio', in memory of its former role as a jaguar refuge. For details, see page 206.

Manizales. A left turn after La Pintada takes an alternative and particularly attractive route to Manizales through Aguadas, Pácora and Salamina, all perched on mountain ridges (for Salamina, see page 224). A right turn from La Pintada, meanwhile, heads northwest to some beautiful country on the west side of the Río Cauca.

This region can also be reached shortly after Caldas, by a road to the west which descends through Amagá to cross the Cauca at Bolombolo. From here, several attractive towns can be visited. **Jericó** is an interesting Antioquian town with a large cathedral, several other churches, two museums and a good view from **Morro El Salvador**. **Andes** is a busy coffee-buying centre, with several places to stay and to eat. **Jardín** is 16 km southeast of Andes. This pretty

> **Fact...**
> Jardín, like Salamina, page 224, is one of the protected Pueblos Patrimonio de Colombia (www. pueblospatrimoniodecolombia.co).

ON THE ROAD
The legends of Marmato

Marmato is known as the 'cradle of Colombian gold'. It is believed that gold has been mined here for more than 500 years. When Sebastián de Belalcázar and Jorge Robledo arrived in 1536, they found the local indigenous Cartamas already mining the mountain and fashioning beautiful *huacas* out of its gold. Belalcázar and Robledo took the Cartamas' bounty and then returned to Marmato in 1539, bringing black slaves from Cartagena to work the mines. Word spread about the fortune under the mountain, and shortly afterwards German mercenaries, who had joined the Spanish hunt for El Dorado, arrived and built their own mines in San Juan, a village just up the mountain from Marmato. In the 19th century, the British came to Marmato at the behest of the Colombian government, which used the gold mines here as collateral to secure funding for its fight for Independence against the Spanish.

Marmato is a place steeped in myth, legend and superstition. A cross at the mountain's peak is meant to ward off beautiful flying witches who have the power to entrance any man. Locals say the witches persuaded the foreign gold prospectors in days gone by to drink from the enchanted waters of the Cascabel spring, so that they would fall in love with the women of Marmato and never want to leave.

The slaves brought in by the Spanish to work the mines brought their own distinct myths. Legend has it that they practised a sacred ritual under an ancient ceiba tree in which they formed a ring around the most beautiful slave girl and made her drink the blood of a sacrificial goat while she undressed. The local Catholic priest, shocked by the practice, denounced the slaves as devil worshippers and cursed them. The ceiba tree is believed to have fallen away in a landslide following the priest's damnation. This is not the only example of divine intervention. The 16th-century Iglesia de Santa Bárbara has collapsed and been rebuilt several times, some say because the town priest cursed the village for its heavy drinking and prostitution; there is an ongoing belief here that the more you drink, the more gold you will find.

Antioquian village is surrounded by cultivated hills, passion-fruit farms, trout farms and good horse riding. The plaza is full of flowering shrubs and trees. There is a delightful Fiesta de las Rosas in January. The Templo Parroquial de la Inmaculada Concepción is a Monumento Nacional and the small museum in the Casa de la Cultura has paintings and local artifacts.

Santa Fe de Antioquia *Colour map 2, B3.*

Santa Fe de Antioquia (usually just called Santa Fe) is 78 km from Medellín, just west of the Río Cauca, surrounded by mountainous green countryside. It is a safe, peaceful, well-preserved colonial town from where it is best to explore on horseback or bicycle. It is a popular weekend haunt with Antioquians.

Santa Fe was founded as a gold-mining town by the Spaniards in 1541 and became famous for its gold jewellery. Today, most of the gold mines have been abandoned but there is still some gold mining in the Río Cauca. In 1813, Santa Fe was declared the capital of the short-lived independent state of Antioquia, but in 1826, its status had collapsed and political control was lost to Medellín.

The lively main plaza is dominated by a fine old cathedral. There are several other churches worth seeing, notably Santa Bárbara. Next door is a **Museo de Arte Religioso/Museo Juan del Corral** ① *C 11, No 9-77, Mon-Fri 0900-1200, 1400-1730, Sat-Sun 1000-1700, closed Wed*, which has a collection of items from colonial and more recent times. Opposite the Plaza Santa Bárbara is the site of a former slave market. Major local festivals are celebrated at Easter, Christmas and New Year.

Listings Around Medellín *map page 211.*

Tourist information

Tourist office
Cra 9 y C 9, T4-853 4139, municipal website http://santafedeantioquia-antioquia.gov.co; see also http://santafedeantioquia.net. Mon-Fri 0800-1200, 1400-1800, Sat 0800-1200.

Where to stay

Southeast from Medellín

$$$-$$ Refugio Río Claro
Reservations in Medellín, T4-268 8855, T311-354 0119, www.rioclaroelrefugio.com.
Tranquil spot, good value, delightful wooden lodges with great views of river (hotel, hostel and cabin accommodation). Includes 3 meals, restaurant service. Book ahead. Rafting trips, zip-lines over canyon and hiking trips are extra. Recommended.

$$-$ Lake View Hostel
Over the bridge at the end of the malecón, Guatapé, T4-861 0023, or T310-378 8743, www.lakeviewhostel.com.
Private rooms and dorms (US$8-11 pp), with Thai restaurant. Activities include boat tours, kayaking, mountain biking, hikes, riding, Spanish classes and fishing.

$ Mi Casa Guatapé
4 mins before Guatapé at foot of El Peñol, behind Restaurante La Mona, T4-861 0632, www.micasaguatape.com.
Smart, bright rooms, private and shared (US$10 pp), good views, use of kitchen, meals extra, plenty of activities can be arranged, Colombian/English owners.

Santa Fe de Antioquia
It's best to book in advance at weekends and public holidays. Rates can be 40% more in high season and bank holiday weekends. Most hotels organize horse rides and town tours and offer weekend packages.

$$$-$$ Caserón del Parque
C 9, No 9-41, T4-853 2040, www.caserondelparque.com
Large colonial building, comfortable rooms, some with balconies looking onto pool or main plaza, cheaper Mon-Fri. Sun deck has fantastic views, bike hire, restaurant, spa, Turkish bath.

$$$-$$ Hostal Tenerife
Cra 8, No 9-50, T4-539 1965, www.hotelcasatenerife.com.co.
Beautifully decorated colonial house, spacious and tastefully decorated

rooms. Free use of house bikes, pool, spa, restaurant, local tours arranged. Recommended.

$$$-$$ Mariscal Robledo
*Cra 10, No 9-70, T4-853 1111,
www.hotelmariscalrobledo.com.*
Stylish hotel in a handsome colonial mansion. Nice pool area with palms. Good weekend lunch buffet. Recommended.

$$$-$$ Tonusco Campestre
C 7 and Cra 7, Barranca 1, El Gualí, T4-853 2258, http://tonuscocampestre.com.

Country lodge resort-style hotel on the edge of town; pleasant grounds with pool, games room, playground, jacuzzi, gym; upmarket cabins with a/c, terrace with hammock, fridge and mod cons, some larger rooms with bunk beds, ideal for families, range of packages available, including half and full board.

$$-$ Hostal Plaza Mayor
Cra 9, No 9-59, Parque Principal, T4-853 3448, hostalplazamayor2011@ hotmail.com.
Popular with backpackers. There are hammocks, a small pool and a small *cabaña* with bunk beds.

$ Pueblito Viejo
Cra 11, No 10-80, T4-853 3763.
Basic rooms, but clean and adequate for price, with pool, reasonable budget choice.

South from Medellín
There are several *residencias* and restaurants by the plaza in Jardín.

$$$ El Despertar
T312-326 1134, Jericó, http://eldespertarhotel.com.
Nice rooms and lovely views, good breakfast, tours arranged, Spanish owner speaks English.

$$$-$$ Hacienda Balandú
Vía Jardín Río Sucio, 800 m from Jardín, T4-444 7110, www.comfenalcoantioquia.com.
Comfortable rooms, pool, gardens, lake, spa, sports, used by birdwatching groups, good restaurant.

Santa Fe de Antioquia

Where to stay 🛏
Caserón del Parque 1
Hostal Tenerife 2
Hostal Plaza Mayor 3
Mariscal Robledo 4
Pueblito Viejo 5
Tonusco Campestre 6

Restaurants 🍴
El Portón del Parque 1
La Comedia 2

Restaurants

Santa Fe de Antioquia

$$ El Portón del Parque
C 10 No 11-03, T4-853 3207.

Local cuisine in an arty setting, decorated wall to wall with artist owner's colourful portraits and sculptures, some outdoor tables in delightful patio garden; specialities include fish, steaks, soups and *bandeja paisa*.

$ La Comedia
C 11, No 8-03, T4-853 1243. 301-596 3032.
Café/bar/restaurant with music and art exhibitions, Colombian and international art house films.

South from Medellín

Dulces del Jardín
C 13 No 5-47, Facebook: dulcesdeljardin.
A very good sweetshop.

Transport

Southeast from Medellín
Bus
From Terminal del Norte in Medellín, desk 14, many buses to **El Peñol**, US$4, and **Guatapé**, US$5 with

Sotransvicente, T4-861 0595, www.sotrasanvicente.com, 1½ hrs. From **Guatapé** to Rionegro, take **Sotransvicente** to Marinilla, US$3. To **Río Claro**, take a Bogotá-bound bus and tell the driver you want to get off at Río Claro, 3 hrs.

Santa Fe de Antioquia
Bus
The station is on the road to Turbo at the north end of Cras 9 and 10 (5 mins' walk to main plaza). To **Medellín** US$3 (numerous companies), 1 hr. To **Turbo**, US$18-23, 8-9 hrs, hourly 0530-2400, with **Sotrauraba** (www.sotrauraba.com).

South from Medellín
Bus
Medellín–Santa Bárbara, US$2.50. Medellín–**Andes**, US$6. From Medellín (Terminal Sur), **Trans Suroeste Antioqueño** and **Rápido Ochoa** to **Jardín**, US$8-11, several daily, 3-4 hrs.

Department
of Chocó

Situated in the heavy rainbelt along Colombia's northwest coast, Chocó is one of the rainiest and most biodiverse regions in the world, densely forested and sparsely inhabited. In the northern part of the department, the mountain ranges rise directly from the ocean to reach a height of about 500 m. Chocó is home to a number of indigenous groups, including the Embera, whose communities are based on hunting, fishing and subsistence farming. The coastline is also dotted with poor Afro-Colombian fishing communities. Tourism centres on the coastal towns of Nuquí and Bahía Solano, with an increasing number of comfortable eco-hotels and hostels dotted along the coastline. Whale watching, fishing, surfing and hiking in pristine jungle are among the highlights. This destination is not cheap, partly because you have to fly, but also because petrol has to be brought in from a long distance, so boat fares are high. However, this is an up-and-coming destination and one of the few unspoilt places where you can experience pristine rainforest next to fine sandy beaches.

Essential Chocó

Finding your feet

If going to the coast, you should fly, and book well ahead during the high season; the planes are small (8-17 seaters) and there are only a few daily scheduled flights. Hotels in Nuquí and Bahía Solano usually offer all-inclusive packages for a three-night stay and arrange boat transport to and from the airport. Road access to Quibdó across the Cordillera Occidental from Medellín is via Bolívar; the road is poor but passable. Travelling beyond Quibdó by road is not safe. Other transport in Chocó is limited to water routes along the Pacific coast from Buenaventura in the south (not safe) and up the rivers.

When to go

The so-called 'dry' season is December to March. The best time to go to Chocó is when humpback whales visit the area from the beginning of July to October. Nuquí holds a **Festival de la Migración Pacífica**, during late August-late September (dates vary), to celebrate the migratory birds, turtles and whales which visit the region from April to October.

> Tip...
> Precautions against mosquito bites, and anti-malarials, are strongly advised.

Quibdó *Colour map 2, B2.*

Quibdó is on the eastern bank of the Río Atrato. There is little to detain the visitor here apart from the unstoppable partying during the city's fiestas. The **San Pacho festival** (September-October, www.sanpachobendito.org), for instance, has parades and a San Francisco de Asís procession. There is an interesting mural in the cathedral. Hordes of birds fly in to roost at dusk and there are magnificent sunsets, which locals watch from the waterfront promenade, *el malecón*. There are ATMs in town, but it is best to buy pesos before arriving.

Nuquí to El Valle *Colour map 2, B1.*

On the Gulf of Tribugá, surrounded by estuaries, mangroves and virgin beaches, the Afro-Colombian town of **Nuquí** gives access to the beaches and ecolodges up and down the Pacific coast. Visitors have to pay a US$2.50 tourism tax. To the south lies the wide curve of Playa Olímpica as well as Playa Guachalito (safe for swimming). Various communities, including Jobí, Coquí, Termales and Jurubidá, welcome visitors. **Termales**, to the south of Nuquí, is a traditional village, with a few basic hostels and a couple of food stores. Its hot baths (entry fee) are in a delightful river setting.

About 50 km north of Nuquí along the coast, **El Valle** has the best bathing and surfing beaches in the area. Between Nuquí and El Valle is **Parque Nacional Ensenada de Utría** ⓘ *entry US$15 (US$6 for Columbian nationals),* home to many aquatic species and birds. The surrounding hillsides are covered with pristine rainforest and there are mangroves and several magnificent beaches. Activities include diving over the coral reefs, swimming, trekking (national park guides obligatory, US$13-30 per day) and whale watching in season. Most hotels organize day trips to the park, or you can hire a boat with a group from El Valle

ON THE ROAD

★ Whale watching

Every year, around 1000 humpback whales migrate northwards from the Antarctic Ocean to the Pacific. Here, along an isolated stretch of the Colombian coastline, where the warm seas are rich with krill and other small fish, the whales find the ideal territory to feed, mate and raise their new-born calves. The spectacle of these giant leviathans of the deep, swimming, diving and breaching through the tranquil waters, is one of Colombia's most thrilling natural sights.

Drawn by one of the world's whale-watching hotspots, groups of nature lovers are taking to the seas to get up close to these magnificent mammals. There are strict rules for whale-watching tours: boats should keep a minimum of 200 m from the nearest whale; no more than three boats at a time should follow one pod of whales, and for no more than 15 minutes. Whales, however, are naturally inquisitive creatures and may suddenly break through the waves close alongside, only to sink back down just as unpredictably, leaving stunned spectators fumbling with their lens caps. They often swim in close groups of two or three, with the adult whale showing its offspring these odd boats, with their camera-snapping passengers. They use their echo-location sensors to bounce off the hull of the boat and check it out. Some have even been known to come so close that when they spout, they drench the occupants with their pungently fishy spray!

Among cetaceans, humpbacks are considered one of the most acrobatic and agile of species; they frequently breach, lifting their immense body almost clear out of the water, and then slamming it down against the surface, with a resounding splash. They also often bob their head out of the water, revealing a barnacle-encrusted and grooved throat, in a display known as spyhopping.

Facts
Size: humpback whales grow up to 18 m in length, and weigh up to 40 tonnes. At birth they weigh 1.5 tonnes and are approximately 4 m long.
Diet: krill and small fish
Reproduction: one calf every two to three years; the calf feeds off its mother's milk for the first year.
Life expectancy: up to 60 years.

Tours
From Bahía Málaga, near Buenaventura, to the Ensenada de Utría National Park, between Nuquí and Bahía Solano, hotels and local agencies offer whale-watching tours, costing around US$50 for three hours, see pages 216-218 for listings.

(one hour), or from Nuquí (minimum 1½ hours). **Isla Playa Blanca** is recommended as part of the trip. Boat prices start at US$150 and vary considerably, depending on time and number of passengers. Ask at hotels and Mano Cambiada (see below) for information. Insist on a life jacket and, on all boat trips, be prepared to get soaked – keep all valuables in watertight bags.

Tip…
Bring plenty of cash. There are no banks or ATMs in Nuquí, though the general store 50 m from the airport may change US dollars.

Bahía Solano *Colour map 2, B1.*

The town lies on a large bay set against jungle-covered hills. As a resort, it gets busy during holiday periods (the whale season is June to October, and the prime sports fishing season, is March to May), otherwise it's a functional fishing town. Good bathing beaches may be reached by launch or by walking about 1½ hours at low tide (for example Playa Mecana; be sure to return before the tide rises or you will be stranded).

Listings Department of Chocó

Tourist information

Nuquí to El Valle

The best place for information is the **NGO Mano Cambiada**, whose office is opposite Nuquí airport (T310-348 6055/T313-7596270, corporacionmanocambiada@yahoo.es, or on Facebook: ManoCambiada, http://manocambiada.org).

Bahía Solano

Tourist information is available from the **Alcaldía** (T4-682 7418, www.bahia solano-choco.gov.co). There are no ATMs in the town.

Where to stay

It is possible to stay in Nuquí and Bahía Solano cheaply if you rent a basic room in a family house. Ask locals or look for rent signs on windows. Negotiate prices during the low season.

Quibdó

There are few decent places to stay.

$$ Camino Real
C28, No1-124, T4-671 2437,
1 block back from the malecón.
Central and safe.

Nuquí to El Valle
Nuquí
Along the beach at the north end of Nuquí are several tourist hotels usually fully booked during the holiday period; it's best to make arrangements through travel agents in Medellín or Bogotá.

$$$-$$ Cabañas Pijiba
Near Nuquí, T4-474 5221 or 311-762 3763,
www.pijibalodge.com.
Award-winning ecotourism development with full board. Comfortable wooden lodges with thatched roofs. Arranges guided trips, diving, forest walks, airport pick-up (45-min boat ride to hotel), from US$250 pp double for 3 nights, longer packages available.

South of Nuquí
South of Nuquí is a great area called **Guachalito**, where you can find simple,

reasonably priced hotels, set back from the fine sandy beach.

$$$-$$ El Cantil
35 mins south of Nuquí, T4-448 0767, www.elcantil.com.
Several packages from about US$360 pp double for a 2-night package, full board, transfers, 2 whale-watching boat trips, and a guided trail walk included. Wooden cabins with sea view, bath, mosquito nets, hammocks; safe swimming off volcanic sandy beach. Also surfing courses, hot springs trips, diving, whale watching in season; excellent tours and meals, well run, friendly and relaxed. From here you can walk to Guachalito beach, safe for swimming, and also, 1 hr away is the village of **Termales** (see above). The lodge is genuinely eco-conscious – guests are given plastic bottles to take their rubbish back home with them. Highly recommended.

$$$-$$ Lodge Piedra Piedra
45 mins south of Nuquí, T315-874 1773, 315-510 8216, www.piedrapiedra.com.
Prices from US$240 double for 3-night package, full board (bed only, US$110). Also all-inclusive, whale-watching and fishing packages, 3-7 days. Organizes local tours, wood and thatched lodges, camping US$20, use of kitchen and kayak rental.

$$$-$$ Punta Brava
Arusi, about 1½ hrs south of Nuquí, T313-768 0804, puntabravachoco.co/
Thatch-roofed *cabañas* on a rocky promontory overlooking the beach; simply but comfortably furnished rooms with terrace and hammock; sun decks, kayaks, whale-watching tours, jungle hikes, fishing, yoga and many other activities, superb meals, 4-night packages, warmly recommended.

North of Nuquí

$$$-$$ Jaibaná (Ensenada de Utría visitor centre)
Run by Mano Cambiada (address above).
On a beautiful inlet in the national park. Comfortable cabins with bath, cold water, mosquito nets, no electricity (but solar power in the main building), good simple fresh food, wonderful staff. Guiding is included in packages.

$$$-$$ Morromico
45 mins north of Nuquí, T313-795 6321, www.morromico.com
5 simple rooms in large *cabaña* right on the beach, family-run for 30 years, very peaceful, excellent meals with organic fruits and fresh juices, wide range of tours available, including whale watching, trips to Utría National Park, kayaking and diving, with very knowledgeable guides, English spoken. Recommended.

El Valle
Hotels along this remote coastline run their own electricity generators, with power supply limited to a few hours a day, so it's worth bringing a torch or reading light.

$$$-$$ Cabañas El Almejal
T4-412 5050, www.almejal.com.co.
Environmentally aware, award-winning and design-oriented cabins with private bath, full board, price depends on the package. In private reserve, turtle conservation programme, educational programmes, lots of wildlife-watching opportunities.

$ Humpback Turtle Lodge/La Tortuga Jorobada
Playa Almejal, T314-766 8708 or 312-756 3439, www.humpbackturtle.com).

Offers surfing, surf kayaking, camping, dorms and private rooms, restaurant and bar, and use of kitchen.

Bahía Solano

$$$$ Mapara Crab

T314-700 8424, www.maparacrab.com. Run by Nancy and Enrique Ramírez, small, comfortable cabins on a private beach, 30 mins by boat from Bahía Solano. Enrique is a master sports fisherman and diving enthusiast, very knowledgeable source of local information. Several packages available. There are also hotels in Bahía Solano itself.

Transport

Note that air passengers pay a US$3 tax on arrival at Nuquí and Bahia Solano airports.

Quibdó
Air

Flights daily to **Medellín**, **Bogotá** and nearby towns with **LATAM**, **Satena**, **ADA** and **EasyFly**.

Bus

Flota Occidental (T4-361 1312, or T4-671 1865 in Quibdó) and **Rápido Ochoa** from **Medellín**, daily, 7-8 hrs, US$15-20.

Nuquí to El Valle
Air

Satena and **ADA** fly to Nuquí from **Medellín**, **Bogotá** and **Quibdó** (daily), from US$200 return. Charters also available with Grupo San Germán, www.gruposangerman.com, T318-400 3777; more expensive but a good alternative during high season when limited scheduled flights fill up fast, about US$365 return from Medellín.

Bahía Solano
Air

There are flights from Medellín, Bogotá, Cali and Quidbó to Bahía Solano with **Satena** and **ADA**.

Pick-up

Pick-ups run from Bahía Solano to **El Valle** throughout the day, 18 km (6 km paved). Check also with **Pacifico Tours**, http://pacificotours.com.

Zona
Cafetera

★ Modern and colonial cities line the fertile western slopes of the Cordillera Central which is the centre of Colombia's coffee production. The three departments of Caldas, Quindío and Risaralda are generally known as the 'Zona Cafetera', recognized by UNESCO as a World Heritage Site, for its cultural, economic and historical significance. Much of the land here is between the critical altitudes for coffee of 800 and 1800 m, and has the right balance of rain and sunshine. The area has beautiful rolling countryside of coffee plantations, interspersed with bamboo, plantain and banana trees. The best way to enjoy the Zona Cafetera is to stay on a coffee farm (finca or hacienda), where you can tour the plantations and see how coffee is produced at harvest time. And of course, there is excellent, fresh coffee all year round. The Zona Cafetera has also built a reputation as an adventure sports destination, including rafting, kayaking and canopying (whizzing across ravines on steel cables), and as a natural hotspot for birdwatchers. The region is overlooked by the high peaks of Los Nevados National Park to the east. Earthquakes and volcanoes remain a feature of this volatile region.

Essential Zona Cafetera

Finding your feet

The three departmental capitals of La Zona Cafetera lie close to each other, flanked to the east by the massif of Los Nevados: Manizales (Caldas) in the north, Pereira (Risaralda), 50 km away in the centre, and Armenia (Quindío) a similar distance to the south. All three can be reached from Bogotá by crossing the Cordillera Central. The most direct route (309 km) heads west through Facatativá and Honda and then over the Páramo de las Letras pass (3700 m, the highest main road pass in Colombia); the alternative is through Girardot to Ibagué and over the high crest of the Quindío pass (3250 m). Both routes involve long winding climbs and descents amid superb scenery.

Getting around

Road and transport facilities are good, although landslides on the steep hills around Manizales can cause significant travel difficulties during the rainy season. The three main cities are connected by the fast Autopista del Café toll road, which has cut journey times. Much of the local transport in this region is by *chiva* (literally 'goat'), simple, brightly coloured buses and jeeps, often called by the historic name 'Willys'; they're usually ancient but lovingly maintained. To get off the beaten track, a hire car is recommended.

Best coffee fincas

When to go

Because of the altitude, the climate in this region is generally very agreeable. The best months of the year are from mid-December through to early March. In Los Nevados National Park the dry seasons are January and February and June to September, but even in those months it can rain for days or be very foggy. The whole upland area is subject to wide temperature changes during the day, depending on cloud cover, and very cold nights.

Time required

You'll need a week to explore this area; add three to four days for trekking in Los Nevados.

Weather Manizales

January	February	March	April	May	June
22°C 11°C 98mm	22°C 12°C 92mm	22°C 12°C 134mm	22°C 12°C 167mm	21°C 13°C 154mm	21°C 12°C 91mm

July	August	September	October	November	December
22°C 12°C 64mm	22°C 12°C 75mm	21°C 12°C 138mm	21°C 12°C 190mm	21°C 12°C 167mm	21°C 11°C 125mm

Manizales, 309 km from Bogotá, is overlooked by the Nevado del Ruiz volcano, which erupted catastrophically in November 1985. The town sits at 2150 m on a mountain saddle, which falls away sharply from the centre into the adjacent valleys. Rich in coffee and flowers, Manizales is one of the principal starting points for excursions to the Parque Nacional Los Nevados.

The city's climate is humid (average temperature is 17°C and annual rainfall is 3560 mm), encouraging prodigious growth in the flowers that line the highways to the suburbs north and south. Frequently the city is covered in cloud. The best months of the year are from mid-December to early March. The city looks down on the small town of Villa María, 'the village of flowers', now almost a suburb.

Sights

Several earthquakes and fires have destroyed parts of the city over the years, so the architecture is predominantly modern with high-rise office and apartment blocks. Traditional styles are still seen in the suburbs and the older sections of the city. The centre is dominated by the enormous concrete **cathedral**. Opposite is the departmental **Gobernación** building in the Parque de Bolívar, an imposing example of neocolonial architecture and a national monument. Inside is a local arts and crafts shop. The **bullring** ⓘ *Av Centenario, T6-883 8124, www.cormanizales. com*, is an impressive copy of the traditional Moorish style. Along Avenida 12 de Octubre to the suburb of Chipre is a park, providing a great view to the west as

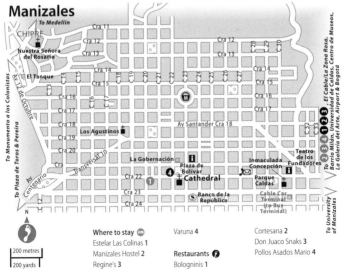

Manizales

Where to stay	Varuna 4	Cortesana 2
Estelar Las Colinas 1		Don Juaco Snaks 3
Manizales Hostel 2	**Restaurants**	Pollos Asados Mario 4
Regine's 3	Bologninis 1	

well as paragliding opportunities (well visited on Sunday); **El Tanque**, on the Avenida, is a popular landmark and viewpoint. The **Centro de Museos** ⓘ *part of Caldas University, Cra 23 No 58-65, T6-885 1374, www.ucaldas.edu.co/portal/tag/centro-de-museos/, Mon-Fri 1000-1800,* has an art gallery, natural history museum and exhibitions on geology and archaeology. To get there take a 'Fátima' bus to the University. The area known as **El Cable**, east of the centre, is the Zona Rosa, with good restaurants and bars.

Reserva Forestal Protectora Río Blanco

Owned by Aguas de Manizales, T6-887 9770, ext 72187, send an email before visiting to reservarioblanco@aguasdemanizales.com.co, or socampo@aguasdemanizales.com.co (Sergio Ocampo, technical director); US$7 entry, and a guide is compulsory, US$10-30 for half or full day, depending on size of group. Tour operators and hostels can arrange visits. The earlier you go (tours start at 0700), the better the birdwatching.

About 8 km from Manizales is the Río Blanco reserve, a 4343-ha protected cloudforest, considered by the World Wildlife Fund the best place for birdwatching in Colombia. To date, 372 species of bird have been identified, including 33 species of hummingbird. There are also 40 types of orchid, 180 species of daytime butterfly and 61 species of mammal, including spectacled bear, ocelot and the white-tailed deer. There are several hikes of between 30 minutes and three hours as well as a rangers' hut where 22 species of hummingbird come to feed. Trails and other facilities are operated by **Fundación Ecológica Gabriel Arango Restrepo** (FUNDEGAR).

★ Parque Nacional Los Nevados

Oficina del Parque de Los Nevados, C 69, No 24-69, Barrio La Camelia, Manizales, T6-887 1611/2273, Mon-Fri 0800-1800, for information and entrance fees, north sector: US$13 for non-Colombians, US$7 for Colombians (children US$5.50), including compulsory guide.

The park has all the wild beauty of the high Cordillera, towering mountains (snow-capped above 4850 m), mostly dormant volcanoes, hot springs and recent memories of tragic eruptions. The park comprises 58,000 ha and straddles the departments of Caldas, Quindío, Risaralda and Tolima. Visitors should come prepared for cold, damp weather, and remember to give themselves time to acclimatize to the altitude.

The northern sector of the park is reached from Manizales along the main highway to Bogotá via a turn-off at La Esperanza. Volcanic activity on **Nevado del Ruiz** (5400 m) has restricted access to Parque de los Nevados in recent years. While the southern section was open in 2017 (0930-1500, US$11, access from Salento, Pereira and Ibagué), the northern section (access from Manizales and Brisas and Murillo in Tolima department) was open only as far as Valle de las Tumbas, from 0800 to 1400; all visitors must leave by 1530. If you wish to enter the northern part of the park or intend to do some serious mountain climbing and/or mountain biking, apply to the above office in advance. The tourist office in Manizales can give advice on which parts of the park are open and can put you in touch with agencies who organize day trips to Nevado del Ruiz. Hotels and hostels offer trips to the park. Guides can be arranged and trips extended to include Nevado del Tolima (Milton César Ocampo is an expert guide to the region, speaks English, French and Portuguese, T311-600 4270, miltoncop@outlook.es). **Mountain Hostels**, see below, has information on trips and provides maps, which are also available at the **Instituto Geográfico** ⓘ *C 21 No 23-22, Edificio Atlas, Manizales, T6-884 5864, Mon-Fri 0700-1200, 1400-1800.*

Los Nevados National Park

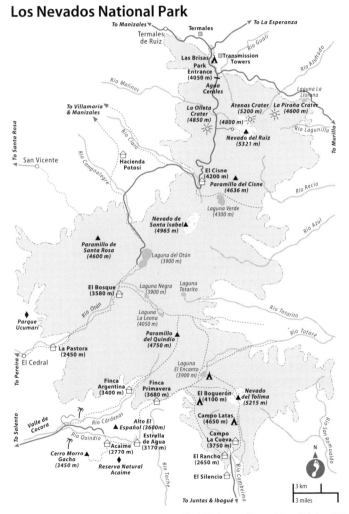

Armero

The main road from Manizales to Bogotá goes east to Honda (see page 69). It passes through **Mariquita**, capital of a fruit-growing region (21 km before Honda). From Mariquita a road turns south to (32 km) Armero, which was devastated by the eruption of the Nevado del Ruiz volcano in November 1985. Over 25,000 people were killed as 10% of the ice core melted, causing landslides and mudflows. Armero can be reached by *colectivo* from Honda; the road heads south to Ibagué via **Lérida**, 12 km south.

Salamina

About two hours' drive north of Manizales, with a stunning mountain-top perch, is probably the most attractive and, as yet, unspoilt town in the whole region. Salamina was declared a national monument in 1982, because of its well-preserved colonial architecture, but its remote location and patchy road have deterred the crowds that pack Salento during peak-season weekends. There's not much to do here, but it's a beautiful place to spend a few days, with a growing clutch of boutique hotels and good restaurants. Nearby is the **Valle de la Samaria**, which has groves of the wax palms in similar quantities to the better-known Valle de Cocora. Local hotels can arrange tours, or take an early-morning bus to the village of **San Félix**, from where it's a two-hour walk or 15-minute taxi ride. Tours are also available to local *trapiches* (mills) showing the production process of the traditional sugarcane syrup.

Listings Manizales and around *map page 221.*

Tourist information

Manizales

There are 3 tourist information points: **Parque Benjamín López**, Cra 22 y C 31, T6-873 3901, **Gobernación de Caldas**, Edif Gobernación, C23 No 22-45, T6-884 9280, and at the **bus terminal**, Cra 43 No 65-100, Los Cámbulos, T6-878 7832.

Instituto de Cultura y Turismo
*Av Alberto Mendoza Hoyos, Km 2
Vía al Magdalena, T6-874 9712, http://
culturayturismomanizales.gov.co/.
Mon-Fri 0700-1200, 1400-1800.*

Salamina

Tourist information kiosk
*Corner of the main plaza.
Mon-Fri 1400-1830.*

Small but very helpful kiosk, with a few maps and leaflets.

Where to stay

Many coffee farms offer a free transfer from Manizales, but check first. When planning a trip here, take into account price rises during the popular Feria de Manizales in Jan.

Manizales

$$$$-$$$ Estelar Las Colinas
*Cra 22, No 20-20, T6-884 2009,
www.hotelesestelar.com.*
Part of the Estelar chain of hotels, Las Colinas has large rooms with cable TV and Wi-Fi. It also has a sauna. Significant discounts at weekends.

$$$ Finca Romelia
Vereda la Cabaña Km 18, 30 mins west of Manizales, up a winding dirt track off the main road to Medellin, T311-701 3438, http://fincaromelia.com.
Half-board, minimum 2 nights' stay. Don Fernando, the owner of this very special finca, insists on keeping his family home first and foremost as a home, so the 3 guest rooms, beautifully decorated with Guatemalan weavings and pre-Columbian artefacts, have shared bathrooms. This is the only compromise, however, as the unique attraction here is the amazing world-class collection of more than 400 species of orchid. Guided tours are available in English or Spanish, also of the cacti and bonsai trees, plus hundreds of birds, in a spectacular hillside setting. Excellent meals, highly recommended.

$$$ Hotel Tinamu
30 mins from centre in Vereda San Peligrino, T311-770 1120, www.hoteltinamu.com.
Former coffee plantation turned nature reserve just outside the city with a firm focus on wildlife watching, especially birds (241 species recorded to date, including 208 native birds); excellent guided birdwatching tours through unspoilt forest. 4 private rooms with Wi-Fi, price includes guiding. Meals other than breakfast extra. Highly recommended.

$$$ Varuna Hotel
C 62, No 23, T314-814 4182, http://varunahotel.com
A slick modern hotel with a minimalist style, rooms large and comfortable, hydro-massage showers, good restaurant, **Tabil**, recommended.

$$$-$ Hacienda Venecia
Vereda El Rosario, 3.5 km off the Chinchiná autopista, T320-636 5719, www.haciendavenecia.com.
Delightful 4th-generation working coffee finca in a beautiful location with 3 different types of accommodation: **hostel** with private and dorm rooms (US$8-9 pp), free pick-up from the road to Medellín, kitchen, small grocery shop, games room, yoga mats, garden with hammocks and barbecue; colonial-style **guesthouse** with comfortable private rooms, restaurant, pool; or the main **hacienda**, with sumptuously furnished rooms, pool and hammocks; breakfast included in guesthouse and hacienda, and other meals can be arranged. Free coffee throughout the day. Attentive, English-speaking hosts. Riding, birdwatching, cooking demonstrations and other tours and workshops are available. The half-day coffee tour is excellent and takes you through the whole process. Day trips can be arranged to Salamina, Manizales and Salento. Highly recommended.

$$ Hotel Regines
C65a, No 23b-113, T6-8875360.
On quiet side street in Cable area. Great location near to restaurants and bars. Clean and comfortable.

$ Mountain Hostel Manizales
C 66, No 23B-91, Barrio Palermo, T6-887 4736, or 300-439 7387, http://manizaleshostel.com.
Popular travellers' hostel next to the Zona Rosa, has all the expected facilities, hammocks, TV room, book exchange, bike rental, hot showers, free coffee, restaurant. Dorms and private rooms with bath. Excellent information about trips to Los Nevados and coffee farms. Recommended.

Salamina

$$$-$$ Casa Carola
Cra 7 No 5-42, T6-834 6262,
http://www.casacarola.com.co/.
A beautiful boutique hotel 2 mins' walk
from the main square, with tasteful
decor and antique furnishings, in
carefully refurbished bahareque-style
19th-century house; spacious rooms
with fan opening onto central courtyard
garden. The US/French managers are
extremely helpful and informative
about local attractions and activities.
Horse riding is available as well as tours
to La Samaria wax palms and panela
mills. Meals are also available, including
vegetarian and gluten-free options.
Recommended.

$$$-$ Casa de Lola García
C No 6-54, T6-859 5919, http://
www.lacasadelolagarcia.com/.
A stylish boutique hotel consisting of
2 converted houses, with 7 sumptuous
rooms of varying prices; some are kitted
out with all mod cons, flat-screen TV and
walk-in rain shower. Family rooms and
dorms also available. Hammocks in patio
garden, jacuzzi, breakfast included.

$$-$ Hotel Colonial
C 5 No 6-74, T6-859 5978, www.facebook.
com/hotelcolonialsalamina.
A charmingly eccentric, labyrinthine
hotel on the main plaza, up narrow
stairs, with nicely furnished rooms and
suites, lots of communal lounge areas
decorated with mix of kitsch ornaments,
bakelite phones and modern art. There's
also a good restaurant downstairs at
the back, open to non-guests, with
excellent-value *menú del día*. Local
tours arranged (see above).

Manizales
Apart from the hotels, the best restaurants
are on or near Cra 23 in El Cable (La Zona
Rosa) and Barrio Milán, a taxi ride from
Cable Plaza, in the east of the city.

$$$-$$ Bologninis
C 77, No 21-116 2, T6-8867799.
Italian/Argentine restaurant with good
pasta, steak and wines. Recommended.

$$ Restaurante Cortesana
Cra 23, No 75-52, T310-3824206.
Great burgers and steaks, wonderful views.

$ Don Juaco Snaks
C 65, No 23A-44.
Typical *paisa* dishes, popular with locals,
also sandwiches and burgers.

$ Il Forno
Cra 23, No 73-86.
Italian and pleasant, serving pastas,
pizzas, salads and good vegetarian dishes.

$ Pollos Asados Mario
Cra 22, No 23-01, T6-8808448.
Traditional Colombian *asadero* with the
best rotisserie chicken in downtown
Manizales. Also burgers and steaks.

Cinema and theatre
Centro Cultural y Convenciones los
Fundadores, *Cra 22 y C 33 No 24-28,*
T6-878 2530, www.ccclosfundadores.com.
Has interesting wood-carved murals
by Guillermo Botero, who also has
murals in the **Club Manizales** and **Hotel
Las Colinas**. Many events held here.

Jan Feria de Manizales includes a coffee
festival, bullfights, beauty parades and folk
dancing as well as general partying.

Sep Festival Internacional de Teatro, www.festivaldemanizales.com.

What to do

Tour operators
Colombia57, *T6-886 8050 or T6-8864333, www.colombia57.com.* Ex-pats Simon Locke, Russell Coleman, Brendan Rayment and team organize tailor-made trips for individuals or groups around the coffee zone and the rest of Colombia. They also arrange adventure activities such as mountain biking in the coffee zone as well as guided day tours to the different villages, some of which are hard to get to without a car. Well organized, thoroughly researched with a commitment to sustainability and quality. Highly recommended.
Colombia Eco Travel, *at The Secret Garden, see Where to stay, above, T311-319 3195, www.colombiaecotravel.com.* Aims to provide responsible tours throughout Colombia, from day trips to longer tours.

Transport

Air
Airport 7 km east; flights are often delayed by fog. Buses to the centre US$1, taxi US$4. There are frequent flights to **Bogotá** and **Medellín**.

Bus
Terminal at Cra 43, No 65-100, T6-878 7858, with a direct cable car system from the station up to the area of El Cable (US$0.75 per journey); taxi to El Cable US$3-4, to centre US$2.50. To **Medellín**, many daily, 5-6 hrs, US$12-17, many companies, including **Expreso Sideral**, T6-878 7533, also non-stop minivans (eg **Flota Ospina**, T314-888 2781, www.flotaospina.com/, **and Tax La Feria**, T6-878 7001, http://taxlaferia.com), 4½ hrs, which also run to **Cali**, 4½ hrs, US$17.50, and **Pereira**, 1½ hrs, US$4. Many buses to **Bogotá**, eg Bolivariano, US$21-23, 9 hrs, also **Tax La Feria**, US$21. To **Honda**, several companies, including **Coopuertos** and **Rápido Tolima**, US$9-11.50, 4 hrs. **Cali**, hourly, US$12-14, 4½-6 hrs, many companies. **Pereira**, every 30 mins, 2 hrs, excellent road, beautiful scenery, US$4. **Armenia**, 3 hrs, US$7, hourly 0600-1800. To **Salamina**, 3 a day with **Expreso Sideral** (see above), 3 hrs, US$6; also shared taxi, maximum 4 passengers, US$8pp, 2 hrs.

Pereira to Ibagué *Colour map 2, C3-C4.*

the heart of the coffee zone

Still in the shadow of the Nevados, this is a region of modern cities (in several cases rebuilt after earthquakes), delightful scenery and botanical parks and gardens. Coffee is still by far the most important agricultural product of the area.

Chinchiná and the coffee fincas *Colour map 2, C3.*
Midway between Manizales and Pereira is Chinchiná, one of the main coffee-producing towns. The surrounding hills are carpeted with coffee bushes and on roasting days the smell of coffee hangs in the air. Many local fincas have diversified into other crops and opened up to tourism, from day visits to overnight stays,

The wild coffee plant originally came from East Africa, possibly first discovered near Kaffa (Kefa) in Ethiopia. A favourite legend is that an Arab goatherd noticed his flock behaving oddly after eating the berries of the bush, so he tried it himself, was exhilarated by the experience and proclaimed his discovery to the world. Coffee was first cultivated in South Arabia in the 15th century, and, in spite of a period when it was decreed intoxicating and therefore prohibited by the Koran, it gained increasing popularity, first among the Arabs and their neighbours, then in Europe, Asia and the Americas. Coffee houses started to open in London and Paris in about 1650, and in North America by about 1690, giving the drink a social dimension. By the end of the 17th century, production was being extended from Arabia (principally Yemen) to Ceylon, Indonesia and the West Indies (about 1715), Brazil (1727) and, towards the end of the century, Colombia.

The two principal types of coffee are arabica and robusta, the latter cultivated mostly in Asia and the Indian sub-continent. Arabica varieties are milder, having about half the level of caffeine, but are less tolerant of warm humid climates and more susceptible to disease. They are, however, more popular with western coffee drinkers and have brought prosperity to many countries in Latin America including Colombia, which grows virtually no *robusta* coffee. It is believed that coffee was brought into Colombia by Jesuit priests who first set up cultivation in Santander Department. Later it was tried in Cauca, and it wasn't until about 1850 that serious production started to take place in what is now known as the Zona Cafetera.

Colombia's coffee has been hit by several serious diseases, notably *roya* (a leaf fungus) and *broca* (a bug that attacks the bean). The latter was particularly destructive in the 1990s, but counter measures including the breeding of resistant plants have improved the situation. The other critical element is the world coffee price which fluctuates wildly. Coffee production in Colombia is done by hand, with an emphasis on quality over quantity. The country can't compete with machine-manufactured, mass-produced coffee sold by such countries as Brazil. So, when the coffee price slumped in 1992 and again in 2002, Colombia was one of the nations that was left struggling, and coffee growers in Caldas, Risaralda and Quindío were forced to diversify into other crops. In 1994, Quindío's tourism board, emulating the success of Spain's countryside haciendas, proposed to the region's finca owners an alternative source of income, and the idea of opening up coffee farms to tourism was born.

From stately post-colonial Antioquian mansions to some pretty primitive accommodation, no two fincas are the same. Some still produce their own coffee – and offer tours where you can learn about the process of coffee-growing – while others have retired that part of the business altogether and give guests the chance to relax, lounge around pools and appreciate the incredible richness of flora and fauna of the region. For our list of recommended fincas, see page 220. For further details, visit www.clubhaciendasdelcafe.com.

highly recommended. No two fincas are the same; they range from beautiful historic country mansions to more modest properties.

Pereira *Colour map 2, C3. See also map, page 230.*

Capital of Risaralda Department and 56 km southwest of Manizales, Pereira stands within sight of the Nevados of the Cordillera Central. It is a pleasant modern city with a large student population. Founded in 1863, its past has been chequered by earthquake damage. The central **Plaza de Bolívar** is noted for the striking sculpture of a nude Bolívar on horseback, by Rodrigo Arenas Betancur. There are other fine works of his in the city. The **Area Cultural Banco de la República** ⓘ *Cra 9 No 18-48, Mon-Fri 0830-1800, Sat 0900-1300, free,* features a library, art exhibitions and an auditorium with a programme of classical music. The **botanical garden** ⓘ *on the campus of the Universidad Tecnológica de Pereria, T6-313 7500, www.utp. edu.co/jardin, US$7, Mon-Fri 0800-1600, Sat-Sun 0900-1400, guided visits weekends and holidays at 1100, US$6,* is good for birdwatching and has bamboo forests and two-hour nature walks. For beautiful views of the city and nature trails, take a bus to El Cedral eco-park, behind Santa Barbara church.

Around Pereira *Colour map 2, C3.*

Fifteen kilometres north of Pereira is **Santa Rosa de Cabal**, from where several thermal pools can be reached. A 9-km unpaved road from Santa Rosa leads to the **Termales de Santa Rosa de Cabal** ⓘ *T6-365 5237, http://termales.com.co, daily 0900-2300, US$14 (US$8.50 midweek and in low season).* The hot baths are surrounded by forests, with waterfalls and nature walks. It's packed at the weekend but quiet during the week. It also has a hotel. An early-morning *chiva* or taxi will charge US$8 to the entrance.

Northwest of Pereira, 30 km towards the Río Cauca, is **Marsella**, and the **Alexander von Humboldt Gardens** ⓘ *T314-623 4941, Tue-Sun 0800-1700,* a carefully maintained botanical display with cobbled paths and bamboo bridges. Just outside the town is the **Ecohotel Los Lagos** ⓘ *T6-368 5298, www. ecohotelloslagos.com.co,* previously a gold mine, then a coffee hacienda, and now restored as a hotel ($$) and nature park with lakes.

Cartago, 25 km southwest of Pereira, is at the northern end of the rich Cauca Valley. Founded in 1540 and noted for its embroidered textiles, Cartago has some colonial buildings, like the fine **Casa del Virrey** (Calle 13, No 4-29) and the **cathedral**. From here, the Panamericana goes south along the Cauca Valley, stretching south for 240 km, to Cali and Popayán.

Parque Ucumarí *Colour map 2, C3.*

Park office, T6-325 4781, www.colparques.net/UCUMARI, daily for information, if visiting for the day and not staying overnight, entrance is free. A chiva leaves from C12, No 9-40 in Pereira daily at 0700, 0900, 1500 (plus 1200 at weekends and more frequently during high season) with Transporte Florida (T6-334-2721) to the village of El Cedral, approximately 2 hrs. The 0700 chiva Mon-Fri only goes to La Suiza for the Otún Quimbaya sanctuary.

From Pereira it is possible to visit the beautiful Parque Ucumarí, one of the few places where the Andean spectacled bear survives. From El Cedral it is a two- to 2½-hour walk to **La Pastora**, the park visitor centre and refuge. There is excellent camping, or lodging at a refuge ($), meals extra. From La Pastora it is a steep, rocky one- to two-day hike to Laguna de Otún through beautiful scenery of changing vegetation. According to the National Parks office, this sector was open in 2017, but check locally for the current situation. The **Otún Quimbaya flora and fauna sanctuary** ① *T314-674 9248, www.parquesnacionales.gov.co and www.yarumoblanco.co, 0800-1700, US$2*, forms a biological corridor between Ucumari and Los Nevados to the east, as well as protecting the last remaining area of Andean tropical forest in Risaralda. There are marked paths and Yarumo Blanco community has **Montaña Hostal-Restaurante** at La Florida with *cabañas* ($) and meals. You can get there by *chiva* (three a day, four on Saturday and Sunday) with **Transporte La Florida**, as above.

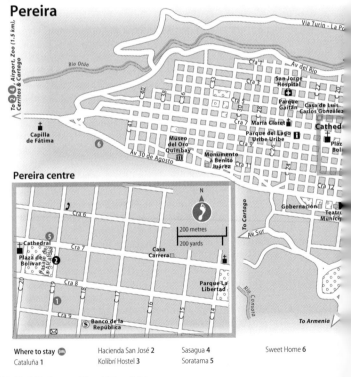

Where to stay 🛏
Cataluña **1**
Hacienda San José **2**
Kolibrí Hostel **3**
Sasagua **4**
Soratama **5**
Sweet Home **6**

Salento and Filandia *Colour map 2, C3.*

A 44-km road runs through the heart of the Zona Cafetera. A turn-off at the **Posada Alemana** goes east for 9 km to Salento, well into the foothills of the Cordillera. This small town is brightly painted with an attractive plaza surrounded by traditional houses, now mostly taken over by hotels, restaurants and souvenir shops. Up Carrera 6 (continuation of the north side of the plaza), is a 250-step climb. The 14 stations of the cross measure your progress to an outstanding viewpoint, overlooking the upper reaches of the Quindío and Cárdenas rivers known as the Cocora valley, one of the finest panoramas in the region. It is a popular weekend resort for Colombians for walking, riding and trekking but is quieter during the week. More places to eat and to stay are opening up constantly, but try to make arrangements early in the day, particularly at the weekend. Fiesta is in the first week of January and every Sunday night after Mass the plaza is taken over by food, drink and craft stalls, with a lively atmosphere. There are ATMs in the main plaza.

Seven kilometres from Salento off the main north–south highway is the small, picturesque town of Filandia, another hub of the coffee industry, and where traditional coffee-picking baskets are made. Its peaceful main plaza is lined with the colourful wooden *paisa* architecture also seen in Salento, but with a more local feel than its neighbour. The town was founded in 1878 by colonizers from Antioquia. For excellent views over the surrounding countryside, make your way to a mirador tower near the cemetery, 1 km from the main square.

Valle de Cocora and the Reserva Natural Acaime

A walk in the Valle de Cocora is one of the main reasons for visiting Salento. The centre of the Cocora valley is 12 km beyond Salento along a road that winds uphill; it's a 35-minute journey by **Willys jeep** from the main plaza (daily 0730-1700; they leave as soon as they fill up – usually every 30 minutes; last return 1800, US$2). There are cafés and souvenir shops in the small village of Cocora, guided horse-riding tours available (mixed reviews). At the start of the walk is a US$1 entrance fee to the **Parque Nacional Los Nevados**. Stretches of the walk can be muddy,

Restaurants 🍴   Pasaje de la Alcaldía **2**
Ambar **1**

partly due to the number of horses (where possible, they are starting to build separate paths for the horses). Some 5 km beyond Cocora, zig-zagging over the river on wobbly footbridges, is the **Acaime Natural Reserve** ① *US2 entry fee*, (at 2770 m) with visitor centre, many hummingbirds (attracted by nectar feeders), ponies for hire, beds for 20 and a small restaurant (entry fee includes a hot drink). Try the hot chocolate with cheese, a local speciality. On the way down, you walk through cloudforest and then the best-known area of wax palms in the country; the valley is stunningly beautiful, with several walks available, from two hours up to Acaime or five-seven hours return via La Montaña high lookout point (La Montaña is quite tough, about 40 to 50 minutes uphill all the way). The reserve borders **Parque Nacional Los Nevados**, and there are many trails into the high mountains above Acaime. Experienced climbers can also make the three-day ascent of Nevado del Tolima (5125 m) from here (see also page 233).

> **Fact...**
> The wax palm is the national tree and one of the tallest trees in the world; the Wax Palm Festival is celebrated in January.

Armenia

To ❶❷❸❺,
Museo Quimbaya
& Pereira

Parque Sucre

San Francisco

Plaza de Mercado

To Calarcá & Bogotá

AV BOLÍVAR

Cathedral

Plaza de Bolívar

Parque Cafetero

To ❸
Bus Station
(7 blocks)
& Airport

To Cali

Parque Uribe Uribe

N

200 metres
200 yards

Where to stay 🛌
Café Plaza **1**
Centenario **2**
Hacienda Bambusa **3**
Zuldemayda **4**

Restaurants 🍴
Café Quindío **1**
Keizaki **2**
La Fogata **3**
La Puerta Quindiana **4**
Natural Food Plaza **5**

Armenia and around *Colour map 2, C3.*
The capital of Quindío Department was founded in 1889. In January 1999, an earthquake flattened much of the city. Impressive reconstruction continues and Armenia is as busy as ever. The fine example of Rodrigo Arenas Betancur's work, the **Monumento al Esfuerzo**, in the Plaza de Bolívar, poignantly portrays the spirit of the local people. The **Museo del Oro Quimbaya** ① *Av Bolívar, Cra 19 No 40-N 80, T6-749 8169 ext 6070, www. banrepcultural.org/armenia, Tue-Sat 0900-1700 free entry*, is worth a visit. **Parque de la Vida**, north of the city, has bamboo structures, waterfalls and a lakeside theatre.

Near Calarcá, 6 km from Armenia, is the **Jardín Botánico y Mariposario del Quindío** ① *T6-742 7254 ext 105, www. jardinbotanicoquindio.org, daily 0900-1600, US$11*, featuring a huge covered butterfly house, with some 50 species of butterfly. There is also an insect zoo and forest walks. Twenty minutes south of Calarcá or Armenia is **Recuca** ① *T310-830 3780, www.recuca.com, daily 0900-*

1500, US$8 for day visit, US$6 for lunch, reserve in advance, US$5 coffee-tasting lesson,
a coffee farm with tours featuring all aspects of coffee-growing, also tastings. To
get there, take the Armenia–Barcelona bus.

Montenegro and around *Colour map 2, C3.*

Some 12 km northwest of Armenia is Montenegro, near which is the **Parque del
Café** ① *1 km from Pueblo Tapao, T6-741 7417, www.parquedelcafe.co, high season
daily 0900-1800, low season Wed-Sun and public holidays 1000-1800, general
entrance US$9, or US$15-20 for additional activities and rides, parking US$2*. There
are restaurants, a coffee shop, a botanical garden, ecological walks, a Quimbaya
cemetery, a tower with a fine view and an interesting museum which covers all
aspects of coffee. A cableway links to a children's theme park (roller coasters,
water rides, etc). To get there, take a bus or *colectivo* (US$2.50) from Armenia to
Montenegro. Beyond Montenegro is **Quimbaya**, known for its **Fiesta de Velas y
Faroles** in December each year. About 7 km away is the **Parque Nacional de la
Cultura Agropecuaria** (Panaca) ① *T01-800 012 3999, www.panaca.com.co, Tue-Sun
0900-1800, US$10-28*, an educational theme park with many varieties of horses
(and a very good show/display), cattle and other animals. A good family outing.

Ibagué and around *Colour map 2, C4.*

The **Quindío Pass**, 3350 m, is on the Armenia to Ibagué road (105 km) across the
Cordillera Central. On the east side of the pass is **Cajamarca**, in a beautiful setting
at 1900 m with an interesting market on Sunday.

　　Ibagué, capital of Tolima Department, lies at the foot of the Quindío mountains
at 1248 m. Visit the Colegio de San Simón and the market for good *tamales*. The
Parque Centenario is pleasant, and there is a famous music conservatory.

　　Just outside town, on the Armenia road, a dirt road leads up the Río Combeima
to **El Silencio** and the slopes of **Nevado del Tolima** (5215 m), the southernmost
nevado in the **Parque Nacional Los Nevados** and the toughest to climb. The ascent
takes two to three days, camping at least one night over 4000 m; ice equipment
is necessary. Entry to the park costs US$9. A milk truck (*lechero*) leaves Ibagué
marketplace for El Silencio between 0630 and 0730, US$2-3, two hours.

Listings Pereira to Ibagué *maps pages 230 and 232.*

Tourist information

Note that tourist offices now
refer to the region as the **Paisaje
Cultural Cafetero**, with a useful
new website suggesting routes and
other tourist information: http://
rutasdelpaisajeculturalcafetero.com/.

Pereira

Centro Cultural Lucy Tejada
*Cra 10, No 16-60, T6-311 6544,
http://pereiraculturayturismo.gov.co.
Mon-Fri 0800-1200, 1400-1830.*
Information is also available at the airport
(daily 0900-1730) and at **Corporación
Autónomo Regional de Risaralda**

(Carder; Av de las Américas and C 46, No 46-40, T6-311 6511, www.carder.gov.co).

Salento

Alcaldía de Salento
Parque Principal, C 6, No 6-30, T6-759 3252, http://salento-quindio.gov.co. Mon-Fri 0800-1200, 1400-1800, Sat 0800-1200.

Armenia

Corporación de Cultura y Turismo
Cra 19A entre C 26 y 29, Edif Republicano, p 2, T6-731 4531, www.armeniacultura yturismo.gov.co. Mon-Fri 0800-1200, 1400-1800.
There are information booths at Centro Comercial Portal del Quindío and the bus terminal.

Secretaría de Turismo
C 20, No 13-22, T6-741 7700 ext 202, www.turismocafeyquindio.com.

Ibagué

Tourist office
Cra 3 entre C 10 y 11, p 2, T8-261 1111, www.desarrolloeconomicotolima.gov.co.

Where to stay

Chinchiná and the coffee fincas
There are far too many coffee farms in the Pereira region to list here. They range from huge traditional haciendas to smaller, more modern farms. See T6-741 3698, www.clubhaciendasdelcafe.com, for a good selection.

$$$ Hacienda Guayabal
Near Chinchiná, T314-772 4856, www.haciendaguayabal.com.
A hacienda that takes day and overnight visitors. Nature trail, swimming pool, games room, beautiful views, ideal for families. Tours include full explanations of the coffee-growing process and delicious lunch. Full board is offered in private bedrooms and dorms. Recommended.

$$ pp Finca Villa María
12 km from Pereira, via Marsella, follow the signs, turning before La Bodega, unpaved 3-km road, 25 mins by taxi from Pereira, US$12, T312-722 3006, fincavillamaria@hotmail.com.
Charming typical coffee hacienda set in beautiful countryside. Large rooms, peaceful, full board. Coffee plantations tours.

Pereira

$$$$ Hacienda San José
Entrada 16 cadena El Tigre, Km 4 Vía Pereira–Cerritos, T6-313 2612, www.haciendahotelsanjose.com.
One of the oldest houses in the region, almost all of its features have been preserved. It is set in delightful grounds and is family friendly. Activities include horse riding and visits to one of the largest bamboo reserves in the region.

$$$$-$$$ Sazagua
Km 7 vía Cerritos, T6-337 9895, www.sazagua.com.
This boutique hotel just outside of town is one of Pereira's oldest and swankiest options. Amenities include a spa and massage services and there is a restaurant serving upscale takes on regional dishes.

$$$ Soratama
Cra 7, No 19-20, T6-335 8650, www.hotelsoratama.com.
On the Plaza Bolívar with helpful staff and lots of services available, 11th-floor **Sky Lounge** restaurant and bar with panoramic views. Discounts available Sat-Sun.

$$-$ Cataluña
C 19, No 8-61, T6-335 4527,
www.hotelcatalunapereira.com.
2 floors up, airy rooms, popular
restaurant, good value.

$ Kolibrí Hostel
C 4, No 16-35, T6-331 3955,
www.kolibrihostel.com.
Close to the centre, with dorms
(US$6.55-7.50 pp), private rooms with
bath and an apartment for up to
8 people. Organizes bike tours through
Retrociclas (see What to do, below).

$ Sweet Home
C 42, No 10-37, T6-345 4453,
www.sweethomehostel.com.
Slightly out of town, but this
backpackers' hostel is worth
the trek. 3 dorms, 1 private room,
breakfast. Handy for the airport.

Around Pereira

$$ Hotel Termales de Santa Rosa de Cabal
Comfortable, chalet style, with restaurant
(see above).

Salento

$$$-$$ La Posada del Café
Cra 6, No 3-08, T6-759 3012,
www.laposadadelcafe.webs.com.
Prettily decorated old *posada* only
3 blocks from main plaza. All rooms have
windows onto the street. Comfortable
lounge areas and patio garden, morning
birdsong; friendly (and quiet) pet dogs,
laundry service, good breakfast. Friendly,
English-speaking owner María Elena is
a mine of information. She will help you
book tours and arrange transfers from
the airport. Recommended.

$$ Hostal Ciudad de Segorbe
C 5, No 4-06, T6-759 3794, www.
hostalciudaddesegorbe.com.
Splendid old *hostal* not far from the main
square. Rooms all have private bath,
including the spacious dorm (US$11.50
pp). Music, TV and reading room and
1 room with disability access. Friendly
and helpful staff with good English.
Recommended.

$$-$ Tralala Hostel
Cra 7, No 6-45, T314-850 5543,
www.hosteltralalasalento.com.
Dutch-run hostel with a dorm
(US$6.50 pp), private rooms and a
studio in the garden, cosy DVD/reading
room, great views, Wellington boot hire.
Recommended.

$ Camping Monteroca
Vereda Boquío, 5 mins before
Salento, before the bridge on
the Río Quindío, T310-422 3720,
www.campingmonteroca.com.
Beside the Río Quindío. Owner Jorge
knows the area, its history and wildlife
well. Well-maintained campsite with
clean showers, communal cooking area,
TV lounge, hammocks. Fantastic themed
cabins, from tree house to 'Hippie Hilton',
all with hot showers; one has a jacuzzi.
Museum of fossils and meteorites, a
room dedicated to Simón Bolívar and a
serpentarium. Camp fires and music in
the evenings.

$ pp La Casa de Lili
C 6, No 3-45, T314-625 1151,
Facebook: hostallacasadelilisalento.
Good beds, tasteful decor, excellent
breakfast, Lili is an enthusiastic hostess.

$ Plantation House
Alto de Coronel, C 7, No 1-04,
T316-285 2603, www.theplantation
housesalento.com.

Popular backpackers' hostel in 2 houses, with private rooms and dorms, outdoor seating area. Gorgeous views, bike hire. English/Colombian-owned, the best local information, also offer tours of their coffee finca nearby. It's possible to stay the night on the top floor of the finca ($). Email reservations only. Highly recommended.

Filandia

$ Hostal el Molino de los Vientos
C 4, No 6-39, T312-6503451.
Simple but clean, comfortable rooms with bath, also family rooms. Flat-screen TV, good location.

$ Hostería de mi Pueblo
Cra 4, No 5-57.
1 block from the main square, traditional style. Price includes bathroom and a good breakfast.

Valle de Cocora

$$ Las Palmas de Cocora
Km 10 Valle de Cocora, T310-455 5400, http://laspalmas decocora.com.
Comfortable rooms with beds and bunks in wooden huts, camping also available. Restaurant serving trout ($$). Horses for hire (US$6 per hr, guide available at extra cost), also guided walks.

Armenia

$$$$-$$$ Hacienda Bambusa
Vía El Caimo–Portugalito Km 93, T301-639 8727, 301-230 2418 in English, www.haciendabambusa.com.
Not strictly a coffee finca, this enchanting traditional hacienda sits amid banana plantations in 160 ha. Very much a place to relax, but there are also plenty of activities on offer, including canopying in a bamboo forest, horse riding or birdwatching. 8 luxurious rooms with a/c, Wi-Fi and hammock on private terrace.Has cable TV, swimming pool, restaurant and free pick-up from airport or bus station. Warmly recommended.

$$$ Centenario
C 21, No 18-20, T6-744 3143, www.hotelcentenario.com.
Bright rooms, attentive staff, gym, sauna, parking.

$$ Café Plaza
Cra 18, No 18-09, T6-741 1500, hotelcafeplaza@hotmail.com.
Near the Plaza Bolívar, a little noisy but simple, clean rooms with bath and TV, breakfast included.

$$ Zuldemayda
C 20, No 15-38, T6-741 0580, http://hotelzuldemayda.co.
A popular central hotel in minimalist style, with restaurant, offers weekend packages.

Montenegro and around

$$$ El Delirio
Km 1 vía Montenegro–Parque del Café, T6-745 0405 / 310 589 6547, casadelirio@hotmail.com.
Beautiful, traditional finca restored with immaculate taste, "a perfect place to unwind", pool, large gardens, delicious food.

$$ El Carriel
Km 1 vía Quimbaya–Filandia, T315-404 2235, http://elcarrielagroturismo.com.
An excellent option if you are looking for an economic stay on a working coffee finca. Simple but comfortable rooms, hot water, restaurant. The coffee tour takes you through the whole coffee-making process.

Ibagué

$$ Lusitania
Cra 2, No 15-55, T8-261 9166.
Smartly modernized old hotel near
historical city centre, with pool and good
restaurant, clean rooms, efficient service,
interesting collection of local antiquities
on display, recommended.

$$ Ukuku
*Corregimiento de Juntas, 17 km from
Ibague, T313-219 3188, http://ukuku.co/.*
Modern eco-lodge in spectacular
isolated location overlooking the Cañón
del Combeima, panoramic views all
around; also camping (US$9pp) and
hiking, horse riding, photo safaris and
many other activities on offer.

Restaurants

Pereira

$$$ Ambar
C 14, No 18-18, T6-344 7444.
Fine dining in colourful modern setting,
traditional dishes served up with
contemporary flair, from rich pepper
steak to succulent ceviche, with outdoor
seating area; very popular as perhaps the
best in town, worth booking ahead.

$$-$ Pasaje de la Alcaldía
In a narrow alleyway next to the Alcaldía.
A number of cheap eating options
including French, Italian, Colombian and
a few cafés.

Salento

$$$ Juan Esteban
*Cra 7, No 5-45, T313-765 5810,
www.fondadelosarrieroscom.*
On the main Plaza Bolívar, with chunky
wooden tables and rustic decor, this
meat-feast haven serves great steaks
and freshwater fish, good wine list; also

owns **La Fonda de los Arrieros**, on the
opposite corner, with similar traditional
cuisine, plus occasional live music.

$$ Café Bernabé
C 3, No 6-03, T318-3933278.
Café and restaurant in quiet location,
cocktails, excellent meals including trout,
meat dishes and pasta, good coffee,
reservation recommended.

$$-$ Balcones del Ayer
*C 6, No 5-40, T6-759 3273,
www.balconesdelayer.com.*
Serving trout, the local speciality, as well
as good quality meat dishes. Efficient and
recommended. Also has rooms to let (**$**).

$ Arte Etnia y Sabor
C 4, No 6-45.
Lovely little café, with artistically
cluttered decor, as its name suggests;
great-value set meals and delicious
juices, highly recommended.

$ Café Jesús Martín
Cra 6, No 6-14. T300-7355679.
Excellent little café with its own coffee
from Señor Bedoya's father's finca. Great
snacks, simple meals and free Wi-Fi (see
also What to do, below); has 2 coffee
shops in Salento and 1 in Armenia. You
can also buy coffee here. Recommended.

$ El Rincón de Lucy
Cra 6, No 4-02.
Excellent breakfasts, lunches and
dinners, limited menu, but great value,
tasty local food. Recommended.

Filandia

$$ Casa de las Orquídeas
Cra 6, No 7-34, T314-4703107.
Steaks, chicken, pasta and fresh
salads. Pleasant atmosphere and
friendly service.

$$ Helena Restaurant
Cra 7a, No 8-01, T320-6659612.
Highly recommended for cocktails and
innovative local food. Portions are large,
the welcome is warm and it has an
attractive patio setting.

Armenia

$$ Café Quindío
Cra 19, No 33N-41, T6-745 4478,
www.cafequindio.com.co.
Gourmet coffee shop and restaurant
next to Parque de la Vida, serving recipes
such as chicken or steak in coffee sauce
as well as international dishes. Also sells
coffee products from its own farm.

$$ Keizaki
*Oasis de Laureles local 10, Cra 15, No 22N-
59, T6-731 2234, www.keizaki.com.*
Sushi and other Asian dishes. There are
several other good restaurants on the
same block, and 2 other Keizaki outlets
in Pereira.

$$ La Fogata
Av Bolívar, No 14N-39, T6-749 5980,
www.lafogata.com.co.
One of Armenia's most popular
restaurants, serving steaks, pork
chops and international dishes,
from Peru to Singapore.

$ La Puerta Quindiana
C 21, No 20-11.
This restaurant serves cheap *comida
corriente*, with dishes such as *sancocho*
a speciality, as well as good fruit juices.

$ Natural Food Plaza
Cra 14, No 4-51, T6-745 1597,
www.naturalfoodplaza.
fundacionlasdelicias.org.
Vegetarian, varied menu and fruit juices.
Also has a wholefood shop.

Festivals

Montenegro
Dec Fiesta de Velas y Faroles,
in Quimbaya.

Ibagué
Jun-Jul National Folklore Festival,
www.festivalfolclorico.com. Tolima
Department commemorates **San Juan**
(24 Jun) and SS Pedro y Pablo (29 Jun)
with fireworks, and music.

What to do

Pereira
Living Trips, *Entrada 16 via Cerritos,
T6-312 8671, www.livingtrips.com.* Offers a
number of multiple-day excursions, such
as rafting and coffee tours, in the region.
Retro Ciclas, *C 4, No 16-36 (at Kolibrí
Hostel), T310-540 7327, www.retrociclas.co.*
Bike tour agency that runs city tours
as well as adventure trips through the
surrounding areas.

Salento
Aldea del Artesano, *C 12A, No 5-148,
book through Alejandro, T320-782
9128, aldeadelartesano@gmail.com.*
Craftworkers community project with
handicraft courses and a shop.
Café Jesús Martín, *Cra 6, No 6-14 (coffee
shop), T6-759 3282, www.cafejesusmartin.
com.* 2-hr tours of local coffee-roasting
factory, fun and informative. Also
3- to 4-hr tours visiting a coffee finca
in Quimbaya, plantation tour with
explanation of coffee-making and coffee
and a brownie in the Salento coffee
shop, minimum 3 participants. There are
outlets in Armenia and Valle de Cocora.
Recommended.
The Colombian Way, *http://the
colombianway.co.* Jeep tours of Salento
and Cocora valley, from US$9 pp.

Armenia

Balsaje Los Remansos, *C 16, No 16-34, Quimbaya, T314-775 4231, see Facebook. Balsaje* excursions (punting on bamboo rafts) on the Río La Vieja.

Transport

Pereira
Air
Matecaña airport is 5 km to the south, bus, US$0.40. Daily flights to **Medellín**, **Bogotá**, **Cali** and **Ibagué**; less frequent to other cities.

Bus
Local taxi and bus services, including the **Megabús**, www.megabus.gov.co, are good. Terminal is at C 17, No 23-157, 1.5 km south of city centre, T6-315 2323, www.terminalpereira.com. Bus to **Armenia**, 1 hr, US$2-3, a beautiful trip. To **Salento**, 1 hr, US$2, frequent, from 0630-1830. To **Cartago**, US$1.50, 45 mins, **Arauca** *buseta* every 10 mins. To **Cali**, US$7-10, 4½-5 hrs, *colectivo* by day, bus by night. To **Medellín**, 6-8 hrs, US$15-22. To/from **Bogotá**, US$18-21, 7 hrs (route is via Girardot, Ibagué – both cities bypassed – and Armenia).

Salento
Bus
To **Armenia** every 20 mins, US$2, 1 hr. To **Pereira**, 4 a day, hourly from 0730 to 1830 at weekends, US$2.50, 1 hr. To **Medellín**, via Pereira, several companies, direct with **Flota Occidental**, 5 a day 0800-1600, US$16, 7-9 hrs.

Filandia
Bus
There are frequent buses from **Pereira** (**Expreso Alcalá**, US$2.50); if coming from **Salento**, change at Las Cruces junction on the main road.

Armenia
Air
El Edén, 13 km from city. Daily to **Bogotá** and **Medellín**. Fog can delay flights.

Bus
Terminal at C 35, No 20-68, T6-747 3355, www.terminalarmenia.com. Bus to **Salento**, 1 hr, US$2, frequent, from 0520-2000. To **Ibagué**, US$6-8, 3 hrs. **Bogotá**, hourly, 7-9 hrs, US$12-18. **Cali**, US$7-9, 3 hrs, frequent.

Ibagué

Air
Daily flights to **Bogotá**, **Cali** and **Medellín**, also to **Pereira**.

Bus
Terminal is between Cra 2, No 20-89, www.terminalibague.com. Tourist police at terminal helpful. Frequent services to **Bogotá**, US$11.50, 4 hrs. To **Cali** US$15-21, 6-7 hrs; **Neiva**, US$12-14, 4 hrs, and many other places.

Southern Colombia

stone statues, sulphur pools and salsa in the steamy south

Much of southern Colombia is characterized by the three mountain ranges that eventually join up to form the high Andes, South America's spine, and people of this region have adapted to the physical obstacles these mountains present.

The sensual city of Cali in the tropical Valle del Cauca has branded itself as the capital of salsa music. To the west lies the Pacific port of Buenaventura, an unlovely place but a handy hub for visiting offshore islands and peaceful Afro-Colombian fishing villages. The Pan-American Highway continues south to the city of Popayán, known for its dazzling white colonial buildings and its solemn Easter processions. Hidden in the mountains east of Popayán are the mysterious archaeological sites of Tierradentro and San Agustín, while next to the Magdalena river lies the geographical anomaly that is the Tatacoa Desert.

From Popayán, the Cordillera Occidental rises even higher to the towns of Pasto and Ipiales on the border with Ecuador. To the west is Colombia's most southerly stretch of Pacific coast, while far to the east is Leticia, the country's toehold on the Amazon and a gateway to Brazil and Peru. Amacayacu National Park and the village of Puerto Nariño allow travellers to observe some of this mighty river's wildlife at close range.

Best for
Archaeology ▪ Festivals ▪ Volcanoes ▪ Wildlife

Footprint
picks

★ **Cali's nightlife**, pages 244 and 251

Dance the night away in a *salsateca*.

★ **The journey to San Cipriano**, page 247

Ride a *brujita* along the rails through thick jungle to this isolated village.

★ **Pre-Columbian archaeology**, pages 257 and 264

Admire the burial mounds at Tierradentro and the carved megaliths at San Agustín.

★ **Parque Nacional Natural de Puracé**, page 262

Soak in the sulphur pools or climb to the summit of a volcano.

★ **Desierto de Tatacoa**, page 265

Spend a night in the desert under countless stars.

★ **Carnaval de los Blancos y Negros**, pages 270 and 275

Get very messy at these lively festivals in Pasto.

★ **Las Lajas**, page 272

Join thousands of pilgrims at the neo-Gothic sanctuary.

★ **Puerto Nariño**, page 278

Use this tranquil riverside village as a base for spotting pink dolphins or visiting the Tikuna tribe.

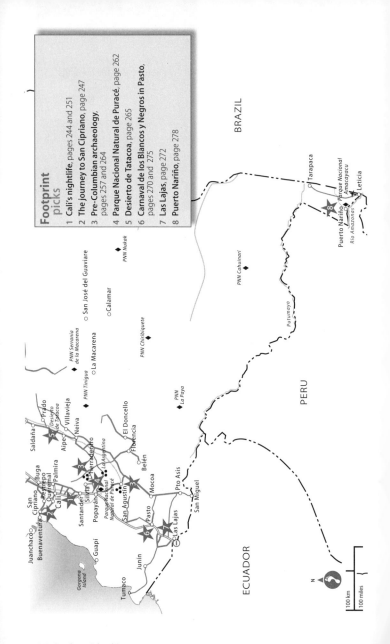

BRAZIL

PERU

ECUADOR

PNN Serranía de la Macarena

San José del Guaviare

PNN Nukak

Calamar

La Macarena

PNN Tinigua

PNN Chiribiquete

PNN Cahuinari

Putumayo

PNN La Paya

Desierto de Tatacoa

Prado

Villavieja

Neiva

Aipe

Saldaña

El Doncello

Florencia

Belén

Mocoa

Pto Asís

San Miguel

San Cipriano

Juanchaco

Buenaventura

Guapi

Gorgona Island

Junín

Tumaco

San Andrés

Buga

Restrepo

Queremal

Cali

Palmira

Santander

Popayán

Parque Nacional Natural de Puracé

Silvia

Tierradentro

La Argentina

San Agustín

Pasto

Las Lajas

Puerto Nariño

Parque Nacional Amacayacu

Río Amazonas

Leticia

Tarapaca

100 km
100 miles

N

Essential Southern Colombia

Finding your feet

The Pan-American Highway provides the quickest access to Cali from the north, continuing to Popayán, Pasto and the Ecuadorean border. Another major route heads southwest from Bogotá, following the Río Magdalena to Neiva, Pitalito (for access to San Agustín) and Mocoa. There are airports at Cali, Popayán and Pasto. Note that there is a malaria risk along the Pacific coast and in the southeast towards Amazonia.

Getting around

Walking is the best way to get around town centres, including Cali, but you'll need taxis to reach the outlying suburbs. Long-distance buses travel around the region; *busetas* and *colectivos* are more expensive but significantly faster and may be the only option in more remote areas.

When to go

Cali and its surroundings are warm throughout the year, with little climate variation. It is hot and humid at midday but a strong breeze that blows up in the afternoon makes the evenings cool and pleasant. Rain can come at more or less any time, although the city is shielded from the heavy rainfall on the Pacific coast by the Cordillera Occidental. To the east, Huila department can be swelteringly hot year round, but the upland areas around Popayán, San Agustín and Tierradentro are noticeably cooler, particularly in the evenings; temperatures drop still further in mountainous regions near the Ecuadorean border. Around San Agustín, the rainy season is April to June/July, but since the weather often comes up from the Amazon to the southeast, it can rain at any time, hence the beautiful green landscape. Festivals are a big deal throughout the region; the biggest celebrations take place in early January in Cali, Popayán and especially Pasto; at Easter in Popayán, and in June in Neiva and San Agustín.

Time required

Spend two to three days in Cali and two to three weeks exploring the rest of the region.

Weather Southern Colombia (Cali)

January	February	March	April	May	June
28°C 19°C 50mm	24°C 19°C 60mm	24°C 19°C 100mm	23°C 19°C 140mm	23°C 19°C 110mm	23°C 19°C 60mm

July	August	September	October	November	December
23°C 18°C 30mm	24°C 18°C 50mm	23°C 18°C 60mm	23°C 18°C 120mm	23°C 18°C 110mm	23°C 19°C 70mm

Cali

The hot, rich agricultural land of the Valle de Cauca is flanked on either side by the slender fingers of two mountain ranges, the Cordillera Occidental and the Cordillera Central. Capital of the department, Cali (population 2,732,000) is Colombia's third city and the country's self-declared salsa capital. If you're looking to join swinging salsa couples on the dance floor, Cali should not to be missed. Sensuous, tropical rhythms are ubiquitous, seeming to seep from every part of the city's being. Cali was founded in 1536, and until 1900 it was a leisurely colonial

Cali

Where to stay 🛏
Acqua Santa Lofts **1** *D1*
Aparta Hotel del Río **2** *C5*
Boutique San Antonio **3** *C1*
Colombian Home Hostel
4 *D1*

El Viajero Cali Hostel **5** *C2*
Hostal Iguana **6** *A4*
Intercontinental **7** *C1*
La Casa Café **8** *C1*
La Pinta Boogaloo **9** *B1*
NOW Hotel **10** *A4*

Pelican Larry Hostel **11** *E*
Posada de San Antonio
12 *C1*
Tostaky **13** *C1*

town. Then the railway came and Cali is now a rapidly expanding industrial complex serving the whole of southern Colombia.

Sights The city's centre is the **Plaza de Caicedo**, with a statue of one of the independence leaders, Joaquín Caicedo y Cuero. Facing the plaza is the elegant **Palacio Nacional** and the **Cathedral**, seat of the influential Archbishop of Cali. Nearby is the renovated church and 18th-century monastery of **San Francisco** ① *Cra 6, C 9/10*, with a splendidly proportioned domed belltower. Cali's oldest church, **La Merced** ① *C 7, between Cras 3 and 4*, has been restored by the Banco Popular. The adjoining convent houses two museums: **Museo de Arte Colonial**

Restaurants 🍴
Antigua Contemporánea
  1 *C1*
El Solar **2** *B4*
El Zaguán de San Antonio
  3 *C1*

Karen's Pizza **4** *D1*
La Tartine **5** *B1*
Lengua de Mariposa **6** *C1*
Tortelli **7** *B1*

Bars & clubs 🍸
Delirio **19** *A6*
Jala Jala **20** *A5*
La Topa Tolondra **23** *D1*
Living Club **24** *A5*
Talbert's Pub **25** *A4*

Tin Tin Deo **26** *D1*
Zaperoco **27** *B4*

BACKGROUND
Cali

After the collapse of the Incas in 1533, Sebastián de Belalcázar left Pizarro's army in Peru and came north, founding Quito in 1534. He established Popayán and (Santiago de) Cali in 1536, intending to continue northwards and establish other new settlements. But around Cali he encountered stiff resistance from the indigenous locals, which delayed him for several years, so that other conquistadors founded Antioquia and Bogotá.

The first site of the city was beside the Río Lili near the present Ciudad Universitaria and Ciudad Jardín, but it was moved north to its present location in 1539. Cali remained a dependency of Popayán and was dominated by Quito for 250 years, due to the fact that north–south communications along the line of the cordillera were so much easier than across the mountain ranges. Indeed, Cali remained a leisurely colonial town until 1900 and the arrival of the railway, when it rapidly expanded into an industrial complex serving the whole of southern Colombia.

The railway has since been eclipsed by road and air links, but today Cali is economically closely tied with the rest of Colombia as the capital of the rich agricultural Valle del Cauca Department, which produces sugar, cotton, rice, coffee and cattle. It sits on the main route north from Ecuador along the Río Cauca and controls the passage to the only important port on Colombia's Pacific coast, Buenaventura. Thanks to the port and the sugar industry, many Afro-Caribbeans and other groups of people have come to the valley over the years and now contribute to the city's wealth and entertainment.

In the early 1990s Cali achieved international notoriety because of its highly successful drug cartel. Known as the 'Gentlemen of Cali', thanks to their high society background, the Rodríguez Orejuela brothers and their associate José Santacruz Londoño profited from Pablo Escobar's war with the government, rising to supersede his Medellín organization. But in 2006 the Rodríguez Orejuela brothers were extradited to the United States, where they were tried and imprisoned for 30 years each, effectively bringing this cartel to an end.

Now Colombia's third city, Cali has largely eradicated the worst of its past crime problems and has become a major destination for visitors, particularly for its reputation as the capital of salsa.

(which includes the church), a collection of 16th- and 17th-century paintings, and the **Museo Arqueológico** ⓘ *Cra 4, No 6-59, T2-885 5309, Mon-Sat 0900-1800, Sun 1000-1600, US$3*, with pre-Columbian pottery. **Museo del Oro Calima** ⓘ *C 7, No 4-69, T2-684 7751, www.banrepcultural.org/cali/museo-del-oro-calima, Tue-Fri 0900-1700, Sat 1000-1700, free*, has pre-Columbian goldwork and pottery.

The **Museo La Tertulia** ⓘ *Av Colombia, No 5-105 Oeste, T2-893 2939 ext 101, www. museolatertulia.com, Tue-Sat 1000-1800, Sun 1400-1800, US$3.50, Sun free*, exhibits South American, including local, modern art and shows unusual films (US$1.50). The neighbourhood of **San Antonio** (behind the Intercontinental Hotel) is the city's oldest area, where Cali's colonial past can still be felt. The area has a relaxed, bohemian atmosphere, especially at weekends when it's livelier. There are good views of the city from the 18th-century church of San Antonio.

Buga and westwards

The pleasant colonial city of **Buga**, 74 km north of Cali on the Panamericana (1¼ hours by bus, US$3-4), has long been popular with Colombians, primarily pilgrims visiting its cathedral, **Basílica del Señor de los Milagros**. More recently, the city has also been attracting visitors from further afield, with hostels opening up, as well an excellent German-run microbrewery, producing the divinely named Holy Water Ale. From Buga, the road west to Buenaventura on the coast passes the **Laguna de Sonso** reserve, good for birdwatching, hiking and biking, before crossing the Río Cauca. Beyond the river, near the crest of the Cordillera, is another park, **Reserva Natural Bosque de Yotoco**, noted for orchids. The road continues to the man-made **Lago Calima**. Many treasures of the Calima culture are said to have been flooded by the lake, when the dam was built. This is an important centre for water sports, riding and other activities. The northern route round the lake goes through **Darién** at 1500 m with an **archaeological museum** ① *Tue-Fri 0800-1200, 1300-1700, Sat-Sun 1000-1800*, with good displays of Calima and other cultures. There are hotels in the village, and cabins at a Centro Náutico on the lakeside. Camping is possible near the village. There are direct buses to Darién from Cali, US$6, 2½ hours.

★ San Cipriano

A popular excursion from Cali is to San Cipriano, 30 km west on the railway line to Buenaventura. The line is now freight-only, so to get to the village, you must get off the bus at Córdoba, from where ingeniously adapted rail cars (man-powered or motorbike-powered) descend to the village through beautiful scenery (US$3, only pay for the return leg when returning). There are crystal-clear rivers and waterfalls and inner tubes can be rented for US$2 for floating downstream. The village and its surroundings are a national reserve of 8564 ha, entry US$0.75. Take insect repellent.

Buenaventura and the islands

The port of Buenaventura is not safe to visit, for this reason it is not included in this edition. **Isla Gorgona**, the former prison island now a national park, is partially open. Entrance fee is US$14 for foreigners, but entry is allowed only for day visits, research or dive boats. There are no facilities for overnight stays and no reservation system. See warning on page 335. **Isla Malpelo**, 506 km west of Buenaventura, was declared a UNESCO site in 2006. It is an acclaimed birdwatching haven with great diving opportunities. The island is considered to be one of the world's best places to observe hammerhead sharks in great numbers. It can only be reached by boat from Buenaventura, a 36-hour bumpy voyage. There are no places to stay on the island and camping is not allowed. If you wish to visit Gorgona or Malpelo contact the National Parks office in Bogotá (T1-353 2400, www.parquesnacionales.gov.co), or the National Parks office in Cali (see page 249). For information on dive boats contact **Embarcaciones Asturias** ① *Harold Botero, T2-242 4620, or 313-7672864,* *barcoasturias@yahoo.com.* **Akua Travel Agency** ⓘ *Cra 30, No 5A-79, San Fernando, T314-880 1607/301 541 7282, www.akua.com.co,* based in Cali, offers whalewatching and other tours in the region.

The nearby fishing villages of **Ladrilleros**, **Juanchaco** and **La Barra** (which are within the Uramba Bahía Málaga Marine National Park) have clean, sandy beaches, accessible only by boat from Buenaventura (arrive early in the day to avoid having to stay overnight in Buenaventura; US$20-23 per person one-way to Juanchaco, one hour, then motorbike taxi available on to Ladrilleros). There are hostels to stay in and facilities are basic, but it's an interesting insight into Afro-Colombian culture. Mangrove trips are available and there is whale watching from June to September.

Around Cali

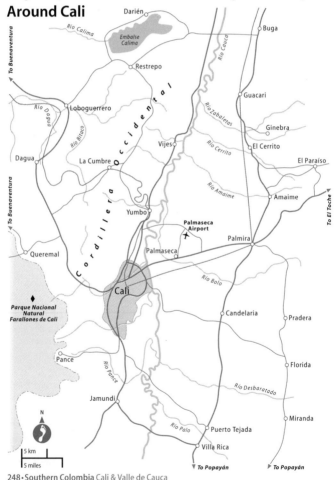

Tourist information

Cali

National Parks office
C 29N, No 6N-43, Santa Mónica,
T2-667 6041.
Very helpful.

Punto de Información Turística (PIT)
Cra 4 C 6 esq. Mon-Fri 0800-1700,
Sat 1000-1400.
Housed inside the large red-brick
Cultural Centre, the PIT has pamphlets
but otherwise isn't much help. The centre
also has free exhibitions in the hallways.

Secretaría de Cultura y Turismo
Cra 5, No 6-05, sala 102, T2-885 4777
ext 102, www.cali.gov.co.
Also has a PIT in reception,
open same hours.

Where to stay

Cali

$$$$-$$$ Acqua Santa Lofts
Cra 106A, No 18-51, Ciudad Jardín, T2-
485 5331/, www.acquasantahotel.com.
Luxurious boutique hotel with modern
loft apartments in smart southern
suburbs; each immaculately furnished
apartment is individually designed and
brimming with mod cons, from high-tech
kitchen to jacuzzi on a private balcony;
with salt-water pool, gym, spa, meals in
adjacent pizzeria (Karen's, see below) or
in-room service. Highly recommended.

$$$$-$$$ Intercontinental
Av Colombia, No 2-72, T2-882 3225,
www.intercontinental.com.
On the edge of San Antonio, this is
the most expensive hotel in town. Big,
modern block with spa, outdoor pool

and elegant restaurant, **La Terraza**,
along with 4 others. Cheaper Sat-
Sun. Good central location, close
to restaurants and nightclubs.

$$$ Hotel Boutique San Antonio
Cra 6, No 2-51, T2-524 6364, www.
hotelboutiquesanantonio.com.
Charming colonial-style hotel with
10 sound-proofed rooms, own security
system, cheaper at weekends and for
5+ nights, rooftop bar, excellent service,
tours and salsa dance classes arranged.

$$$ NOW Hotel
Av 9A N, No 10N-74, T2-2488 9797,
www.nowhotel.com.co.
Colourful, modern boutique hotel in
cosmopolitan Barrio Granada; spacious
rooms with wide-screen TV and the
usual mod cons, split-level rooftop
restaurant and pool, with great views
over the city, upstairs bar attracts trendy
local crowd, huge lobby festooned
with parasols and hanging plants.
Recommended.

$$ Aparta Hotel Del Río
Av 2N, No 16N-30, T2-660 2713,
www.apartahoteldelrio.com.
Modern, business-style hotel, with
comfortable suites and rooms, good
facilities (gym, sauna, pool, laundry), safe,
restaurant, parking, in financial district,
plenty of riverside restaurants nearby.

$$ Posada de San Antonio
Cra 5, No 3-37, T2-893 7413,
www.posadadesanantonio.com.
Rooms set around a couple of
patios in pretty colonial building,
decorated with Calima artefacts
and modern art, good value.
10% discount for Footprint readers.

$$-$ El Viajero Cali Hostel
Cra 5 No 4-56, San Antonio, T2-893 8342, www.elviajerohostels.com.
Doubles (cheaper with shared bath) with TV, dorms (US$9-10 pp), salsa school, pool, open-air bar, cinema room and a stage for shows. Breakfast, internet and Wi-Fi included.

$$-$ La Pinta Boogaloo
Cra 3 Oeste, No 11-49, Bellavista, T2-892 2448, www.lapinta.com.co.
In a mansion in a quiet neighbourhood, private rooms (cheaper with shared bath), dorms (US$7-10) and camping, restaurant, bar, pool, garden, cinema room, kitchen available, salsa classes arranged, newest hostel in chain also in Bogotá, Cartagena, San Andrés and Chinauta.

$ Colombian Home Hostel
C 3bis, No 35A-70, San Fernando Viejo, T320-629 7879/315-705 2343, colombianhostecolombian@hotmail. com, Facebook: Colombian Home Hostel.
Colombian-owned hostel, dorms with and without bath and a private room, hot water, welcoming and helpful, also offer salsa classes.

$ Hostal Iguana
Av 9 Norte, No 22N-22, T2-382 5364, or 313-768 6024, www.iguana.com.co.
In 2 suburban houses on the edge of fashionable Barrio Granada, dorm US$9 pp, popular backpackers' hostel so there can be a lot of *movimiento*. Private rooms, some with bath, garden, TV room with DVDs, Spanish and free salsa classes and good local information.

$ La Casa Café
Cra 6, No 2-13, T316-521 7388, www.lacasacafecali.blogspot.com.
Nice backpackers' hostel and café. Simple rooms with high ceilings, wooden floorboards and shared baths,

bed in dorm US$8. Next door they have rooms with bath; café hosts cultural and music evenings.

$ Pelican Larry Hostel
C 20 Norte, No 6AN-44, Barrio Granada, T2-382 7226, www.hostelpelicanlarry.com.
Rooms with and without bath, also has dorms. Close to Zona Rosa restaurants and bars, 15 mins' walk from bus terminal and centre, hot water, laundry and internet extra, Sun night barebecue, Spanish lessons and free salsa classes arranged, TV room, helpful staff. Recommended.

$ Tostaky
Cra 10, No 1-76, T2-893 0651, www.tostakycali.com.
At the bottom of San Antonio park, good backpackers' hostel, French/Colombian-run, airy rooms and dorms (US$8.50) above a café open only to guests, hot water, shared bath, breakfast extra. There is also a studio with private bath. Recommended.

Buga

$ Buga Hostel
Cra 13, No 4-83, T2-236 7752, http://bugahostel.com.
German-run hostel, which also owns a microbrewery (see page 247); with dorms (US$9 pp) and private rooms, kitchen, roof terrace, free Wi-Fi and coffee, bike rental, laundry service, guided tours.

Restaurants

In the centre, Parque de Peñón, just north of San Antonio, has an excellent selection of restaurants serving all types of international food, while San Antonio itself has many good restaurants and cafés. In the north, Barrio Granada has an enormous number of eating places to choose from. In the south, Parque del Perro (C3A, Cra 34) is ringed by lively bars and restaurants with outdoor tables, popular with groups of young locals.

$$$ Antigua Contemporánea
C 10, No 1-39, T2-893 6809.
Classy San Antonio restaurant in rambling colonial house, with cosy nooks and crannies, softly lit with brass lanterns, bubbling fountains and Buddha statues; the good food is not the main attraction but the romantic ambience definitely is; also with a shop selling antiques and chic designer fashion.

$$$ El Solar
C 15 Norte, No 9N-62, Barrio Granada, T318-348 9327.
Great atmosphere and a varied menu, mix of Italian and Latin American, occasional live music, outdoor eating area, popular.

$$$ La Tartine
C 3 Oeste, No 1-74, T2-893 6617.
Classic French-owned restaurant in a tasteful setting, with mix of modern and classic artworks; traditional cuisine such as fondues and Coquilles Saint Jacques.

$$$ Tortelli
C 3 Oeste, No 3-15, T2-893 3227, www.restaurantetortelli.com.
Smart Italian restaurant serving great home-made pasta, fresh seafood, steaks and risottos, overlooking Parque del Peñón, pretty little square between San Antonio and the river. 3 more branches in the city.

$$ Karen's Pizza
C 18, No 106A, T2-312 6868, https://www. facebook.com/KarensPizzaOficial.
Excellent freshly baked pizzas and fruity ice creams in airy open-sided restaurant

in leafy Ciudad Jardín; fun kids' club upstairs for parties, with cooking classes, climbing wall and games area. Highly recommended.

$$-$ El Zaguán de San Antonio
Cra 12, No 1-29, San Antonio, T2-893 8021.
Long-established favourite with locals, walls covered with photos and messages from regulars past and present; imaginative local dishes such as *puerquita* – tamales stuffed with *chicharrón* pork rinds – and *aborrajados* – deep-fried plantains stuffed with cheese.

$ Lengua de Mariposa
Cra 6, No 1-19, T2- 378 9301, https://lenguademariposacom. wordpress.com/. Tue-Sun from 1300.
Lovely little café serving delicious artisan ice creams; try exotic fruit flavours such as *chontadura*, *champus*, *apiche*, or the simple but refreshing ginger and lemon; outdoor tables in the shade of a giant mango tree, in a quiet corner of San Antonio.

★ Bars and clubs

Cali's nightlife is legendary, especially the *salsatecas* – salsa-playing discos. Many places have a cover charge, around US$4-6 for men, US$3-5 for women, which includes a drinks voucher. The most popular with *caleños* can be found on Av 6 Norte where there are dozens to choose from. Barrios Juanchito and Menga also have a range of salsa bars and huge, hi-tech *salsatecas*. It is worth visiting just to watch couples dancing salsa and to join in, if you dare! Go with locals and couples; groups of foreign male tourists might have a hard time getting in. If heading to Juanchito or Menga, it's advisable to take a registered radio

Salsa may have its roots in Cuba and have developed its sound in the Latin barrios of New York, but the people of Cali claim that it's in their city that it has found its true home. It can be heard everywhere – on radios, in taxis, bars and nightclubs. So all-pervasive is its reach that it can be said that this horn-led music with its complex, syncopated beats has, literally, become part of the rhythm of everyday life.

Local groups such as Orquesta Guayacán, Grupo Niche and Jairo Varela have helped develop a distinctive sound, which is mirrored on the dance floor by a style that is characterized by an upright upper body and intricate movements of the feet.

'No salsa, no dates', say the locals. At the weekend, sexual attraction is measured in moves on the dance floors of Juanchito's enormous *salsatecas*. But salsa purists also head for traditional salsa bars nearer the centre, such as **Zaperoco**, where the dancing is the most important thing.

taxi there and back (15 mins), across the bridge over the Río Cauca.

Delirio
*Cra 26 No 12-328 T2-8937610, delirio.com.
co/en. Last Fri of the month.*
A spectacular mix of salsa and circus. Try to arrive early and get seats near the front. The show is popular with locals as well as tourists. Expensive but highly recommended. Also runs a non-profit salsa school foundation.

Jala Jala
C10, No 36A-154, Acopi Menga, T315-847 6696, www.jalajalaclub.com.
High-tech and heaving club in Menga, bristling with laser lights and video screens; crossover range of music, including hip hop, reggaeton, *merengue*, *bachata*, electronica, but most of all salsa; good and fairly priced bottle service.

La Topa Tolondra
*C5, No 13-27, T323-597 2646, https://
www.facebook.com/Latopabar.*
High-energy salsa bar, great for dancing, learning or just watching the experts;

down-to-earth atmosphere and reasonably priced drinks, salsa lessons on Mon nights.

Living Club
Cra 40 No 11-83, Barrio Menga, T300-787 0335, Facebook: livingclubcali.
Massive and lively nightclub, with wide range of music from salsa to electronica.

Talbert's Pub
C 17N, No 8N-60, T2-660 5080/8371, and Bourbon St, Av 9N, No 15AN-27, T2-381 6398, Barrio Granada, Facebook: bourbonstcol. Open from 1700.
English- and American-themed bars, with same owner, English music generally, good live bands on Fri and good atmosphere in general.

Tin Tin Deo
*C 5, No 38-71, T2-514 1537,
www.tintindeo.com.*
Long-established top salsa venue, attracts salsa pros, students and teachers and is more forgiving of beginners; packed most nights, but good table service and welcoming to all.

Zaperoco
*Av 5N, No 16-46, T313-661 2040,
Facebook: zaperoco.*
The place for salsa purists, live bands on
Thu, with cover charge, otherwise free
entry; small and smart club, but with big
friendly atmosphere.

Entertainment

Theatre
Teatro Experimental, *C 7, No 8-63,
T314-600 3332, Facebook: tec Enrique
Buenaventura.* Repertory drama, poetry
and art, non-profit avant-garde group
founded in 1950s.
Teatro Jorge Isaacs, *Cra 3, No 12-28,
T2-889 9322, www.teatrojorgeisaacs.com.
co.* Neoclassical 1930s building declared
a National Monument in 1984. Hosts
live jazz and pop music events as well as
circus, pantos and comedy nights.
Teatro La Máscara, *Cra 10, No 3-40, T2-
893 6640, Facebook: Teatro-La-Mascara.*
Principally a women's theatre ensemble
that stages alternative productions.
Teatro Municipal, *Cra 5, No 6-64,
T2-881 3131, www.teatromunicipal.gov.
co.* Since 1918, opera, ballet and weekly
classical concerts, also home to the Cali
Symphony Orchestra.

Festivals

**Jun Festival de Música Andina Mono
Núñez**, www.funmusica.org. 4 days
of traditional Andean musical events
and contests.
Aug/Sep Festival Petronio Alvarez,
Facebook: FestivalPetronioAlvarez.
A week-long celebration of Afro-Latino
and Pacific music, dance and culture.
Sep AjazzGo festival, www.ajazzgo
festival.com. From trad jazz to
experimental and fusion, with
Colombian and international artists.

25-31 Dec Feria de Cali, www.feria
decali.com. The biggest salsa festival
in Latin America, carnival in streets and
at the purpose-built Salsadrome, horse
parades, masquerade balls, sporting
contests and general heavy partying.

Shopping

The best shopping districts are Av 6N,
from Río Cali to C 30 Norte, and
Cra 5 in the south with several new
shopping malls including **Centenario**
(C 8N, No 7N-46), **La Pasarela** (Av 5AN,
No 23DN-68) and **Chipichape**, at the end
of Av 6N, which has cinemas and a good
choice of restaurants and shops.

Handicrafts
Artesanías Pacandé, *Av 6N, No 17A-53,
Facebook: artesaniaspacande.* Typical
regional handicrafts, Mon-Sat 0800-1830.
La Caleñita, *Cr 24, No 8-53/49, Barrio La
Alameda, www.lacalenita.com.* Good
selection of typical handicrafts, home
decor and furnishings.
Parque Artesenal Loma de la Cruz, *C 5,
Cras 14/16. Daily 0900-2200.* Permanent
handicraft market in a pleasant, safe
neighbourhood, with cafés around the
park, best in the mornings.
Platería Ramírez, *5 outlets including
CC Unicentro, T2-660 5460, www.plateria
ramirez.com.* Good selection of jewellery,
from ethnic to modern designs.

Transport

Air
**Alfonso Bonilla Aragón (Palmaseca)
airport**, 20 km from city. Minibus from
airport, from far end of pick-up road
outside arrivals, to bus terminal (ground
floor), every 15 mins from 0430 up to
2020, approximately 30 mins, US$1.50-2;
taxis from here to city centre US$2-3.

Minibuses to airport from 2nd floor of bus terminal until 2020. Taxi to city US$15-25, 20 mins. Frequent services to **Bogotá**, **Medellín**, **Cartagena**, **Ipiales** and other Colombian cities. International flights to **Miami**, **New York**, and **Panama**.

Bus

Urban MIO metro buses, with exclusive city-centre lanes avoiding heavy rush-hour traffic jams, US$0.75 a ride, single tickets sold at the stations; for multiple journeys and to use pre-trunk routes you need a **MIO** smart card (http://mio.com.co), which you pre-charge (minimum US$1), also with handy **Moovit** phone app for route guides.

Long distance Terminal is at C 30N, No 2AN-29, T2-668 3655, www.terminal cali.com, 25 mins' walk from the centre (leave terminal by the taxi stands, take 1st right, go under railway and follow river to centre, or go through tunnel, marked *túnel*, from the terminal itself). Left luggage (US$1.25), ATMs, showers, supermarket and good food outlets. Buses between the bus station and the centre, US$0.75. Taxi from bus station to centre as above. To **Popayán**, many buses, **Belalcazar** have small, comfortable buses, US$7-9, 3 hrs. To **Pasto**, US$18-22, 8-9 hrs. To **Ipiales** (direct), US$24-27, 10-11 hrs; to **San Agustín**, 9 hrs, US$16-20. To **Cartago**, US$9-11, 3-4 hrs. To **Armenia**, US$8-12, 3-4 hrs. To **Manizales**, US$13-16, 4-6 hrs. To **Medellín**, US$21-24, 8-10 hrs. To **Bogotá**, 9-11 hrs, 4 companies, US$22-26. *Busetas* charge more than buses but save time; taxi-*colectivos* charge even more and are even quicker.

Taxi

Ensure that taxi meters are used. Prices, posted in the window, minimum fare US$2. Extra charge on holidays, Sun and at night.

Popayán to Tierradentro

colonial architecture and pre-Columbian archaeology

The Pan-American Highway climbs out of the valley to Popayán, a historic city that gives access to the *páramo* of Puracé in the Cordillera Central and serves as a good base for visiting some of Colombia's most intriguing sights, including the burial caves of Tierradentro and the archaeological site of San Agustín. The Cauca Valley has strong indigenous cultures, notably the Páez people.

Popayán *Colour map 3, B3.*

Founded by Sebastián de Belalcázar, Francisco Pizarro's lieutenant, in 1536, Popayán became the regional seat of government, subject until 1717 to the Audiencia of Quito and, later, to the Audiencia of Bogotá. It is now the capital of the Department of Cauca. The city lies in the Pubenza Valley, a peaceful landscape of palm, bamboo, and the sharp-leaved agave. The early settlers, after setting up their sugar estates in the hot, damp Cauca Valley, retreated to Popayán to live, for the city is high enough to give it a delightful climate. To the north, south and east the broken green plain is bounded by mountains. The flattened cone of the volcano Puracé (4646 m) rises to the southeast, its steaming sulphur vents sometimes visible from the town.

Sights Popayán has retained its colonial character, even though it had to be fully restored after the March 1983 earthquake. The streets of two-storey buildings are in rococo Andalucían style, with beautiful old monasteries and cloisters of pure Spanish classic architecture. The **cathedral** ① *C 5, Cra 6*, has been beautifully restored and has a fine marble Madonna sculpture behind the altar by Buenaventura Malagón and the unusual statue of Christ kneeling on the globe. Among the other churches are **San Agustín** ① *C 7, Cra 6*, note the gilt altarpiece; **Santo Domingo** ① *C 4, Cra 5*, used by the Universidad del Cauca; and **La Encarnación** ① *C 5, Cra 5*, also used for religious music festivals. Walk to **Belén chapel** ① *C4, Cra 0*, seeing the statues en route, and then continue to **El Cerro de las Tres Cruces** if you have the energy, and on to the equestrian statue of Belalcázar on the **Morro de Tulcán**, which overlooks the city; this hill is the site of a pre-Columbian pyramid. Warning: occasional robberies have occurred beyond Belén; it's safer to go in a group. A fine arcaded bridge, **Puente del Humilladero**, crosses the Río Molino at Carrera 6. Public concerts and events are given in the gardens below. **Museo Negret y Museo Iberoamericano de Arte** (MIAMP) ① *C 5, No 10-23, T2-824 4546, http://museonegret.wordpress.com, Wed-Mon 0800-1200, 1400-1800, Sat and Sun 0900-1200, 1400-1700, closed Tue, free*, has works, photographs and

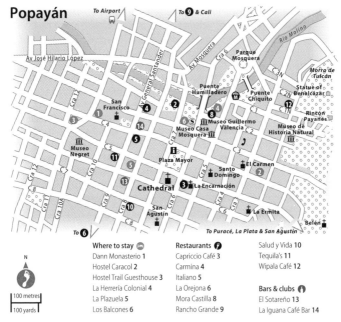

Popayán

To Airport

To ⑨ & Cali

Río Molino

Av José Hilario López

Parque Mosquera

Morro de Tulcán

Statue of Belalcázar

Puente Humilladero

Puente Chiquito

Rincón Payanés

San Francisco

Museo Guillermo Valencia

Museo de Historia Natural

Museo Casa Mosquera

Museo Negret

Plaza Mayor

Santo Domingo

El Carmen

Cathedral

La Encarnación

San Agustín

La Ermita

Belén

To ⑥

To Puracé, La Plata & San Agustín

N

100 metres
100 yards

Where to stay 🛏
Dann Monasterio **1**
Hostel Caracol **2**
Hostel Trail Guesthouse **3**
La Herrería Colonial **4**
La Plazuela **5**
Los Balcones **6**

Restaurants 🍴
Capriccio Café **3**
Carmina **4**
Italiano **5**
La Orejona **6**
Mora Castilla **8**
Rancho Grande **9**

Salud y Vida **10**
Tequila's **11**
Wipala Café **12**

Bars & clubs 🍸
El Sotareño **13**
La Iguana Café Bar **14**

BACKGROUND
Popayán

Popayán was founded by Sebastián de Belalcázar, Francisco Pizarro's lieutenant, in 1536, in the valley of the Pubenza. After establishing their sugar estates in the hot, damp Cauca Valley, early settlers retreated to Popayán to live. The city was high enough to give it a delightful climate, and it was surrounded by a peaceful landscape of palm, bamboo and the sharp-leaved agave. After the conquest of the indigenous Pijao, Popayán became the regional seat of government, subject until 1717 to the Audiencia of Quito, and later to the Audiencia of Bogotá.

Popayán has given no fewer than eleven presidents to the Republic. It is also the birthplace of the scientist Francisco José de Caldas (1768-1816), who discovered how to determine altitude by variations in the boiling point of water. It was to him that Mutis (of the famous *Expedición Botánica*) entrusted the directorship of the newly founded Observatory at Bogotá. Caldas was a passionate partisan of Independence and was executed in 1815 during Morillo's 'Reign of Terror'.

The city has also produced many celebrated poets, most notably the leading Modernist, Maestro Guillermo Valencia (1873-1943). More recently, Popayán has achieved recognition for its outstanding cuisine, named in 2005 as UNESCO's first ever City of Gastronomy.

furniture of Negret and exhibitions of contemporary art. **Casa Mosquera** ⓘ *C 3, No 5-14, www.unicauca.edu.co/museos/museomosq/info.html, Tue-Sun 0800-1200, 1400-1800, US$0.75*, has collections of colonial religious art and historical objects in the house of four-times president Tomás Cipriano de Mosquera. The **Museo de Historia Natural** ⓘ *Cra 2, No 1A-25, www.unicauca.edu.co/museonatural, daily 0900-1100, 1400-1600, US$1*, has good displays of archaeological and geological items with sections on insects (particularly good on butterflies), reptiles, mammals and birds. Providing a great introduction to the town, free **walking tours** ⓘ *Mon-Sat 1000 and 1600 (tips appreciated) in English and Spanish (and sometimes Italian and French)*, are run by university students. They leave from the TO kiosk in front of Juan Valdez café on the main plaza. A highly recommended **coffee tour** ⓘ *US$11 including lunch with the children*, is run by **Fundación Fedar** (www.fedar.org/), a charity-run school in Popayán for children with special needs; departing at 0700, *chiva* buses take visitors to a local coffee finca, where the pupils guide them around, showing the production process and plantation; bookings through **Hostal Trail Guesthouse** or **Hostal Caracol**, see below.

East from Popayán *Colour map 3, A3-A4.*
The road from Popayán to Tierradentro is difficult and narrow, but with beautiful scenery. At Piendamó, on the road towards Cali, there is a turning to **Silvia** in a high valley at 2520 m, 59 km northeast of Popayán. The town is best known for its **Tuesday market** when the friendly local Misak (aka Guambianos, their Spanish colonial name) come to town in their distinctive blue and fuchsia clothes. The

market (also full of Otavalo from Ecuador) is at its best between 0600 and 0830 and is very colourful. Information is available at the **Municipio** ① *C 9, No 2-49, on the plaza, T2-825 1168, http://silvia-cauca.gov.co, 0800-1200, 1400-1800*. For horse riding enquire at the tourist office or hotels.

Inzá, 134 km east of Popayán via Totoró, has several stone statues in its plaza. Nearby, via a signposted turning on the road north towards San Andrés, is the **Pirámide de San Francisco**, a huge rock perforated with tunnels, with spectacular views over the canyon from its peak. Some 9 km beyond Inzá is the Cruce de Pisimbalá (or Cruce de San Andrés or just El Cruce), where a road turns off to **San Andrés de Pisimbalá** (4 km) and the archaeological park (see below).

★ Parque Arqueológico Tierradentro *Colour map 3, A4.*
Park and museum daily 0800-1600 (closed 1st Tue of the month), US$7, under-7s and over-60s free, students half price, children 7-14 US$2, www.icanh.gov.co. When walking between the sites, take a hat and plenty of water. It gets crowded at Easter.

Tierradentro is one of Colombia's great pre-Columbian attractions and a World Heritage Site. Scattered throughout the area are man-made burial caves dating from the sixth to the 10th centuries AD. The tombs are decorated with red, black and white geometric patterns; some are shallow, others up to 8 m deep.

The **Tierradentro Museum** has exhibits on indigenous culture and very good local information. The second floor is dedicated to the work of the Páez; not to be missed. At the archway opposite the museum or at Pisimbalá village you can hire horses (US$3 an hour US$24 per day with guide; make sure they are in good condition) to explore the site, or you can walk. There are four cave sites: Segovia, El Duende, Alto de San Andrés and El Aguacate. The main caves are lit, but a torch is advisable. At **Segovia** (15 minutes' walk up behind the museum across the river), the guards are very informative (Spanish only) and turn lights on in the main tombs. Segovia has about 30 tombs,

Tierradentro

To Santa Rosa

El Duende (1700m)
Quebrada Chapequis
Quebrada Los Guacas
El Tablón (1700m)
Segovia (1650m)
Quebrada La Virgen
San Andrés de Pisimbalá
Quebrada San Andrés
Alto de San Andrés (1750m)
Museum & Administration
To La Pirámide
To El Cruce, Inzá & La Plata
Quebrada El Escaño
El Aguacate (2000m)
N
500 metres
500 yards

five of which can be lit. Fifteen minutes up the hill beyond Segovia is **El Duende** (two of four tombs are very good, faint paintings can be seen but take torch/flashlight). From El Duende continue directly up to a rough road descending to **Pisimbalá** (40 minutes). **El Tablón**, with eight stone statues, is just off the road 20-30 minutes' walk down. **El Alto de San Andrés** is 20 minutes from Pisimbalá. From the back of El Alto it is 1½ hours up and down hill, with a long climb to **El Aguacate** (superb views). Only one tomb is maintained although there may be 30 more. Guides are available.

The village of **San Andrés de Pisimbalá** lies at the far end of the Tierradentro Park (2 km from the museum). It has a unique and beautiful colonial church with a thatched roof; for the key ask behind the church. The surrounding scenery is spectacular, with small indigenous mountain villages to explore (get exact directions before setting out). The Páez people in the Tierradentro region can be seen on market days at Inzá (Saturday) and Belalcázar (Saturday); both start at 0600. The area is also good for birdwatching.

Listings Popayán and Tierradentro *map page 255.*

Tourist information

Popayán

Alcaldía
Cra 6 No 4-21, www.popayanmas.co.
Has set up 10 interactive information posts at strategic sites in the city.

Cultura y Turismo
Cra 7, No 4-36, T2-824 3625, www.cccauca.org.co.
Daily 0800-1200, 1400-2000.

Punto de Información Turística (PIT)
Next door to the Cámara de Comercio de Cauca.

Tourist office
Cra 5, No 4-68, T2-824 2251.
Has a good selection of maps and brochures.

Tourist police
T2-822 0916.
You can ask the tourist police which areas of the city are unsafe.

Where to stay

Popayán
Prices can rise by 100% for Holy Week and festivals, eg 5-6 Jan, when it's essential to book in advance. It is not safe walking alone at night outside the central area.

$$$ Dann Monasterio
C 4, No 10-14, T2-824 2191, www. hoteldannmonasteriopopayan.com.
In what was the monastery of San Francisco, with classically furnished rooms and suites, lovely grounds, pool, spa, gym and restaurant; very good.

$$$-$$ La Plazuela
C 5, No 8-13, T2-824 1084, www.hotellaplazuela.com.co.
Opposite Iglesia San José, beautiful colonial building very near the main plaza. Good-sized rooms with antique furniture set around a courtyard, laundry service available, restaurant, breakfast included.

$$ Los Balcones
Cra 7, No 2-75, T2-824 2030, www. hotellosbalconespopayan.com.
Charming, old-fashioned little hotel, with some huge and other small rooms, antique furniture in lovely leafy patios and lounge areas; but up-to-date services and helpful with local information; good breakfast. Recommended.

$$-$ La Herrería Colonial
C 5, No 2-08, T2-831 8135, www.laherreriapopayan.com.
Small hotel in refurbished colonial mansion, on quiet corner of old district, with restaurant, Wi-Fi, attentive and friendly service. Recommended.

$ Hostel Caracol
C 4, No 2-21, T2-820 7335/311-626 8840,
www.hostelcaracol.com.
Private single and double rooms and
dorms (US$9 pp), shared bath, all smart
and clean, cheaper rates for longer stays,
café open to non-residents (a great
place to meet locals and students), book
exchange, laundry service, kitchen, bike
hire and tours, for example to Volcán
Puracé, Coconuco thermal springs and
Tierradentro (run by owners of **Hostel
Trail**, below). Highly recommended.

$ Hostel Trail Guesthouse
*Cra 11, No 4-16, T2-831 7871/314-696
0805, www.hosteltrailpopayan.com.*
This excellent, efficient backpackers'
hostel is run by Scottish couple Tony
and Kim. The rooms are comfortable
(cheaper with shared bath), cheaper
dorms (US$9 pp), good communal areas,
DVD room, bike hire (free bike loan
for residents), book shop and lockers.
Extensive knowledge of the local area.
Bike tours from nearby thermal springs,
30 km downhill back to Popayán, a great
way to explore the local countryside on
traffic-free backroads. Recommended.

Tierradentro

$$ Albergue El Refugio
T321-811 2395.
Cottages situated around a large pool.
Basic rooms with private bathrooms
and hot water (sporadic), peaceful with
lots of birdlife.

$ Hospedaje Lucerna
Next to the museum, T312-764 7333.
Run by a lovely couple, this little place
has clean, basic rooms and good
showers (with 30 mins' notice).

$ Hospedaje Ricabet
Near the museum, T312-795 4636.

Flower-filled courtyard, clean rooms with
bath and hot water. Rooms with a shared
bath are a little cheaper.

$ La Portada
San Andrés de Pisimbalá, T311-601 7884,
http://laportadahotel.com/
Bamboo building 30 m from the jeep/
bus stop in the village. Rooms with bath
and hot water. Owners can arrange local
tours and horse riding. Restaurant with
excellent *menú del día*, fresh soups.

Restaurants

Popayán
There is a good selection of typical food
from the Cauca region in Popayán.

$$ Rancho Grande
Autopista Norte 32N-50, T2-820 5219. Sun.
A short taxi ride from the city on the
road to Cali. 2 thatched restaurants,
delicious *chuzos* (barbecued beef),
credit cards accepted.

$$-$ Carmina
C 3, No 8-58, 3 blocks from Parque Caldas,
T310-515 4934. Mon-Sat 0800-1500, plus
Thu-Sat 1830-2200.
Mediterranean-themed cuisine run
by charming Spanish/Colombian
couple, delicious crêpes, pasta,
Spanish tortilla, with a small but
tempting selection of desserts,
including home-made ice cream.

$$-$ Italiano
C 4, No 8-83, T2-824 0607.
Swiss-run, excellent selection of pastas,
pizzas, crêpes and fondues, cheap
lunches. Recommended.

$$-$ Salud y Vida
C 8, No 7-19, T2-822 1118.
Popular vegetarian place, with a wide
choice of set lunches for about US$2.50,
simple but great value for money.

$$-$ Tequila's
C 5, No 9-25.
Decent little Mexican-run *cantina* with authentic and reasonably priced cuisine, including burritos, enchiladas, and veggie options, such as quesadillas; tasty mojitos too. Recommended.

$ La Orejona
Cra 9, No 14-10, next to Plaza de Toros.
This restaurant, with eccentric, pig-related decor, specializes in cuisine from the Tolima region, particularly the traditional *lechona tolimense* (stuffed pork, with *tamales*); delicious, huge portions, recommended.

Cafés
Popayán has a thriving café culture, with many in colonial buildings.

Capriccio
Centro Comercial Campanario, local 25, Av Panamericana No 24 AN-21.
Popular with the locals, in shopping mall out of town beyond the airport, serving excellent frappés, brownies and ice creams.

Mora Castilla
C 2, No 4-44, T2-838 1979, www. moracastilla.com. Mon-Sat 0900-1900, Sun 1300-1900.
A brilliant little gastro-café a couple of blocks from the main plaza, above the owners' home, specializing in local cuisine, with snacks, cakes and life-enhancing fruit juices. Try the *tamales* and *empanaditas* with tangy tomato sauce and spicy peanut dip; fruit smoothies including *salpicón payanés* (with blackberries, *lulo* and soursop). They also sell locally produced fruit wines, coffee, chocolates and preserves.

Wipala
Cra 2, No 2-38, see Facebook.
Community-based café, with art and local handicrafts for sale, and occasional live music. Good for snacks, burgers, coffee and cocktails.

Bars and clubs

Popayán

El Sotareño
C 6, No 8-05.
This eccentric bar plays old tango LPs from the 1940s and 50s as well as *bolero* and *ranchero* music. The owner has a huge collection of vinyl records.

La Iguana Café Bar
C 4, No 9-67.
Good music, jazz, salsa, loud and lively, friendly owner.

Festivals

Popayán
Jan Fiestas de Pubenza. Plenty of local music, incorporating **Día de los Negros** on 5 Jan and **Día de los Blancos** on 6 Jan (as in Pasto but less violent); drenching with water is not very common.
Mar/Apr Semana Santa. Spectacular processions take place every night until Good Fri; at the same time there is an **International Religious Music Festival** and local handicraft fairs. The city is very crowded. The children's processions the following week are easier to see.
Sep Congreso Gastronómico de Popayán (www.gastronomicopopayan. org). Food stalls offer examples of the traditional cuisine of the area, plus special themes each year (for example Indian cuisine in 2017); a major event that helped Popayán get UNESCO status as regional gastronomic hub.

Shopping

Popayán
During the week, the open markets are interesting. **Mercado Bolívar** (C 1N, Cra 5) is best in the early morning for local foods such as *pipián, tamales* and *empanadas*. Another, better market, is **Mercado Esmeralda** on C 5 and Autopista.

Transport

Popayán
Air
The airport is 20 mins' walk from the centre, T2-823 1671. Service twice daily to **Bogotá**. All passengers need a Migración Colombia stamp on their boarding pass from Migración Colombia (see page 339), a quick formality.

Bus
The bus terminal is opposite the airport, T2-823 1817, 15 mins' walk from the centre (Ruta 2-Centro bus, terminal to centre, US$0.50, or taxi, US$2 in the day, US$2.50 at night), www.terminal popayan.com. Luggage can be stored safely (receipt given). From the bus station, walk up Cra 11 and take a left at C 4 to reach the centre. Take care if you cross any of the bridges over the river going north, especially at night. To **Bogotá**, **Continental**, US$33, 12-16 hrs, also **Expreso Bolivariano**. To **Cali**, US$7-9, 2½-3 hrs, **Belalcázar** have small comfortable buses, *colectivos* leave from the main plaza. To **Pasto**, US$12-15, 4-6 hrs, spectacular scenery (sit on right – night buses are not safe). To **Ipiales**, **Expreso Bolivariano**,

Cootranar and **Transipiales**, US$14-20, 6-8 hrs, frequent services, but some buses arrive full from Cali, book in advance. To **San Agustín**: several companies go to **Pitalito**, US$9-11, 7 hrs (eg **Cootranshuila**) from where you can catch a taxi *colectivo*, US$2. Via Isnos **Cootranshuila**, US$10-13, and others, several a day mainly mid-morning to afternoon, 5-7 hrs. Sit on the left for the best views. To **Puracé**, **Cootranshuila** US$5, 2½ hrs, hourly. To **Silvia**, daily **Coomotorista**, **Sotracauca** and **Belalcázar**, several *busetas* in the morning, US$2.50 direct, also via Piendamó with the same companies.

Taxi
Meters, minimum charge approximately US$1.50 (extra US$0.20 at night); normal price within city is US$2.

Tierradentro
Bus
From Popayán, 4-5 daily 0430-1330, US$7-9, 4-6 hrs to **Cruce Pisimbalá**. Best to take early buses, as afternoon buses will leave you at the Cruce in the dark. Walk uphill (about 2 km, 30 mins) to the museum and on, 20 mins, to the village. Returning to Popayán, there are 4 daily buses from Pisimbalá, but services are erratic. Otherwise, you must go to El Cruce. Buses and *camionetas* also go from El Cruce south to **La Plata** (en route to San Agustín, see below), US$3, 4-5 hrs or more frequent *colectivo* jeeps, US$4.50. The roads from Totoró and La Plata to Inzá are being paved.

There are two routes from Popayán to San Agustín, both of which go through the highlands of the Puracé National Park, with its volcanoes, hot springs and the sources of four great rivers. One route goes east to join the main highway from Bogotá, while the other, with a quicker, direct bus service, heads due south. The goal of the journey is one of South America's most mysterious archaeological sites, which is also one of Colombia's main tourist destinations.

★ Parque Nacional Puracé/Resguardo Indígena de Puracé

Following long-running tension between the national park authorities and the indigenous community, the latter has taken over the park, now renamed the Resguardo Indígena de Puracé, but still open to visitors, with guides and other services available. For information contact Parque Nacional Puracé office in Popayán, Sr Diomar Castro, T8-521 2578, or 313-424 6563, purace@parquesnacionales.gov.co, or the Parques Nacionales headquarters in Bogotá. Compulsory guides cost about US$12 per group per day, entry fee for foreigners US$14 during the week, US$17 at weekends and holidays.

The national park contains **Volcán Puracé** (4640 m), **Pan de Azúcar** (4670 m), and the line of nine craters known as the **Cadena Volcánica de los Kokonukos**. The park also encompasses the sources of four of Colombia's greatest rivers: the Magdalena, Cauca, Caquetá and Patía. Virtually all the park is over 3000 m. The Andean condor is being reintroduced to the wild here from Californian zoos. There are many other birds to be seen and fauna includes the spectacled bear and mountain tapir. **Pilimbalá** is a good base from which to explore the northern end of the park.

Before climbing or hiking in the national park get advice on which areas are safe and hire a guide (compulsory, prices above). The terrain can be difficult, but the path keeps a safe distance from potentially dangerous volcanic fumes. Although the best weather is reported to be December to March and July to August, this massif makes its own climate, and high winds, rain and sub-zero temperatures can come in quickly at any time.

Tip...
Military areas have been cleared of land mines, but walkers must keep to paths, accompanied by the guide.

Puracé to La Plata

Some 30 km from Popayán is the small town of Puracé, which has several old buildings. Behind the school a 500-m-long path leads to **Chorrera de las Monjas** waterfalls on the Río Vinagre, which is notable for the milky white water due to concentrations of sulphur and other minerals. At Km 22, look for the spectacular San Francisco waterfall on the opposite side of the valley. About 1 km along this road is a turning left leading in 1.5 km to Puente Tierra in the **Parque Nacional Puracé** at 3350 m. Ordinary cars will struggle up this last stretch, but it's an easy walk from Km 23. Here there is a park office, a restaurant and lodging (see Where to stay, page 266).

Continuing on the main road to La Plata, there is a viewpoint for Laguna Rafael at Km 31, the **Cascada de Bedón** (also chemically charged water) at Km 35, and another entrance to the most northerly part of the Parque Nacional Puracé at Km 37. Here you'll find the very interesting **Termales de San Juan** ⓘ *700 m from the road, US$0.50*, where 112 hot sulphur springs combine with icy mountain creeks to produce spectacular arrays of multicoloured mosses, algae and lichens, a must if you are in the area (bathing strictly prohibited).

In the central plaza in **La Plata** is an enormous ceiba tree, planted in 1901. La Plata is an important road junction in the region, with transport north to El Cruce for Tierradentro (see above). Another road goes 41 km east to join the main Bogotá–Neiva–Pitalito highway, some 60 km south of Neiva (see page 265), while a southerly road through Pital joins the same highway some 42 km before Pitalito.

Pitalito and Parque Nacional Cueva de los Guácharos

Permission to visit the park must be obtained from the National Parks office, Cra 4, No 9-25, Acevedo, T8-831 7487/313-258 0268, guacharos@parquesnacionales.gov.co, or in Bogotá.

Pitalito has little to offer the tourist, save convenient access to the **Parque Nacional Cueva de los Guácharos**, which lies to the south. Between December and June swarms of oilbirds (*guácharos*) may be seen; they are nocturnal, with a unique radar-location system. The reserve also contains many of the unusual and spectacular cocks-of-the-rock and the limestone caves are among the most interesting in Colombia. The rangers are particularly friendly, providing tours and basic accommodation.

Popayán to San Agustín direct

South of Puracé towards San Agustín is **Coconuco** (altitude 2460 m; bus from Popayán US$1.50). Coconuco's baths, **Agua Hirviendo** ⓘ *T321-934 1746, http://aguahirviendo1. wixsite.com/coconuco, 1.5 km beyond the Hostería Coconuco (see Where to stay, page 266), on a mostly paved road, US$3.50, children 5-8 years US$2.50*, have one major and many individual pools with an initial temperature of at least 80°C. There is one pool where you can boil an egg in five minutes. There are cabins for overnight stays ($). A track from town is quicker than the road. It gets crowded at weekends, but during the week it is a fine area for walking and relaxing in the waters. In Coconuco there are several restaurants, such as **Restaurante Sofi**, selling local trout. About 6 km beyond Coconuco, near the road, are **Aguas Tibias** ⓘ *T310-543 7172, www. termalesaguatibia.com US$6, children US$3*, warm rather than hot, with various pools, including one of mud, waterslide, zip-line, restaurant and accommodation ($$). Note that at the time of writing Aguas Tibias were closed to visitors, because of an ongoing dispute between the owner and the indigenous community.

South of Coconuco by Km 24 is **Paletará** with high grassland on a grand scale with the Puracé/Pan de Azúcar volcanoes in the background. Below the village (roadside restaurant and national park post) flows the infant Río Cauca. Ten kilometres south of Paletará, the road enters the **Parque Nacional Puracé** and there is a track northeast to Laguna del Buey. The road then enters a long stretch of virgin cloudforest. Some 62 km from Paletará at the end of the cloudforest is San José de Isnos (see opposite), followed by a steep drop to a dramatic bridge over the Río Magdalena and shortly after to the main road between Pitalito and San Agustín.

★ San Agustín *Colour map 3, B3.*

The little town of San Agustín, near the source of the Río Magdalena, is a peaceful place with a few colonial houses and cobbled streets still intact. It is on every traveller's itinerary because of its proximity to the '**Valley of the Statues**', where hundreds of large rough-hewn stone figures of men, animals and gods can be found, dating from approximately 3300 BC to just before the Spanish conquest.

Little is known of the culture which produced them or what exactly the stone sculptures represent. One theory suggests that this culture came from the Amazon region. The sculptures also display indigenous and Asian influences. No evidence of writing has been discovered, but traces of small circular bamboo straw-thatched houses have been found. The sites were burial and ceremonial sites where it is thought sacrifices, including of children, were made to the gods. Some sites were also residential areas. Various sculptures found here are exhibited at the National Museum in Bogotá. Only about 30% of the burial mounds in the area have been excavated and many of those that have been opened had been previously ransacked by grave diggers, who had looted their precious statues. There are about 20 well-kept sites.

The area offers excellent opportunities for hiking (although some trails to remote sites are not well marked) and other adventure sports. The rainy season is April to June/July, but it rains almost all year – hence the beautiful green landscape; the driest months are November to March. The whole area leaves an unforgettable impression: the strength and strangeness of the statues set against the great beauty of the rolling countryside.

Parque Arqueológico ⓘ *Wed-Mon 0800-1700, closed Tue. US$9.50 including museum, Parque Arqueológico and Fuente de Lavapatas, students US$4, under 12s and over 60s free; if, at the end of the day, you wish to visit the following day for free, enquire first at the ticket office. It is recommended you hire a guide to gain a better understanding of the statues and what they represent. Guidebook in Spanish/English US$4 (available online for free at www.icanh.gov.co).* The nearest archaeological sites are in the Parque Arqueológico, 3 km from San Agustín. At the entrance is the **Museo Arqueológico**, which displays pottery and information about San Agustín culture (Spanish only). The 130 statues and graves in the Parque are *in situ*, though those in the Bosque (a little wood) have been moved and rearranged, and linked by gravel footpaths. Originally, the statues were found lying down and covered in the graves. Those excavated have been placed upright next to the graves and fenced in. Beyond the central area are the carved rocks in and around the stream at the **Fuente de Lavapatas** in the park, where the water runs through carved channels. The **Alto de Lavapatas**, above the Fuente, has an extensive view. You can get a good idea of the Parque, the Bosque and the museum in the course of three hours' walking, or add in El Tablón and La Chaquira (see below) for a full day.

Other sites around San Agustín El Tablón is reached up Carrera 14, over the brow of the hill and 250 m to a marked track to the right. El Tablón (five sculptures brought together under a bamboo roof) is shortly down to the left. Continue down the path, muddy in wet weather, ford a stream and follow signs to the Río Magdalena Canyon. La Chaquira (figures carved on rocks) is dramatically set halfway down to the river. It takes two hours to walk to and from San Agustín.

At La Pelota, two painted statues were found in 1984 (three-hour return trip, six hours if you include El Tablón and La Chaquira, 15 km in all). Discoveries from 1984/1986 include some unique polychromed sculptures at El Purutal near La Pelota and a series of at least 30 stones carved with animals and other designs in high relief. These are known as Los Petroglifos and can be found on the right bank of the Río Magdalena, near the Estrecho (narrows) to which jeeps run.

Alto de los Idolos ⓘ *6 km from San Agustín, daily 0800-1630, US$9.50, students US$4, under 12s and over 60s free*, can be reached by horse or on foot, a lovely (if strenuous) walk, steep in places, via **Puente de la Chaquira**. Here on a levelled hill overlooking San Agustín are 13 uncovered tombs and statues dating from 100 BC-AD 600. Each of these statues, known as *vigilantes*, guards a burial mound. One is an unusual rat totem; stone crocodiles are believed by some to have strong links with the Amazon region. The few excavated have disclosed large stone sarcophagi. It is not certain whether the *vigilantes* bear a sculpted resemblance to the inmate they guard.

San José de Isnos and around *Colour map 3, B3.*
Alto de los Idolos can also be reached from San José de Isnos, 22 km northeast or 27 km by road from San Agustín. The road passes the **Salto del Mortiño**, a 170-m fall 7 km before Isnos, 500 m off the road. The main plaza in Isnos has restaurants and cafés and a **Cootranshuila** bus office. Isnos' market day is Saturday (bus 0500, US$2, return 1100, 1300, otherwise bus from Cruce on Pitalito road).

About 6 km north of Isnos is **Alto de las Piedras** (included on same ticket as Alto de los Idolos), which has seven interesting tombs and monoliths, including the famous 'Doble Yo' and the tombs of two children. There are still over 90 tombs to be excavated. Only less remarkable than the statues are the orchids growing nearby. Some 8 km further is Bordones; turn left at end of the village and there is (500 m) parking for the **Salto de Bordones** falls, which are good for birdwatching.

Bogotá to San Agustín *Colour map 2, C5-3, B3.*
The route south from Bogotá to San Agustín passes through **Neiva**, the capital of Huila Department. Neiva is a modern city on the east bank of the Río Magdalena, surrounded by rich coffee plantations, with a large and colourful daily market. **Villavieja**, 45 km north of Neiva, provides access to the ★ **Desierto de Tatacoa**, a small area (300 sq km) of scrub and arid eroded red soil with large cacti, isolated mesas and unusual wildlife. Four- or five-hour guided walks through the desert cost US$12 per person per day. There is also a **museum** ⓘ *in the Casa de la Cultura on the main plaza, daily 0800-1800, US$2*, showing prehistoric finds from the area. On top of a small incline some 15 minutes' drive from Villavieja is the **Observatorio Astronómico de la Tatacoa** ⓘ *T310-465 6765, Facebook: Tatacoa.Astronomia*, run

by Javier Fernando Rua who gives an excellent talk every evening at 1900, US$10 per person. There are also daytime observances of solar flares and eruptions, US$2.

Tourist information

San Agustín

Oficina Municipal de Turismo
Plaza Cívica, C 3 y Cra 12, T316-472 5248, www.sanagustin-huila.gov.co. Mon-Fri 0800-1200, 1400-1700.

Oficina de Policía de Turismo
C 3, No 11-86.
Tourist police.

There are also 4 tour agencies calling themselves 'tourist offices'. They give out useful advice, but they also hold contracts with hotels and other operators. There are 2 banks with ATMs, but don't arrive short of cash.

Where to stay

Puracé to La Plata
In **Pilimbalá** there are picnic shelters, restaurant, lodging in room with bath (**$** pp) and camping (tents and sleeping bags can be hired). Firewood is provided. Sleeping bags or warm clothing recommended to supplement bedding.
    Other basic places to stay in La Plata are **Berlín** (C 4, No 4-76 on the Plaza, T8-837 0229), and **El Portal de Valencia** (C 6, No 3-58, T8-837 6304).

Pitalito

$$ Hotel Calamó Plaza
Cra 5, No 5-45, T8-836 0603, www.hotelcalamoplaza.com.
Smart modern hotel overlooking main plaza, large and plush rooms, small

pool, *cafetería*, parking, free Wi-Fi and breakfast included.

$ Hotel Hostal Ullumbe
C 2, No 4-45, T8-836 6368.
Quiet hotel just a couple of blocks from the main plaza, cosy rooms with colourful decor, plant-filled central patio and communal areas, friendly family atmosphere; good breakfast.

Popayán to San Agustín direct

$$$-$$ Hostería Coconuco
500 m south of Coconuco, T2-827 1014, or 313-652 6179, www.comfandi. com.co. 10 mins' drive to the baths, transport arranged.
The best option, part of chain run by local cooperative fund, comfortable rooms, hot water, price is full board, colonial-style hotel, restful atmosphere, activities arranged, games room, good for families. There are several other modest hotels and restaurants in town.

San Agustín
Some hotels increase prices during Easter and Christmas by around 10-20%.

$$$ Hostal Huaka-Yo
200 m from entrance to San Agustín. T571-489 9269, www.huakayo.com.
Large rooms in wooden terraced buildings in spacious manicured grounds close to the archaeological site, popular with school groups.

$$ Hacienda Anacaona
Vía al Estrecho del Magdalena, 2 km from town, T311-231 7128, www.anacaona-colombia.com.
Elegant traditional finca, attractive, beautiful views and garden, hammocks, good restaurant, quiet. Camping allowed on grounds. Recommended.

$$-$ Casa de Nelly
Km 2 Vía Parque Archeológico, T310-215 9067, www.hosteltrail.com/hostels/hotelcasadenelly.
On top of the hill on the road to the archaeological park, 4 colourful rooms and *cabañas* set in a gorgeous garden, home-cooked pastas and pizzas, hammocks.

$$-$ El Jardín
Cra 11, No 4-10, T8-837 3455, www.hosteltrail.com/hostels/eljardin.
In town, colonial house with a colourful patio, simple rooms, some with private bath, dorms, airy central courtyard, restaurant with fixed-menu lunches, helpful owner good source of local information.

$$-$ pp Finca El Maco
1 km from town, 400 m past Piscina Las Moyas, T8-837 3437, www.elmaco.ch.
Swiss-owned, working organic farm with colourful gardens, rustic, peaceful, cosy cabins and Maloka dorms for 1-6 (from US$9 pp), also teepee, welcoming, laundry service, very good restaurant (reserve ahead), great local information; see **Chaska Tours**, below.

$ pp Finca El Cielo
3 km from San Agustín, Vía El Estrecho/Obando, T313-493 7446, Facebook: fincaelcielosanagustin.
Guesthouse and organic farm, overlooking Río Magdalena, restaurant serving great home cooking, good breakfasts too, camping, swimming pool,

tours organized in the area and beyond, also live music, dance and riding classes.

$ La Casa de François
T8-837 3847, T314-358 2930, 200 m via El Tablón, www.lacasadefrancois.com.
Just outside town, French-run, private rooms, dorms (US$9-11.50) and camping set in 2 ha of gardens, good breakfast, meals, crêpes and home-baked bread available, use of kitchen, bike and horse hire.

$ Posada Campesina
Cra 14, Camino al Estrecho (on the route to El Tablón), 1 km from town, T312-562 0826, https://posadacampesinasan agustin.jimdo.com.
Nicely furnished rooms in this recommended farmhouse, owned by Doña Silvina Patiño, who makes good pizza and cheese bread, meals with family, simple working farm, shared bath, hot water, Wi-Fi, use of kitchen, camping possible, good walks nearby.

Camping

Camping San Agustín Gamcelat
1 km from town towards Parque Arqueológico, opposite clean public swimming pool, Las Moyas, T311-509 2933/805 8066.
US$7, plus charge pp with own tent, US$6 pp to hire tent, clean, pleasant, safe (guards), showers, toilets, lights, laundry service, horse hire.

Bogotá to San Agustín
Neiva

$$$ Neiva Plaza
C 7, No 4-62, T8-871 0806, www.hotelneivaplaza.com.
Neiva's traditional smart hotel for some 60 years, good location overlooking the main plaza, comfortable rooms,

restaurant, café, gym and indoor pool, business facilities.

$ Panorama Neiva
C 2, No 9-24, T8-872 0396.
Basic rooms but clean and quiet, fan or a/c, free Wi-Fi, breakfast, central location just a few blocks from main plaza with restaurants nearby, good value for money.

Villavieja and Desierto de Tatacoa
Camping is permitted at the observatory (US$3.50 to hire tent) or accommodation is available in Villavieja (**$**). There are also several *posadas nativas*, run by local families, enquire at the **Asociación de Operadores Turísticos** (on the Parque Principal, T313-804 9580, www.villavieja-huila.gov.co).

Restaurants

San Agustín

$$ Donde Richard
C 5, No 23-45, T312-432 6399.
On the outskirts of town, but handy if going to/from archaeological site. Big, airy place dishing up decent steaks, chicken and fish, soups and salads, agreeable surroundings with prices to match. Recommended.

$$-$ Pepe Nero
C 5, No 18-287, T319-258 4556.
Italian fare in a pleasant environment, with red-checkered tablecloths and rustic bamboo beams, serves tasty traditional favourites, including seafood pasta, tiramisu and panna cotta, also a good wine selection.

$ Brahama
C 5, No 15-21, T310-750 5934.
This small restaurant serves pretty decent typical local fare, as well as

Mexican dishes, pizzas and some good vegetarian options.

$ El Fogón
C 5, No 14-30.
Family-run, good fish, steaks, *comida* and juices, fresh salads. Out of centre, on the road towards the archaeological site. Recommended.

$ Tomate Restaurante Vegetariano
C 5, No 16-04. Closed Tue and Wed.
Delicious vegetarian food, German owner, excellent-value set lunches about US$3, also good fruit juices and home-made wholewheat bread, a bit far from the centre, near the archaeological site, but well worth the walk.

Festivals

San Agustín
24 Jun San Juan, horse races and dances.
29 Jun San Pedro, horse races, dances, fancy dress and more.
Mid-Jul Santa María del Carmen.
1st week of Oct La Semana Cultural Integrada at the Casa de Cultura, with folklore performances from all parts of the country.

Bogotá to San Agustín
Neiva
Late Jun/early Jul Festival Nacional del Reinado del Bambuco, incorporating San Juan and San Pedro: dancing competitions, parades on the river and through the streets.

What to do

San Agustín
Guides
There are countless guides in town offering tours of the various sites. Some give a better service than others. Enquire at your hotel or at the tourist office for

advice. Recommended are: **Marino Bravo** (T311-835 6736), takes walking, riding and minibus tours, authorized, professional, speaks English, French and Italian; **Gloria Amparo Palacios** (T311-459 5753), and **Carlos Bolaños** (T311-459 5753); **Fabio Burbano** (T8-837 3592, 311-867 5665), professional, reliable and knowledgeable; **Luis Alfredo Salazar** (T8-837 3426), speaks English, French, Italian. They charge US$15 for a half day, US$30 for a full day.

Horse riding
For trips around San Agustín you are strongly advised to hire horses through hotels. These cost about US$6 per hr, per rider, or US$25 per day with guide. **Pacho** (T311-827 7972, pachitocampesinito@yahoo.es) who also does tours to Lago Magdalena, the source of the Río Magdalena (US$27 for guidance plus US$20 pp), is recommended and is contactable through **La Casa de Nelly**.

Rafting
Magdelana Rafting, *C 5, No 16-04, T311-271 5333, www.magdalenarafting.com*. Run by experienced Frenchman Amid Bouselahane, offers various rafting, kayaking and caving tours, also day-trips to the Tatacoa Desert.

Tours
Jeeps may be hired for 4-5 people. Prices vary according to the number of sites to be visited, but the rate is about US$20 per person per day with a minimum of 4 people.
Chaska Tours, *T8-837 3437, 311-271 4802, www.chaskatours.net*. Run by Swiss René Suter (who also owns **Finca El Maco**), organizes tours around San Agustín, Tierradentro and throughout Colombia. English and German spoken.

Transport

Puracé to La Plata
Bus and colectivo
Several buses daily to Puracé from **Popayán**, last returning 1700, US$5, 2½ hrs. Bus stops 3.5 km from Pilimbalá. All the places beyond Puracé village can be reached by bus from **Popayán** to La Plata. The bus service can be erratic so check time of last daylight bus to Popayán and be prepared to spend a cold night at 3000 m. The rangers will allow you to stay in the centre.

From La Plata there are buses to **Bogotá**, via Neiva, **Coomotor**, 9 hrs, in the evening, **Cootranshuila**, 5 a day, US$21-25. To **Popayán** 0500 and others, US$12.50, 5½ hrs. To **San Agustín**, direct US$10 or take a *colectivo* to Pitalito and change. For **Tierradentro** take a bus towards Popayán (leaves 0600-0630) and alight at the Cruce US$3. Private jeep hire La Plata–Tierradentro US$50, cheaper if you pick up other passengers. To **Pitalito**, 3½ hrs, US$7.50-10.

Pitalito
Bus and colectivo
Plenty of buses and *colectivos* to **San Agustín**, US$3-4. Bus to **La Plata**, 3½ hrs, US$7.50-10. Bus to **Bogotá**, 9-10 hrs, US$25-28. Bus to **Mocoa** (in the Putumayo), US$8, 3-4 hrs. To **Tierradentro**, catch a *colectivo* jeep to La Plata, US$9, 3½ hrs, from where you can usually get a *chiva*, bus or *colectivo*, 2-3 hrs to San Andrés de Pisimbalá the same day. To **Parque Nacional Cueva de los Guácharos**, take a bus/*chiva* to Palestina, US$2, 1 hr, then a 40-min *chiva* to Mensura. From there, 8-km walk or horse ride to visitor centre.

San Agustín
Bus and taxi

To **Bogotá** by *colectivo* with **Taxis Verdes** (C 3, No 11-27, T8-837 3068, or C 17, No 68D-54, T1-411 1152 in Bogotá, www.taxisverdes.net) daily, direct or change at Neiva, US$22-28, 9-11 hrs (go early); or by bus with **Coomotor** (C 3, No 10-71), 4 a day, US$22-26, 10-12 hrs. Most services going to Bogotá will also stop at Neiva, 6 hrs, US$10-15. From **Bogotá**, **Taxis Verdes** will pick up at hotels (extra charge); alternatively, travel to Pitalito (30 mins, see above), then change.

To **Tierradentro**, check first if any of the tourist offices is running a jeep, otherwise travel via Pitalito. Do not take a night bus to Tierradentro. There are several daily buses from San Agustín to **Popayán** via Isnos with **Cootranshuila** (office on C 3, No 10-81) and others, 4-5 hrs, US$10-12. Do not travel between San Agustín and Popayán at night; the road is isolated and dangerous. Some Popayán–San Agustín buses drop passengers outside San Agustín. It's best to book seats the day before.

Bogotá to San Agustín
Neiva

Air La Marguita, 1.5 km from city. Daily flights to/from **Bogotá** and principal cities. Taxi to bus terminal US$4.

Bus Station out of town, www.elterminalneiva.com; bus from the centre leaves from the old terminal (Cra 2, Cs 5 y 6). To **Bogotá**, 6 hrs, US$16-19. To **San Agustín**, US$12-14, 6 hrs. To **Pitalito**, US$8-11, 3 hrs. To **La Plata**, for Tierradentro, US$7.50-10, 2 hrs, frequent services (especially early morning, 0400, 0500). To **Popayán**, US$18-21, 8-11 hrs, poor road in parts. All services with **Coomotor** and **Cootranshuila**. To **Villavieja**, daily with **Flotahuila** and **Coomotor** from Neiva bus terminal, 1 hr, US$3-5.

Villavieja

Canoe You can cross the Río Magdalena by motorized canoe near Villavieja for US$1, then it's 1.5 km to Aipe for buses on the Neiva–Bogotá road.

Taxi From Villavieja hire a taxi to the **Tatacoa Desert**, US$12 return.

South to Ecuador

dramatic journeys through the cordillera

From Popayán to Ecuador is scenic highland country, with spectacular deep ravines intersecting lush pastures and, higher up, open *páramo*. From Popayán to Pasto is 285 km (five hours' driving). The road drops to 700 m in the valley of the Río Patía before climbing to Pasto with big temperature changes. To the west is the long slope down to the Pacific. To the east is the continental divide of the Cordillera Oriental and the beginning of the great Amazonian basin.

★ Pasto and around *Colour map 3, B2.*

Pasto, 88 km from Ecuador, is in a very attractive setting, overlooked from the west by Volcán Galeras and from the east by green hills not yet suburbanized by the city. It was founded in the early days of the conquest and retains some of its colonial character. During the Wars of Independence, it was a stronghold of the Royalists and the last town to fall into the hands of the patriots after a bitter struggle. The people of Nariño Department, of which Pasto is capital, wanted to join Ecuador when that country split off from Gran Colombia in 1830, but were prevented by Colombian troops.

There are several churches worth visiting: ornate **San Juan Bautista** and **La Merced** ① *C 18A, No 25-11*, **Cristo Rey** ① *C 20, No 24-64* and **Santiago** ① *Cra 23*

Pasto

Where to stay 🛏
Don Saúl **1**
Fernando Plaza **2**
Koala Inn **3**
Loft **4**

Restaurants 🍴
Guadalquivir Café **2**
Inca Cuy **3**
Loto Verde **4**
Parrilla Chipichape **5**
Picantería Ipiales **6**

y C 13, which has good views over the city to the mountains. The **Museo de Oro del Banco de la República** ⓘ *C 19, No 21-27, T2-721 3001, www.banrepcultural. org/pasto, Tue-Sat 1000-1700, free*, has a small well-displayed collection of pre-Columbian pieces from the cultures of southern Colombia. **Museo Zambrano** ⓘ *C 20, No 29-78, Mon-Sat 0800-1200, 1400-1600, free*, houses indigenous and colonial period arts, especially *quiteño* (from Quito).

Volcán Galeras (4276 m) has been erupting frequently since 1989, and most recently in 2010. Check at the **tourist office** ⓘ *open 0800-1400, information as for Isla de La Corota below, entry US$1*, whether it is safe to climb on the mountain and whether you need a permit. A road climbs up the mountain to a ranger station and police post at 3700 m, beyond which you are not permitted.

On the north side of the volcano lies the village of **Sandoná**, where panama hats are made; they can be seen lying in the streets in the process of being finished. Sandoná market day is Saturday. Buses and *colectivos* are frequent from Pasto daily, US$3, 1½ to two hours.

The Putumayo *Colour map 3, B2-B3.*

About 25 km east of Pasto, on the road to **Mocoa** is **Laguna La Cocha**, the largest lake in south Colombia (sometimes called Lago Guamuez). In the lake is the **Isla de La Corota Nature Reserve** ⓘ *open 0800-1600, 10 mins by boat from the Hotel Sindanamoy, information T2-732 0493, corota@parquesnacionales.gov.co, or from the National Parks office in Bogotá, US$1*, with interesting trees; camping is possible.

A steep climb over the Sierra leads to a large statue of the Virgin marking the entry into the Putumayo. The road then descends steeply to Sibundoy and Mocoa, in the transitional zone between Andes and Amazon. Beyond are the lowlands and the river towns of Puerto Asís and San Miguel (a crossing to Lago Agrio in Ecuador). For many years this was guerrilla territory, but it is opening up for ecotourism with lots of potential for visiting rivers and waterfalls and nature-watching. Seek local advice before heading to Ecuador this way.

Ipiales and Las Lajas *Colour map 3, C2.*

Passing through deep valleys and a spectacular gorge, buses on the paved Pan-American Highway cover the 84 km from Pasto to Ipiales in 1½ to two hours. The road crosses the spectacular gorge of the Río Guáitara at 1750 m, near El Pedregal, where *choclo* (corn) is cooked in many forms by the roadside. **Ipiales**, 'the city of the three volcanoes', is famous for its colourful Friday morning indigenous market but the main attraction is the ★ **Santuario de la Virgen de Las Lajas**, about 7 km to the east. Seen from the approach road, looking down into the canyon, the sanctuary is a magnificent architectural conception, set on a bridge over the Río Guáitara: close up, it is very heavily ornamented in the gothic style. The altar is set into the rock face of the canyon, which forms one end of the sanctuary with the façade facing a wide plaza that completes the bridge over the canyon. There are walks to nearby shrines in dramatic scenery. It is 10-15 minutes' walk down to the sanctuary from the village. Also you can cross the canyon via a **cable car** ⓘ *T316-693 7675, www.telefericodelaslajas.com, Mon-Fri 0900-1900, US$5.50 return, Sat, Sun*

ON THE ROAD

Las Lajas

In 1754 María Mueces de Quiñonez was travelling from the village of Potosí to Ipiales with her deaf-mute daughter Rosa when she stopped to rest by a cave next to the Guáitara river. Rosa escaped her clutches and ran into the cave. Some moments later she emerged and spoke for the first time in her life, saying: "Mother, look at the *mestiza* over there holding a boy in her arms". María did not look in the cave but grabbed Rosa and continued on her way. When she reached Ipiales, she recounted what had happened, though no one took what she said seriously.

A few days later, Rosa disappeared from home. María guessed that her daughter must have gone to the cave, as Rosa had often said that the Lady was calling her. María ran to Las Lajas and found her daughter in front of a lady and playing with a child. María fell to her knees before the Virgin Mary and Baby Jesus.

From that day, she and Rosa often went to the cave to place wild flowers and candles in the cracks in the rocks. One day Rosa fell gravely ill and died. A distraught María decided to take her daughter's body to Las Lajas to ask the Lady to restore Rosa to life.

The Virgin resurrected Rosa, and María returned home brimming with joy. Crowds began to visit the cave, curious about what had happened. They discovered a picture of the mysterious Lady on the wall of the grotto that is still there to this day.

That same year Fray Gabriel Villafuerte returned to the cave and built a straw church. As more pilgrims visited the miraculous spot, a new cathedral was planned on the other side of the river. The first stone was laid in 1899 and the extraordinary Gothic Revival structure was finally finished in 1949. Today it is a popular destination for religious believers from all parts of Latin America.

---

and hols 0700-2000, US$7 return. There are great pilgrimages to the sanctuary from Colombia and Ecuador (very crowded at Easter) and it is said to be second only to Lourdes in the number of miracles claimed for it.

Border with Ecuador

Ipiales is 2 km from the Rumichaca bridge across the Río Carchi into Ecuador. The border post stands on a concrete bridge, beside a natural bridge, where customs and passport examinations take place 24 hours. All Colombian offices are in one modern complex: **Migración Colombia** (immigration, exit stamp given here), customs, **INTRA** (Department of Transport, car papers stamped here; if leaving Colombia you must show your vehicle entry permit) and **ICA** (Department of Agriculture for plant and animal quarantine). There is also a restaurant, Telecom, clean bathrooms (US$0.10) and ample parking. The **Ecuadorean consulate** ⓘ *Cra 7, No 14-10, p2, T2-773 2292/4801, cecuipiales@mmrree.gob.ec, weekdays 0830-1700*, is in the Migración Colombia complex. There are many money changers near the bridge on both sides; rates are better on the Colombian side but check all calculations.

Tourist information

Pasto

Tourist office
Just off the main plaza, C 18, No 25-25, p 2, T2-723 4962, http://turismo.narino. gov.co. Mon-Fri 0800-1200, 1400-1800.
Friendly and helpful. See also the state tourist information website: www.cultura pasto.gov.co, which is quite useful.

Where to stay

Pasto

$$$-$$ Fernando Plaza
C 20, No 21B-16, T2-729 1432, www.hotelfernandoplaza.com.
Smart, lots of good details such as orthopaedic mattresses, some bigger family rooms, restaurant.

$$$-$$ Loft Hotel
C 18, No 22-33, T2-722 6737, www.lofthotelpasto.com.
Comfortable upscale hotel, with minimalist decor, restaurant, spa, gym. 20% discount if you show a copy of a Footprint guide.

$$ Don Saúl
C 17, No 23-52, T2-722 4480, www.hoteldonsaul.com.
This elegant hotel stays true to its Jordanian owner's roots, with murals depicting Arabic scenes and its restaurant serves Middle Eastern food. Rooms with large beds, cable TV and Wi-Fi, Turkish bath and sauna, breakfast included. Recommended as good value.

$ Koala Inn
C 18, No 22-37, T2-722 1101, www.hosteltrail.com/hostels/koalainn.
The best backpackers' option in town. Large, antiquated but clean rooms, some

with bath, laundry, cable TV, free Wi-Fi, good local information. There is a small café serving decent breakfasts (US$2-3).

The Putumayo
There are hotels on the plaza in **Mocoa**.

$ Hostal Casa del Río
Vereda Caliyaco, 2.5 km from Mocoa, T8-420 4004, T314-304 5050, www. hosteltrail.com/hostels/casadelrio.
Belgian-owned, dorms from US$6pp, out of town, taxi from bus station US$1.50.

Ipiales and Las Lajas
Several basic hotels and a small number of restaurants at Las Lajas. The following are in Ipiales:

$$-$ Santa Isabel 2
Cra 7, No 14-27, T2-773 4172.
Smart, central, good services, Wi-Fi, hot showers, parking, restaurant. Sister hotel **Santa Isabel** (1, Cra 7, No 14-27), also **$$-$**, and similar standard, also recommended.

$ Avanty
Cra 11, No 15-19, T2-725 2894.
Centrally located modern hotel with small but comfortable rooms, very clean, attentive and helpful service, decent breakfast, restaurant open for dinner too, good value. Recommended.

$ Emperador
Cra 5, No 14-43, T2-773 2311.
Central, best budget option, good rooms, hot water, parking.

Restaurants

Pasto

$ Guadalquivir Café
C 19, No 24-84, T2-723 9504, see Facebook: GuadalquivirCafeSAS/.

A Pasto stalwart with more than 44 years' experience, this colourful and arty café serves home-made snacks such as *tamales*, *empanadas de añejo* and *envueltos de choclo*, open from 0700 for breakfast too.

$ Inca Cuy
C 29, No 13-65, T2-723 8050.
Down a narrow corridor behind the Plaza de Bombona, specializes in fried guinea pig (*cuy*); book ahead as it takes an hour to prepare.

$ Picantería Ipiales
C 19, No 23-37, T2-723 0393, Facebook: Picanteria Ipiales.
Typical food from Nariño in this long-established restaurant, specializing in pork-based dishes, served in tortilla wraps, with salads, and *almuerzos*.

Festivals

Pasto
★ **5 Jan** New Year festivities include **Día de los Negros** and **Día de los Blancos** the next day. On 'black day' people smear each others' faces in black grease. On 'white day' they throw talc or flour at each other. Local people wear their oldest clothes.
5 Feb and 28 Dec **Fiesta de las Aguas**, when anything that moves gets drenched with water from balconies and even from fire engines' hoses. All towns in the region are involved in this legalized water war!
31 Dec **Concurso de Años Viejos**, in Pasto and Ipiales huge dolls are burnt; they represent the old year and sometimes lampoon local people.

Shopping

Pasto
Handicrafts
Pasto varnish (*barniz*) is mixed locally, to embellish the colourful local wooden bowls. Leather goods shops are on C 17 and C 18. Try the **municipal market** for handicrafts, **Mercado Potrerillo** (between C15C and C15D), open daily, also **Artesanía Bombona** (C14, No 28-109).

Transport

Pasto
Air
Daily flights to **Bogotá** and **Cali**. The airport is at Cano, 35 km from Pasto; by *colectivo* (beautiful drive), 45 mins, US$3 or US$18 by taxi.

Bus
Bus terminal at Cra 6, No 16D-50, T2-732 4935, 4 km from centre, taxi, US$2. **Bogotá**, 18-23 hrs, US$36-50. **Ipiales**, 2-3 hrs, US$6-9, sit on the left for the views. **Popayán**, US$11-15. **Cali**, US$17-20, 8½-10 hrs. To La Cocha, take a taxi, a *colectivo* from C 20 y Cra 20, or a bus to **El Encano** and walk 20 mins from bus stop direct to lake shore.

Ipiales and Las Lajas
Air
San Luis airport is 6.5 km out of town. Flights to **Cali** and **Puerto Asís**. Taxi to Ipiales centre, US$6.

Bus
Companies have individual departure points: *busetas/colectivos* mostly leave from main plaza. *Colectivo* taxis go direct to Las Lajas, 10 mins, US$1 one way, or US$5 return by taxi. To **Popayán**, Expreso **Bolivariano**, **Transipiales**, US$14-20, 6-8 hrs, hourly 0800-2000; also *colectivo*

taxis, US$25. **Expreso Bolivariano** to **Cali**, US$20-27, 10-12 hrs. To **Pasto** US$6-9, 2-3 hrs. Frequent buses to **Bogotá** every 2 hrs, 20-24 hrs, US$49-52 (check if you have to change buses in Cali).

Border with Ecuador
Car
If entering Colombia by car, the vehicle should be fumigated against diseases that affect coffee trees, at the ICA office. The certificate must be presented in El Pedregal, 40 km beyond Ipiales on the road to Pasto. (This fumigation process is not always carried out.) You can buy insurance for your car in Colombia at Banco Agrario, in the plaza.

Taxi
It is easiest to take a taxi from Ipiales to the border, about US$7, although there are also *colectivos* from C 14 y Cra 11 to the border, US$1.50, and from the border to Tulcán, US$1.50.

Leticia and the Amazon

explore the Colombian Amazon en route to Peru or Brazil

Leticia, Colombia's port on the Amazon, is on the southern tip of a spur of territory which gives Colombia access to the great river, 3200 km upstream from the Atlantic. At the east edge of town is the land border with Brazil; the Brazilian port of Tabatinga starts directly at the border and the two cities function as one unit, although Leticia is safer and has better tourist services than Tabatinga; it's more expensive too. Across the river and downstream is a more relaxed and pleasant Brazilian town, Benjamin Constant, at the confluence of the Amazon and the Rio Javari. On an island across from Leticia and Tabatinga is the small Peruvian town of Santa Rosa, which is prone to severe flooding in the rainy season. The best time to visit the area is in July or August, during the early months of the dry season.

Leticia *Colour map 4, C2.*
Capital of Amazonas Department, the city is clean and modern. Changes in the height of the river sometimes mean that the water is quite a distance from town and port facilities. Parque Santander y Orellana is pleasant and is a popular meeting place. Leticia is a good place to buy typical products made by the Amazon *indígenas*, which are sold at **Museo Artesanal Uirapurú** ⓘ *C 8, 10-35*. Housed in the beautiful Biblioteca del Banco de la República is the **Museo Etnográfico** ⓘ *Cra 11 9-43, T8-592 7213 ext 8053, www.banrepcultural.org/leticia/museo, Tue-Sat 0900-1700, free,* which has displays on local ethnography and archaeology. The **Hospital San Rafael** ⓘ *Av Vásquez Cobo, Cra 1013-78, T8-592 7826,* is well equipped. There are several banks with ATMs in Leticia, and this is the best place to change money in the border area (cash only): good rates for US dollars and Brazilian reais, poor rates for Peruvian soles. Many street changers and *cambios* on Calle 8, near the market and port; beware of tricks.

Jungle trips from Leticia
Full-day trips (eg to Puerto Nariño and Lago de Tarapoto) cost about US$75 per person. Colombian operators also run tours to several jungle reserves and lodges in Colombian, Brazilian and Peruvian territory; see What to do, page 281.

Essential Amazonia

Finding your feet

Leticia is in the far southeast of Colombia on the border with both Brazil and Peru; crossing between these countries is straightforward as long as your paperwork is in order. There are onward boat services to Manaus (Brazil) and Iquitos (Peru). Transport to/from elsewhere in Colombia is by air or boat only. There is an obligatory US$9.50 environment tax payable on arrival in Leticia. You may also be asked for a yellow fever certificate, although this is only compulsory if you're travelling from Peru. Take water purification tablets with you since almost all the water here is taken from the river.

Getting around

You can get around Leticia on foot. River taxis or organized boat tours travel to destinations on the Amazon.

When to go

The Colombian Amazon is very hot all year round. The best time to visit the area is from June to August, during the early months of the dry season. The river is at its highest level in May, when some areas may be flooded and inaccessible. The river is lowest in September. At weekends, accommodation may be difficult to find.

Time required

One week is enough to explore the area around Leticia, but you'll need more time if you want to venture into Brazil or Peru.

Weather Amazonia (Leticia)

January	February	March	April	May	June
31°C	31°C	31°C	31°C	30°C	30°C
23°C	23°C	23°C	23°C	23°C	22°C
368mm	313mm	351mm	329mm	291mm	203mm

July	August	September	October	November	December
30°C	31°C	32°C	32°C	32°C	31°C
22°C	22°C	22°C	23°C	23°C	23°C
136mm	172mm	231mm	259mm	286mm	314mm

Reserva Natural Isla de los Micos ⓘ *Entry US$10; Decameron has the concession for the restaurant here.* Upriver from Leticia, this island has few monkeys now, and those left are semi-tame. Native communities can be visited in the area: Huacarí of the Yagua people, opposite the island; Santa Sofía, upriver from the island, and Nazareth downriver, the latter two of the Ticuna people.

Amazon forests

It may all look the same from above as you fly into Leticia, but the Amazon has three types of tropical forest, each with distinct ecosystems. *Terra firme*, which is dry all year round and characterized by an abundance of tropical hardwoods, is where you are most likely to see large mammals. *Várzea*, which is flooded for half the year, contains fewer mammals but an abundance of birds. *Igapo*, which is always flooded and grows to a height of 3 m, is where you are likely to see reptiles such as anacondas, caimans, boa constrictors and large fish.

The area immediately around Leticia is characterized by *várzea* and *igapo* forests; for *terra firme* you will have to venture inland from the river or into Brazil or Peru.

Parque Nacional Amacayacu ⓘ *Partly open again since flood damage caused its closure in 2016. For the latest information write to amacayacu@parquesnacionales. gov.co, or contact the National Parks office in Bogotá, www.parquesnacionales.gov. co.* The national park is located 60 km upstream, at the mouth of the Matamata Creek, two hours from Leticia. There is a jungle walk to a lookout and a rope bridge over the forest canopy, with wonderful views over the surrounding jungle. There are various other guided day treks through the jungle.

Leticia

★ **Puerto Nariño** This is a small, attractive settlement on the Río Loretoyacu, a tributary of the Amazon, beyond the Parque Nacional Amacayacu. It is becoming a more popular destination for jungle trips, with its more isolated location, 75 km from Leticia, about two hours by boat. Where the two rivers meet is a popular place to watch dolphins. Tours include Lago de Tarapoto to see pink and grey river dolphin – the latter when the water level is high (US$70 per person by motorized canoe) and walks to indigenous communities. **Fundación Natütama** ⓘ *T313-456 8657, http://natutama.org, daily except Tue 0800-1230, 1400-1700, US$6,* works to preserve the marine life of this part

Mahatu Hostel **2**
Yurupary **3**

Restaurants 🍴
El Cielo **1**
Numae Bistro **2**
Tierras Amazónicas **3**
Waira Suites **4**

Where to stay 🛏
Malokamazonas **1**

of the Amazon by organizing educational programmes with local communities. They have an informative visitor centre with an elaborate display of underwater life. Internet and international calls (expensive) can be made next to the school.

Listings Leticia and the Amazon *map page 278 and below.*

Tourist information

Leticia

Secretaría de Turísmo y Cultura
C 8, No 9-75, T2-592 7569.
Mon-Fri 0700-1200, 1400-1700,
see www.amazonas.gov.co.
There is also an office at the airport.

Policía de Turismo del Amazonas
T99-592 7569.
Tourist police.

Where to stay

Leticia

$$$ Malokamazonas
C 8, No 5-49, T8-592 6642,
www.hotelmalokamazonas.es.tl.
Family-run, close to the border, a variety of rooms in 9 nicely furnished thatched cabins with hammocks, welcome drink, meals apart from breakfast extra, jacuzzi, laundry, cable TV, garden, range of tours and river trips available.

$$$-$$ Yurupary
C 8, No 7-26, T8-592 4743,
www.hotelyurupary.com.

Around Leticia

Good, large rooms, pool fringed with tropical plants, dinner available. Also arranges tours into the Amazon through **Yurupary Amazonas Tours** and runs **Aldea Yurupary**, thatch-roofed *cabañas*, in Puerto Nariño.

$ Mahatu Hostel
Cra 7, No 1-40, T311-539 1265, see Facebook: Mahatu-Hostel-568839959808864.
On the edge of town, towards the border with Tabatinga, a couple of private rooms with bath and dorms with fan (US$7-12 pp), kitchen, bar, nice ample grounds with ponds, small pool, hammocks, quiet location. Owner speaks English, Flemish, French and Portuguese and organizes alternative tours of the Amazon.

Puerto Nariño
Increasingly travellers are choosing to stay in Puerto Nariño. Several options are available, see www.puertonarino-amazonas.gov.co/turismo.shtml, T321-454 7752.

$$$-$$ Casa Selva
Cra 6, No 6-78, T311-201 2153.
Comfortable, airy, spotless rooms, with breakfast, good food and pleasant grounds, quiet location. Tours to Lago de Tarapoto and other destinations through their operator **AT Amazonas Turismo Ecológico**.

$$-$ Maloca Napu
C 4, No 5-72, 2 blocks from river, T315-607 4044, www.malocanapu.com.
Simple private wooden rooms in thatch-roofed cabins, dorms (US$7), separate cabins available for group rental, quiet and relaxing. Breakfast provided.

$ Hospedaje Manguaré
C 4, No 5-52, T311-276 4873, claudia_alzate81@hotmail.com.

Comfortable cabin-style rooms with fans and bath, also has bunks in dorms. It doubles up as the town chemist.

$ Hostal Alto del Aguila
Km 2 salida de Puerto Nariño, T320-244 0187.
Basic but clean *cabañas* in peaceful setting by the riverside, 15 mins from the village; kayaks available free to guests, and good guided tours arranged. Warmly recommended.

$ Paraíso Ayahuasca
C 4 No 2-135, T311-234 7292, paraisoayahuasca@gmail.com.
Sturdily built *cabaña* overlooking the river, with 5 rooms, simply furnished but clean and comfortable, also cheaper dorms, breakfast (US$2.50). Recommended.

Restaurants

Leticia
Several popular sidewalk restaurants near the corner of Cra 9 and C 8 serve good-value set lunches (*comida corriente*) and à la carte in the evening.

$$ El Cielo
C 7, No 6-50.
Leticia's only 'gourmet fusion' restaurant, doing interesting things with local ingredients, such as yuca-based pizza and stuffed mojojo palm tree worms.

$$-$ Tierras Amazónicas
Cra 8, No 7-50, T8-592 4748.
Has an a/c dining room, faux jungle decor, but most of all great fresh fish (including crunchy piranha), plus tasty steaks and wide range of Amazonian fruits. Can be lively and popular with groups.

$$-$ Waira Suites
Cra 10, No 7-36, T8-592 4428.
Upmarket hotel/restaurant in town centre, dining room with a/c, poolside

buffet; excellent fresh fish and ceviche, pasta and salads.

$ Numae Bistro
Cra 11 No 4A-32, T8-839 5856,
Facebook: NUMAE Bistro.
Tapas and other imaginative snacks and cocktails from this contemporary bistro, with stunning views over the Amazon.

What to do

Leticia
Tour operators
Isaac Rodríguez, *Cra 6N, No 7-91 apto 117, T312-314 0311, isaacdrc@gmail.com.*
Ministry of Tourism-registered guide.
Reserva Natural Palmarí, *Cra 10, No 93-72, Bogotá, T01-610 3514, Facebook: Reserva Natural Palmari.* They operate a reserve on the Río Javarí, rich in local wildlife, with range of accommodation and many tours available.
SelvAventura, *Cra 9, No 6-85, T8-592 3977, 311-287 1307, www.selvaventura.org.*
Jungle tours and expeditions to natural reserves and indigenous territories, activities such as kayaking, trekking and canopying. English and several other languages spoken. Also run (**$**) **Casa del Kurupira** hostel (Cra 9, No 6-100), with dorms (US$9 pp) and private rooms.
Turismo Verde, *no storefront, Leticia, T311-508 5666, www.amazonheliconia. com.* Run **Kurupira** floating hotel on the Colombian Amazon, with range of tours and alternative activities (such as indigenous tattooing) and packages from Bogotá.

Puerto Nariño
Tour guides
Ever Sinarahua (a boatman), **Clarindo López** and **Milciades Peña** are recommended for their local knowledge of flora and fauna and indigenous

customs; they work with tour operators. Also recommended is **Pedro Nel Cuello**, enquire through **Fundación Natútama** (see page 278).

Transport

Leticia
Air
Airport is 1.5 km north of the city; small terminal, few facilities, T8-592 8133. Expect to be searched before leaving Leticia airport, and on arrival in Bogotá from Leticia. Daily flights from **Bogotá**.

Boat
Different docks are used at different times depending on water levels; ask around. Motorboat to **Santa Rosa**, Peru, daily 0700-1800, US$2 pp; to cross at night arrange ahead with a boatman, US$6.50 pp, beware overcharging and negotiate. If crossing to Santa Rosa in the early morning to catch the *rápido* to Iquitos, better to take a taxi to Tabatinga docks (it is not safe to walk) where a motorboat shuttles passengers starting 0230 (Colombia/Peru time), US$3 pp. Speedboats to **Puerto Nariño**, daily 0800, 1100 and 1500, return 0730, 1100 and 1600 (check times as they often change), 2 hrs, US$14-18. These will take passengers to the **Parque Nacional Amacayacu**, US$16 one way; let them know when you wish to return; 2 companies on alternate days, make sure that your operator travels the day you want to return.

Taxi
Airport to the centre US$3.50; Leticia (including airport) to **Tabatinga** (including Brazilian immigration and ports) US$14 during the day, US$18 at night, mototaxi US$2.70; mototaxi (1 passenger only) within Leticia US$1.

Background

History

Pre-Columbian

Colombia was inhabited by various indigenous groups before the Spanish conquest. The most highly developed were the **Tayronas**, who had settlements along the Caribbean coast and on the slopes of the Sierra Nevada de Santa Marta. The Tayronas had a complex social organization, with an economy based on fishing, agriculture and commerce. They built paved roads, aqueducts, stone stairways and public plazas for ceremonies.

Another major group were the **Muisca**, a Chibcha-speaking people who dominated the central highlands of Colombia at the time of the conquest. Muisca and Chibcha can be considered the same language. Philologists identify the 'Chibchan' language as referring to a series of dialects extending from Nicaragua in Central America to Ecuador, almost all of which have now disappeared. Carbon dating places their earliest settlements at around BC 545. Their village confederation was ruled by the **Zipa** at Bogotá, and the **Zaque** at Hunza (now Tunja). The Zipas believed that they were descended from the Moon, and the Zaques from the Sun. Their livelihood came from trading at markets in corn, potatoes and beans. They were also accomplished goldsmiths, and traded emeralds, ceramics and textiles with other societies.

The **Sinú** had their chiefdoms in the present-day Department of Córdoba and parts of Antioquia and Sucre. They farmed yuca and maize on artificial mounds in the local marshlands with complex drainage systems to make the best use of high and low water levels. They also cultivated reeds used for textiles and basket-weaving, as well as working with gold. Much wealth was plundered from their tombs, known as 'guacas', by the Spaniards during the conquest.

The **Quimbayas** inhabited parts of the Valle del Cauca. They had a class system and society similar to that of the Muisca and Tayronas, except that some evidence suggests they practised ritual cannibalism.

'**Calima**' is a term used to classify the other indigenous groups living in the department of Valle del Cauca. They include the **Liles** (based near present-day Cali) and the **Gorrones** (based in the Cordillera Occidental). They were organized into small chiefdoms with economies based on fishing, hunting and cultivating beans, yuca and corn. They traded in gold, salt, textiles and slaves. Two other significant groups prospered in San Agustín and Tierradentro, in what is now the south of Colombia. Both left fascinating monuments but they had disappeared well before the conquest.

Spanish colonization

The first permanent Spanish settlement in Colombia was established in 1500-1507 by **Rodrigo de Bastidas** (1460-1527). He reached the country by sailing south along the Caribbean coast. After his return to Spain to face trial for insubordination, he was given permission to establish a colony. In 1525 he founded Santa Marta and named the river Magdalena. Cartagena was founded in 1533 by **Pedro de Heredia** and used as a central stockpile for the growing Spanish collection of treasure. Massive fortifications were built to protect it from pirate attacks. Santa Fe de Bogotá was founded by **Gonzalo Jiménez de Quesada** (c 1495-1579) in 1538. He arrived in Santa Marta in 1535 and continued up to the high plateau of Sabana de Bogotá with his men: 200 made the trip by boat, 670 by land. **Sebastián de Belalcázar** (c 1480-1551), the lieutenant of Francisco Pizarro, was given instructions to explore southern Colombia and the Cauca Valley in 1535. He founded Cali and Popayán in 1536 and 1537 respectively, and was made governor of Popayán in 1540. **Nicolás Federmann** (1506-1541), acting on behalf of the Welser financiers of Germany, led an expedition east to Coro and Cabo de la Vela, then back to Barquisimeto and Meta. He arrived in the Sabana de Bogotá in 1538, where he met Belalcázar and Jiménez de Quesada.

Jiménez de Quesada named the territory he had conquered Nuevo Reino de Granada, because it reminded him of Granada in Spain. Santa Fe de Bogotá was named after the city of Santa Fe in Granada. The first secular government to be established after the conquest was the Audiencia de Santa Fe de Bogotá, in 1550. After 1594, it shared ruling authority with the president of the New Kingdom of New Granada, the name given to the whole conquered area, which included Panama. The presidency was replaced in 1718 by a viceroyalty at Bogotá, which also controlled the provinces now known as Venezuela; it was independent of the viceroyalty of Peru, to which this vast area had previously belonged.

Independence from Spain

In 1793, a translation of *Rights of Man* was published in Colombia by **Antonio Nariño** (1765-1823), an administrator and journalist, known as 'el Precursor' for his important role in the Independence movement. He was imprisoned in Spain in 1794, but escaped and returned to Nueva Granada (as Colombia was then called) in 1797. He joined the patriot forces in 1810 and became president of Cundinamarca in 1812. In 1813 he led a military campaign in the south and was again imprisoned by the Spanish. Meanwhile **Simón Bolívar** (1783-1830) was leading a campaign for Venezuelan Independence. Following the collapse of the First Republic of Venezuela in 1812, he joined the Independence movement in Cartagena and had early successes in his 1812 Magdalena Campaign, which ended in Caracas, where the Second Republic was proclaimed. Again, the patriots lost control and Bolívar returned to Colombia, but was forced to flee to the West Indies when **General Pablo Morillo** launched the Spanish re-conquest.

Changes in Europe were also to affect the situation in Colombia. In 1808, Napoleon replaced Ferdinand VII of Spain with his own brother Joseph. The New World refused to recognize this, and several revolts erupted in Nueva Granada, culminating in a revolt at Bogotá and the establishment of a junta on 20 July 1810. Cartagena also bound itself to a junta set up at Tunja.

Simón Bolívar returned to the Llanos in 1816 and formed a new army. Their campaign for liberation involved a forced march over the Andes, in the face of incredible hardship. After joining forces with **Francisco de Paula Santander**'s Nueva Granada army, he defeated the royalists at the Battle of the Pantano de Vargas in July of 1819, winning the decisive victory at the Battle of Boyacá on 7 August. From

1819 to 1828 Bolívar was president of Gran Colombia, the new name for the union of Colombia, Venezuela, Panama and Ecuador, which lasted until the 1830s.

After the fall of Napoleon in 1815, the Spanish set about trying to reconquer the independent territories. The main Spanish general behind the task was Pablo Morillo (1775-1837), known as 'the Pacifier'. During his reign of terror (1816-1819), more than 300 patriot supporters were executed. Morillo set up the 'Consejo de Guerra Permanente' and the 'Consejo de Purificación'. The latter's aim was to punish crimes of treason. There was also a board of confiscations known as the 'Junta de Secuestros'. Morillo was linked to the re-establishment of the Inquisition, which saw many priests tried in military courts in South America.

The Spaniards created a considerable legacy in Colombia. Their main objective was to amass riches, notably gold, and ship everything back to Spain. Protecting what they had collected from their English, French and Dutch rivals led to the massive fortifications of their main port, Cartagena. Most of what they built is still intact and has to be experienced to be fully appreciated. However, they also brought with them culture and lifestyle, and some of their best colonial public and domestic architecture can be found in Colombia. Furthermore they brought their language, religion and many institutions, including universities, that continue to thrive today. The towns they planned and built are now being preserved. What they did not create, however, were political institutions, and the search for a durable formula continues, 200 years after Independence.

Gran Colombia

La República de Gran Colombia was established by the revolutionary congress at present-day Ciudad Bolívar (Venezuela) on 17 December 1819. A general congress was held at Cúcuta on 1 January 1821, and it was here that the two opposing views that later sowed such dissent in Colombia first became apparent. Bolívar and Nariño were in favour of centralization; Santander, a realist, wanted a federation of sovereign states. Bolívar succeeded in enforcing his view and the 1821 Constitution was drawn up, dividing Gran Colombia into 12 departments and 26 provinces. New laws were introduced to abolish the slave trade and allow free birth for the children of slaves born in Colombia, to redistribute indigenous lands and to abolish the Inquisition. This constitution lasted until 1830 when, following the breakaway of Venezuela and Ecuador, a new constitution was drawn up.

The next president after Bolívar was Francisco de Paula Santander, from 1832 to 1837. Formerly the vice-president, he had led a campaign of dissent against the alleged dictatorship of Bolívar, culminating in an assassination attempt on Bolívar on 25 September 1828. Suspected of having had a hand in the attempt, Santander was sentenced to death, but pardoned by Bolívar himself and instead sent into exile. later returning to hold the presidency. He played an important role in establishing the administrative structure of the new republic of Colombia, and went on to become leader of the congressional opposition from 1837 to 1840.

Colombia's civil wars

The new country, which still included present-day Panama, was the scene of much dissent between the centralizing pro-clerical Conservatives and the federalizing anti-clerical Liberals. The Liberals were dominant from 1849, and the next 30 years saw countless insurrections and civil wars. In 1885 the Conservatives imposed a highly centralized constitution that was not modified for over 100 years. Civil war had a disastrous effect on the economy, leading to the Paper Money Crisis of 1885, when Colombian currency suffered a dramatic fall in value and circulation had to be reduced to 12 million pesos in notes. Gold was not established as the standard for currency until 1903.

A Liberal revolt of 1899 against the rigidly partisan government of the Conservatives turned into the 'War of the Thousand Days', also known as 'La Rebelión'. It lasted from 17 October 1899 to 1 June 1903. The first Liberal victory was at Norte de Santander in December 1899, when government forces were defeated by rebel leader General Benjamín Herrera. The Battle of Palonegro, 11-26 May 1900, was won by the government forces, led by General Próspero Pinzón. This proved to be the decisive victory of the 'War of a Thousand Days'. 100,000 people had died before the Liberals were finally defeated.

During the Independence Wars, Panama remained loyal to Spain. Although it had been a state in Nueva Granada since 1855, it was practically self-governing until 1886, when the new Colombian constitution reduced it to a mere department. A bid for Independence in 1903 was supported by the USA. The revolution lasted only four days (3-6 November) and by 18 November the USA had signed a treaty allowing them to build the Panama Canal.

The authoritarian government of General **Rafael Reyes** (1850-1921), from 1904 to 1909, was known as the Quinquenio dictatorship. He created his own extra-legal national assembly in 1904. His territorial reorganization and his negotiations with the USA over Panama increased his unpopularity, leading to an assassination attempt in 1906. The new president from 1910 to 1914, **Carlos Eugenio Restrepo** (1867-1937), restored a legal form of government and began negotiations with the USA for the Urrutia-Thomson Treaty of 1914. This resulted in a US$25 million indemnity payment to Colombia over US involvement in the Panamanian Revolution.

Colombia was also engaged in a dispute with its southern neighbour, Peru, over Leticia, capital of the Commissariat of Amazonas. Peru had repudiated the Salomón-Lozano Treaty of 1922 by occupying Leticia, a part of Colombia according to the treaty. The dispute was submitted to the League of Nations in 1933, who took over the Leticia area and handed it back to Colombia in 1934.

La Violencia

The late 1940s to mid-1960s were dominated by a period known as 'La Violencia', incited by the assassination of the socialist mayor of Bogotá, **Jorge Eliécer Gaitán**, on 9 April 1948. The riots that ensued were known as the 'Bogotazo'. La Violencia was characterized by terrorism, murder and destruction of property. Simultaneous, though uncoordinated, outbursts persisted throughout the 1950s. Among the many victims were Protestants, who were persecuted 1948-1959. Some 115 Protestants were murdered and 42 of their buildings destroyed. Other contributing factors to La Violencia were anti-communist sentiments, economic deprivation and the prevailing partisan political system. In 1957 a unique political truce was formed, putting an end to the violence. The Liberal and Conservative parties became the Frente Nacional, a coalition under which the two parties supported a single presidential candidate and divided all political offices equally between them. Political stability was maintained for 16 years. Ultimately the Conservatives gained more from this accord, and unforeseen opposition was provoked in parties not involved in the agreement.

Guerrilla movements

One of the biggest guerrilla organizations active after La Violencia was the Movimiento 19 de Abril, known as M19. Their political wing was the Alianza Nacional Popular (ANAPO), founded by followers of the dictator **General Gustavo Rojas Pinilla** (1900-1975). His Peronist tactics during his 1953-1957 presidency had resulted in his trial by national tribunal and he was overthrown on 10 May 1957. ANAPO opposed both Liberals and Conservatives. They became a major protest force during the late 1960s and 1970s, believing that the 1970 presidential elections, in which Rojas Pinilla was a candidate, had been rigged, and that fraudulent results had placed **Misael Pastrana Borrero** in power. M19 took their name from the date of the election, 19 April 1970.

M19's agenda was to achieve a democratic socialist society. Seeking to identify themselves with the legacy of the hero of the Independence movement, their first public act was the theft of Bolívar's sword from Quinta de Bolívar in Bogotá. They also kidnapped José Rafael Mercado, president of the Confederation of Workers, in 1976, accusing him of fraud and misconduct in office, for which they tried and executed him. They then kidnapped Alvaro Gómez Hurtado, Communist Party leader and son of earlier president Gómez, to publicize demands for renewed talks with the government.

It was not until the late 1980s that negotiations got under way. A peace accord was reached in late 1989. The following year, M19 members surrendered their weapons and turned themselves into a bona fide political party, named Alianza Democrática, or M19-AD, with which they gained a significant percentage of the vote in the 1990 elections.

The other main terrorist organization after La Violencia was Fuerzas Armadas Revolucionarias de Colombia (FARC). Formed in 1964 under leader **Pedro Antonio Marín**, known as Manuel Marulanda or 'Tirofijo' ('Sureshot'), they were aligned with the Communist Party. After 20 years of guerrilla activity they signed a truce with the government on 24 May 1984. FARC joined forces with the legitimate Unión Patriótica and went on to win 10 seats in the 1986 election, while the Liberals took the majority.

In 1985 many of Colombia's guerrilla movements merged into the 'Coordinadora Guerrillera Simón Bolívar' (CGSB), together with all organizations that had refused to sign the government amnesty offered by **President Belisario Betancur** in 1985. Their aim was to co-ordinate their actions against the government and the armed forces. Most of their actions were based along the upper Río Cauca and the department of Antioquia. Peace talks with the government in the early 1990s collapsed, followed in 1992-1993 by several indecisive but destructive offences on the part of both the guerrillas and the armed forces.

The 1994 presidential elections were won by another Liberal, **Ernesto Samper**. The main thrust of his programme was that Colombia's current economic strength should provide resources to tackle the social deprivation that was causing drug use and insurgency. He placed emphasis on bringing the FARC and the other main guerrilla group, the **Ejército de Liberación Nacional (ELN)**, to the negotiating table, while also increasing public spending on social welfare. Revelations during 1995-1997 that Samper's election campaign had been financed partly by a US$6 million donation from the Cali cartel saw the government's popularity decline. In 1996 further charges were brought against the president for links with the drugs mafia, although he was acquitted. The charges led to political instability and the attempted killing of Samper's lawyer. With the assassination of opposition leader Alvaro Gómez, Samper declared a state of emergency.

When it was revealed that other ministers had links with the drugs mafia, suspicion arose that Samper's acquittal had only been to protect their own positions. International confidence was lost. The USA decided, in March 1996, to remove (decertify) Colombia from its list of countries making progress against drug trafficking. This made Colombia ineligible for US aid.

Colombia was decertified for the second time in March 1997 partly because the Cali leaders were continuing their business from prison, having been given light sentences. Whatever progress was being made to eradicate drugs plantations and stocks, the denial of US aid permitted little scope for the establishment of alternative crops. Many rural communities were therefore left without any means of support.

In May 1997 the government admitted for the first time to the escalating problem of paramilitary groups and their links with members of the armed forces. The most infamous of these is 'Autodefensas Campesinas de Córdoba y Urabá' (ACCU), who receive financial support from drugs cartels. The state department admitted that 48% of violent episodes in 1997 were carried out by paramilitaries. This was confirmed by the annual report of the Inter-American Human Rights Commission in June 1997. In March 1998, congressional elections were relatively peaceful; and the US withdrawal of decertification restrictions the same month, were a welcome boost of confidence. Two rounds of presidential elections in May and June 1998 also passed without excessive guerrilla disruption. The new president, **Andrés Pastrana**, voted in on a promise to find a formula for peace, immediately devoted his efforts to bringing the guerrilla groups to the negotiating table. After a long, tortuous process with FARC, a large *zona de despeje* (demilitarized zone), was conceded, centred on San Vicente del Caguán in Caquetá. Not everyone was in favour of Pastrana's initiative, not least because FARC violence and extortion did not cease. In April 2000, the government proposed the ceding of a similar but smaller demilitarized zone to the ELN, situated on the west side of the Río Magdalena in the department of Bolívar and a small section of Antioquia, a *zona de encuentro*. Local communities of this agricultural area were dismayed and peacefully demonstrated by closing roads and causing disruption.

After a series of high-profile guerrilla terrorist actions, including the hijacking of a plane, attacks on several small towns and cities, and the kidnapping of several political figures, Pastrana ended the peace talks on 21 February 2002 and ordered the armed forces to start retaking the FARC-controlled zone.

Modern Colombia

Recent history

Alvaro Uribe succeeded Andrés Pastrana as president in May 2002, holding office for two terms, until 2010. A Harvard- and Oxford-educated lawyer, he came to power promising to eradicate the left-wing guerrillas' and right-wing paramilitaries' hold on the country.

To a large extent he succeeded. Using US funding from Plan Colombia (see below) and helped by the CIA, he boosted spending on the military, targeted FARC leaders and armed peasants in vulnerable regions. He held formal peace talks with far-right paramilitaries and managed to bring security to most of the urban areas of the country within the mountainous centre. In so doing he effectively pushed the guerrillas, who at one point held territory within an hour of Bogotá, to the margins of the country – to the dense jungles around the borders with Venezuela, Ecuador and Panama.

In terms of the state's fight against the FARC, which has been going on for more than 40 years, 2008 was Colombia's *annus mirabilis*. Three major successes – each of which would have been considered a major, standalone coup in their own right – shifted the balance of the conflict overwhelmingly in favour of the government.

In March of that year, the Colombian army executed a raid just over the border into Ecuador in which Luis Edgar Devia Silva (normally known by his nom de guerre, Raúl Reyes), the FARC's spokesperson and a member of the Secretariat, was killed.

In May, it was revealed that the FARC's founder and leader, Pedro Antonio Marín Marín, aka Manuel Marulanda or Tirofijo ('Sureshot'), had died of a heart attack.

Then in July came the biggest blow of all – the dramatic rescue of Senator Ingrid Betancourt, who had been kidnapped six years previously while campaigning for the presidency.

These three strikes put the FARC firmly on the defensive. Alfonso Cano took over command after Marulanda's death, but Colombia continued to target high-level FARC leaders and decimate rebel camps through airstrikes. The FARC officially entered peace talks with the Colombian government in Havana, Cuba in 2012, which gave many Colombians hope that five decades of conflict might soon come to an end. However, despite releasing 10 of the longest-held hostages in the world in 2012, the FARC continues to kidnap and bomb, with major incidents occurring in 2008 and 2013.

Overall, Uribe managed to improve security in most areas in Colombia during his eight years in office. His successor, Santos, a Harvard economist and former minister, took office in August 2010 and appears to be following in Uribe's footsteps in terms of national security policies, while also recommencing a long-awaited land redistribution programme. The major success of the Santos presidency was his signing of a historic peace agreement with FARC in September 2016, following four years of sometimes fractious negotiations held in Havana, Cuba. It nearly failed at the first hurdle, however, when the public narrowly voted against in a surprise referendum. Nevertheless, Santos held firm and Congress ratified it in December, winning the Nobel Peace Prize for his efforts. The agreement brought an end to a war that had lasted 52 years, and cost an estimated 220,000 lives. FARC rebels began handing over their weapons to the UN, a lengthy process that is expected to continue for many months.

Presidential elections are to be held in 2018, with president Santos stepping down. At the time of writing, polls show a close-fought contest between six candidates, with the current favourite, left-wing Gustavo Petro (Progressive Movement) just ahead of centrist Sergio Fajardo (Citizens' Commitment Movement). Former presidents Alvaro Uribe and Andrés Pastrana have joined forces in a coalition, hinting at a renegotiation of the FARC peace agreement. Nevertheless, most Colombians polled have highlighted jobs, political corruption and healthcare as their main concerns.

Meanwhile, just two days before the visit of Pope Francis to Colombia in September 2017, the government made the dramatic announcement that a bilateral ceasefire had been agreed with the ELN, the first time that the country's second-largest guerrilla group had called a formal halt to their activities."

Relations with neighbours

In the last few years, diplomatic relations between Colombia and her neighbours have been at best frosty, at worst volatile. While much of Latin America has experienced a swing toward socialism and anti-American sentiment, Colombia has strengthened its ties with the USA and pursued a neo-liberal economical model. Uribe and the former president of Venezuela, Hugo Chávez, one of the more outspoken critics of US 'imperialism', displayed a barely disguised disdain for each other and their diametrically opposed ideologies. Considerable tension has risen between the two countries recently, sparked by the ongoing crisis in Venezuela. Many thousands of Venezuelans have fled into Colombia, with sporadic violence a daily occurrence along border areas.

Border relations with Ecuador and Panama have at times also been fraught, due to guerrilla and drug-trafficking activities in the border areas.

Paz Colombia

Formerly known as Plan Colombia, Paz Colombia is a US-Colombian initiative designed to reduce the flow of cocaine into the USA. Conceived during the presidency of Andrés Pastrana, the original Plan Colombia asked for US aid to address the problem of social exclusion that has plagued Colombia since Independence from the Spanish and that has forced peasant farmers to cultivate coca, giving birth to guerrilla movements like the FARC in the first place.

A second draft, presided over by US President Bill Clinton's advisers, had an entirely more militaristic slant and aimed to reduce the drug supply by providing extra firepower to the Colombian army in its pursuit of drug-traffickers and supplying equipment and civilian agents for the destruction of coca plantations.

The plan has come under heavy criticism for its fumigation policy, which has seen farmers' legal crops destroyed alongside illegal ones, as well as causing adverse health effects on those exposed. NGOs also claim that the money provided by the US government, which tallies up to several billion dollars, has funded Colombian army units involved in extra judicial killings and other human rights abuses.

Despite the billions of dollars ploughed into the project, the plan has failed in its primary objective. A UN analysis has found that the eradication of coca plantations has been on a smaller scale than anticipated. What's more, the market price of cocaine has not increased significantly, something that would be expected if there were a shortage of the drug on the streets of the USA. Critics of the plan also argue that any eradication of coca production in Colombia would simply push cultivation back to countries such as Bolivia and Peru.

But the initiative has had a huge tangential success in that the money provided by the US government has helped the Colombian army in its victories over the FARC and for that has gained much approval in the eyes of many Colombians. The 2018 budget for Paz Colombia is for US$251.4 million, cut from the previous year's US$299.4 million, part of US president Donald Trump's worldwide reduction of foreign aid. Nevertheless, despite its shortcomings, particularly the persistent increase in coca cultivation throughout Colombia, the plan remains in operation.

The drugs trade

In Medellín and Cali, two cartels transformed Colombia's drugs trade into a major force in worldwide business and crime. Their methods were very different; Medellín's was violent and ostentatious, while Cali's was much more low-key. The Medellín cartel processed and distributed 60-70% of cocaine exported to the USA during the 1980s. It was headed by **Pablo Escobar Gaviria** (see box, page 194) and **Jorge Luis Ochoa Vásquez**. In the late 1980s both Jorge Luis Ochoa and Pablo Escobar were listed as billionaires by *Forbes Magazine*.

In 1981, **Marta Nieves Ochoa Vásquez**, Jorge's sister, was kidnapped. M19 were believed responsible. In response to the kidnapping, 'Muerte a Secuestradores' (Death to Kidnappers) was formed by leaders of the drugs trade. Their strong anti-Communist beliefs led to alleged support from factions of the military. In 1984 Muerte a Secuestradores assassinated Carlos Toledo Plata, an ANAPO congressman who had later joined M19.

President César Gaviria Trujillo, the Liberal candidate who had won the 1990 presidential election, put into motion a pacification plan to end the drugs cartels' offensive and establish a peace agreement with the guerrillas. In a further display of reformist government, he appointed **Antonio Navarro Wolff**, former guerrilla leader now of the M19-AD, to the post of health minister.

As a result of the reform of the constitution in 1991, a further general election was held in October 1991 and the Liberals retained a majority in the Senate and the House of Representatives. By 1991 the government had secured the surrender, under secret terms, of senior members of the Medellín cartel, namely Pablo Escobar and Jorge Luis Ochoa. One of the publicized conditions for their surrender was immunity from extradition and reduced sentences. Some of the senior traffickers and murderers got only five to eight years. President Gaviria received international support, including from the USA, for his stance against the drugs problem, which contrasted with previous president Barco's tougher and unsuccessful stand.

In the National Constituent Assembly elections of 1991 the M19-AD won 19 of the 70 contested seats; the Liberals won 24; combined Conservative factions won 20. These results were followed by attempts to legitimize and modernize the political system, in an effort to deny remaining guerrilla groups any cause for protest and therefore lead to peace. The judicial system was strengthened and extradition was banned. However, the early 1990s saw high abstention rates in elections: 60-70% of the electorate didn't vote. This was blamed on loss of confidence in the political system and disruption of voting by guerrillas in some rural areas.

During the Gaviria term, it was reported that Pablo Escobar was continuing to direct the Medellín cartel from inside his purpose-built prison at Envigado. The Cali cartel's trade was in turn growing in the wake of reduced activity by the Medellín cartel. In July 1992, Escobar escaped during a transfer to army barracks. Drug-related violence in Bogotá increased in 1993; thought to be Escobar's way of persuading the government to offer better surrender conditions for him. A paramilitary vigilante group was formed, called 'Perseguidos Por Pablo Escobar' (Los Pepes). This was allegedly made up of relatives of Escobar's murder victims and members of the Cali cartel, and it targeted Escobar's family. Escobar was finally shot by the armed forces on 2 December 1993 in Medellín, giving a temporary boost to the government's popularity. The Cali cartel capitalized on the death of Escobar and the dismantling of his empire. By the mid-1990s they controlled 70% of the world market in cocaine. But in June and July 1995, six of the seven heads of the cartel were arrested. In 2006, the Rodríguez brothers, Gilberto and Miguel, were extradited to the USA and pleaded guilty in Miami, Florida, to charges of conspiracy to import cocaine. This put an end to cartel control over the Colombian drug trade and it has now splintered into many individual groups, including paramilitary and guerrilla forces, although this has not stopped production in any significant way.

Government

Senators and Representatives are elected by popular vote. The Senate has 102 members, and the Chamber of Representatives has 166. The president, who appoints his 13 ministers, is elected by direct vote for a term of four years, but cannot succeed himself in the next term. Every citizen over 18 can vote. Reform of the 1886 Constitution was undertaken by a Constituent Assembly in 1991 (see History, above). Administratively, the country is divided into 32 departments and the Special Capital District of Bogotá. Liberty of speech and the freedom of the press are in theory absolute but in practice more limited. The official language of Colombia is Spanish. Its religion is Roman Catholicism. There is complete freedom for all other creeds not contravening Christian morals or the law.

People

The regions vary greatly in their racial make-up. Antioquia and Caldas are largely of European descent; Nariño has more indigenous roots; while people from the Cauca Valley are more African, descending from the slaves brought to the area when sugar was introduced. Afro-Caribbeans are also prominent in the rural area near the Caribbean and the northwest Pacific coastline. No colour bar is legally recognized but is not entirely absent in certain centres.

The birth, death and infant mortality rates vary greatly from one area of the country to another, but in general they are similar to those of neighbouring countries. Hospitals and clinics are few in relation to the population. About 66% of the doctors are in the departmental capitals, which contain about half of the population, though all doctors have to spend a year in the country before they can get their final diploma. The best hospitals, notably in Bogotá and Medellín, are well equipped and have fine reputations attracting patients from other countries of Latin America.

An estimated 1,340,000 tribal people – some 3.4% of the population – from 84 ethnic groups, live in Colombia. Groups include the Wayúu (in the Guajira), the Kogui and Arhauco (Sierra Nevada de Santa Marta), indigenous Amazonians such as the Huitoto, the nomadic Nukak and the Tikuna, indigenous Andean and groups of the Llanos and in the Pacific coast rainforest.

Although the national and official language of Colombia is overwhelmingly Spanish, many indigenous groups still use only their own languages. The largest ethno-linguistic group are the 150,000 Chibchas. On the Caribbean coast,

Indigenous cultures

Santa Marta
Guajira
Barranquilla
(Wayúu)
Cartagena
Tayrona
(Kogi)
(Arhuaco)
PANAMA
Sinú
(Cuna) Turbo Cúcuta
VENEZUELA
(Embera-Wunan) Sinú
(Cholo) Bucaramanga
Medellín Muisca
Chibcha (U'wa)
Quimbaya Tunja
Pereira Tolima
Calima (Páez) BOGOTÁ
Maypure
Cali Tierradentro (Puihave)
(Guambiano) Neiva
Tumaco Popayán
Tumaco San Agustín
Pasto
BRAZIL
(Huitoto)
ECUADOR
PERU
(Tikuna)
Leticia
Guajira...... Pre-Columbian
Not to scale (Wayúu)..... Present day

especially the islands, English or Creole are widely spoken. The diversity and importance of indigenous peoples was recognized in the 1991 constitutional reforms when Indigenous Colombians were granted the right to two senate seats; the National Colombian Indian Organization (ONIC) won a third seat in the October 1991 ballot. State recognition and the right to bilingual education has not, however, solved major problems of land rights, training and education, and justice.

The vast majority of Colombians (90%) are nominal Roman Catholics, though observance is not particularly high. As elsewhere in Latin America, Protestant Evangelical Churches have made some progress in Colombia in recent years.

Culture

Arts and crafts

With the wide variety of climate, topography and geology, it is not surprising that Colombia has virtually all the materials, fibres, minerals and incentives to create useful and artistic products. Many of the techniques practised today have been inherited from the indigenous peoples who lived here before the conquest, some indeed have not changed much in the intervening centuries and are as appropriate now as they were then.

Gold

Gold is very much associated with Colombia. It was gold that brought the Europeans to the New World, and where they found it first. The indigenous peoples had been using it for many centuries though not as a simple 'store of value'. Only when it had been made into jewellery, body ornaments or items to be used for sacrificial rites for their gods did gold have value for them. It must have seemed incomprehensible to them, as well as a tragedy for posterity, when the Spaniards melted down the gold they obtained in order to ship it back to Europe.

Many of the *sierras* in the west of the country have traces of gold in the strata. Through erosion in the rainy climates of the region, panning for gold in the rivers was productive and has probably been practised here since around 800 BC. Even some deep shaft mines have been found in west Colombia.

The Quimbaya of the Cauca Valley produced 24 carat gold containers, helmets and pendants in their ascendancy from 1000-1500 AD and also worked with *tumbaga*, a gold-copper alloy. The Tolima of the Magdalena Valley made artefacts of pure gold, while the Wayúu of the Guajira made string beads, sometimes covered with gold, a tradition that continues today. When the Spaniards arrived, the Muisca of the Boyacá/Bogotá area were modelling figures in wax and covering them with clay. They then fired them, removed the melted wax and filled the mould with gold. By carefully prizing open the mould, they were able to make many replicas, thus inventing an early form of mass production.

Virtually all of today's techniques of the goldsmith were known to the early peoples of Colombia and there is a fine presentation on this subject at the museum in the Parque Arqueológico in Sogamoso, Boyacá.

There are some good gold item bargains to be had in Colombia, notably in Bogotá and Cartagena. Perhaps the most interesting place, however, is Mompós, Bolívar, where there is a tradition of fine gold filigree work.

No one visiting Colombia should miss the Banco de la República's wonderful gold museums. The central collection of gold artefacts is in Bogotá but there are other smaller presentations in the main cities around the country, always worth a visit.

Textiles

Although Colombian textiles cannot rival those of Guatemala or Peru in terms of design and spectacular colour, certain areas of the country have very fine traditions. For the Wayúu, *'ser mujer es saber tejer'* (to be a woman is to know how to weave). Cotton was available in north Colombia and textiles were traded for wool from the Santa Marta *sierra* nearby, also used as a raw material. The Cuna of northwest Colombia still make the decorative panels for garments known as *molas*. A speciality is the *mola* made of many layers of coloured cloth sewn together, then cut out using the different colours to create a pattern or motif.

One striking costume is found in the south near Silvia, Cauca, where the indigenous Guambiano weave their own blue and fuchsia costumes as well as many other wool garments and blankets.

Basketry

By its nature, articles made of vegetable fibres do not survive for very long, but we know that the Spaniards found many examples of indigenous work in Colombia. The basket-weaving techniques of the Muisca have continued in Tenza, Boyacá, where people still use the giant reed *caña de castilla* (*Arundo donax*), which is easier to work with than bamboo. The whole local village works in this cottage industry.

Another similar community enterprise is in Sandoná, Nariño, where, in addition to basket weaving, Panama hats are a speciality. Panama hats are so named for where they were initially sold and shipped from, rather than where they were made. The workers on the canal in the early part of the 20th century were the first customers, followed by those passing through. They were made in Ecuador and in Sandoná where the local *iraca* palm fibre is used. Hats are also made in Sampués, Sucre, from 'arrowcane' which grows in the river lowlands nearby and good basket weaving using palma iraca can be found at Usiacurí, south of Barranquilla.

The finest quality basket weaving in the country is to be found along the northwest Pacific coast of Chocó where the women of the indigenous Waunana use *werregue* palm to weave a texture so fine that the finished product can look like clay and be used to carry water. They have a flourishing trade nowadays in coarser but more colourful palm weaving products.

Wood

The indigenous people of Chocó also make interesting 'healing sticks', said to have magical as well as healing powers. These are about 50 cm long with a pointed end and carved figures above. Held against the stomach of the patient, they can drive away evil spirits and cure illnesses. Carved wooden masks are a feature of indigenous crafts in the Sierra Nevada de Santa Marta in the north and the Sibundoy people of Putumayo in the extreme south of the country, used them for festivities and rituals. Interesting wood carvings are made by the Puinave people near Inírida. Wooden masks appear in the carnival in Barranquilla.

Perhaps the most important wood *artesanía* is found in Chiquinquirá (Boyacá). Carved musical instruments are a speciality and many other items including all sorts of items made of *tagua* nuts gathered in the forests of Chocó and Amazonas. Guitars are also found in Marinilla near Medellín.

Leather
Leather and woodwork often go together, and the arrival of cattle brought the necessary raw material. Now, finely engraved leather covering carved wooden chairs and other furniture is made in Pasto (Nariño), an important centre.

Barniz
An additional craft is that of the resin locally called *barniz*. This comes from seed pods of *Eleagia utilis*, which grows at altitudes of over 2000 m in Putumayo. Nowadays, the resin is extracted by passing through a mill or by hammering. Previously this was done by chewing the seeds, commonly known as *mopa-mopa*, supposedly because of the strange sound made by the chewers attempting to speak as well as chew at the same time. After extraction, the resin is dyed and expertly stretched to paper thin sheets into which designs are cut to decorate wooden objects including masks, each colour produced individually, finally covered with a protective lacquer. Pasto is the most important centre for *barniz*.

Pottery
The best known pottery centre in Colombia is Ráquira, Boyacá. A large selection of products is made for household and ornamental use including many small items, all sold here and in surrounding towns. The large earthenware pots made here today are identical to those made by the Chibcha centuries ago. A similar pottery centre across the country, Carmen de Viboral, Antioquia, also produces ceramics that are known throughout Colombia.

Imaginative and amusing ceramics are made in Pitalito, Huila. This form of popular art, pottery adorned with scenes of everyday life, is typified by representations of the *chiva*, the omnipresent brightly coloured bus seen in many parts of Colombia.

A more unusual line of production is the 'blackware' made at La Chamba, Tolima. This small village, beside the Río Magdalena near Guamo, is not generally marked on maps. The process involves using closed kilns, thus cutting down the use of oxygen which thereby causes the iron in the clay to turn from red to black. La Chamba is now a household name in Colombia and is also becoming better known abroad.

Fine art and sculpture

The colonial art of Colombia is rich and diverse, perhaps reflecting its geographical position between the Caribbean and the Pacific, but also because of the early rivalry between the two first important colonial settlements of Bogotá and Tunja. Both cities boast numerous museums and religious foundations with good collections of painting, sculpture and decorative arts. Throughout the colonial period works of art were imported from Europe and elsewhere in the Spanish territories, particularly from Quito in the south. Artists came from far afield to work in the wealthy Colombian centres. In contrast to colonial practices in Mexico and

Ecuador there seems to have been little attempt to train native craftsmen in the dominant European artistic modes of painting and sculpture, perhaps because indigenous expertise lay in pottery and metalwork rather than carving or painting.

Early art from Spain

The conquerors brought the Christian religion and, along with it, Christian art. The cathedral sacristy in Bogotá preserves what must be one of the first European imports: a fragile silk standard traditionally believed to have been carried by Jiménez de Quesada's troops at the foundation of Bogotá in 1538, and known as the **Cristo de la Conquista**. The emaciated, bloody figure of Christ is in a mixture of paint and appliqué, with a swirling length of loin cloth around his hips. This seems to billow in the breeze, an impression that would have been all the stronger in its original context. It is hard to imagine anything more alien to native beliefs or native forms of art. Other early Christian images, especially pictures of the Virgin, must have tapped into local beliefs because they soon became the focus of popular cults: the **Virgen de Monguí**, for example, is a 16th-century Spanish painting, which tradition holds was sent over by Philip II, while the **Virgen de Chiquinquirá**, the patron saint of Colombia, was painted by the Andalucían **Alonso de Narváez** who settled in Tunja in the 1550s. Neither is outstanding as a work of art but both have been attributed with miraculous powers and versions can be found all over Colombia.

Although religious commissions dominated artistic production throughout the colonial period some remarkable secular wall paintings survive in Tunja that show another side to colonial society. In the late 16th and 17th centuries the houses of the city's founder, Gonzalo Suárez Rendón, of poet Juan de Castellanos and of city notary Juan de Vargas were decorated with colourful murals based on a wide range of printed sources. Those in the **Casa Vargas** are the most sophisticated, the combination of mythological figures, exotic animals, grotesques, heraldic cartouches and occasional Christian monograms resulting in a complex humanistic programme, probably devised by Castellanos. The diversity of styles reflects the diversity of sources, which can be traced to French, Flemish, German and Spanish originals. The rhinoceros, for example, is derived from Dürer's famous woodcut of 1515 but reached Tunja via a Spanish architectural treatise by Juan de Arfe, published in Seville in 1587. The murals in the **Casa Suárez Rendón** derive in part from those in the Casa Vargas, but are less philosophical, more straightforwardly decorative. Nevertheless, these paintings imply that a highly cultured society imported the most-up-to-date books and prints from Europe.

Woodcarvings and sculpture

The new religious foundations in the Americas created a huge market for paintings and sculptures with which to adorn their altarpieces, and workshops in Andalucía flourished as a result. An outstanding example of imported polychrome sculpture is the dignified Crucifixion group of 1583 on the high altar of the chapel of the wealthy Mancipe family in the cathedral in Tunja, sent by **Juan Bautista Vázquez** (died 1589) from his workshop in Seville. Sculpture workshops were soon established in the Americas, however, and Colombian churches preserve a wealth of carved and polychrome wooden altarpieces, choir stalls, confessionals and pulpits, as well as decorative wooden ceilings, screens and wall panels. An early example is the ambitious high altar of the church of San Francisco in Bogotá. The central bays were redesigned in the late 18th century but the wings date from about 1620. The tightly ordered Renaissance structure frames panels of relief carving in two distinctive styles: in the upper storey each has a single, clearly defined saint, while in the lower storey the panels contain crowded narrative scenes, overflowing with energy (the torso of the figure of St Jerome leans right out towards the high altar) and lush vegetation. The unknown artist was probably trained in Andalucía.

Such altarpieces usually involved several different craftsmen. The carvings for that in the Jesuit church of San Ignacio in Bogotá (1635-1640), for example, were by an Italian, **Gian Battista Loessing**. Another important sculptor working in Colombia in the 17th century was **Pedro de Lugo Albarracín**, whose devotional images of the suffering Christ appealed to popular piety, and several, such as the powerful figure of the fallen Christ known as **El Señor de Monserrate** (1656) in the eponymous shrine on the hill above Bogotá, have become pilgrimage destinations. Records of other sculptors with the same surname working in Bogotá and Tunja in the 17th century suggest that Pedro de Lugo was the father of a dynasty of craftsmen. **Lorenzo de Lugo**, for example, executed the eight large reliefs for the high altar of the chapel of Rosary in Santo Domingo, Tunja (c 1686). The architectural frame of this outstanding altarpiece includes numerous anthropomorphic supporting figures, *atlantes*, a common feature of colonial church furnishings in Colombia, and a chance for craftsmen to indulge in fanciful invention constrained by Christian orthodoxy. A famous example is the androgynous figure on the pulpit stairs in San Francisco, Popayán, a basket of exotic fruit on its head, and a pineapple in its hand, but grotesque figures, sometimes semi-angelic, sometimes semi-demonic, can be spotted amongst the fronds of tropical foliage on almost any baroque altarpiece. In the 18th century, figure sculptor **Pedro Laboria** from Andalucía introduced a new lightness of touch with his sinuous, almost dancing saints and angels (examples in Tunja cathedral and Santo Domingo, Bogotá).

Early paintings

As with sculpture, the demand for painting was met from a variety of sources. Works were imported from Europe, particularly from Andalucía and from the Netherlands. In the 17th century, enterprising sea captains would find room in their holds for a roll or two of canvases from the workshops of Zurbarán or Rubens to sell in the colonial ports. Itinerant artists worked their way round the viceregal centres in pursuit of lucrative commissions such as **Angelino Medoro** (c 1567-1631) from Rome who also worked in Quito and Lima before returning to Europe (see the two large canvases in the Mancipe chapel in Tunja Cathedral, 1598). Quito was an important source both of artists and of works of art. Born in Quito, the Dominican **Pedro Bedón** (c 1556-1621) worked in Tunja in the late 16th century and his influence can be seen in the Bogotano miniaturist **Francisco de Páramo** (active in the early 17th century), while **Miguel de Santiago** (c 1625-1706) sent numerous works to Colombia, including his esoteric 'Articles of the Faith' paintings now in Bogotá's cathedral museum.

Santiago was an important influence on Colombia's best 17th-century artist, **Gregorio Vásquez de Arce y Ceballos** (1638-1711) who trained in the workshop of the extensive Figueroa family of painters but who was working independently by the time he was 20. A prolific and eclectic artist, Vásquez drew on a variety of sources: sometimes his stiff, hieratic figures reveal his debt to popular prints, sometimes his soft landscapes and sweet-faced Virgins demonstrate his familiarity with the work of Zurbarán and Murillo (good examples in the Museo de Arte Colonial, Bogotá). Eighteenth-century painting in Colombia follows the well-trodden paths of earlier generations of artists, with none of the confident exuberance found in sculpture. You will find his work in many of Bogotá's churches.

After Independence

Independence from Spain did not bring independence from the traditions of colonial art. A survey of the galleries of ponderous churchmen and other civic dignitaries in the various museums suggests a more or less seamless production from the 17th to the 19th centuries: some appear sophisticated, some brutish, and the artist is not necessarily to blame. But if artistic style changed little the struggle for independence did provide some new subject matter. Bolívar is endlessly celebrated in painting. An inventive example is that of 1819 in the Quinta de Bolívar in Bogotá, by **Pedro José Figueroa** (1770-1838), where he stands with a protective arm around the shoulders of a diminutive female figure personifying the new and newly tamed republic, dressed in a silk gown, but still with bow, arrows and feather headdress, and seated on a caiman. The events of the Wars of Independence are recorded by **José María Espinosa** (1796-1883) in a series of paintings of the 1813-1816 campaigns (examples in the Quinta de Bolívar and the Academia de Historia, Bogotá). The painting of the death of General Santander in 1840 by **Luis García Hevia** in the Museo Nacional is sincere in its naïveté, whereas **Alberto Urdaneta** (1845-1887) who studied in Paris with Meissonier and is a much more versatile artist, sometimes makes his subjects from recent history seem artificial and melodramatic (*Caldas marchando al patíbulo*, Museo Nacional). But Urdaneta is also remembered as an uncompromising caricaturist, so much so that on one occasion he was expelled from the country. The Museo Nacional in Bogotá has two contrasting portraits of the heroine Policarpa Salavarrieta, executed by the Spanish in 1817; one popular anecdotal version shows her *en route* to the scaffold, the other attributed to **Epifanio Garay** (1849-1903) nicely contrasts the formal society portrait with the drama of the event: she sits poised and beautiful while the ominously shadowy figure of a soldier appears in a doorway behind.

Interest in Colombia's natural resources produced scientific missions that, although organized by foreigners (the first by the Spanish botanist **Celestino Mutis** in the 18th century and the next by the Italian geographer **Agustín Codazzi** in the 19th), nevertheless helped to awaken an appreciation of the landscape, peoples and cultures of Colombia, past and present. The Venezuelan **Carmelo Fernández** (1809-1887) worked for Codazzi in 1851, producing carefully observed watercolours of the peoples and traditions of different provinces (examples in the Biblioteca Nacional). **Manuel María Paz** (1820-1902) held the same position in 1853 and his drawings of the pre-Columbian culture of San Agustín are the first of their kind. **Ramón Torres Méndez** (1809-1895) was not a member of the mission, but like them he travelled extensively in the countryside and his scenes from everyday life helped to make *costumbrista* subjects respectable.

20th century

During the first decades of the 20th century Colombian artists preferred to ignore the upheavals of the European art scene and hold on to the established traditions of academic figure and landscape painting. Almost the only interesting figure, **Andrés de Santa María** (1860-1945), spent most of his life in Europe and developed a style that owed something to Cezanne and something to 17th-century Spanish art, but with an overriding concern for a thickly textured painted surface that is entirely personal (*Self-portrait*, 1923, Museo Nacional, Bogotá). During the 1930s the more liberal political climate in Colombia encouraged the younger generation of Colombian artists to look for a more socially and politically relevant form of art which, conveniently, they found in the Mexican muralists. Instead of having to embrace the violent rupture with the past represented by modern European movements such as Cubism and Futurism, the muralists offered a way of continuing in a figurative tradition but now with a social conscience expressed in images of workers and peasants struggling against the forces of oppression. **Pedro Nel Gómez** (1899-1984) was the first to paint murals inside public buildings, particularly in his native Medellín, and he was followed by others such as **Alipio Jaramillo** (1913-1999) and **Carlos Correa** (1912-1985). The sculptor **Rómulo Rozo** (1899-1964) was also influenced by the rhetoric of the Mexican muralists, as well as by forms of Aztec and Mayan sculpture, and strove to achieve a comparable combination of simplicity and monumentality.

Only in the 1950s did Abstraction have any impact in Colombia. Born in Munich, **Guillermo Wiedemann** (1905-1969) arrived from Germany in 1939 and after a spell painting tropical landscapes began to experiment with an expressionist form of abstraction, full of light, space and colour. **Eduardo Ramírez Villamizar** (1922-2004) also began painting in a figurative mode but moved into abstraction in the 1950s and subsequently into sculpture, to create, alongside his contemporary **Edgar Negret** (1920-2012), some of the most interesting Constructivist work in Latin America. Both work in metal and have produced large, often brightly painted pieces for public spaces. Another important artist of this generation was Barcelona-born **Alejandro Obregón** (1920-1992), who avoided pure abstraction, preferring instead to include colourful figurative references with nationalistic overtones: carnations, guitars, condors. The slightly younger and internationally famous **Fernando Botero** (born 1932) has also tended to favour national themes. Working both as a painter and a sculptor he takes figures from Colombian society – dictators, drug barons, smug priests, autocratic matrons, prostitutes, spoilt children – and inflates them to ludicrous proportions. His gigantic bronze figures and the angular, two-dimensional sheets of metal of Negret and Ramírez Villamizar represent the two poles of 20th-century artistic expression.

For the subsequent generation of artists Colombia's turbulent political history remains a recurrent preoccupation. **Luis Caballero** (1943-1995) was a masterful draughtsman who expressed his sympathy for the victims of officially sanctioned violence by the tender attention he devotes to their tortured, naked bodies. **Beatriz González** (born 1938) uses a pop idiom to present military and political leaders as big and bold but essentially empty. **Juan Camillo Uribe** (1945-2005) manipulates the paraphernalia of popular religion – prayer cards, plastic angels, metallic trinkets – to construct wittily disturbing collages. Younger artists are exploring the tensions between the national and international demands of art, and are experimenting with a tremendous diversity of styles and media. There is certainly no shortage of talent. Many cities in Colombia now boast a lively art scene with regular public exhibitions of contemporary art and a good range of commercial galleries.

Rodrigo Arenas Betancur (1919-1995) followed in Rozo's footsteps (see above) to become Colombia's best known sculptor of nationalistic public monuments. His gigantic and often rather melodramatic bronzes can be found in towns and cities throughout the country, as, for example his heroically naked *Bolívar* in Pereira, *Monumento a la Vida* in the Centro Suramericano in Medellín and the complex *Lanceros del Pantano de Vargas* near Paipa which must have been quite a challenge to the foundrymen. His sculptures are eminently worth seeking out.

Literature

The indigenous Colombian written language was discovered to be at its earliest stages at the time of the Spanish conquest in the 16th century. Consequently there are practically no records of pre-conquest literature. The poetic tradition was oral; one of the few transcribed examples of spoken poetry is 'El Yurupay', an oral epic gathered from *indígena* in the Vaupés region in the 16th century, though not published until 1890.

The literature produced during the colonial period (1500-1816) was mainly by an ecclesiastical elite, written for the benefit of an upper-class minority. The predominant themes were the conquest itself, Catholicism and observations of the New World. The two major writers of this period had themselves been renowned conquistadors. **Gonzalo Jiménez de Quesada** (1495-1579), the founder of Bogotá in 1538, wrote *Antijovio* in 1567. The main purpose of this book was to defend Spain's reputation against accusations made by the Italian Paolo Giovio in his *Historiarum sui temporis libri XLV* (1552). Quesada sought to put the record straight on matters concerning the behaviour of his nation during the conquest of the New World.

Juan de Castellanos (c 1522-1607) wrote a lengthy chronicle of the conquest called *Elegías de varones ilustres de Indias* (*Elegy of Illustrious Men of the Indies*, 1589). It was written in the Italian verse style popular at the time, and has been called one of the longest poems ever written, 113,609 verses. The most important piece of narrative prose written during this period was *El carnero* (*The Butcher*, 1638) by **Juan Rodríguez Freyle** (1566-1640). This is a picaresque account of a year in the life of Santa Fe de Bogotá, using a blend of historical fact and scandalous invention to create a deliciously amoral book for its time. Mystic writing was also popular during the middle years of the conquest. **Sor Francisca Josefa de Castillo y Guevara** (1671-1742) was a nun who wrote baroque poetry, but was best known for her intimate spiritual diary *Afectos espirituales* (date unknown). Another Baroque poet of renown was **Hernando Domínguez Camargo** (1606-1659), who chronicled the life of Saint Ignatius in his epic *Poema heróica de San Ignacio de Loyola* (*Heroic Poem of St Ignatius of Loyola*, 1666).

The first major Colombian writer after the declaration of Independence in 1824 was **Juan José Nieto** (1805-1866). His *Ingermina, o la hija de Calamar* (*Ingermina, or the Child of Calamar*, 1844) is a historical novel about the conquest of the Calamar Indians in the 16th century. The mid-19th century saw the publication in Bogotá of *El Mosaico*, a review centred around a literary group of the same name, founded by **José María Vergara y Vergara** (1831-1872). The prevailing style in the capital was *costumbrismo*, the depiction of local life and customs in realistic detail. Major *costumbrista* novels were *Manuela* (1858) by **Eugenio Díaz** (1803-1865) and *María* (1867), by **Jorge Isaacs** (1837-1895). Romantic poetry also defined the early years of Independence, reflecting the strong influence Europe still had over Colombia. One of the exceptions was a poet from Mompós, **Candelario Obeso** (1849-1884), the first Colombian poet to use Afro-American colloquialisms in poetry. His *Cantos populares de mi tierrra* (*Popular Songs of my Land*, 1877) marked a progressive shift from the Romantic style, into a poetic language which reflected the true variety of Colombia's indigenous population.

An important region in the development of Colombian literature was Antioquia, the main city of which is Medellín. This region spawned the first crop of writers who were not of the upper-class elite which had dominated Colombian letters until the late 19th century. **Tomás Carrasquilla** (1858-1940) produced three major novels which reflected his humble middle-class background, and used a casual, spoken style to portray local customs and speech, and above all a love of the land. Another Antioquian of renown was **Samuel Velásquez** (1865-1941), whose novel *Madre* (*Mother*, 1897) gives a strong sense of the simple life of the countryside coupled with the religious passion of its inhabitants.

The beginning of the avant-garde in Colombia is marked by the publication of *Tergiversaciones* (*Distortions*) in 1925 by **León de Greiff** (1895-1976), in which he experimented with new techniques to create a completely original poetic idiom. Another important Modernist poet was **Porfirio Barba-Jacob** (the pseudonym of Miguel Angel Osorio, 1883-l942), who was influenced by the French Parnassian poets and published melancholic verse, typified by *Rosas negras* (*Black Roses*, 1935).

Other novelists of the same era were pursuing a much more social realist style than their avant-garde counterparts. *La vorágine* (*The Vortex*, 1924) by **José Eustasio Rivera** (1888-1928) deals with the narrator's own struggle for literary expression against a backdrop of the Amazonian rubber workers' struggle for survival. **César Uribe Piedrahita** (1897-1951) also chronicled the plight of rubber workers, and in *Mancha de aceite* (*Oil Stain*, 1935) he looks at the effects of the oil industry on the land and people of his country. The problems facing indigenous people began to get more attention from socially aware writers and **Bernardo Arías Trujillo** (1903-1939) examined the lives of Afro-Americans in Colombia in *Risaralda*.

The late 1940s to the mid-1960s in Colombian society were dominated by La Violencia (see History, page 286). Literary output during this intensely violent period reflected the political concerns which had led to the violence; among the novels to stand out from the many personal tales of anger and disbelief was *El jardín de las Hartmann* (*The Garden of the Hartmanns*, 1978) by **Jorge Eliécer Pardo** (born 1945), which charts the history of La Violencia in Tolima, one of the most severely affected regions. What makes this book readable is the lack of historical facts and figures, typical of books set during La Violencia, and a more generalized view of the troubles.

Two important poetry movements to come out of La Violencia were the 'Mito' group and the 'Nadaistas'. *Mito* was a poetry magazine founded in 1955 by **Jorge Gaitán Durán** (1924-1962). It included **Eduardo Cote Lemus** (1928-1964), **Carlos Obregón** (1929-1965) and **Dora Castellanos** (born 1924). Their influences were contemporary French writers such as Genet and Sartre, and the Argentinean José Luis Borges. *Mito* came out during the dictatorship of Rojas Pinilla, and was one of the few outlets for free literary expression in the country. The Nadaista group was concerned with changing the elitist role of literature in the face of the violent conflict which affected everyone, and they felt should be addressed directly; they used avant-garde styles and techniques to achieve this.

By far the biggest influence on Colombian fiction was the publication, in 1967, of *Cien años de soledad* (*A Hundred Years of Solitude*) by **Gabriel García Márquez** (1927-2014). He had published many short stories and novels in the 1950s and early 1960s. Among the most significant were *La hojarasca* (*Leaf Storm* in 1955) and *El coronel no tiene quien le escriba* (*No one Writes to the Colonel*, 1958), a portrayal of a colonel and his wife struggling to cope with the tropical heat, political oppression and economic deprivation in their final years. But it was with *Cien años de soledad* that he became recognized as the major exponent of a new style generic to Latin American writers. Events were chronicled in a deadpan style; historical facts were blended with pure fantasy, the latter written matter-of-factly as if it were the truth; characters were vividly portrayed through their actions and brief dialogues rather than internal monologues. The style came to be known as Magical Realism in English, a translation of the Spanish 'Lo real maravilloso'. In 1975 García Márquez published *El otoño del patriarca* (*The Autumn of the Patriarch*), which was a return to a favourite theme of his, the loneliness that power can bring. *Crónica de una muerte anunciada* (*Chronicle of a Death Foretold*, 1981) was set in an unnamed coastal city, but no doubt not far from the author's birthplace of Aracataca. It captures the docility and traditional stubbornness of the people of Colombia's Caribbean seaboard, an area in which García Márquez had worked as a journalist in the 1950s. *El amor en los tiempos de cólera* (*Love in the Time of Cholera*, 1985) is set at the turn of the century, and depicts the affair between a couple of septuagenarians against the backdrop of another fictional city; García Márquez skillfully blends Cartagena, Barranquilla and Santa Marta into one coastal town. He published 23 works in total, as well as articles, essays and an autobiography. See also page 165.

Other important writers in the 1970s and 1980s include **Fanny Buitrago** (born 1945) and **Manuel Zapata Olivella** (1920-2004). In novels such as *Los Pañamanes* (1979) and *Los amores de Afrodita* (*The Loves of Aphrodite*, 1983), Buitrago contrasts the legends and culture of the Caribbean coast with the needs of young people to move

BACKGROUND

Recommended reading

Fiction

María (1867), Jorge Isaac's 19th-century romance of young lovers María and Efraín, perhaps the first work of Colombian fiction to achieve world-wide acclaim.

Risaralda (1935), by Bernardo Arias Trujillo, one of the first socially aware accounts of Afro-Caribbean life in Colombia.

El jardín de las Hartmann (*The Garden of the Hartmanns*, 1945), by Jorge Eliecer Pardo; one of Pardo's series of novels charting the Violencia era, seen through the eyes of a family from Tolima, one of the worst-hit regions.

Cien años de soledad (*100 Years of Solitude*, 1967) by Gabriel García Márquez; classic saga of the Buendía family, with pioneering infusion of magic realism. García Márquez's all-time literary masterpiece.

Los amores de Afrodita (*The Loves of Aphrodite*, 1983), by Fanny Buitrago; a novel ultimately about love and power, based in the Caribbean, where a new generation is torn between their traditional culture and that of modern US consumerist society.

El fusilamiento del Diablo (*Shooting the Devil*, 1986) by Manuel Zapata Olivella, a monumental novel covering the six centuries of African and Afro-American history.

Delirio (*Delirium*, 2011) by Laura Restrepo; a husband tries to deal with his wife's descent into insanity, reflecting the collective madness of Colombian society in the 1990s.

El ruido de las cosas al caer (*The Sound of Things Falling*, 2013), by Juan Gabriel Vásquez, a dark thriller set in 1980s Bogotá, in the grip of Pablo Escobar's drug empire.

La oculta (*The Occult*, 2014), by Héctor Abad Faciolince, a typically inventive novel by the bestselling author of *Oblivion*, following the interwoven lives of the Angel family.

Los Ejércitos (*The Armies*, 2014), by Evelio Roselio; with a respectful nod towards García Márquez's magic realism, this novel creates a fantastical nightmare vision of disappearing villagers.

on, at the risk of being swallowed up by modern North American culture. Zapata Olivella has published a monumental novel, *El fusilamiento del diablo* (*The Shooting of the Devil*, 1986), covering the six centuries of African and Afro-American history.

Colombian post-modern literature has followed European theoretical trends, with many of Colombia's more avant-garde writers living and working in Europe. While retaining the Magical Realist tradition of dispensing with a subjective, authoritative narrator, the post-modernists have greatly distanced themselves from the Colombian tradition of orally based, colloquial storytelling. Despite these developments it is García Márquez who continues to dominate the public imagination. By borrowing from Colombian traditions with a modernist approach, he created a style that made him an internationally renowned literary figure and a national icon in both life and death.

Non-fiction

Biblioburro (2011), by Jeanette Winter, based on the true story of a Colombian teacher who carried library books to remote rural neighbourhoods riding on his donkey, a beautifully illustrated story for children of all ages, or those just young at heart.

The Colombia Reader (2017, Duke University Press), Editors Ann Farnsworth-Alvear, Marco Palacios and Ana María Gómez López; essays and stories about modern Colombian history, culture and politics; a weighty tome – in both senses of the word.

The Fruit Palace (1998), by Charles Nicholls, a highly entertaining travelogue, charting the author's travels around Colombia, in search of the 'great cocaine story'.

Killing Pablo (2002), by Mark Bowden, a gripping, pacy account of the hunt for Pablo Escobar, the world's most wanted criminal in the 1980s.

Law of the Jungle (2011), by John Otis, a dramatized re-telling of the true story of the kidnapping of three US servicemen by FARC guerrillas.

My Colombian War (2013), by Silvana Paternostro, a family biography set in Barranquilla, combined with insights into modern Colombian society, gripped between guerrilla warfare and drug cartel violence.

The Robber of Memories (2013), by Michael Jacobs, following the author's journey up the Magdalena river, intertwining the political complexities of modern Colombia with his family struggles, as his mother falls ills with Alzheimer's disease.

The Search for El Dorado (2001), by John Hemming, an authoritative history of the conquistadors' obsessive hunt for the legendary golden king.

Short walks in Bogotá (2012), by Tom Feiling, a journalist's travels in the countryside surrounding the Colombian capital, meeting key locals and revealing insights into life during the troubled guerrilla war years.

Was Gabo an Irishman? (2013), edited and contributed to by Richard McColl; a collection of tales from Gabriel García Márquez's Colombia.

Music and dance

No South American country has a greater variety of music than Colombia, strategically placed where the Andes meet the Caribbean. The four major musical areas are: the mountain heartland; the Pacific coast; the Caribbean coast; and the Llanos or eastern plains.

Mountain heartland

The heartland covers the Andean highlands and intervening valleys of the Cauca and Magdalena rivers and includes the country's three largest cities, Bogotá, Medellín and Cali. The music here is relatively gentle and sentimental, accompanied largely by string instruments, with an occasional flute and a *chucho* or *carángano* shaker to create the rhythm. The preferred instrument of the highlands and by extension

Colombia's national instrument, is the *tiple*, a small 12-stringed guitar, most of which are manufactured at Chiquinquirá in Boyacá. The national dance is the **bambuco**, whose lilting sounds are said to have inspired Colombian troops at the Battle of Ayacucho in 1824. This dance can be found throughout the country's heartland and has long transcended its folk origins. The choreography is complex, including many movements, such as Los Ochos, La Invitación, Los Codos, Los Coqueteos, La Perseguida and La Arrodilla. Other related dances are the **torbellino**, where the woman whirls like a top, the more stately Guabina, the Pasillo, Bunde, Sanjuanero and the picaresque **rajaleña**. Particularly celebrated melodies are the *Guabina Chiquinquireña* and the *Bunde Tolimense*. The following fiestas, among others, provide a good opportunity to experience the music and dancing: **La Fiesta del Campesino**, ubiquitous on the first Sunday in June, the **Fiesta del Bambuco** in Neiva and **Festival Folclórico Colombiano** in Ibagué later in the month, the **Fiesta Nacional de la Guabina y el Tiple**, held in Vélez in early August, the **Desfile de Silleteros** in Medellín in the same month and **Las Fiestas de Pubenza** in Popayán just after the New Year, where the Conjuntos de Chirimía process through the streets.

Pacific coast

On Colombia's tropical Pacific coast (and extending down into Esmeraldas in Ecuador) is to be found some of the most African sounding black music in all South America. The **currulao** and its variants, the **berejú** and **patacoré**, are extremely energetic recreational dances and the vocals are typically African-style call-and-response. This is the home of the *marimba* and the music is very percussion driven, including the upright *cununo* drum plus *bombos* and *redoblantes*. Wakes are important in this region and at these the **bundes**, **arrullos** and **alabaos** are sung. Best known is the 'Bunde de San Antonio'. The **jota chocoana** is a fine example of a Spanish dance taken by black people and turned into a satirical weapon against their masters. The regional fiestas are the **Festival Folclórico del Litoral** at Buenaventura in July and **San Francisco de Asís** at Quibdó in September.

Caribbean coast

The music of Colombia's Caribbean lowlands became popular for dancing throughout Latin America more than 30 years ago under the name of **Música Tropical** and has much more recently become an integral part of the salsa repertoire. It can be very roughly divided into cumbia and *vallenato*. The **cumbia** is a heavily black influenced dance form for several couples, the men forming an outer circle and the women an inner. The men hold aloft a bottle of rum and the women a bundle of slim candles called *espermas*. The dance probably originated in what is now Panama, moved east into Cartagena, where it is now centred and quite recently further east to Barranquilla and Santa Marta. The most celebrated cumbias are those of Ciénaga, Mompós, Sampués, San Jacinto and Sincelejo. The instrumental accompaniment consists of *gaitas* or *flautas de caña de millo*, backed by drums. The *gaitas* ('male' and 'female') are vertical cactus flutes with beeswax heads, while the *cañas de millo* are smaller transverse flutes. The most famous conjuntos are the Gaiteros de San Jacinto, the Cumbia Soledeña and the Indios Selectos. Variants of the cumbia are the **porro**, gaita, puya, **bullerengue** and **mapalé**, these last two being much faster and more energetic. Lately cumbia has also become very much part of the *vallenato* repertoire and is therefore often played on the accordion. Cumbia has been superseded by *vallenato* in Colombia and today is probably heard more outside the country than in it, with Colombian migrants taking it with them to cities like Buenos Aires, Mexico City, Los Angeles – even London. While it has travelled, it has picked up influences to create new sub-genres such as **techno-cumbia** and **cumbia villera**, both popular in Peru and Argentina. **Vallenato** music comes from Valledupar in the department of César and is of relatively recent origin. It is built around one instrument, the accordion, albeit backed by *guacharaca* rasps and *caja* drums. The most popular rhythms are the paseo and the merengue, the latter having arrived from the Dominican Republic, where it is the national dance. Perhaps the first virtuoso accordionist was the legendary 'Francisco El Hombre', playing around the turn of the century. Today's best known *vallenato* names are those of Rafael Escalona (1927-2009), Alejandro Durán (1919-1989), Los Gigantes del Vallento and Calixto Ochoa. In April the **Festival de la Leyenda Vallenata** is held in Valledupar and attended by thousands.

Barranquilla is the scene of South America's second most celebrated **carnival**, after that of Rio de Janeiro, with innumerable traditional masked groups, such as the *congos*, *toros*, *diablos* and *caimanes*. The **garabato** is a dance in which death is defeated. Barranquilla's carnival is less commercialized and more traditional than that of Rio and should be a 'must' for anyone with the opportunity to attend. Other important festivals in the region are the **Corralejas de Sincelejo** with its bullfights in January, **La Candelaria** (Candlemas) in Cartagena on 2 February, the **Festival de la Cumbia** in El Banco in June, **Fiesta del Caimán Cienaguero** in Ciénaga in January and **Festival del Porro** in San Pelayo (Córdoba). To complete the music of the Caribbean region, the Colombian islands of San Andrés and Providencia, off the coast of Nicaragua, have a fascinating mix of mainland Colombian and Jamaican island music, with the calypso naturally a prominent feature. More recently two other genres have gained increasing popularity. **Champeta** originates in Cartagena and has roots in soukous, compas and reggae. It is characterized by very provocative dancing. **Reggaeton** has become a phenomenon throughout Latin America. Believed to have originated in Puerto Rico, it blends a merengue beat with rapping and influences from ragga and Spanish-style reggae from Panama.

Llanos

The fourth musical region is that of the great eastern plains, the so-called Llanos Orientales between the Ríos Arauca and Guaviare, a region where there is really no musical frontier between the two republics of Colombia and Venezuela. Here the **Joropo** reigns supreme as a dance, with its close relatives the **galerón**, the slower and more romantic **pasaje** and the breathlessly fast **corrido** and **zumba que zumba**. These are dances for couples, with a lot of heel tapping, the arms hanging down loosely to the sides. Arnulfo Briceño (1938-1989) and Pentagrama Llanera are the big names and the harp is the only instrument that matters, although normally backed by *cuatro*, guitar, *tiple* and *maracas*. Where to see and hear it all is at the **Torneo Internacional del Joropo** at Villavicencio in December.

Land &
environment

Geology and landscape

Colombia is the fourth largest in size of the 10 principal countries of South America, slightly smaller than Peru and slightly larger than Bolivia at 1,142,000 sq km. In terms of Europe, that is the size of France and Spain combined. The latest estimate of population is 49.5 million (2017), marginally more than Argentina and second only to Brazil in the continent. The people are concentrated in the western third of the country: nevertheless, the population density of 39.3 per sq km is only greater in Ecuador within South America. To the east, it is bounded by Venezuela and Brazil, to the south, by Peru and Ecuador and in the northwest by Panama. It is the only South American country with a coastline on the Pacific (1306 km) and the Caribbean (1600 km), with two small offshore islands in the Pacific. In the Caribbean, there are various coastal islands including the Rosario and San Bernardo groups and the more substantial San Andrés/Providencia archipelago off the coast of Nicaragua, plus several cays towards Jamaica.

Its greatest width east–west is 1200 km and it stretches 1800 km north–south, from 12°N to 4°S of the equator, with virtually all of one of its departments, Amazonas, south of the equator. The borders of Colombia have been stable since 1903 when Panama seceded, though Nicaragua occasionally revives a claim for the San Andrés group of islands and there are three minute uninhabited reefs claimed by Colombia and by the USA: Quita Sueño Bank, Roncador Cay and Serrana Bank.

Structure

As with other countries on the west side of the continent, Colombia is on the line of collision between the west moving South American Plate, and the Nasca Plate, moving east and sinking beneath it thus creating the Andes. Almost 55% of the country to the east is alluvial plains on top of ancient rocks of the Guiana Shield dating from the Pre-Cambrian era over 500 million years ago. This was at one time part of the landmass called 'Pangea' which geologists believe broke up between 150 and 125 million years ago and the Americas floated away from what became Africa and Europe. It is presumed that prior to this, what is now the Caribbean Sea was an extension of the Mediterranean Sea and in the course of time this expanded to separate the two halves of the Americas. During the Cretaceous period, around 100 million years ago, the Atlantic was undoubtedly connected to the Pacific Ocean, at least from time to time, but by the end of the Cretaceous, the Tertiary mountain building had begun and the emergence of Central America and eventually the Isthmus of Panama, sealed off the connection.

All the rest of Colombia to the west, apart from the islands, is the product of the Andean mountain building activity, which continues today. This began earlier in the Jurassic and Cretaceous eras with intense volcanic activity, but the maximum was in the late Tertiary (around 25 million years ago). Large areas of molten material were formed beneath the surface and were pushed up to form the large high plateaux with peaks formed from later volcanic activity. Some areas were folded and contorted and the original rocks metamorphosed to lose their former identity. In general, it is the mountain ranges to the west that were most affected in this way. Continuous weathering, especially during the ice ages of which the most recent was in the Pleistocene up to 10,000 years ago, has been responsible for deep deposits in the valleys and the plains of north Colombia and in the inland slopes of the Andes towards the Orinoco and Amazon.

Other than the coral islands just off the north coast, the Colombian islands of the Caribbean are all on a submarine ridge, which extends from Honduras and Nicaragua to Haiti, known as the Jamaica Ridge, which separates the Cayman Trench from the Colombia Basin, two of the deepest areas of the Caribbean Sea. Providencia is probably volcanic in origin but San Andrés has a less certain past, perhaps being an undersea mount which has been colonized by coral for millions of years, evidenced by the white sands and the limestone features. Little is known about the other reefs, banks and cays that belong to Colombia. The two Colombian island groups in the Pacific are quite different. Isla Gorgona is one of the few islands off the South American Pacific coast which is on the continental shelf and no more than 30 km from the mainland. There is evidence of past volcanic activity on the island and it may represent a point on an otherwise submerged ridge parallel to the coast. By contrast, the Isla de Malpelo is on one of the structural lines of the east Pacific which runs due south from west Panama along the line of longitude 81°W which peters out off the coast of Ecuador. There is a deep trench between this line and the coast with depths down to 5000 m and clear signs of tectonic activity along the ridge including Malpelo which is the top of a volcanic structure. Further to the west there is another ridge running south from Central America, the Cocos Ridge, which leads to the Galápagos Islands.

Andes

To the south of Colombia, the Andes of Ecuador are a single high range with volcanic peaks up to nearly 5000 m, but north of the border they quickly split into three distinct cordilleras named Occidental, Central and Oriental. The first two are close together for 400 km but separated by a fault line occupied by the Río Patía in the south and the Cauca in the north. The Cordillera Oriental gradually pulls eastwards creating a valley basin for Colombia's most important river, the Magdalena. This range crosses the northeast border into Venezuela and continues as the Cordillera de Mérida. A subsidiary range, called the Sierra de Perijá, continues north within Colombia to reach the Caribbean at Punta Gallinas on the Península de Guajira, the northernmost point of the South American mainland. Near this point is the Santa Marta massif, one of the biggest volcanic structures in the world with the highest mountain peak in Colombia at 5775 m.

All three of the cordilleras have peaks, mostly volcanic, over 4000 m, the Central and Oriental over 5000 m, with permanent snow on the highest. Many are active and have caused great destruction in the past, both with gas and ash explosions and by creating ice and mud slides. The whole of the western half of the country is subject to earthquakes, demonstrating the unstable nature of the underlying geology, and the significant situation of the country at the point where the Andes make a dramatic turn to the east. Also, in the northwest, another range to the west of the Cordillera Occidental appears, the Serranía de Baudó, which becomes the spine of the Darién isthmus of Panama, eventually continuing westwards. Thus north Colombia is at the tectonic crossroads of the Americas.

Valleys

A glance at the map of Colombia will show the physical dominance of the cordilleras and the human dependence on the valleys between them. The fact that they run more or less north–south was a great advantage to the earlier explorers interested in finding gold and silver and the later settlers looking for good arable land. Even the earliest inhabitants were interested in the protection that the rugged land offered them but also in ways to migrate further south. As a consequence, the eastern half of the country has, until very recently, been ignored and still remains largely unexplored.

The valleys are structural basins between the cordilleras and not simply products of river erosion. In some places they are many kilometres broad, as for example between Cali and Popayán, yet the Patía and Cauca rivers flow in opposite directions. Elsewhere, the rivers go through narrow passages, eg near Honda on the Magdalena where rapids interrupt river navigation. However, the basins have been filled many metres thick with volcanic ash and dust which has produced very fertile terrain. This, together with the height above sea level has made for an agreeable environment and one of the most productive zones of the tropics worldwide.

By contrast, the cordilleras create formidable obstacles to lateral movements. The main routes from Bogotá to Cali and Manizales must cross the Cordillera Central by passes at 3250 m and 3700 m respectively, and virtually all the passes over the Cordillera Oriental exceed 3000 m. Many of the volcanic peaks in these ranges are over 5000 m and are capped with snow, hence the name *nevados*. Such is the nature of the terrain that no railway was ever built to cross the cordilleras, except from Cali to Buenaventura.

The rivers themselves do not provide the most attractive human corridors as can be seen by the frequent diversions from the rivers by the main trunk roads. Fortunately, the surrounding countryside is frequently dominated by plateaux. These make good level sites for towns and cities (Bogotá itself is the best example). They also give long stretches of easy surface travel but are interrupted by spectacular descents and climbs where there are natural rifts or subsidiary river gorges. This makes for dramatic, but time-consuming scenic trips by road throughout this area of Colombia.

Caribbean lowlands

From the Sierra de Perijá and the Sierra Nevada de Santa Marta westwards are the great plains of the Lower Magdalena, which collects most of the water flowing north in Colombia to the Caribbean. The Cordilleras Central and Occidental finish at about 4°N, 350 km from the mouth of the river at Barranquilla. About 200 km from the sea, both the Magdalena and the Cauca flow into an area of swamps and lagoons which becomes a vast lake when water levels are high. This lowland is the result of the huge quantities of alluvium that has been brought down over the years from the mountains in the south of Colombia. While not comparable in length with the major rivers of the world, the average discharge at the mouth of the Magdalena is 7500 cu m per second similar to that of the Danube or about one third of that of the Orinoco. To the north, the land slopes gently to the sandy beaches of the Caribbean and a string of inshore islands of considerable touristic appeal.

Beyond Barranquilla to the east, a sandbar encloses a salt lake that was formerly part of the Magdalena delta, now abandoned by the river which flows to the sea further west. On the far side of the lake, the Santa Marta massif comes down to the sea creating a interesting stretch of rocky bays and headlands. Further east again, the flatter land returns extending finally to the low hills of the Guajira peninsula at the northernmost tip of the continent. This is a sandy, arid region, and the modest northern end of the Cordillera Oriental.

At the west end of this section is the Gulf of Urabá and the border with Panama. The Río Atrato, which drains most of the area between the Cordillera Oriental and the Serranía de Baudó, reaches the sea here via another large swampy area where no land transport is possible. It is probable that this was formerly linked to the Gulf of Urabá which is itself now being filled up with material brought down by the Atrato and many other small streams. This was also probably an area where, in a much more distant past, the Atlantic was joined to the Pacific, a point not lost on the Colombians who periodically quote this as the site of a future rival to the Panama Canal. There is little seismic activity in this region though there are occasional earthquakes and the mud lakes near Arboletes, Galerazamba and elsewhere near the coast are volcanic in origin.

Pacific coast

The Serranía de Baudó runs from Panama south to 4°N just north of Buenaventura. The basin between it and the Cordillera Occidental is drained by the Río Atrato to the north and the San Juan to the south with another river, the Baudó assisting the centre. This is an area of very high rainfall and access by any means is difficult. This coastline is very different from the north coast. Most of it is heavily forested but with very attractive small beaches interspersed with rocky stretches and affected with a wide tidal range, absent from the Caribbean. It has only recently been 'discovered' by the tourist industry and remains quiet owing to the difficulties and cost of getting there.

South of Buenaventura, there is another 300 km of coastline to Ecuador, but reasonable access is only possible at Buenaventura (see page 247), and **Tumaco** in the extreme south. Rainfall here is still copious with many short rivers coming down from the Cordillera Occidental and creating alluvial plains along the coast typically with mangrove swamps, which continue into Ecuador. This part of the Colombian coast is also remote and unspoilt with a few fishing communities though tourism is beginning to take hold at the end of the two access roads. Further inland there are a few mineral deposits and gold mines which have attracted interest. There is no range of Tertiary hills here between the Andes and the coastline as in Ecuador.

Eastern plains

This section, representing more than half of Colombia, is divided into two parts. In the north are the grasslands known as *los llanos*, which stretch from the Cordillera Oriental across into Venezuela and on to the mouth of the Orinoco. Around 40% of the *llanos*, which means 'plains', are in Colombia. They are noted in both countries for the quality of the land for cattle raising which has been going on since the 16th century and are second only to the *Pampas* in Argentina for ranching in South America. Several important rivers, eg the Meta, flow from the mountains through this region to the Orinoco and act as transport routes. Slowly roads are being made into the interior but all-weather surfaces are virtually non-existent and land transport in the wet season is impossible. All important towns and villages and many fincas have their own airstrips. In the extreme north of the area, near the border with Venezuela, oil was found some years ago and new finds are still being made.

The southern part of the section is tropical forest associated with the Amazon Basin. As far as the vegetation is concerned, the transition is, of course, gradual. However, the Río Guaviare is the southernmost tributary of the Orinoco and, with headwaters (here called the Guayabero) rising near Neiva in the Cordillera Oriental, has its source some 350 km further from the sea than those of the official source of the Orinoco in the Sierra Parima on the Brazil/Venezuela border. Two important rivers join to form the Guaviare near the town of San José, the Guayabero and the Ariari. Between them is an extraordinary geological anomaly, the Serranía de Macarena. It is a huge dissected block of crystalline rocks partly covered with stratified later formations, 140 km long and 30 km wide, that stands isolated 2000 m above the surrounding undulating forest and has been identified as a chunk of the Guiana Shield, the rest of which is hundreds of kilometres to the east, forming the border area between The Guianas, Venezuela and Brazil. Although there are some other low formations in this area of the country which are founded on the ancient basalt rocks, as a remnant of 'Pangea', Macarena displays by far the oldest exposed rocks of Colombia.

South of the Guaviare Basin, all the waters of the region flow into the Amazon system. However, in the extreme east of the country, the Río Guainía drains the south part of the department of the same name which connects with another geographical curiosity, discovered by the great explorer Alexander von Humboldt. Some 250 km before joining the Guaviare, the Orinoco divides, with part of its flow going southwest as the 'Brazo Casiquiare', which eventually joins the Guainía to form the Negro and thence the Amazon. Other Colombian rivers feed the Negro, in particular the Vaupés, the longest tributary. Colombia therefore has the distinction of providing the true sources of the Orinoco and the Negro.

In the southern area, the climate becomes progressively wetter. Thick jungle covers much of it, though Colombia is no exception to the gradual destruction of the environment. The rivers Caquetá and Putumayo are important water routes to the Amazon proper but there is virtually no tourist traffic.

In the extreme south of Colombia is Leticia, on the Amazon itself, a reminder of the original drawing of the maps which allowed all the western countries of South America except Chile to have access to the river and an exit to the South Atlantic.

Climate

Temperatures in Colombia are mainly affected by altitude and distance from the north and west coasts. The highest average temperatures in South America are in the Maracaibo lowlands of which Colombia has the southwest corner and the northwest extension into the Guajira Peninsula. Average annual temperatures in the Caribbean Lowlands are typically in excess of 25°C, modified downwards on the coast, yet, within sight of the coast are the permanent snows of Sierra Nevada de Santa Marta due to its altitude of over 5500 m. The temperature becomes oppressive where there is also high humidity.

Rainfall depends on the migrating northwest and southeast trade wind systems, the effect of the Andes acting as a weather barrier and also on local situations along the coasts. There is high rainfall in the southeast where the southeast trade winds bring moisture all year into the Amazon Basin that is continually recycled to produce heavy daily precipitation all along the east edge of the Andes. This however tails off northwards into the *llanos* especially November to March when the wind systems move south and the southeast Trades are replaced by the northeast system. This is less effective in bringing moisture to the area because of the protection of the Venezuelan Andes. The rainfall in the lower reaches of the Magdalena Basin is also high, aided by the large swampy area which keeps the air saturated. The highest rainfall in the country is in the northwest near the border with Panama, brought about by the convergence of the trade wind systems interacting with warm, saturated air coming in from the Pacific. Here it rains daily most of the year with some respite from January to March but with a total on average of 10,000 mm. This is one of the highest in the world. This heavy rain belt extends down the coast tailing off as Ecuador is approached. Unlike further south, the ocean here is warm and air over it readily condenses when it moves on to the land. However, this is a generalized pattern only.

Aberrations in the weather systems between November and March, when less rain normally falls, now labelled the *El Niño* phenomenon, also affect the western part of Colombia at least as far east as Bogotá. Large parts of the country, particularly the Caribbean coast and la Zona Cafetera, suffered from unusually heavy and prolonged rains in the autumn and winter of 2010, leading to extensive flooding, mud- and landslides. Further mud slides from heavy rains killed more than 270 people in Mocoa, southwest Colombia, in April 2017, leading to predictions of damaging El Niño storms later that year.

Inland local features often determine the level of precipitation. To the east of Nevado de Huila (5750 m), for example, there is a small area of near desert caused by the effect of rain shadow. Near desert conditions also can be found on the tip of the continent, between Riohacha and Punta Gallinas which is probably caused by descending air collecting rather than expelling moisture. Although there are occasional storms here (Colombia was marginally affected by the heavy rains that brought disaster to the Venezuelan coast in 1999), the normal Caribbean hurricane track fortunately passes well to the north of the Colombian coast.

Wildlife and vegetation

This neotropical zone is a land of superlatives. It contains the most extensive tropical rainforest in the world; the Amazon has by far the largest volume of any of the world's rivers and the Andes are the longest uninterrupted mountain chain. The fauna and flora are to a large extent determined by the influence of those mountains and the great rivers, particularly the Amazon and the Orinoco. There are also huge expanses of open terrain, tree-covered savannahs and arid regions. It is this immense range of habitats which makes Colombia one of the world's regions of high biodiversity.

This diversity arises not only from the wide range of habitats available, but also from the history of the continent. South America has essentially been an island for much of its geological past, joined only by a narrow isthmus to Central and North America at various times between 50 million and 25 million years ago. The present connection has been stable only for a few million years. Land passage played a significant role in the gradual colonization of South America by both flora and fauna from the north. When the land-link was broken these colonists evolved into a wide variety of forms free from the competitive pressures that prevailed elsewhere. When the land-bridge was re-established a new invasion of species took place from North America, adding to the diversity but also leading to numerous extinctions. Comparative stability has now ensued and guaranteed the survival of many primitive groups like the opossums.

There are three cordilleras of the Andes dominating the western part of Colombia. The rivers draining the area are referred to as white water (although more frequently brown because they contain a lot of sediment). This is in contrast to the rivers that drain the Guiana shield in neighbouring Venezuela, which are referred to as black or clear waters. The forests of the latter are of considerably lower productivity than those of the Andean countries.

Llanos

Northeast of the Andes and extending almost to the Caribbean coast, the lowland habitat characterized by open grasslands and small islands of trees is called the *llanos*. Poor drainage leads to the alternation between standing water and extreme desiccation, leading to large areas being devoid of trees except for some species of palm. Fire has also been responsible for maintaining this habitat type. Above 100 m this gives way to predominantly dry forest with seasonal rainfall and a pronounced drought. Gallery forest persists only in the regions surrounding rivers and streams. In contrast, arid conditions are also found in the vicinity of the northern Caribbean coast.

Pacific West

The wet forests of the Pacific slopes of the western Andes provide an interesting contrast with the Amazon region by virtue of their high degree of endemism – species unique to an area. The region is often referred to as the Chocó and extends from the Darién Gap in Panama to northern Ecuador. The natural vegetation is

ON THE ROAD

Floral Colombia

An overabundance of floral species has helped make Colombia the world's second largest exporter of flowers, with over US$1 billion in sales annually. You name it, Colombia has it, everything from garden-variety roses and carnations to more exotic species like the bird of paradise and the heliconia. However, this country's undisputed crown jewel is the orchid. Over 3000 species of orchid are known to exist in Colombia, including the national flower, the majestic *Flor de Mayo*. A passion for these flowers led botanist Tom Hart Dyke into the treacherous Darién Gap in 2000, a harrowing journey, including kidnap by guerrillas, that he recounts in his bestselling book, *The Cloud Garden*. For those who do not wish to risk life and limb to experience the best of Colombia's flora, check out the José Celestino Mutis Botanical Gardens in Bogotá or the Joaquín Antonio Uribe Botanical Gardens in Medellín. The latter is particularly spectacular and contains a newly built orquideorama that is not to be missed by orchid lovers. **Finca Romelia**, near Manizales in the Zona Cafetera (see page 225), also has one of the biggest private collections of orchids in Colombia, as well as impressive displays of cacti and bonsai plants. If you are lucky enough to be in Medellín during August, be sure to check out the flower festival that the city hosts every year.

tropical wet forest. Clouds that hang over the forest provide condensation, and this almost constant drenching by mist, fog and rain leads to a profusion of plants with intense competition for space, such that the trees and shrubs are all covered with a great variety of epiphytes – orchids, mosses, lichens and bromeliads. The area has been referred to by birders as the 'tanager coast', owing to the large mixed flocks of these colourful birds. There are many other species of endemic birds here apart from the tanagers. At La Planada, between Pasto and Tumaco, there is one of the highest concentrations of native birds in the continent and the forest reserve contains an immense diversity of orchids.

Overall, the fauna shows some interesting biogeographic patterns. Some species found here are those more common to Central and North America than to South America. The westernmost range defines a coastal strip with a fauna similar to Panama. Meanwhile, to the southeast, the fauna south of the river Guaviare is more typical of the upper Amazon Basin of Brazil and Peru.

High Andes

From about 3600 m to 4400 m, the high Andes are covered by *páramo* typified by the grass (*Stipa-ichu*) or *pajonal* which grows here. *Páramo* is a distinct type of high-altitude moorland vegetation comprised of tall grasses and *frailejones (Espeletia)* a member of the Compositae family, which are only found in the Colombian cordilleras and the Sierra Nevada de Mérida in Venezuela. These extraordinary plants that grow as high as 12 m, also frequently attract hummingbirds such as the black-tailed trainbearer and the great sapphirewing. Lakes and marshes are also a common feature since the ground is generally level. Interspersed among the grasses are clumps of club-moss and chuquiraguas. In the zone of the high *páramo* there are many lakes. Birds frequently seen in this area include the Andean teal, Andean coot and a variety of hummingbird species. **Andean condor** (*Vultur gryphus*) the largest land bird, weighing 12 kg and with a wingspan of 3 m, may be seen effortlessly gliding on the updraft from the warmer valleys below.

Some protection from the severe climate and the icy winds that can blast this harsh environment may be provided in the deeply incised gorges. Here there may be a lush growth of shrubs, orchids, reeds and dwarf trees providing a marked visual contrast to the superficially drier *páramo*. In the favourable sheltered micro-climatic conditions provided in the gaps between the tall clumps of grass, there nestle compact colonies of gentians, lupines and prostrate mosses. There is little evidence of mammal life here save for the occasional paw print of the Andean fox. **White-tailed deer**, once common has been over-hunted.

Under 3600 m, the condensation of the moisture-laden upwelling air from the warm humid jungles to the east creates cloudforest, with a similar wide variety of epiphytes as found near the west coast. Both giant and dwarf tree ferns are characteristic. These are highly resistant to fire, the traditional manner of maintaining grazing lands. Pollination is effected by a variety of agents. Fragrant odours and bright colours are used by some orchids to attract nectivorous birds, including some species of humming birds and insects. Others exude putrid smells to attract flies to carry out the same process. Tangled stands of bamboo intermingled with the *polylepis* forest are the dominant vegetation feature.

At high altitude *polylepis* forest clothes the deeply incised canyons and sides of the valleys. This is a tangled, lichen and fern be-decked world, dripping water from the moisture-laden air on to a mid-storey of tangled bamboo and lush tree ferns. A plentiful supply of bromeliads provide food for **spectacled bears**, now an endangered species. The steep slopes of the gullies are clothed in a dense blanket of giant cabbage-like *paraguillas* or umbrella plant. Tracks of mountain tapir are commonly found along river beaches, and the prints of the diminutive **pudu**, a small **Andean deer**, are also occasionally found. Mammals are rarely seen on the *páramo* during the day since most seek refuge in the fringing cloudforest, only venturing out on the open moors at night or under the protection of the swirling mists. But their presence is demonstrated by the tracks of **Andean fox** and marauding puma. Birds of the *páramo* include the mountain **caracara** and a variety of other raptors such as the **red-backed hawk**. Andean swifts, tapaculos, hummingbirds, finches and thrushes are common.

Masked **trogons** are also abundant in the *aliso* (birch) forests, evidence of recent colonization of areas devastated by the frequent landslides. Colourful tanagers and tiny hummingbirds are often encountered flitting between the myriad of flowers. At night the hills reverberate with the incessant croaks of frogs and toads.

Eastern slopes of the Andes

The cloudforests of South America are found in a narrow strip that runs along the spine of the Andes from Colombia, through Ecuador and into Peru. On the western side of the Central Cordillera between 2000 m and 3000 m are the remaining stands of the **wax palm** (*Ceroxylon alpinum*), the tallest variety of palm tree that grows dramatically above the surrounding forest and often appears above the cloud blanket. On the eastern side of the Cordillera Oriental the dense, often impenetrable, forests clothing the steep slopes protect the headwaters of the streams and rivers that cascade from the Andes to form the mighty Amazon as it begins its slow 8000 km journey to the sea. A verdant kingdom of dripping epiphytic mosses, lichens, ferns and orchids grow in profusion despite the plummeting overnight temperatures. The high humidity resulting from the 2 m of rain that can fall in a year is responsible for the maintenance of the forest and it accumulates and leaks from the ground in a constant trickle that combines to form myriad icy, crystal-clear tumbling streams that cascade over precipitous waterfalls. In secluded areas flame-red Andean **cock-of-the-rock** give their spectacular display to females in the early morning mists. **Woolly monkeys** are also occasionally sighted as they descend the wooded slopes. Mixed flocks of colourful tanagers are commonly encountered, and the golden-headed **quetzal** and **Amazon umbrella bird** are occasionally seen.

At about 1500 m there is a gradual transition to the vast lowland forests of the Amazon Basin; surprisingly less jungle-like but warmer and more equable than the cloudforests clothing the mountains above. The daily temperature varies little during the year with a high of 23-32°C falling slightly to 20-26°C overnight. This lowland region also receives some 2 m of rainfall per year, most of it falling from November to April. The rest of the year is sufficiently dry, at least in the lowland areas, to inhibit the growth of epiphytes and orchids which are so characteristic of the highland areas. For a week or two in the rainy season the rivers flood the forest. The zone immediately surrounding this seasonally flooded forest is referred to as *terra firme* forest.

Colombian Amazonas

The lowland Amazon region can be seen at its best as the river passes the Amacayacu National Park. Flood waters from the Peruvian catchment area inundate the forest for a short period starting in January in its upper reaches to create a unique habitat called *várzea*. *Várzea* is a highly productive seasonally inundated forest found along the banks of the whitewater rivers; it is very rich as a consequence of the huge amount of silt and nutrients washed out of the mountains and trapped by the massive buttress-rooted trees. One of the commonest trees of the *várzea*, the Pará rubber tree, is the source of latex. The Brazilian rubber industry foundered in the 19th century when seeds of this tree were illegally taken to Asia to form the basis of huge rubber plantations and flourished in the absence of pest species. In the still-flowing reaches of the *várzea*, permanently flooded areas are frequently found where vast carpets of floating water lilies, water lettuce and water hyacinth are home to the Amazonian manatee, a large herbivorous aquatic mammal which is the fresh-water relative of the dugong of the Caribbean. Vast numbers of spectacled caiman populate the lakes feeding on the highly productive fish community.

In the lowland forests, many of the trees are buttress rooted, with flanges extending 3-4 m up the trunk of the tree. Among the smaller trees stilt-like prop roots are also common. Frequently flowers are not well developed, and some emerge directly from the branches and even the trunk. This is possibly an adaptation for pollination by the profusion of bats, giving easier access than if they were obscured by leaves.

The vast river basin of the Amazon is home to an immense variety of species. The environment has largely dictated the lifestyle. Life in or around rivers, lakes, swamps and forest depend on the ability to swim and climb; amphibious and tree-dwelling animals are common. Once the entire Amazon Basin was a great inland sea and the river still contains mammals more typical of the coast, for example manatees and dolphins.

National parks & reserves

National parks

Colombia established its first protected area in 1960 (Cueva de los Guácharos) and now has 59 reserves comprising National Nature Parks (PNN), Flora and Fauna Sanctuaries (SFF), National Nature Reserves, a Vía Parque, a Fauna Sanctuary and a Unique Natural Area (ANU), spread throughout the country and in virtually every department. They vary in size from the tiny island of Corota in the Laguna de la Cocha near the border with Ecuador to large areas of forest in the eastern lowlands. All the significant mountain areas are National Parks including the Sierra Nevada de Santa Marta, El Cocuy, El Nevado de Huila, Los Nevados (Tolima and Ruiz) and Puracé. There are 15 on or near the Caribbean and Pacific coasts including the off-shore islands.

All except the smallest parks normally have one or more centres staffed with rangers (*guardaparques*) who offer information and guidance for visitors. Most, however, are remote with difficult access and few facilities. Unlike some Latin American countries, many national parks in Colombia are virtually free of 'tourism' and are thus of particular interest to those looking for unspoilt natural surroundings.

For various reasons, unlike many countries where the main problem for national parks is visitor overcrowding, many of the parks in Colombia are difficult to visit. Unfortunately, because of their remoteness, some have been sanctuary to guerrilla groups or drug traffickers, some are sensitive indigenous territories and many are of difficult access and have few or no facilities. Lovers of wilderness, however, will enjoy the richness of the natural attractions and the freedom from oppressive tourism.

Apart from the national parks, there are a considerable number of private nature reserves, some exclusively for research, others open to the general public. Many of these are worth visiting: details are given in the text.

Practicalities

Getting there

Air

International flights arrive principally at Bogotá and Cartagena, but there are also direct flights to Medellín, Cali, Pereira, Barranquilla and San Andrés; information on all these airports is given in the relevant chapters. Fares are significantly lower outside the peaks times of Easter, July, August and December to mid-January. You no longer need to reconfirm most flights, especially if booked online, but double check with your travel agent at the time of booking. On departure, allow at least two hours for checking in and going through the comprehensive security procedures.

From Europe
There are direct flights to Bogotá from London with **British Airways** (www.britishairways.com) and Avianca (www.avianca.com), from Paris with **Air France** (www.airfrance.com), from Frankfurt with **Lufthansa** (www.lufthansa.com), from Madrid with **Avianca** (www.avianca.com) and **Iberia** (www.iberia.com).

From North America
United (www.united.com) has direct flights from New York, Cleveland, Los Angeles and Houston. **Delta** (www.delta.com) has flights from New York, Atlanta and Cleveland. **Avianca** and **LATAM** (www.latam.com) fly direct from Miami to Bogotá. **Spirit Air** (www.spiritair.com) has flights from Fort Lauderdale to Cartagena, Medellín and Bogotá. **Air Canada** (www.aircanada.com) flies direct to Bogotá and San Andrés Island from Toronto.

From Australia and New Zealand
LATAM and **Avianca** have connections with Auckland and Sydney via Santiago in Chile.

From Latin America
Avianca has direct connections with Bogotá from Buenos Aires, Caracas, Lima, Mexico City, Panama City, Quito, Santiago and San José. **Copa** (www.copaair.com) has direct flights from Panama City. **Aerolíneas Argentinas** (www.aerolineas.com. ar) has 12 flights a week between Buenos Aires and Bogotá. **LATAM** has direct connections from Santiago.

River

Colombia shares borders with Brazil and Peru at Leticia on the Amazon. It is possible to cross into Colombia from these countries by ferry, but the journey can be time consuming: eight days from Manaus (Brazil); eight (by speedboat, US$80) to 36 hours (by cargo boat, US$40) from Iquitos (Peru).

Road

The main overland **Venezuela–Colombia** crossings are at San Antonio–Cúcuta (page 94) and Paraguachón–Maicao (page 172). There are plenty of buses from Maracaibo (Venezuela) to Maicao, Santa Marta and Cartagena. See warning page 172. The **Ecuador–Colombia** border is crossed at Rumichaca–Ipiales (page 273). **Cruz del Sur** and **Expreso Internacional** offer direct bus services from Quito to Bogotá, but it takes 36 hours. The 20-hour ride from Quito to Cali (from US$107) is a popular alternative. For details of this and other international services, see www.andestransit.com. See also Visas and immigration, page 337.

Driving

To bring a car into Colombia, you must have documents proving ownership of the vehicle, and a tourist card/transit visa. These are normally valid for 90 days and must be applied for at the Colombian consulate in the country that you are leaving to enter Colombia. A carnet de passages is recommended when entering with a European registered vehicle. When you cross an overland border into Colombia, make sure you keep any vehicle papers you are given as you will be asked to produce them when you leave.

Foot

If travelling independently on foot, there are many more places for entering Colombia, including from Panama via Sapzurro in the Darién (page 137). The border crossings from Ecuador at Puerto Asís, and from Venezuela across the Río Orinoco are not advised at the moment due to security concerns.

Sea

Colombia can be reached from Ecuador via Tumaco (page 311). There are various ways to reach Colombia from Panama by sea but only the Puerto Obaldía–Capurganá route is currently considered safe (pages 137-138).

Getting around

Air

Colombia has a well-established national airline network with several competing airlines. Internal flights are increasingly competitively priced and if you're short of time, flying may be your best option. **Avianca**, **Satena**, **Viva Colombia** and **Easyfly** are the main carriers; the latter two are low-cost airlines, with an expanding network of routes. There are also several regional airlines, such as **Aerolíneas de Antioquia (ADA)**, which serve smaller destinations.

Travel agents often have discount arrangements with certain airlines: **Vivir Volando** ① T1-601 4676, www.vivirvolando.co, in Bogotá, and **Destino Colombia** ① T574-268 6868, www.destinocolombia.com, in Medellín and Cartagena, are recommended. Otherwise, book online for advance purchase fares and last-minute deals. A useful search engine for sourcing cheap flights is www.despegar.com.

Domestic airlines

Avianca, El Dorado airport, Bogotá, T1-587 7700, ext 1875, www.avianca.com. The country's national airline, with offices in every major city in Colombia, **Avianca** flies to most destinations. The drawback is that all connections must go via Bogotá.

Copa Airlines, Cra 10, No 27-51, Local 165, Bogotá, T1-320 9090, www.copaair.com. Colombia's 2nd-largest airline is owned by Panamanian carrier **Copa**. Flies to most of the main destinations, with the same proviso that all flights route via Panama City.

Easyfly, T1-414 8111, www.easyfly.com.co. Budget airline with cheap flights to obscure destinations near popular tourist cities.

Satena, Av El Dorado 103-08, Entrada 1, interior 11, Bogotá, T1-423 8530/T01-800 091 2034, www.satena.com. Government-owned airline with flights to most destinations.

Viva Colombia, T1-743 3999 (Bogotá), vivacolombia.co. Newer budget airline serving most of the main cities, including Bogotá, Medellín, Cartagena and Santa Marta. It is cheap, but reliable and efficient, though there are no ticket offices.

Rail

Colombia used to have an extensive railway system but due to lack of funding most of the lines have fallen into disrepair or are used purely for cargo. The one exception is the tourist train that runs at weekends north from La Sabana station in downtown Bogotá, stopping at Usaquén and continuing to the salt cathedral at Zipaquirá and Cajicá. See www.turistren.com.co for more information and page 72.

Road

While there are few motorways, the main roads in Colombia are mostly in good condition and journeys are generally comfortable, although landslides frequently close roads after rains.

From Bogotá two roads run north towards the coast. To the northeast, a road (45A) heads high over the mountains of Boyacá and up to Bucaramanga before straightening up as it makes for the Sierra Nevada de Santa Marta. Another road forks northeast from here toward Cúcuta and the Venezuelan border. The second road (50) leaves Bogotá to the northwest and joins the Magdalena river valley at Honda. It follows the river until it reaches a fork at Puerto Triunfo. The eastern artery cuts back towards Bucaramanga. The western branch leads to Medellín.

Medellín is on the route of the Pan-American Highway (Panamericana). This single continuous road links most of the countries in the Americas, beginning in Canada and ending in Chile (interrupted only by the Darién Gap jungle between Panama and Colombia). In Colombia, after Darién, it begins again at Necoclí and runs due south, passing through Medellín, the Zona Cafetera, Cali, Popayán, Pasto and reaches Ecuador via Ipiales.

There are two further main roads exiting Bogotá. One (40) runs southeast over (and under) high mountain passes towards Villavicencio and the Llanos. The other (45) heads south towards Neiva. It eventually joins up with the Pan-American Highway at Pasto but not before tackling some treacherous terrain around Mocoa.

Bus and minibus

On the main routes, the bus network is comprehensive and buses are generally comfortable and efficient. Arriving at one of the large bus stations, the huge choice of carriers can be daunting, but it also has its advantages in that there are frequent services and competition between different companies can sometimes allow for a bit of haggling. The cost of tickets is relatively high by Latin American standards; fares shown in the text are middle of the range but should be treated as no more than a guide. Some of the best known operators include: **Berlinas del Fonce**, www.berlinasdelfonce.com; **Bolivariano**, www.bolivariano.com.co; **Copetran**, www.copetran.com.co; **Expreso Brasilia**, www.expresobrasilia.com, and **Expreso Palmira**, www.expresopalmira.com.co.

There is usually a variety of services on offer, with varying levels of price, quality and speed. The cheapest, *corrientes*, are essentially local buses, stopping frequently, uncomfortable and slow but offering plenty of local colour. *Pullman* or *servicio de*

Driving in Colombia

If there is one rule that is always adhered to on Colombian roads it is that 'might is right'. Colombians may have impeccable manners in personal exchanges, but when they step into a car, like Dr Jekyll, their character transforms. Overtaking around blind corners, ignoring traffic lights – anything goes. The worst culprits are truck drivers who seem to treat their job as a permanent rally. They are closely followed by bus drivers, with the rest not far behind. In cities, especially Bogotá, pedestrians have few rights, so mind how you go. Look both ways twice when crossing the road, sit tight on the bus or in a taxi, and cross your fingers. The upside may be that after a week of travelling around the country by bus, you will be cured of any fear of flying – air travel is never more attractive than after just a few days on Colombia's roads.

lujo (luxury) are long-distance buses, usually with air conditioning, toilets and DVDs (mostly rom-coms, but occasionally other films dubbed into Spanish). *Colectivos*, also known as *vans* or *busetas*, are usually 12- to 20-seat vehicles but also seven-seater cars, pick-up trucks or taxis; they are rather cramped but fast, saving several hours on long journeys. *Busetas* may also be known as *por puestos* (pay-by-the-seat) and will not leave until all the places have been filled. It is worth checking too that your fellow passengers are going the whole way as, if not, you may find yourself waiting again somewhere en route, for others to take their place. Some *colectivo* companies will offer a '*puerta-a-puerta*' (door-to-door) service.

Car

With a good road network, self-driving is driving is a viable alternative (bearing in mind the warnings above about Colombian motorists). It's an especially good way of exploring rural areas such as the Zona Cafetera where public transport will only take you between the main cities. However, driving in these rural areas is a test of nerve, as speeding cars and buses frequently pass one another on blind corners.

The kind of motoring you do will depend on your car of choice. While a normal car will reach most places of interest, a high-clearance vehicle is useful for badly surfaced or unsurfaced roads and for fording rivers. Four-wheel drive vehicles are recommended for flexibility in mountain and jungle territory. Wherever you travel you should expect to find roads that are badly maintained, damaged or closed during the wet season; expect delays because of floods and landslides from time to time. There is also the possibility of delays due to major roadworks so do not plan your schedule too tightly.

There are *peajes* (toll stations) every 60-100 km or so on major roads: tolls depend on distance and type of vehicle, but start around US$3. For excellent information (in Spanish only), including all the toll costs, see www.viajaporcolombia.com. Fuel prices are around US$3 per gallon for standard petrol, US$3.50 per gallon for super and US$2.75 per gallon for diesel. Prices are likely to fluctuate in the current economic climate.

Safety Before taking a long journey, ask locally about the state of the road and check if there are any safety issues. Roads are not always signposted. Avoid night journeys, as the roads may not be in good condition, lorry and bus drivers are notoriously reckless, and animals often stray onto the roads. Police and military checks can be frequent in troubled areas, so keep your documents handy. In the event of a vehicle accident in which someone is injured, all drivers involved are usually detained until blame has been established; this may take several weeks.

Spare no ingenuity in making your car impenetrable to deter the determined and skilled thief. Be sure to note down key numbers and carry spares of the most important ones (but don't keep all spares inside the vehicle). Avoid leaving your car unattended except in a locked garage or guarded parking space (*parqueadero*), especially at night; the better hotels all have safe parking. Only park in the street if there is someone on guard; adult minders will generally protect your car fiercely in exchange for a tip, US$1-2.

Documents Carry driving documents with you at all times. National or international driving licences may be used by foreigners in Colombia. For information on bringing a car into Colombia, see page 322. Bringing a car in by sea or air is much more complicated: you will usually be required to hire an agent to clear it through customs, which can be a slow and expensive process.

Insurance for the vehicle against accident, damage or theft is best arranged in the country of origin, but it is getting increasingly difficult to find agencies who offer this service.

Car hire Car hire is convenient for touring Colombia, though it is relatively expensive, especially if you are going to the more remote areas and need a 4WD or specialist vehicle. The main international car rental companies are represented at principal airports but may be closed on Saturday afternoons and Sundays. There are also local firms in most of the departmental capitals. In addition to passport and driver's licence, a credit card may be asked for as additional proof of identity (Visa, MasterCard, American Express) and to secure a returnable deposit to cover any liability not covered by the insurance. Check the insurance carefully; it may not cover you beyond a certain figure, nor for 'natural' damage such as flooding. Ask if extra cover is available. You should be given a diagram showing any scratches and other damage on the car before you hire it.

Maps

A decent map can be difficult to find in Colombia. There are few road maps, although the *Guía Rutas de Colombia* (www.rutascolombia.com in Spanish), available at all toll booths, is relatively decent. The **Instituto Geográfico Agustín Codazzi** (www.igac.gov.co) produces general and specialist maps of the country but is receiving increasingly less funding from the government and many of its maps may be out of date. Tourist offices should be able to provide town maps. Try also major bookstores such as **Pan-Americana** (Calle 12, No 34-30, Bogotá, www.panamericana.com.co).

Essentials A-Z

Accident and emergency

Contact the relevant emergency service and your embassy in Bogotá. Make sure you obtain police/medical reports in order to file insurance claims.

Emergency services

CAI Police: T156 (to report a crime and obtain the necessary paperwork); **Fire**: T123; **Police**: T123; **Red Cross ambulance**: T123; **Traffic accidents**: T127.

Children

Travelling with children can bring you into closer contact with Colombian families and presents no special problems. In fact your trip may be even smoother, since officials are sometimes more amenable where children are concerned and are particularly pleased if your child knows a little Spanish. Local comic strips are a good way for older children to get to grips with the language. For more detailed advice on travelling with children, see Footprint's *Travel with Kids*.

Facilities

Despite genuine good will towards younger visitors, Colombia's tourist industry does not generally offer dedicated family-friendly or children's facilities. Large, upscale chain hotels are likely to have babysitting or nanny services but you should not expect any independent hotels or haciendas to offer these. Baby-changing facilities can be found only in the larger airports. On the plus side, many museums and attractions offer discounts for children.

Bus travel

On long-distance buses you pay for each seat and there are no half-price fares. For shorter trips it is therefore cheaper, if less comfortable, to seat small children on your knee. Sometimes there are spare seats that children can occupy after tickets have been collected. Local buses are often crowded and uncomfortable. Remember that a lot of time can be spent waiting around in bus stations and airports; take your own reading material to while away the hours since children's books are difficult to find and expensive in Colombia. Reading on the bus itself, especially on winding mountain roads, is not recommended!

Food

It is better to take food with you on longer trips rather than to rely on meal stops, although there's an almost constant stream of hawkers touting snacks and drinks en route. Stick to simple things like bread and fruit while you are on the road. In restaurants, you may be able to buy a *media porción* (half portion), or divide a full-size helping between 2 children.

Health

Be extra vigilant to avoid sun burn and heat exhaustion.

Customs

Travellers can bring up to US$1500 worth of the goods into the country. Customs checks take place at airports and land frontiers for all arriving and departing travellers (see Visas and immigration, page 337). There are sometimes additional checks at the flight gate before departure. Do not carry drugs or firearms of any kind and take care that no-one tampers with your baggage. On departure, foreigners must pay an exit tax of around US$35 (some airlines, such as **Avianca**, include taxes in the cost of the ticket).

Disabled travellers

Provision for the disabled in Colombia is limited, but increasing. Wheelchairs and assistance are available at major airports; modern public buildings are provided with ramps and lifts, and some streets have pavement breaks that are usually adequate for wheelchairs. An increasing number of hotels and restaurants (in the upper price range) now have disabled access, rooms and toilets.

Some travel companies specialize in exciting holidays, tailor-made for individuals with a variety of disabilities. For general information, consult www.disabledtravelers.com.

Drugs

As is all too well known, Colombia is a major drug-producing and smuggling nation that produces most of the world's cocaine. Police and customs activities have greatly intensified in recent years, and criminals increasingly try to use innocent carriers to smuggle drugs out of the country. Pack all luggage yourself; do not leave any bags unattended, and under no circumstances carry packages for other people without checking the contents; indeed, taking any suspicious-looking packages or gift-wrapped presents through customs should be avoided, even if they are your own. Be very polite to customs staff and policemen, particularly if your hotel room is raided by police looking for drugs. Colombians who offer

you drugs may well be framing you for the police, who are very active on the north coast, on San Andrés island and at other tourist resorts. Any foreigner caught using any drug can expect to face prison, fines and/or deportation.

Electricity

110 volts AC, alternating at 60 cycles per second. A converter may be required if your device does not run on 110 volts. Most sockets accept both continental European (round) and North American (flat) 2-pin plugs.

Embassies and consulates

For a list of both Colombian embassies abroad, and foreign embassies/consulates in Colombia, see http://embassy.goabroad.com. Note that only the UK embassy in Bogotá has public attention duties.

Health

See your GP or travel clinic at least 6 weeks before departure for general advice on travel risks and vaccinations. Try phoning a specialist travel clinic if your own doctor is unfamiliar with health conditions in Colombia. Make sure you have sufficient medical travel insurance, get a dental check, know your own blood group and if you suffer a long-term condition, such as diabetes or epilepsy, obtain a Medic Alert bracelet/necklace (www.medicalert.org.uk). If you wear glasses, take a copy of your prescription.

Vaccinations

Confirm that your primary courses and boosters are up to date. It is advisable to vaccinate against polio, tetanus, typhoid, hepatitis A, and also rabies if going to more remote areas. Vaccinations for diphtheria, hepatitis B and yellow fever should also be considered. Although a yellow fever certificate is not compulsory for visiting Colombia, if you travel to the Amazon you are likely to be asked for one at the airport in Leticia. You may well be turned away if you can't produce one, or you will be made to have the vaccination on the spot (not recommended). The bus terminal in Bogotá now offers professional and free yellow fever vaccinations for foreigners.

Health risks

The most common cause of **traveller's diarrhoea** in Colombia is eating contaminated food. Tap water in the major cities is in theory safe to drink, but it may be advisable to err on the side of caution and drink only bottled or boiled water. Avoid having ice in drinks unless you trust that it is from a reliable source. Swimming in sea or river water that has been contaminated by sewage can also result in stomach upset; ask locally if water is safe. Diarrhoea may also be caused by a virus, bacteria (such as E-coli), protozoal (such as giardia), salmonella and cholera. It may be accompanied by vomiting or by severe abdominal pain. Any kind of diarrhoea responds well to the replacement of water and salts. Sachets of rehydration salts can be bought in most chemists and can be dissolved in boiled water. If the symptoms persist, consult a doctor.

Travelling in high altitudes can bring on **altitude sickness**. On reaching heights above 3000 m, the heart may start pounding and the traveller may experience shortness of breath. Smokers and those with underlying heart or lung disease are often hardest hit. Take it easy for the first few days, rest and drink plenty of water;

you will feel better soon. It is essential to get acclimatized before undertaking long treks or arduous activities.

Mosquitoes are a nuisance and some are carriers of serious diseases. **Malaria** and **dengue fever** are a danger in the Amazon and in other tropical areas along the Pacific coast including the Darién and Chocó. Cases of the **Zika virus** have also been reported. Take specialist advice on the best anti-malarials to use, and try to avoid being bitten as much as possible by sleeping off the ground and using a mosquito net and some kind of insecticide. Mosquito coils are available in many shops, as are tablets of insecticide, which are placed on a heated mat plugged into a wall socket.

Finally, remember that the sun in tropical areas and at high altitude can be fierce, so take precautions to avoid **heat exhaustion** and **sunburn**.

If you get sick

Contact your embassy or consulate for a list of doctors and dentists who speak your language, or at least some English. Your hotel may also be able to recommend good local medical services. Good-quality healthcare is available in the larger centres of Colombia, but it can be expensive, especially hospitalization. Make sure you have adequate insurance (see below).

Useful websites

www.cdc.gov US government site that gives excellent advice on travel health and details of disease outbreaks.
www.fco.gov.uk British Foreign and Commonwealth Office travel site has useful information on each country, people, climate and a list of UK embassies/consulates abroad.
www.fitfortravel.scot.nhs.uk A-Z of vaccine/health advice for each country.

www.travelhealth.co.uk Independent travel health site with advice on vaccination, travel insurance and health risks.

ID

It is highly recommended that you photocopy your passport details, including entry stamps which, for added insurance, you can have witnessed by a notary. Always carry your passport or a photocopy with you, as you may be asked for identification at any time. A photocopy is a valid substitute for most purposes but not, for example, for getting a cash advance on a credit card. A driving licence, provided it is plastic, of credit card size and has a photograph, is generally an acceptable form of ID (eg to enter government buildings). For more information, check with your consulate.

Insurance

Travel insurance is a must for all visitors to Colombia. Always take out insurance that covers both medical expenses and baggage loss, and read the small print carefully before you set off. Check that all the activities you may end up doing are covered; diving, kayaking, mountaineering (especially at high altitude), whitewater rafting, etc, may require additional or specialist insurance. Check if medical coverage includes air ambulance and emergency flights back home.

Be aware of the payment protocol: in Colombia you will have to pay out of your own pocket and later request reimbursement from the insurance company. Before paying for any medical services, insist on getting a fully itemized invoice. In case of baggage loss, have the receipts for expensive personal effects like cameras and laptops on file, take photos of these items, note the serial numbers and be sure to leave unnecessary valuables at home. Keep the insurance company's telephone number with you and get a police report for any lost or stolen items.

Internet

The internet has largely replaced postal and telephone services for the majority of travellers. Public internet access is available in most areas of Colombia, although the cost and speed of access varies. Small towns and villages may not have connectivity, or it may be slow; the best service is generally available in the largest cities. Most hotels and major airports now have free Wi-Fi, as do cafés, bars, restaurants and some public spaces, but connectivity can be erratic. Keep your wits about you if using Wi-Fi spots outdoors; not all are safe. Likewise, cyber cafés sometimes get crowded and noisy, so keep an eye on your belongings.

Language

For a list of useful Spanish words and phrases, see page 342.

The official language of Colombia is Spanish and it is spoken by the majority of the population. However, there are also some 60 aboriginal languages spoken by the indigenous communities. A form of creole English is spoken on the islands of San Andrés and Providencia. An increasing number of Colombians can speak and understand a little English, even in more remote areas, but a basic knowledge of Spanish will infinitely enhance your journey and make communication that much easier. It's well worth learning the basics before you arrive or taking a course at the start of your trip (see below). Language exchanges with students wishing to learn English are also popular. Note that if you are intending to do any formal language or other studies, then you must get a student visa (see Visas and immigration, page 337), which can be obtained once you're in the country.

Language courses

Amerispan, 1334 Walnut St, 6th floor, Philadelphia, PA 19107, USA, T215-7511100/T1-800-511 0179, www.amerispan.com. Spanish immersion and volunteer programmes throughout Latin America, including in Bogotá and Cartagena.
Cactus Language Travel Holidays, T0845-130 4775 (UK), www.cactuslanguage.com. Spanish language courses often combined with activities such as salsa or gastronomy in different parts of Colombia, including Bogotá and Cartagena.

Universities in Bogotá also provide Spanish language courses: **Pontificia Universidad Javeriana**, T1-320 8320 ext 4563, www.javeriana.edu.co; **Universidad de los Andes**, T1-339 4949, www.uniandes.edu.co (US$460 for 45/90-hr summer courses); **Universidad Nacional**, T1-316 5000, www.unal.edu.co (high-quality intensive courses for about US$500, group discount available); **Universidad Pedagógica**, C 72, No 11-86, T1-594 1894.

see Visas and immigration, page 337

LGBT travellers

Colombia has some of the most progressive laws regarding homosexuality in Latin America. While same-sex marriages and civil unions are yet to be legalized, common-law marriage (registered partnership), property rights and inheritance rights for same-sex couples were approved by the Constitutional Court in 2007. Since then the courts have often ruled in favour of gay plaintiffs and the Constitutional Court continues to be progressive on the subject of gay rights. Most of the big cities have gay neighbourhoods; Bogotá in particular has a large and thriving gay scene, centred around Chapinero. Gay travellers should not experience any difficulty booking a double room, say, in most hotels around the country. However, it may be wise to be discreet and respect local sensibilities in more conservative, remote locations.

Media

Newspapers and magazines

Bogotá has an excellent English-language magazine, *The City Paper*, www.thecitypaperbogota.com, distributed in hotels, hostels and bars. The best national magazine is probably *Semana*, www.semana.com. Most of the major cities have their own newspaper, usually with a regional bias; most of these have an online presence.
Bogotá: *El Tiempo*, www.eltiempo.com; *El Espectador*, www.elespectador.com; *La República*, www.larepublica.com.
Cartagena: *El Heraldo*, www.elheraldo.co.
Cali: *El País*, www.elpais.com.co; *Nuevo Diario Occidente*, www.diariooccidente.com.co; *El Pueblo*.
Medellín: *El Mundo*, www.elmundo.com; *El Colombiano*, www.elcolombiano.com.

Radio

Colombia has a wealth of radio stations. Try **W Radio**, www.wradio.com.co, for up-to-the-minute news. You may be able to pick up the **BBC World Service** or **Voice of America** with a long-wave or digital radio.

Television

Colombia has some 25 TV stations including regional ones, but the

2 principal stations are **RCN** (state owned) and **Caracol** (private). All of the major stations have websites which enable live streaming and on-demand viewing. Colombian TV is well known for its 'soaps' (*telenovelas*), which are exported to other Spanish-speaking countries. Satellite TV with access to **CNN** and **CNN en Español** is available in even the cheapest hotels.

Money

US$1 = COP$3005; UK£1 = COP$3966; €1 = COP$3499 (Nov 2017). See www.xe.com.
Colombia's currency is the *peso* ($). Banknotes are available in the following denominations: 50,000, 20,000, 10,000, 5000, 2000 and 1000, as well as coins worth 500, 200, 100 and 50. Large bills may be hard to use in small towns so carry notes in small dominations (10,000 and below). Watch out for forged notes. The 50,000-peso note should smudge colour if it is real; if not, refuse to accept it.

There is a variety of ways for visitors to bring their funds into Colombia; you are strongly advised to combine 2 or more of these, so as not to be stuck without money. Always carry some US$ cash, which can be used when and where all else fails. Avoid carrying large quantities of cash on your person.

ATMs and credit cards

Credit cards are widely used, especially MasterCard and Visa; Diners Club is also accepted, but American Express (Amex) is only accepted in upmarket places in Bogotá. Many banks accept Visa (Visaplus and ATH logos) and Cirrus/MasterCard (Maestro and Multicolor logos) for peso cash advances; these cards can also be used in ATMs. There are ATMs for Visa and MasterCard everywhere, including in **Carulla** and **Exito** supermarkets, but you may have

to try several machines before you find one that works.

Note that ATMs in Colombia do not retain your card during the withdrawal. Insert your card for scanning and withdraw it immediately, then proceed as normal. If your card is not given back straight away, do not proceed with the transaction and do not type in your pin number. Money has been stolen from accounts when cards have been retained. Only use ATMs in supermarkets, malls or where a security guard is present. Don't ask a taxi driver to wait while you use an ATM. Be particularly vigilant around Christmas time when thieves may be on the prowl.

ATMs dispense a frustratingly small amount of cash at a time. The maximum withdrawal is often 300,000 pesos (about US$150). You can make several withdrawals each day, but this will accrue heavy transaction charges over a period of time. For larger amounts try: **Davivienda** (occasionally 500,000 pesos per visit) and **Bancolombia** (400,000 pesos per visit).

If planning to use credit and debit cards abroad, be sure to warn your bank back at home in advance to prevent them blocking your card. It is also worth finding out how much your bank charges for foreign withdrawals; some banks have much higher fees than others. In case of credit card loss or theft, call your bank or contact Visa T01800-912 5713, or MasterCard T0800-96-4767.

Currency exchange

Cash (preferably US$ or euros) and TCs can, in theory, be exchanged in any bank, except the **Banco de la República**. Take your passport (a photocopy is not normally accepted) and, in smaller places, get there early. It can be difficult to buy and sell large amounts of pounds sterling, even in Bogotá.

In most sizeable towns there are *casas de cambio* (exchange bureaux), which are quicker to use than banks but may charge higher commission. US$ and Euro are readily accepted but other international currencies can be harder to change. Hotels usually give very poor rates of exchange, especially if you are paying in dollars. On Sun currency exchange is virtually impossible except at Bogotá airport. Do not be tempted to change money on the streets; it is dangerous and you may well be given counterfeit pesos. Counterfeit US$ bills are also in circulation.

When leaving Colombia, try to sell your pesos before or at the border, as it may be difficult to change them in other countries.

Cost of living

Prices are generally lower than Europe and North America for services and locally produced items, but more expensive for imported and luxury goods. Modest, basic accommodation costs about US$15-25 per person per night in Bogotá, Cartagena, Santa Marta and colonial cities like Villa de Leiva, Popayán or Santa Fe de Antioquia, but is cheaper elsewhere. A *menú del día* (set lunch) costs about US$3-5 and breakfast US$2-3. A la carte meals are usually good value as fierce competition keeps prices relatively low. Internet cafés charge US$1-2 per hr.

Opening hours

Business hours are generally Mon-Fri 0800-1200, 1400-1700, and Sat 0900-1200. A longer siesta may be taken in small towns and tropical areas. **Banks** in larger cities do not close for lunch. Most businesses, such as banks and **airline**

offices, close for official holidays, while **supermarkets** and street markets may stay open. This depends a lot on where you are, so enquire locally. The best time to visit **churches** for sightseeing is before or after Mass (not during).

Police and the law

You are required to carry your passport at all times; you will seldom be asked for it outside border areas but there are occasional police and military checks on main roads. In general, most police are helpful to travellers and you are unlikely to experience any hassle as long as you are polite and cooperative. Remain calm and courteous if your hotel room is raided by police looking for drugs. Never offer to bribe a police officer; if an official suggests that a bribe must be paid before you can proceed on your way, be patient and they may relent.

Note that if you are the victim of theft or other forms of crime, contact a **Centro de Atención Inmediata** (**CAI**) office for assistance, T156, not a standard police station. The CAI police office is the only place that will carry out the relevant paperwork. In Bogotá there are **CAI** offices at Cra 24, No 82-77, Downtown, T1-552 4840; at C 60 y Cra 9, Downtown, T1-217 7472, and at C 62, No 42C-07 Sur, La Candelaria, T1-715 1934.

Post and courier

There are 2 parallel services: **Deprisa**, operated by the national airline **Avianca**, and **4-72**, previously known as Correos de Colombia or Adpostal. Both have offices in major cities but only **4-72** can be found in small towns and rural areas. Both offer an overseas parcel service; anything important should be registered. **Servientrega**, DHL and

Fedex also handle overseas parcels.
Portal Oficial, 4-72 Diagonal 25G
No 95A-55B, T1-472 2000, www.4-72.
com.co. Bogota's main postal centre.

Public holidays

Public holidays are known as
puentes (bridges).
1 Jan   New Year's Day
6 Jan   Epiphany*
19 Mar   St Joseph*
Mar/Apr   Maundy Thu; Good Fri
1 May   Labour Day
May   Ascension Day* (6 weeks and
a day after Easter Sun)
May/Jun   Corpus Christi* (9 weeks
and a day after Easter Sun)
29 Jun   St Peter and St Paul*
30 Jun   Sacred Heart*
20 Jul   Independence Day
7 Aug   Battle of Boyacá
15 Aug   Assumption*
12 Oct   Columbus' arrival in America*
1 Nov   All Saints' Day*
11 Nov   Independence of Cartagena*
8 Dec   Immaculate Conception
25 Dec   Christmas Day

* When these do not fall on a Mon,
the public holiday is held on the
following Mon.

Safety

Travellers confirm that the vast majority
of Colombians are polite, honest and
will go out of their way to help visitors
and make them feel welcome. In
general, anti-gringo sentiments are
rare. However, visitors should always
keep in mind that Colombia is part of a
major cocaine-smuggling route and take
suitable precautions; for specific advice
on drugs in Colombia, see page 328.

Drug-based scams

There have been reports of travellers
being victims of *burundanga*, a drug
obtained from a native white flower,
which is used to contaminate cigarettes,
food or drink. It is almost impossible
to see or smell but leaves the victim
helpless. Usually, the victim is taken to
an ATM to draw out money. At present,
the use of this drug appears to be
confined to major cities. Be wary of
accepting cigarettes, food and drink from
strangers at sports events or on buses.
In bars watch your drinks very carefully.
Other Colombian scams may involve fake
police and taxicabs; there are variations
in most major cities. For advice on safety
in Bogotá, see page 41.

Guerrillas

The government has had considerable
success in its fight against left-wing
guerrillas such as the **FARC**, but the
internal armed conflict in Colombia is
almost impossible to predict and the
security situation changes from day
to day. For this reason, it is essential
to consult with locals for up-to-date
information. Taxi and bus drivers, local
journalists, soldiers at checkpoints, hotel
owners and Colombians who actually
travel around their country are usually
good sources of reliable information.
Since 2002, incidents of kidnapping
and homicide in major cities have been
declining. Travelling overland between
towns, especially during the holiday
season and bank holiday weekends, has
become much safer due to increased
military and police presence along main
roads. With the recent signing of the
peace agreement with FARC, armed
hostilities have largely ceased. Conflicts
remain, however, particularly with the
ELN guerrillas, who were not included in

the agreement, so visitors should seek updated local advice.

Hotel security

The cheapest hotels are usually found near markets and bus stations but these are also the least safe. Look for something a little better if you can afford it; if you must stay in a suspect area, try to return to your hotel before dark. If you trust your hotel, then you can leave any valuables you don't need in their safe-deposit box, but always keep an inventory of what you have deposited. An alternative to leaving valuables with the hotel administration is to lock everything in your pack and secure that in your room; a light bicycle chain or cable and a small padlock will provide at least a psychological deterrent for would-be thieves. Even in an apparently safe hotel, never leave valuable objects strewn about your room.

Theft

Pickpockets, bag snatchers and bag slashers are always a hazard for tourists, especially in crowded areas such as markets or the downtown cores of major cities. There have been reports of assaults in the Candelaria area of Bogotá, especially at night. Keep alert and avoid crowds of people. You should likewise avoid deserted areas, such as parks or plazas after hours. Be especially careful around bus stations, as these are often the most dangerous areas of town and are obvious places to catch people carrying a lot of important belongings.

To limit your chances of being robbed, leave unnecessary documents and valuables at home. Those you bring should be carried in a money-belt or pouch, including your passport, airline tickets, credit and debit cards. Hide your main cash supply in several different places. If one stash is lost or stolen, you will still have the others to fall back on. Never carry valuables in an ordinary pocket, purse or day-pack. Keep cameras in bags or day-packs and generally out of sight. Do not wear expensive wrist watches or jewellery. If you are wearing a shoulder-bag or day-pack in a crowd, carry it in front of you.

Women travellers

Unaccompanied foreign women may be objects of curiosity in Colombia; don't be unduly scared – or flattered – but do take sensible precautions. Avoid arriving anywhere after dark. Remember that for a single woman a taxi at night can be as dangerous as wandering around alone. During the day, a good general rule is to always look confident and pretend you know where you are going, even if you do not. If you accept a social invitation, make sure that someone knows the address of where you are going and the time you left; ask if you can bring a friend (even if you do not). Watch your alcohol intake at parties, especially if you are on your own, and keep a close eye on your drink. Don't tell strangers where you are staying.

Student travellers

If you are in full-time education you are entitled to an **International Student Identity Card (ISIC)**, which is sold by student travel offices and agencies in 70 countries. The ISIC may give you special prices on transport and access to a variety of other concessions and services, although these are relatively uncommon in Colombia. Teachers are entitled to an **International Teacher Identity Card (ITIC)**. Both are available from www.isic.org. If undertaking any form of study in Colombia, you will need a student visa (see Visas and immigration, page 337).

Tax

Departure tax is US$35, sometimes included in the cost of the ticket.

VAT/IVA is 16%. Ask for an official receipt if you want it documented. Some hotels and restaurants add IVA onto bills, but foreigners do not officially have to pay (see page 26).

Telephone *Country code +57.*

To call a landline in Colombia from outside the area, dial the 1-digit area code, followed by the 7-digit number. To make an international call from Colombia, dial the IDD code of the carrier – Orbitel 005; ETB 007; Telecom 009 – followed by the country code.

Phone boxes are widespread but are not recommended for long-distance calls. Instead, national and international calls can be made from the many public phone offices found in all major cities (eg in the **Tequendama Hotel** complex in Bogotá, Cra 13, No 26-45) and even in rural towns. You are assigned a cabin, place your calls and pay on the way out. There is usually a screen that tells you how much you are spending. Prices vary considerably. You can also make calls from street vendors who hire out their mobile phones (usually signposted '*minutos*'). Another cost-effective way to make an international call is to use Skype (www.skype.com), available in most internet cafés.

It is relatively inexpensive to buy a pay-as-you go SIM card for your mobile phone. Calls are on the whole cheap but making international calls from mobiles can be complicated.

Time

GMT -5 all year round.

Tipping

A voluntary charge is added to most bills but you can ask to have this taken off if you are not happy with the service. Otherwise a 10% tip is customary.

Tourist information

Contact details for tourist offices and other information resources are given throughout the text. The Colombian government is making a big push to promote tourism and most *alcaldías* (municipalities) have some sort of tourist office, whose staff are invariably very well meaning. However, the qualifications of the staff, the resources available and the standards of service vary enormously in smaller towns. Keep your expectations modest and you may be pleasantly surprised. For further information, contact the **Colombia Tourist Board – Proexport**, C 28, No 13A-15, piso 36, Bogotá, T1-427 9000, www.colombia.travel; its website is useful, comprehensive and up to date. For information on the national parks, see box, page 22.

Useful websites
www.clubhaciendasdelcafe.com Extensive list of coffee fincas in the Zona Cafetera.

www.colombianhostels.com.co Network of Colombian backpackers' hostels. Also publishes a thorough guidebook, available for free in most major hostels.

www.conexcol.com Colombian search engine (Spanish only).

www.despegar.com Cheap flights website for travel within Latin America.

www.gobiernoenlinea.gov.co Government website with information on new laws and citizen rights, in Spanish and English.

www.hosteltrail.com/colombia Reviews of hostels, tour agencies and destinations.

www.ideam.gov.co Weather and climate information.

www.igac.gov.co Instituto Geográfico Agustín Codazzi Official maps of Colombia.

www.invias.gov.co Instituto Nacional de Vías (National Road Institute). Current details on the state of the roads with maps, etc.

www.lab.org.uk Latin American Bureau site, based in the UK. Publishes online articles, in-depth news reports and holds talks on Latin American issues.

www.quehubo.com Listings site.

Tour operators

In the UK
Dragoman, T01728-862211, www.dragoman.com.

Exodus Travels, T0845-805 5459, www.exodus.co.uk.

Explore, T01252-883 790, www.explore.co.uk.

Intrepid Travel, T0808-274 5111, www.intrepidtravel.com.

Journey Latin America, T020-3432 9346, www.journeylatinamerica.co.uk.

LATA (Latin American Travel Association), T020-3713 6688, www.lata.org. Useful country information and listing of UK operators specializing in Latin America.

Senderos, T0117-223 2321, www.senderos.co.uk. UK-based portal for exclusive Latin American hotels and adventure tour companies.

South America Travel, T0800-011 9170, www.southamerica.travel.

In North America
GAP Adventures, T1-416 260 0999, www.gapadventures.com.

See Colombia Travel, 11491 SW 20th St, Miami Fl, 33025-6639, T1-800-553-8701 (toll free), T020-7101 9467 (UK), www.seecolombia.travel.

South America Travel, T1-800-747 4540, www.southamerica.travel.

In South America
Colombian Highlands Tours & Expeditions, Av Cra 10-21, Finca Renacer, Villa de Leiva, Colombia, T310-552 9079, www.colombianhighlands.com.

De Una Colombia Tours, Cra 24, No 39b-25, of 501, La Soledad-Bogotá, Colombia, T1-368 1915, www.deunacolombia.com.

Surtrek, Av Amazonas 897 y Wilson, Quito, Ecuador, T1-866 978 7398 (US) T080 8189 0438, www.surtrek.com.

Visas and immigration

Before you go
To visit Colombia as a tourist, nationals of countries of the Middle East (except Israel and UAE), Asian countries (except Japan, South Korea, Philippines, Indonesia and Singapore), Cuba, Haiti, Nicaragua, Serbia, Bosnia and Herzegovina, Kosovo, Macedonia, Montenegro and all African countries (except South Africa) need a **visa**. Always check for changes in regulations before leaving your home country. Visas are issued only by Colombian consulates. When a visa is required you must present a valid passport, 2 photos on a white background, the application form (in duplicate), US$80, onward tickets, and a photocopy of all the documents (allow

2 weeks maximum). A non-refundable charge of US$52 is made for any study made by the Colombian authorities prior to a visa being issued. Canadian citizens have to pay a fee of COP$160,000 (about US$53) for a business visa.

All other nationals with a valid passport are issued a standard 90-day tourist visa on arrival. If you intend to stay more than 90 days, extensions can be granted through **Migración Colombia** (www. migracioncolombia.gov.co; see below).

On arrival
Normally, passports are scanned by a computer and stamped on entry; sometimes a landing card is issued. If you receive an entry card when flying in and lose it while in Colombia, apply to any **Migración Colombia** office (see below) who should issue one and re-stamp your passport for free. It is highly recommended that you photocopy your passport details, including entry stamps which, for added insurance, you can have witnessed by a notary. Always carry a photocopy of your passport with you (see page 330).

Visa extensions
If you wish to stay longer than 90 days as a tourist, go to a **Migración Colombia** office in any major city with your onward ticket and they will usually grant you a free extension (*salvoconducto*) on the spot. You may be asked to prove that you have sufficient funds for your stay. The *salvoconducto* is only issued once for a period of 30 days, costs around US$23.50 and is usually processed within 24 hrs. It is best to apply 2-3 days before your tourist stay expires. Bring 2 recent photos and copies of your passport. Arrive early in the morning; expect long queues and

a painfully slow bureaucratic process. Migración Colombia now accepts cash and credit card payments on site.

Alternatively, if you have good reason to stay longer (eg for medical treatment), you should apply to the Colombian embassy in your home country before leaving for Colombia.

If you overstay on any type of visa without an official extension, you will be charged a fine, minimum US$55 up to thousands of dollars.

Student and business visas
If you are going to take a Spanish course, you must have a student visa; a tourist visa is not valid for study. A student visa can be obtained once you're in Colombia on a tourist visa. You must be enrolled on a course at a bona fide university and have proof of sufficient funds; US$400-600 for a 6-month stay is usually deemed sufficient.

Various business and other temporary visas are needed for foreigners who wish to reside in Colombia for a length of time. The **Ministerio de Relaciones Exteriores** (not **Migración Colombia**), C 10 No 5-51, Palacio de San Carlos, T01800-097 9899 or 382 6999, www. cancilleria.gov.co, Mon-Fri 0730-1600, processes student and some work visas, but in general, Colombian work visas can only be obtained outside Colombia at the appropriate consulate or embassy.

You must register work and student visas at a **Migración Colombia** office within 15 days of obtaining them; otherwise you will be liable to pay a hefty fine. Visas must be used within 3 months. Supporting documentary requirements for visas change frequently, so check with the consulate in good time before your trip.

Leaving Colombia

To leave Colombia you must get an exit stamp. These are issued automatically at the airport as long as you haven't overstayed your visa. If you're leaving overland, get the exit stamp from a **Migración Colombia** office, but bear in mind that they may not have an office at the small border towns, so try to get your stamp in a main city.

Migración Colombia offices

Barranquilla Cra 42, No 54-77, T5-351 3401.

Bogotá C 26, No 59-51, Edif Argos Torre 3, Piso 4, T1-605 5454, Mon-Fri 0800-1600.

Cali Av 3N, No 50N-20, T2-397 3510.

Cartagena Cra 20B, No 29-18, T5-670 0555, daily 0800-1200, 1400-1700.

Cúcuta Av 1, No 28-57, T7-572 0033, daily 0800-1130, 1400-1700; also at the airport.

Ipiales Cra 7, No 14-10 esq C 14 piso 3, Mon-Fri 0900-1200, 1400-1700. There's also an Ecuadorean consulate here.

Leticia C 9, No 9-62, T8-592 5930; also at the airport.

Manizales C 53, No 25A-35, T6-887 9600, cf.manizales@migracioncolombia. gov.co, Mon-Fri 0800-1200, 1400-1700.

Medellín C 19, No 80A-40, Belén La Gloria, T4-340 5800; and at airport, T4-562 2903.

Pasto C 29-76. Will issue exit stamps if you are going on to Ecuador.

Riohacha C 5, No 4-48, daily 0800-1200, 1400-1700.

Santa Marta C 22, No 13A-88, Santa Marta, T5-421 7794. Mon-Fri 0800-1200, 1400-1700.

Volunteering

Volunteers can apply to work as park rangers at some national parks (see box, page 22). Other agencies offering volunteer placements include:

Colombia Ministry of the Environment, www.minambiente. gov.co. Environmental legislation and general information.

Conservation International, www. conservation.org. Click on 'Get Involved' of 'Join Us' to start the process.

Fundación Natura, www.natura.org. co. For scientific information on several national parks where they have projects.

Goals for Peace, www.goalsfor peace.com. **Kasa Guane** hostel in Bucaramaranga (see page 98) runs this social project which dedicated to improving opportunities for low-income children in the city. Local and international volunteers can get involved with teaching, coaching, mentoring and administrative work.

Institute Von Humboldt, www. humboldt.org.co (in Spanish). Probably the most important environment research organization in Colombia. An excellent site with descriptions of the different ecosystems in the country and details of projects with ethnic communities.

International Union for the Conservation of Nature, www.iucn.org. One of the best sites for information on biodiversity protection worldwide with links to South America/Colombia including projects in protected areas and national parks.

Survival International, www.survival international.org. Information on indigenous communities in Colombia.

Weights and measures

Colombia uses the metric system, but uses US gallons for petrol.

Footnotes

Basic Spanish for travellers

Learning Spanish is a useful part of the preparation for a trip to Latin America and no volumes of dictionaries, phrase books or word lists will provide the same enjoyment as being able to communicate directly with the people of the country you are visiting. It is a good idea to make an effort to grasp the basics before you go. As you travel you will pick up more of the language and the more you know, the more you will benefit from your stay.

Colombian Spanish

Colombians display a sometimes excessive inclination for politeness. Nowhere is this more evident than in their language, which is characterized by a punctilious, sometimes archaic, courteousness. Step inside any shop or taxi in the interior (the coast has its own rules, separate from the rest of the country) and you are likely to be bombarded by forms of address such as *'a la orden'* (at your service), *'que esté bien'* (may you be well), *'con mucho gusto'* (with pleasure); in departments such as Boyacá, you may even be addressed as *'su merced'* (your mercy). And politeness isn't only for strangers. They even use the third person, formal *usted* (you) with their children or spouses.

Although more and more Colombians speak a few phrases of English, you shouldn't rely on this, particular in more remote or rural areas. Instead, make the effort to learn some Spanish, either before you arrive or by signing up for a language course as part of your trip. Without any language skills, you will feel like someone peering through a keyhole at the country. But Colombians are so gregarious that with just a modest knowledge of the language you will soon be engaged in conversation, and, helpfully, the Colombian accent is one of the easiest to understand, save for the more choppy intonations heard on the coast.

General pronunciation

Whether you have been taught the 'Castilian' pronunciation (*z* and *c* followed by *i* or *e* are pronounced as the *th* in think) or the 'American' pronunciation (they are pronounced as *s*), you will encounter little difficulty in understanding either. Regional accents and usages vary, but the basic language is essentially the same everywhere.

Vowels

a as in English *cat*
e as in English *best*
i as the *ee* in English *feet*
o as in English *shop*
u as the *oo* in English *food*
ai as the *i* in English *ride*
ei as *ey* in English *they*
oi as *oy* in English *toy*

Consonants

Most consonants can be pronounced more or less as they are in English. The exceptions are:

g before *e* or *i* is the same as *j*
h is always silent (except in *ch* as in *chair*)
j as the *ch* in Scottish *loch*
ll as the *y* in *yellow*
ñ as the *ni* in English *onion*
rr trilled much more than in English
x depending on its location, pronounced *x*, *s*, *sh* or *j*

Spanish words and phrases

Greetings, courtesies

hello *hola*
good morning *buenos días*
good afternoon/evening/night
  buenas tardes/noches
goodbye *adiós/chao*
pleased to meet you *mucho gusto*
see you later *hasta luego*
how are you? *¿cómo está?/¿cómo estás?*
I'm fine, thanks *estoy muy bien, gracias*
I'm called... *me llamo...*
what is your name? *¿cómo se llama?/*
  ¿cómo te llamas?
yes/no *sí/no*
please *por favor*
thank you (very much) *(muchas) gracias*

I speak Spanish *hablo español*
I don't speak Spanish *no hablo español*
do you speak English? *¿habla inglés?*
I don't understand *no entiendo/*
  no comprendo
please speak slowly *hable despacio*
  por favor
I am very sorry *lo siento mucho/disculpe*
what do you want? *¿qué quiere?/*
  ¿qué quieres?
I want *quiero*
I don't want it *no lo quiero*
good/bad *bueno/malo*
leave me alone *déjeme en paz/*
  no me moleste

Questions and requests

Have you got a room for two people?
  ¿Tiene una habitación para dos personas?
How do I get to_? *¿Cómo llego a_?*
How much does it cost?
  ¿Cuánto cuesta? ¿cuánto es?
I'd like to make a long-distance
  phone call *Quisiera hacer una llamada*
  de larga distancia
Is service included? *¿Está incluido*
  el servicio?

Is tax included? *¿Están incluidos*
  los impuestos?
When does the bus leave (arrive)?
  ¿A qué hora sale (llega) el autobús?
When? *¿cuándo?*
Where is_? *¿dónde está_?*
Where can I buy tickets?
  ¿Dónde puedo comprar boletos?
Where is the nearest petrol station?
  ¿Dónde está la gasolinera más cercana?
Why? *¿por qué?*

Basics

bank *el banco*
bathroom/toilet *el baño*
bill *la factura/la cuenta*
cash *el efectivo*
cheap *barato/a*
credit card *la tarjeta de crédito*
exchange house *la casa de cambio*
exchange rate *el tipo de cambio*

expensive *caro/a*
market *el mercado*
note/coin *le billete/la moneda*
police (policeman) *la policía (el policía)*
post office *el correo*
public telephone *el teléfono público*
supermarket *el supermercado*
ticket office *la taquilla*

Getting around

aeroplane *el avión*
airport *el aeropuerto*

arrival/departure *la llegada/salida*
avenue *la avenida*

block *la cuadra*
border *la frontera*
bus station *la terminal de autobuses/ camiones*
bus *el bus/el autobús/el camión*
collective/fixed-route taxi *el colectivo*
corner *la esquina*
customs *la aduana*
first/second class *primera/segunda clase*
left/right *izquierda/derecha*
ticket *el boleto*
empty/full *vacío/lleno*
highway, main road *la carretera*
immigration *la inmigración*
insurance *el seguro*
insured person *el/la asegurado/a*
to insure yourself against *asegurarse contra*

luggage *el equipaje*
motorway, freeway *el autopista/ la carretera*
north, south, east, west *norte, sur, este (oriente), oeste (occidente)*
oil *el aceite*
to park *estacionarse*
passport *el pasaporte*
petrol/gasoline *la gasolina*
puncture *el pinchazo/la ponchadura*
street *la calle*
that way *por allí/por allá*
this way *por aquí/por acá*
tourist card/visa *la tarjeta de turista*
tyre *la llanta*
unleaded *sin plomo*
to walk *caminar/andar*

Accommodation

air conditioning *el aire acondicionado*
all-inclusive *todo incluido*
bathroom, private *el baño privado*
bed, double/single *la cama matrimonial/ sencilla*
blankets *las cobijas/mantas*
to clean *limpiar*
dining room *el comedor*
guesthouse *la casa de huéspedes*
hotel *el hotel*
noisy *ruidoso*
pillows *las almohadas*

power cut *el apagón/corte*
restaurant *el restaurante*
room/bedroom *el cuarto/la habitación*
sheets *las sábanas*
shower *la ducha/regadera*
soap *el jabón*
toilet *el sanitario/excusado*
toilet paper *el papel higiénico*
towels, clean/dirty *las toallas limpias/ sucias*
water, hot/cold *el agua caliente/fría*

Health

aspirin *la aspirina*
blood *la sangre*
chemist *la farmacia*
condoms *los preservativos, los condones*
contact lenses *los lentes de contacto*
contraceptives *los anticonceptivos*
contraceptive pill *la píldora anti-conceptiva*
diarrhoea *la diarrea*

doctor *el médico*
fever/sweat *la fiebre/el sudor*
pain *el dolor*
head *la cabeza*
period/sanitary towels *la regla/las toallas femeninas*
stomach *el estómago*
altitude sickness *el soroche*

Family

family *la familia*	husband/wife *el esposo (marido)/ la esposa*
friend *el amigo/la amiga*	boyfriend/girlfriend *el novio/la novia*
brother/sister *el hermano/la hermana*	married *casado/a*
daughter/son *la hija/el hijo*	single/unmarried *soltero/a*
father/mother *el padre/la madre*	

Months, days and time

January *enero*	Thursday *jueves*
February *febrero*	Friday *viernes*
March *marzo*	Saturday *sábado*
April *abril*	Sunday *domingo*
May *mayo*	
June *junio*	at one o'clock *a la una*
July *julio*	at half past two *a las dos y media*
August *agosto*	at a quarter to three *a cuarto para las tres/a las tres menos quince*
September *septiembre*	
October *octubre*	it's one o'clock *es la una*
November *noviembre*	it's seven o'clock *son las siete*
December *diciembre*	it's six twenty *son las seis y veinte*
	it's five to nine *son las nueve menos cinco*
Monday *lunes*	in ten minutes *en diez minutos*
Tuesday *martes*	five hours *cinco horas*
Wednesday *miércoles*	does it take long? *¿tarda mucho?*

Numbers

one *uno/una*	sixteen *dieciséis*
two *dos*	seventeen *diecisiete*
three *tres*	eighteen *dieciocho*
four *cuatro*	nineteen *diecinueve*
five *cinco*	twenty *veinte*
six *seis*	twenty-one *veintiuno*
seven *siete*	thirty *treinta*
eight *ocho*	forty *cuarenta*
nine *nueve*	fifty *cincuenta*
ten *diez*	sixty *sesenta*
eleven *once*	seventy *setenta*
twelve *doce*	eighty *ochenta*
thirteen *trece*	ninety *noventa*
fourteen *catorce*	hundred *cien/ciento*
fifteen *quince*	thousand *mil*

Food

avocado *el aguacate*
baked *al horno*
bakery *la panadería*
banana *la banana*
banana passion-fruit *la curuba*
beans *los frijoles/las habichuelas*
beef *la carne de res*
beef steak *el lomo*
blackberry *la mora*
boiled rice *el arroz blanco*
bread *el pan*
breakfast *el desayuno*
butter *la manteca*
cake *la torta*
cape gooseberry (physalis) *la uchuva*
chewing gum *el chicle*
chicken *el pollo*
chilli or green pepper *el ají/pimiento*
clear soup, stock *el caldo*
cooked *cocido*
dining room *el comedor*
dragon fruit *la pitaya*

egg *el huevo*
fish *el pescado*
fork *el tenedor*
fried *frito*
garlic *el ajo*
goat *el chivo*
grapefruit *la toronja/el pomelo*
grill *la parrilla*
grilled/griddled *a la plancha*
guava *la guayaba*
ham *el jamón*
hamburger *la hamburguesa*
hot, spicy *picante*
ice cream *el helado*
jam *la mermelada*
knife *el cuchillo*
lulo fruit *el lulo* (tangy orange-coloured
fruit with green pulp)
passion-fruit *la maracuyá*
soursop *la guanábana*
star fruit *la carambola*

Drink

beer *la cerveza*
boiled *hervido/a*
bottled *en botella*
camomile tea *la manzanilla*
canned *en lata*
coffee *el café*
coffee, white *el café con leche*
cold *frío*
cup *la taza*
drink *la bebida*
drunk *borracho/a*
firewater *el aguardiente*
fruit milkshake *el batido/licuado*
glass *el vaso*
hot *caliente*
ice/without ice *el hielo/sin hielo*

juice *el jugo*
lemonade *la limonada*
milk *la leche*
mint *la menta*
rum *el ron*
soft drink *el refresco*
sugar *el azúcar*
tea *el té*
to drink *beber/tomar*
water *el agua*
water, carbonated *el agua mineral
con gas*
water, still mineral *el agua mineral
sin gas*
wine, red *el vino tinto*
wine, white *el vino blanco*

Index

*Entries in **bold** refer to maps*

FOOTPRINT

Features

Advertisers' index

Acknowledgements

For Brendan Hennessy and Madeleine Hennessy, who paved the way.

We would like to thank the following people, without whose help and advice this book would not have been possible: Thomas Doyer, Erik Rupert, Russell Coleman, Juliana Torres Nieto and everyone at ProColombia, Natalia Henríquez and Claudia Valencia at Medellín Convention and Visitors' Bureau, Pamela Ludwig, Milton César Ocampo, Richard McColl, Lothar Berg, Tony Clark, Kim Macphee, Dayana Conrado, Diana María Guevara and José Fernández Villaquirán of Cali TB, Diana Tamayo, Nadia Diamond, Melissa Montoya, Juan Pablo Echeverri, Laura Pérez (VivaColombia), and Catalina Carrizosa Isaza. Finally, thanks to Ben Box, Felicity Laughton and the team at Footprint.

About the authors

Huw and Caitlin Hennessy

Modern Languages graduates from the University of London, Caitlin and Huw Hennessy first met as tour leaders for Journey Latin America in 1985, running group adventure tours to this 'undiscovered' new travel destination. In their 'down time', they began to help update the South American Handbook, poring over readers' letters, with their minutiae of bus routes, timetables and colourful anecdotes. The travel writing bug soon took over from the tour leading and now they have accumulated more years than they care to count, editing, writing and updating numerous Footprint Handbooks on Latin America. They have also ventured out into the wider world of journalism, from local newspaper reporting to editing for a wide range of publishers in London, as well as writing for various magazines and newspapers, including Wanderlust, The Independent and The Times. Latin America remains their abiding passion, however, and between the two of them they have covered pretty much every highway and byway from Ciudad Juárez to Ushuaia.

At home in Devon, they keep fit walking the South West Coast Path together. Kate is also an accomplished artist, recently completing her MA in Fine Arts, while Huw releases his inner Tigger paddling in his kayak and pedalling his road bike up and down the country lanes.

Credits

Footprint credits
Editor: Felicity Laughton
Production and layout: Emma Bryers
Maps: Kevin Feeney
Colour section: John Hendry

Publisher: John Sadler
Head of Publishing: Felicity Laughton
Marketing: Kirsty Holmes
Advertising and Partnerships:
Debbie Wylde

Photography credits
Front cover: Barna Tanko/
Shutterstock.com
Back cover top: Gary C Tognoni/
Shutterstock.com
Back cover bottom: Ste Lane/
Shutterstock.com
Inside front cover: Casey French,
Caitlin Hennessy.

Colour section
Page 1: Jess Kraft/Shutterstock.com.
Page 2: Jess Kraft/Shutterstock.com.
Page 4: Caitlin Hennessy, Christian Kober/
Superstock.com, Jess Kraft/Shutterstock.
com. **Page 5**: Matyas Rehak/Shutterstock.
com, Scott Biales/Shutterstock.com.
Page 6: GIUGLIO Gil/Superstock.com,
imageBROKER/Superstock.com, Matyas
Rehak/Shutterstock.com. **Page 7**:
Casey French, VWPics/Superstock.com,
mundosemfim/Shutterstock.com,
Jenny Leonard/Shutterstock.com.
Page 10: Venturelli Luca/Shutterstock.
com. **Page 11**: Casey French. **Page 12**:
Casey French, Diego Grandi/Shutterstock.
com. **Page 13**: Casey French. **Page 14**:
rafcha/Shutterstock.com. **Page 15**:
Casey French, Thomas Marent/
Superstock.com. **Page 16**: Ondrej
Prosicky/Shutterstock.com.

Publishing information
Footprint Colombia
6th edition
© Compass Maps Ltd
March 2018

ISBN: 978 1 911082 53 8
CIP DATA: A catalogue record for this
book is available from the British Library

® Footprint Handbooks and the
Footprint mark are a registered
trademark of Compass Maps Ltd

Published by Footprint
5 Riverside Court
Lower Bristol Road
Bath BA2 3DZ, UK
T +44 (0)1225 469141
footprinttravelguides.com

Every effort has been made to ensure
that the facts in this guidebook are
accurate. However, travellers should still
obtain advice from consulates, airlines,
etc about travel and visa requirements
before travelling. The authors and
publishers cannot accept responsibility
for any loss, injury or inconvenience
however caused.

Printed in India by Replika Press Pvt Ltd